Interdisciplinary and Trans Failures

Unlike other volumes in the current literature, this book provides insight for interdisciplinary and transdisciplinary researchers and practitioners into what *doesn't* work. Documenting detailed case studies of project failure matters, not only as an illustration of experienced challenges but also as projects do not always follow step-by-step protocols of preconceived and theorised processes.

Bookended by a framing introduction from the editors and a conclusion written by Julie Thompson Klein, each chapter ends with a reflexive section that synthesizes lessons learned and key take-away points for the reader. Drawing on a wide range of international case studies and with a strong environmental thread throughout, the book reveals a range of failure scenarios for interdisciplinary and transdisciplinary projects, including:

- Projects that did not get off the ground
- Projects that did not have the correct personnel for specified objectives
- Projects that did not reach their original objectives but met other objectives
- Projects that failed to anticipate important differences among collaborators

Illustrating causal links in real-life projects, this volume will be of significant relevance to scholars and practitioners looking to overcome the challenges of conducting interdisciplinary and transdisciplinary research.

Dena Fam is Associate Professor and Research Director at the Institute for Sustainable Futures, University of Technology Sydney. She has a decade of experience developing transdisciplinary programmes and projects with an interest in negotiating the challenges of cross sectoral integration of knowledge.

Michael O'Rourke is Professor of Philosophy and faculty member in AgBioResearch and Environmental Science and Policy at Michigan State University. He is Director of the Center for Interdisciplinarity and Director of the Toolbox Dialogue Initiative, an NSF-sponsored research initiative that investigates philosophical approaches to facilitating interdisciplinary research.

Research and Teaching in Environmental Studies

This series brings together international educators and researchers working from a variety of perspectives to explore and present best practices for research and teaching in environmental studies.

Given the urgency of environmental problems, our approach to the research and teaching of environmental studies is crucial. Reflecting on examples of success and failure within the field, this collection showcases authors from a diverse range of environmental disciplines including climate change, environmental communication and sustainable development. Lessons learned from interdisciplinary and transdisciplinary research are presented, as well as teaching and classroom methodology for specific countries and disciplines.

Titles in this series include:

Sustainable Energy Education in the Arctic
The Role of Higher Education
Gisele Arruda

Interdisciplinary and Transdisciplinary Failures
Lessons Learned from Cautionary Tales
Edited by Dena Fam and Michael O'Rourke

For more information about this series, please visit: https://www.routledge.com/Research-and-Teaching-in-Environmental-Studies/book-series/RTES

Interdisciplinary and Transdisciplinary Failures
Lessons Learned from Cautionary Tales

**Edited by Dena Fam and
Michael O'Rourke**

First published 2021
by Routledge
2 Park Square, Milton Park, Abingdon, Oxon OX14 4RN

and by Routledge
52 Vanderbilt Avenue, New York, NY 10017

Routledge is an imprint of the Taylor & Francis Group, an informa business

© 2021 selection and editorial matter, Dena Fam and Michael O'Rourke; individual chapters, the contributors

The right of Dena Fam and Michael O'Rourke to be identified as the authors of the editorial material, and of the authors for their individual chapters, has been asserted in accordance with sections 77 and 78 of the Copyright, Designs and Patents Act 1988.

All rights reserved. No part of this book may be reprinted or reproduced or utilised in any form or by any electronic, mechanical, or other means, now known or hereafter invented, including photocopying and recording, or in any information storage or retrieval system, without permission in writing from the publishers.

Trademark notice: Product or corporate names may be trademarks or registered trademarks, and are used only for identification and explanation without intent to infringe.

British Library Cataloguing-in-Publication Data
A catalogue record for this book is available from the British Library

Library of Congress Cataloging-in-Publication Data
A catalog record has been requested for this book

ISBN: 978-0-367-20703-8 (hbk)
ISBN: 978-0-367-20704-5 (ebk)

Typeset in Times New Roman
by Deanta Global Publishing Services, Chennai, India

Contents

List of figures	viii
List of tables	x
List of contributors	xi
Preface	xx
Acknowledgements	xxi

1 Theoretical and empirical perspectives on failure:
An introduction   1
MICHAEL O'ROURKE AND DENA FAM

2 Re-thinking failure: Using design science theory and
methods, including design-thinking, for successful
transdisciplinary health and social interventions   21
LINDA NEUHAUSER, TALYA BRETTLER AND DENNIS BOYLE

PART I
Institutional environments associated with failure   43

3 Stem cells and serendipity: Unburdening social scientists'
feelings of failure   45
ISABEL FLETCHER AND CATHERINE LYALL

4 A fragile existence: A transdisciplinary food systems
research program cut short   62
BILL BELLOTTI AND FRED D'AGOSTINO

5 Over-promising and under-delivering: Institutional and
social networks influencing the emergence of urine diversion
systems in Queensland, Australia   78
CARA BEAL, DENA FAM AND STEWART CLEGG

vi *Contents*

PART II
Failures and responses associated with collaboration and stakeholder engagement

95

6 Failure and what to do next: Lessons from the Toolbox
   Dialogue Initiative

97

   MICHAEL O'ROURKE, STEPHEN CROWLEY, SANFORD D. EIGENBRODE
   AND STEPHANIE E. VASKO

7 Failure to consider local political processes and power
   relations in the development of a transdisciplinary research
   project plan: Learning lessons from a stormy start

114

   IRENA LEISBET CERIDWEN CONNON

8 A week in the life of a transdisciplinary researcher: Failures
   in research to support policy for water-quality management
   in New Zealand's South Island

131

   MELISSA ROBSON-WILLIAMS, BRUCE SMALL AND ROGER ROBSON-WILLIAMS

PART III
Personal reflection on failed initiatives through an autoethnographic lens

147

9 Reframing failure and the Indigenous doctoral journey

149

   JASON DE SANTOLO (GARRWA AND BARUNGGAM)

10 Transdisciplinary research – challenges, excessive
   demands and a story of disquiet

165

   MARTINA UKOWITZ

PART IV
Failure in interdisciplinary and transdisciplinary educational programs

179

11 The challenges of studying place: Learning from the failures
   of an experimental, interdisciplinary and community-
   engaged environmental studies course

181

   VALERIE IMBRUCE AND MIROSLAVA PRAZAK

Contents vii

12 Transdisciplinary learning within tertiary institutions – a
space to skin your knees 198
DENA FAM, ABBY MELLICK LOPES AND CYNTHIA MITCHELL

13 Learning to fail forward – operationalizing productive failure
for tackling complex environmental problems 217
BINBIN J. PEARCE

14 Failing and the perception of failure in student-driven
transdisciplinary projects 237
ULLI VILSMAIER AND ANNIKA THALHEIMER

Coda 253

15 Failure *is* an option: Lessons for success 255
JULIE THOMPSON KLEIN

Index 269

Figures

2.1 The general design process (Roschuni 2012). Courtesy of Celeste Nicole Roschuni — 26

2.2 Workers use the Changzhou Wellness Guide to plan worker educational activities in their factory wellness house. Source: Neuhauser — 29

2.3 Design-thinking and innovation Venn diagram. Innovation occurs at the intersection of desirability, viability, and feasibility. Courtesy of IDEO — 32

2.4 The phases of the design-thinking process. The design-thinking process occurs as a series of divergences and convergences. Courtesy of IDEO — 33

2.5 Iterative and cyclical design-thinking process. Progressive learning and innovation occur through repetitions of this cycle. Courtesy of IDEO — 33

2.6 The Medela Symphony breast pump weighs 7.05 pounds (3.2 kilos) and is 10 ¼" × 8 ¼" × 12 ½" (26 cm × 21 cm × 32 cm). Photo credit: Thomas Wucherpfennig — 34

2.7 Willow breast pump prototyping process. Creating physical prototypes early in the design process allows users to see and feel an example product, generating guidance for designers. Courtesy of IDEO — 35

4.1 Interconnectedness of key challenges. Each of the separate challenges is potentially influenced by the other. For illustrative purposes, and to avoid overcomplicating the figure, only one example of interconnectedness is shown — 68

5.1 Urine-diverting toilet installed at the Ecovillage at Currumbin, Queensland, Australia — 79

8.1 New Zealand, with the Canterbury region highlighted — 132

8.2 Selwyn Waihora and Matrix of Good Management project timelines — 134

8.3 A summary of the three domains and five questions of the integration and implementation sciences (i2S) framework — 136

Figures ix

8.4	A week of salutary lessons for transdisciplinary researchers	144
12.1	Outcomes achieved in the trial of urine diversion systems at UTS	202
12.2	Images of documented pipe blockages from struvite build-up in piping for conventional urinals	204
12.3	Illustration of UD toilet and sampling system (Mitchell et al. 2013)	207
12.4	Graffiti board in situ and detail: used to collect end-users' feedback on the system, Designer: Yana Mokmargana (WSU)	209
12.5	Development of a visual communication strategy building collaborative input across strands of research (Mellick Lopes et al. 2012)	210
13.1	A learning ecosystem for productive failure	222
13.2	Failure potential of learning activities	226
13.3	Modelled prototype of a "floating mosaic" to enhance biodiversity in the Birs River software. (Source: Report from Clivaz, Eberli, Furrer, Holman, Hotz, Luz, Scherrer 2019)	229
15.1	"Top Impediments to IDR," _Facilitating Interdisciplinary Research_, 2005, p. 76	259

Tables

6.1   A representation of how success conditions vary across four Toolbox contexts. Toolbox workshops in each category draw their purposes from the set of purposes marked with a checkmark. "(ind)" indicates that the individual but not the group purpose is pursued   98

6.2   The Values module from Eigenbrode et al. (2007), with questions, is above the bar, while the Values module from Looney et al. (2014), with statements, is below it   100

12.1   Collaborators involved in the UTS trial across academia, industry and government   200

13.1   ESD competences in Bloom's Taxonomy   221

13.2   Corresponding learning activities and assessment tasks. Activities marked with a "*" are ungraded. Shaded assessment methods are graded cumulatively   230

15.1   Barriers and disincentives related to failure in cross-disciplinary and cross-sector work (Klein 2020)   257

Contributors

Cara Beal is an Associate Professor in Environmental Health at the School of Medicine at Griffith University, Queensland, and the Cities Research Institute. Cara teaches and researches in the fields of sustainable environmental management; environmental health; water, sanitation, hygiene; and socio-technically driven behaviour change. Although her research background is in the physical sciences, Cara has recognized the critical role that human behaviour and environmental psychology play in achieving truly sustainable, inclusive, and transformative outcomes for global planetary health and wellbeing. Apart from urine-diverting toilets, Cara has been involved in a number of innovative socio-technical research topics including the introduction of high-resolution smart water and energy meters in peri-urban subdivisions and remote First Nations communities in Australia, and the use of digital/geospatial tools to improve community water management in rural Pacific Island villages.

Bill Bellotti has more than 30 years' experience in leading agricultural production system research in southern Australia, western China and eastern India. His expertise includes agronomy, climate variability and change, farming systems and integrated approaches to food systems. Professor Bellotti's research in China and India has focused on sustainability and food security, and more recently on the linkages between diversification of cropping systems, dietary diversity and empowerment of women farmers. His research interests include the application of Life Cycle Assessment approaches to Australian food systems. This interest includes the development of concepts such as sustainable diets and food footprints. At the Global Change Institute, he looks forward to engaging the diversity of views and expertise across the University of Queensland and other stakeholders to promote more healthy, sustainable and equitable food systems.

Dennis Boyle is a partner and a founding team member of IDEO. Dennis helps lead the Design for Health Studio at IDEO and works in its San Francisco office. Design for Health is the part of IDEO's business that works with clients in medical and health-related industries to develop innovative products, software, services and strategies. Dennis is also an adjunct professor at Stanford's d.school and in the Design Division of the engineering school, where he has

xii Contributors

taught courses in product design, human factors design, design for sustainability and creativity and innovation. He established and co-teaches "Design for Healthy Behaviors" at the d.school, a course that draws students from each of the university's graduate schools. Students in this class learn and use the design thinking process to help patient-volunteers with chronic conditions build healthy behaviours and thrive in their daily lives.

Talya Brettler is a public health trained paediatrician serving as Medical Director at IDEO's Design for Health Studio in San Francisco. In that role, she helps bring innovation to health products, services and experiences. Talya especially enjoys demonstrating the value of human-centred design in an industry that is hesitant to accept change. She is passionate about exploring questions that challenge the status quo and improve health and wellness for the community. Talya holds a BA in philosophy from Harvard University, an MD from the University of Massachusetts Medical School and a Master's of Public Health from University of California, Berkeley. She completed her clinical training in paediatrics at Kaiser Oakland Medical Center.

Stewart Clegg is Distinguished Professor at the University of Technology Sydney, and a Visiting Professor at Nova School of Business and Economics, Lisbon. His research is driven by a fascination with power and theorizing. Stewart is a prolific writer and is the author or editor of a number of books, including recent volumes on *Strategy: Theory and Practice, Managing and Organizations, Positive Organizational Behaviour, Media Management and Digital Transformation, Theories of Organizational Resilience* and *Management, Organizations and Contemporary Social Theory* with various colleagues. He is also a prolific contributor to journals of note.

Irena Leisbet Ceridwen Connon (PhD, MRes, MA(Hons), FHEA, PG Cert) is a social anthropologist and transdisciplinary researcher whose research expertise and interests focus on: understanding the human responses to and management of environmental hazards, disasters, and climate risks; enhancing inclusion in disaster risk reduction strategy development; urban geography and healthy sustainable development, particularly in the context of high density urban development; planetary health and critical perspectives of sustainable development; water cycle management and the remediation of contaminated land and groundwater; transdisciplinary research methodologies; and policy-relevant qualitative, quantitative and mixed-method research. Her research has been published extensively in peer-reviewed academic journals and has been used to inform a number of national government strategic developments, including for improving institutional responses to weather emergencies and other environmental hazards. Irena is a Research Fellow with the Discipline of Geography at the University of Dundee in Scotland and with the Institute of Sustainable Futures at the University of Technology Sydney in Australia. She holds a PhD from the University of Aberdeen and is a Fellow of the Higher Education Academy.

Contributors xiii

Stephen Crowley is a Professor of Philosophy at Boise State University in Idaho. He has been part of the Toolbox Dialogue Initiative (TDI) since 2007 and TDI's focus on both theoretical and applied approaches to facilitating cross-disciplinary research forms a large part of his research agenda. As far as Stephen is concerned these interests flow naturally into his work on epistemology more generally, where he focuses on aspects of social epistemology using virtue theoretic perspectives and experimental methods.

Fred D'Agostino was educated at Amherst College (BA, 1968), Princeton University (MA, 1973), and the London School of Economics (PhD, 1978). He was Research Fellow in Philosophy at the Australian National University from 1978 to 1984 and worked at the University of New England in Australia from 1984 to 2004, where he was Associate Professor of Philosophy, Associate Dean of Arts, Head of the School of Social Science, and Member of the University Council. He is now Professor of Humanities and President of the Academic Board at the University of Queensland, Australia. He has edited the *Australasian Journal of Philosophy* and *Politics, Philosophy and Economics* and has published four books: *Chomsky's System of Ideas* (1986), *Free Public Reason* (1996), *Incommensurability and Commensuration* (2003), and *Naturalizing Epistemology* (2010). He recently completed work on an Australian Research Council (ARC) Discovery Grant project in social epistemology, and on an Australian Learning and Teaching Institute grant for educational leadership development. He is co-editor of the *Routledge Companion to Political and Social Philosophy.* His current research is on disciplinarity. He is a Fellow of the Australian Academy of the Humanities.

Jason De Santolo (Garrwa and Barunggam) is a producer, writer/director and researcher. He is Associate Professor in the School of Design and Director of Indigenous Excellence in the Faculty of Design, Architecture and Building at the University of Technology Sydney. Jason's latest film *Warburdar Bununu* screened in 2019 at the Sydney Film Festival and the Melbourne International Film Festival and received a Special Mention for Australian Shorts at the Antenna International Documentary Festival. His latest co-edited book (with Professor Jo-Ann Archibald and Professor Jenny Lee Morgan), *Decolonizing Research: Indigenous Storywork as Methodology*, was published in 2019 by Zed Books London.

Sanford D. Eigenbrode is Professor of Entomology and University Distinguished Professor at the University of Idaho. He conducts primary research on chemical ecology, landscape ecology, the management of pests, beneficial insects and insect vectors of plant pathogens affecting crops. The broader context of this work is food production as a social-ecological system, in which insects play a part. This has led to his involvement in and leadership of interdisciplinary projects addressing the sustainability of agricultural systems. As an outgrowth of his interdisciplinary endeavours, Sanford works with philosophers

xiv *Contributors*

to conduct research and provide consulting to improve communication within collaborative science and its applications.

Dena Fam is a system thinker and transdisciplinary collaborator at the Institute for Sustainable Futures at the University of Technology Sydney. Over the last decade, Dena has worked with industry, government and community actors to collaboratively manage, design, research and trial alternative water and sanitation systems with the aim of sustainably managing sewage and reducing its environmental impact on the water cycle. Her consulting/research experience has spanned the socio-cultural (learning for sustainability), institutional (policy analysis) and technological aspects of environmental management. With experience in transdisciplinary project development, Dena has increasingly been involved in developing processes for teaching and learning in transdisciplinary programmes and projects. In particular, she has been involved in documenting and synthesizing processes/methods/techniques supporting the development of transdisciplinary educational programmes and projects. Dena has led and co-led international transdisciplinary networking events, grants and projects including an Australian Government-funded teaching and learning grant.

Isabel Fletcher is a qualitative social scientist, based at the University of Edinburgh, whose research is located within science and technology studies, incorporating approaches from sociology, food policy and public health policy. She pursues two main research interests: British and European policy approaches to food, nutrition and eating, and the ways in which interdisciplinary research is used to address complex social problems. Her research contributions span public health models of obesity, food security policy, commercial actors' responses to public health regulation and sustainable diets. She is currently contributing to the Horizon 2020-funded SHAPE-ID project ("Shaping Interdisciplinary Practices in Europe") and co-convenes the interdisciplinary network Food Researchers in Edinburgh (FRIED).

Valerie Imbruce is the Director of the External Scholarships and Undergraduate Research Center and a Research Associate of Environmental Studies at Binghamton University in New York State. She specializes in educational programme design and the development of a first-year research immersion initiative in humanities and social sciences, interdisciplinary initiatives and scholarship programmes for academically talented, low-income, first generation and under-represented students. Her research investigates how Asian-Americans create and maintain food supply networks that suit their needs under changing social, economic and environmental circumstances. She is author of the book *From Farm to Canal Street: Chinatown's Alternative Food Network in the Global Marketplace* with Cornell University Press. She collaborates with colleagues through the Sustainable Communities Transdisciplinary Area of Excellence to measure environmental, social and economic health across communities. Imbruce teaches a first-year research course in which students investigate the intersections between culture, environment and politics in their newfound college hometown. Her work has been supported by the National Science Foundation and the National Endowment for the Humanities.

Julie Thompson Klein is Professor of Humanities Emerita at Wayne State University, Detroit. She has also been a Visiting Foreign Professor in Japan, a Fulbright Professor in Nepal, a Foundation Visitor at the University of Auckland in New Zealand and Mellon Fellow in Digital Humanities at the University of Michigan. Holder of a PhD in English from the University of Oregon, Klein is past president of the Association for Interdisciplinary Studies (AIS), former editor of the AIS journal *Issues in Interdisciplinary Studies* and recipient of the Kenneth Boulding Award for outstanding scholarship on interdisciplinarity. Her books include *Interdisciplinarity* (1990), *Interdisciplinary Studies Today* (1994), *Crossing Boundaries* (1996), *Transdisciplinarity* (2001), *Interdisciplinary Education in K-12 and College* (2002), *Humanities, Culture, and Interdisciplinarity* (2005), *Creating Interdisciplinary Campus Cultures* (2010) and *Interdisciplining Digital Humanities* (2015). She is also Associate Editor of the *Oxford Handbook on Interdisciplinarity* (2010, 2017) and co-editor of the University of Michigan Press series *Digital Humanities@ digitalculturebooks*.

Abby Mellick Lopes is a design theorist with 15 years' practical and academic experience in the field of design for sustainability. She is currently Associate Professor in the School of Design, University of Technology Sydney. Her current research projects explore the liveability of Western Sydney in a climate-changed future, and repair cultures in Sydney. She also researches in visual communications and has a long-standing interest in how image ecologies mediate socio-material relationships, which was the topic of her PhD titled "Ecology of the Image" (2005). She publishes widely, most recently contributing several chapters to *The Bloomsbury Encyclopedia of Design* (2016). In 2015 she co-edited a special issue on design and social practice theory for the international *Journal of Design Research* (with Dr. Dena Fam), and another for the *Global Media Journal: Australian Edition*, entitled "Initiating change by design."

Catherine Lyall is Professor of Science and Public Policy at the University of Edinburgh. She is an experienced science policy researcher and evaluator of knowledge exchange and interdisciplinary research who has acted as a consultant to public bodies including the UK Economic and Social Research Council (ESRC), the Scottish Funding Council and the European Commission. She is Co-Investigator on an EU-funded project, Shaping Interdisciplinary Practices in Europe (SHAPE-ID) addressing the challenge of improving interdisciplinary cooperation between the arts, humanities and social sciences (AHSS) and STEM (sciences, technology, engineering and mathematics) and other disciplines. Her publications include *Interdisciplinary Research Journeys* (2011) and a paper in *Futures* that explores the UK research community's engagement with "transdisciplinarity." Her latest book *Being an Interdisciplinary* xvi *Contributors*

Academic: How Institutions Shape University Careers highlights the enduring challenges faced by researchers attempting to embed interdisciplinarity in their own career trajectories.

Cynthia Mitchell's passion for improving our collective ability to articulate, do and value transdisciplinary research began when an engineering professor said of her research student's work, "I just can't see a PhD in this," and an education professor said, "I can see three." Cynthia is Deputy Director and Professor of Sustainability at the Institute for Sustainable Futures at the University of Technology Sydney, where she has been pioneering transdisciplinary research since 2001, principally in learning, water services and international development. She founded, and for 13 years directed, the Institute's higher degree research programme. Her research has won national and international awards from academia and industry. She has an honorary doctorate from Chalmers University in Sweden for her interdisciplinary work for the environment, and is a fellow of the Academy of Technological Sciences and Engineering, a fellow of Engineers Australia and a fellow of the Institute of Community Directors of Australia.

Linda Neuhauser (Dr PH, MPH) is Clinical Professor of Community Health Sciences at the School of Public Health, University of California, Berkeley (California, USA) and is Visiting Professor at the Department of Humanities and Social Sciences at Nanjing Youdian University (Nanjing, China). She is also Co-Principal Investigator of the Health Research for Action Center (HRA) at the UC Berkeley School of Public Health. Her teaching, research and practice are focused on using participatory methods across disciplines and societal sectors to engage diverse groups to identify and solve problems. She and her Center colleagues have used participatory and transdisciplinary methods to co-create and test many kinds of health and social interventions in many countries worldwide spanning diverse topics from large-scale efforts to educate parents of young children, to transforming approaches to address childhood asthma, to working closely with factory workers in China to improve their life situations. She has authored over 100 publications about participatory design, transdisciplinary research and action and health interventions.

Michael O'Rourke is Professor of Philosophy and faculty member in AgBioResearch and Environmental Science and Policy at Michigan State University. He is Director of the Center for Interdisciplinarity (http://c4i.msu.edu/) and Director of the Toolbox Dialogue Initiative, an NSF-sponsored research initiative that investigates philosophical approaches to facilitating interdisciplinary research (http://tdi.msu.edu/). His research interests include epistemology, communication and epistemic integration in collaborative, cross-disciplinary research and linguistic communication between intelligent agents.

BinBin Pearce is a senior scientist and lecturer at ETH Zurich in the Transdisciplinarity Lab in the Department of Environmental Systems Science.

Making use of a mental models approach, cognitive mapping, soft systems methodology, qualitative systems modelling and institutional analysis and design thinking, her research interest is in developing and evaluating methods for collaborative decision-making. She is also an educator who has developed new curriculum and learning environments that enable students to understand and critically challenge the world around them by building skills for insightful observation and problem-solving. She has been involved in research and engineering projects on waste management, energy, and agriculture projects in Singapore, India, China, and the United States. She has a doctorate from the Yale School of Forestry and Environmental Studies, and BSc and MSc degrees in Environmental Engineering from Stanford University.

Miroslava Prazak teaches anthropology at Bennington College in Vermont. Her longitudinal research in East Africa focuses on gender-, age-, social- and economy-based inequalities, particularly the impact of economic development on various cultural institutions, including family, education and health care systems. In addition, her interests include ways of knowing, and their relevance to institutional organization and change. Her book *Making the Mark: Gender, Identity and Genital Cutting* was published in 2016 and her more recent publications include: the entry on "Women, Gender, and Sexuality" for the *Oxford Encyclopedia of African Women's History*; a chapter on "Doing Good and Doing It Quickly in East African Study Abroad Programs," co-authored with Jennifer Coffman in *Study Abroad: Service, Student Travel, and the Quest for an Anti-Tourism Experience*; and a special issue of *The Walloomsack Review* titled *Bennington: View from Bingham Hill*, showcasing the writings of students in the 2018 iteration of the "Studying Place by Metes and Bounds."

Melissa Robson-Williams works at Manaaki Whenua Landcare Research in Lincoln, New Zealand, as an environmental scientist and transdisciplinary researcher. Melissa works in the Landscape, People and Governance team and manages the Integrated Land and Water Management research area. Since 2018 she has had an additional role as an integration architect. After completing a PhD in plant and soil science and an MSc in integrated water management and advanced irrigation, Melissa worked at the Environment Agency in the United Kingdom in regulatory and catchment-based water quality initiatives. In 2008, Melissa moved to New Zealand and after leading a large multidisciplinary project on the environmental impacts of irrigation development, she began a joint appointment between AgResearch and Environment Canterbury to facilitate science and policy interactions in managing water quality. She specializes in managing the impacts of land use on water, science and policy interactions and the practice of transdisciplinary research.

Roger Robson-Williams works at the New Zealand Institute of Plant and Food Research, where he has been the General Manager of Science – Sustainable Production since early 2014 and Chief Sustainability Officer since 2019. Roger studied applied biological sciences at graduate and postgraduate levels in the

xviii *Contributors*

United Kingdom, gaining a PhD from the University of Sheffield. He worked as a plant pathologist in a range of crops in the United Kingdom at Horticulture Research International and Rothamsted Research before taking up senior science management positions at the UK's Home-Grown Cereals Authority and latterly the Royal Horticultural Society. Roger moved to New Zealand in 2012 to join the Foundation for Arable Research as Director of Research Development. While there, he developed a keen interest in sustainability issues and particularly the impacts of primary production on the environment. He is the chairman of the Precision Agriculture Association of New Zealand.

Bruce Small was born in 1955 in Hamilton, New Zealand. He did his PhD on the social responsibility of scientists in a high technology world, based on research conducted in the departments of philosophy and psychology at the University of Waikato. Currently, Bruce is a senior scientist (social science and bioethics) with AgResearch Ltd, a New Zealand Crown Research Institute. His research interests include: technological foresight, digital technologies, sustainability science, interdisciplinary and transdisciplinary research processes and ethics and socially responsible science.

Annika Thalheimer has an MSc in Sustainability Science. She has been a member of the Faculty of Sustainability Sciences at Leuphana University Lüneburg in Germany since 2014. From 2016 to 2018 she was a student assistant in the Transdisciplinary Research Projects module of the faculty's Master's programme. Annika has participated as both a student and a tutor and helped to organize and manage the module and its consolidation. Recently, she worked in the transdisciplinary project "Zukunftsstadt Lüneburg 2030+" a collaboration between Leuphana University and the City of Lüneburg. Her research focuses on education for sustainable development and sustainable consumption as well as creative approaches to sustainable transformation. The title of her Master's thesis was "Corporations in our Heads: The Potential of an Interactive Theatre Method in Education for Sustainable Consumption." In September 2018 she began work as Project and Education Consultant for the Earth Charter Initiative Germany.

Martina Ukowitz is an Associate Professor at Klagenfurt University, Austria. Her research interests include transdisciplinary research, intervention research, organizational research and development, the theory of science, and process ethics. She is conducting transdisciplinary research projects in various interdisciplinary constellations in the fields of sustainable development, education, nature conservation and public health. In 2003, after her studies at Graz University and 12 years of working as a trainer in vocational adult education and teacher training, she began her scientific work as a freelance staff member in several research projects at the University of Klagenfurt. In 2006 she became Assistant Professor and after her Habilitation in Transdisciplinary Intervention Research in 2012, she became an Associate Professor at the Department of Organizational Development, Group Dynamics and Intervention

Research at the University of Klagenfurt, where she also had management tasks. In 2017 she moved to the Department of Personnel, Leadership and Organizational Behaviour, where she holds a part-time position. Her teaching activities currently cover qualitative social research, transdisciplinary research, and organizational research in study programmes for business management and the education sciences.

Stephanie E. Vasko is the Managing Director at the Center for Interdisciplinarity at Michigan State University. She holds a PhD in chemistry and nanotechnology (2012) and an MSc in chemistry (2009). She builds community and collaborative capacity among academic, community and blended academic/community research teams by developing and delivering philosophically informed team-based workshops as part of the Toolbox Dialogue Initiative. She also researches the application of machine learning to team science and artistic practice, and she conducts research around ceramics and mixed media sculptures. She is a former American Association for the Advancement of Science Community Engagement Fellow.

Ulli Vilsmaier trained as a geographer and is currently a member of the Institute of Philosophy and Sciences of Art, and of the Methodology Center at Leuphana University Lüneburg. She was a Junior Professor for Transdisciplinary Methods and President's Delegate for Transdisciplinarity at Leuphana University from 2011 to 2017 and member of the Institute of Geography and Geology of Salzburg University from 2001 to 2011. Her research and teaching focus is on epistemological and methodological foundations, and methods for inter- and transdisciplinary research. She is working on the design of spaces for inter- and transdisciplinary research. Her particular interests are in concept-, image- and artefact-based methods of boundary work and interface design, as well as new modes of research for inter- and transdisciplinary teams. Her thematic research fields are: sustainability and sustainability science, sustainable urban and rural development, climate change adaptation and area protection. Her further research deals with inter- and transdisciplinary research-based learning, the concept of global learning, and theory–praxis relations in education. Research approaches that have emerged from pedagogies of liberation in Latin America, strongly grounded in civil society organizations, have recently become important in her work.

Preface

Failures and successes, in all their messiness ...

During a light-hearted conversation in the campus cafeteria at Leuphana University in Germany in 2017, we pondered the need for a book on interdisciplinary and transdisciplinary failures. As with many academics and practitioners working across disciplines, we have both experienced failures, yet had not openly and explicitly shared the details of those failures in a public forum. Also, while it was our sense that interdisciplinary and transdisciplinary, or more generally, *cross-disciplinary* projects fail more often than they succeed, we had not encountered much discussion of these failures. This book therefore emerged as a way of reflecting on our own failures while also remedying our concern about the lack of communication about unsuccessful cross-disciplinary projects.

With these goals in mind, we have brought together a collection of highly experienced and emerging international academics and practitioners to share their failures across a broad range of interdisciplinary and transdisciplinary projects and programmes. This book has been structured to ensure each chapter not only details a project failure but also identifies recommendations for mitigating these failures, ensuring that learning can take place through our shared experience and communication.

Finally, there is no shortage of published works available espousing successful models, frameworks and practices for interdisciplinary and transdisciplinary practitioners. In our view, these works reflect a "success" bias in scientific publication which contributes to the formation of the unrealistic expectation that complex cross-disciplinary projects are only valuable if they are successful, and that they should otherwise be hidden in the shadows, never to be heard from again. This book is offered in opposition to this bias. By sharing the messy and complicated details of failed projects, we position the reader to engage more effectively in cross-disciplinary practice by learning from the failure of others.

Acknowledgements

We would like to acknowledge the authors contributing chapters to this book who have boldly delved into the messy details of their past to retrieve recommendations for others to learn from their failures. This is a risky form of research communication, given the stigma that can attach to failure in research practice, and we are grateful to them for their willingness to accept that risk with a view to improving cross-disciplinary research and practice.

1 Theoretical and empirical perspectives on failure

An introduction

Michael O'Rourke and Dena Fam

Introduction

Consider the following example. A two-day meeting of highly motivated university researchers in a large metropolitan area was convened by city managers, planners and engineers to address concerns about the resilience of downtown infrastructure in the context of a changing climate. Specifically, it wasn't clear whether the city had the ability to manage stormwater drainage in a new climate regime that included higher-than-normal precipitation. A recent close call with flooding had raised concerns, and the city leadership was now convinced that they needed a research-based plan to address these concerns. The group of researchers was multi-disciplinary, ranging over disciplines such as hydrology, civil engineering, urban planning and even philosophy. The goal of the meeting was to find common interests among the different disciplines and then use that as a staging ground for a research project that would both document existing infrastructural inadequacies and identify promising directions for sustainable improvement.

It began with promise, first with presentations by city officials and then disciplinary, research-focused presentations from the academics. But as the meeting unfolded, it began to dawn on both city officials and university researchers that the priorities which motivated them were different and, perhaps, incommensurable. To provide funding for the work through their budgets, city officials needed quick responses to their concerns and a set of findings that they could use to write policy and initiate change. The academics, on the other hand, needed peer-reviewed research products to justify their time to administrators back at the university. By the time the group got to the "next steps" part of the meeting at the end of day two, it was clear that there was no way this particular collection of experts could take any further steps together.

This transdisciplinary effort failed before it could get started, but its failure is instructive. Efforts like this one are complex, involving a variety of different perspectives, values and priorities. Even the enthusiastic embrace of a common objective, like planning for a city's resilient future, is insufficient to ensure project success. What could have been done differently? Recognition in this case of the different cultures would have been a good start, since that might have revealed the differences among the incentives and rewards that motivated the different

2   *Michael O'Rourke and Dena Fam*

participants to attend the meeting. Initiating the meeting with a conversation about the deliverables required by the city officials and the academics would have helped, as such a conversation would likely have highlighted differences and perhaps motivated early compromises and the pursuit of common ground.

In general, the published research literature exhibits a bias towards positive outcomes because, for the most part, only what *works* gets published. Research failures such as the one described above less commonly contribute to the literature, since many projects are dropped before they come to fruition. Much can be learned, however, from what *doesn't* work. For example, cautionary tales about what to avoid could help researchers save valuable time and resources, especially in research projects that are intrinsically complex. In this volume, we assemble the first set of original essays that concern failure in intrinsically complex projects, focusing on those that are interdisciplinary and transdisciplinary in character.

Interdisciplinary and transdisciplinary modes of research involve the integration of different perspectives, and for this reason they are notoriously challenging. *Interdisciplinary* research combines insights from different academic disciplines, and so it is not uncommon that it requires the integration of different types of data collected using different methods in the service of different explanations. *Transdisciplinary* research involves the integration of knowledge and expertise from academic and other sectors of society, such as non-governmental organizations (NGOs), policymakers and community members. In addition to any challenges that derive from the presence of different disciplinary experts, transdisciplinary projects confront large differences in the values, priorities and cultures of participants. These challenges manifest at all stages in the lifecycles of these projects, creating the potential for failure at all points along the way.

Documenting details of failure in interdisciplinary and transdisciplinary projects matters, not only as an illustration of how challenges are experienced in these complex contexts, but also since projects do not always follow step-by-step protocols that generate preconceived and theorized processes. While clearly defined processes can be invaluable for guiding the development of complex projects, in reality practice may diverge from theory. Case studies that illustrate failure illuminate causal links in real-life projects that can help researchers and practitioners avoid pitfalls in their own work.

In this introduction, we set the stage for the case studies to follow in subsequent chapters. We begin by reflecting on *failure* in general before considering the results of a preliminary survey we have conducted on the incidence of failure in cross-disciplinary projects. The survey results position us to describe how we conceive of failure in this volume, a conception that we then use to introduce each chapter in turn.

What is *failure*?

One goal of this introduction is to provide a systematic and informed way of thinking about what counts as *failure* in the context of interdisciplinary and transdisciplinary projects. As we noted above, these are typically complex projects designed to do justice to the manifold challenges of complex problems. They involve many moving parts, and so there are many potential sites of failure. In this section, we provide a review of the literature on failure, which draws on a number of different disciplinary perspectives, ranging from engineering to philosophy to organizational behavior. After discussing a number of different ways that one might think about failure, we highlight why failure is often identified by educators as a powerful instructional tool.

Ways of thinking about failure

Why spend time developing a conceptual understanding of failure? After all, surely we all know what failure is – we've experienced it personally and we've observed that others experience it, and we typically work hard to minimize it in our lives. While it is certainly true that we are all personally acquainted with failure, it is precisely with respect to quotidian concepts like this that a systematic, theoretical understanding can help. It allows us to be consistent and reliable in reflecting on past experience and planning future experience, and it also supports the interpersonal exchange of information about failure. Without theoretical coordination, we lack firm ground to compare our experiences and learn from one another.

A good place to start is with a definition of the term "failure." One might think pursuing a definition is a fool's errand, given that the term "can take on different meanings in different contexts" (Petroski 2012, p. 134) and given the very broad "class of things it represents" (Firestein 2016, p. 7). But we can grant that no compact definition is going to provide individually necessary and jointly sufficient conditions encompassing all and only those things that count as failure while nevertheless recognizing that efforts to delimit the application of the concept by defining it can be very informative. Because so many things count, the attempts at defining failure are often quite general:

1. "a state where reality is inferior to the goal"; "reality is worse than expectations" (Lee and Miesing 2017, p. 159)
2. "deviation from expected and desired results" (Cannon and Edmondson 2005, p. 300)
3. "an unacceptable difference between expected and observed performance" (Carper 1996, p. 57, as quoted in Petroski 2018, p. 50)

More specific definitions are also available that focus on failure in particular contexts:

4. *Education*: "students will typically not be able to generate or discover the correct solution(s) by themselves" (Kapur 2016, p. 289)
5. *Academia*: "the authoring faculty members' inability to collaboratively create our intended, idealized manuscript product in a timely fashion" (Vanasupa et al. 2011, p. 173)

In each of these definitions, failure is understood relative to a norm or ideal, for example, a "goal," an "expected ... performance," or the "correct solution(s)." Furthermore, each definition highlights falling short of meeting the norm or realizing the ideal. *Falling short* by itself is not necessarily a problem – it is not just *failure* by another term; what constitutes an outcome as a failure is that meeting the norm is "desired," "intended," or "expected," which means that the effort has led to disappointment. Of course, what it means to *fall short* is going to depend heavily on the nature of the norm and the associated expectations, which will vary significantly by context.

Definitions help us distinguish failure from non-failure, but once we have identified failure as a category, there is still analytic work to be done before we fully understand it. Failures differ along several dimensions, such as how *avoidable* a failure was, its *size*, whether it is a failure in *product* or *process*, and how *objective* it is. We might think that we should avoid failure if we can, and only accept it if it is unavoidable; however, whether or not the failure is avoidable will turn on many factors, and it is important to recognize that *avoidable* failures can be laudable – for example, if they reflect experiments aimed at innovation (Cannon and Edmondson 2005) – and *unavoidable* failures can be criticizable – for example, if they reflect broader systemic problems that need to be addressed (Baumard and Starbuck 2005).

The *size* of a failure is one of its more obvious characteristics, since the catastrophic failures we notice tend to be large ones, for example the Hyatt Regency Hotel Disaster of 1981 or the Tacoma Narrows Bridge failure (Petroski 1992). Failure doesn't need to be catastrophic, though, as there are also "small losses" (Sitkin 1992) and even "micro-failures" (Tawfik et al. 2015; Lam 2019).

Failure can also be analyzed in terms of *product* and *process*. The concept *failure* is typically used to highlight the *product* of falling short, as is evinced in the general definitions (1) to (3) above which emphasize the outcome's "state," "deviation," or "difference." It is also possible, however, to highlight the *process* of falling short, as is clear from the more specific definitions (4) and (5) above that focus on the inability of people to produce a successful product.

A final dimension that can help us understand failure concerns whether or not we are thinking of it *objectively* or *subjectively*. The larger the failure, the more likely it will strike people as an objective failure, that is, one that is a failure no matter how you look at it. But failure can be in the "eyes of the beholder" (Lee and Miesing 2017, p. 158) – what seems a failure to one person might not strike another in those terms. For example, if you conceive of a project as one that embeds principles of adaptation, the events that force project adjustment may be regarded as felicitous parts of the natural development of the project towards your objectives rather than instances of failure.

Disciplinary perspectives on failure

The observation that failures come in different shapes and sizes is further reinforced by looking at how failure is treated in disciplines that explicitly thematize it. Failures are found in all disciplines, of course, but only a few disciplines explicitly identify failure as part of their process. Pausing to consider how failure is understood and harnessed by these disciplines can foreground strategies for dealing with failure that are applicable in interdisciplinary and transdisciplinary contexts. We will briefly consider six disciplines: engineering, logic, the philosophy of science, empirical science, education and learning and organizational behavior.

- *Engineering*: Because the failure of bridges or structures can lead to injury and death, it is incumbent on engineers to design with failure in mind. Engineering is in fact home to *forensic engineering*, or the investigation of engineering failures, and *failure analysis,* a field that aims to provide "critical feedback into the design process thereby contributing to the prevention of engineering failures in the future" (Engineering Failure Analysis 2020). Henry Petroski, a civil engineer who has spent a career writing about the importance of failure to engineering and design, argues that success is "foreseeing failure" (Petroski 1992, p. 53), and that the "paradox of engineering and design" is that we will learn more from failure than we will from success (Petroski 2018, p. 96).
- *Logic*: Although contradictions, that is, propositions that are necessarily false, are not failures, they can indicate the presence of failure. When you derive a contradiction from a set of propositions that you believe to be consistent and collectively significant, you establish that the set is inconsistent and meaningless, since it will in fact entail any proposition at all. An important historical example of this involves Bertrand Russell noticing that his set-theoretic paradox could be derived from the axioms that formed the foundation of Gottlob Frege's logical work (Irvine and Deutsch 2016). Logic, though, harnesses failure of this sort as a proof technique against the backdrop of bivalence in the form of *reductio ad absurdum*, which directs us to assert the proposition $\sim p$ if we can establish that the proposition p leads to contradiction.
- *Philosophy of science*: It would seem that the goal of scientific inquiry is to propose hypotheses that get the world right and then confirm them via experiment. It is not uncommon, though, that the world rejects our hypotheses, and this can certainly feel like failure if you have devoted significant time to preparing the test for that hypothesis (Parkes 2019). The philosopher Karl Popper understood science to differ from non-science precisely by virtue of its relationship to this sort of "failure." Popper argued that science is dependent for its success on scientists formulating risky hypotheses that are *falsifiable* in the sense that they could be undermined in principle by empirical evidence (Popper 1999).
- *Empirical science*: Another general lesson for empirical science that derives from the concept of failure concerns *negative results* (Firestein 2016). There is a bias in the direction of positive results in the scientific literature, as one might expect; however, scientists often get things wrong and occasionally they get things wrong in ways that are instructive (e.g., the Michelson-Morley experiment). Until recently, though, there was little to be done with

interesting negative results. It has become increasingly possible to publish negative or null results, enabling the scientific community to profit from the apparent failures of others (JNRBM 2020).

- *Education and learning*: Successful learning is marked by the acquisition of knowledge or abilities – for example, the ability to solve a certain kind of problem. Failure in this context is the familiar experience of falling short in performance, which is an expected and regular feature of the process of learning. In fact, failure has been harnessed by educational theory in a "paradigm of learning from failure" (Lam 2019, p. 1), which recognizes that failure can create the kind of "impasse" or "disequilibrium" that motivates inquiry and results in informed adjustments to mental models (Tawfik et al. 2015). Paradoxically, because failure can be so productive in the learning process, there are those who argue that it should be built into that process as a required part (Tawfik et al. 2015; Kapur 2016; see Chapter 13, Pearce).
- *Organizational behavior*: Organizations are also capable of learning from experience and adapting their operation to changing circumstances (Cyert and March 1963; Baumard and Starbuck 2005). As with individuals, though, there are reasons why this is not inevitable (Baumard and Starbuck 2005). However, if an organization creates a culture that encourages the identification and analysis of failure, and even experimentation designed to generate failure, then failure can be an engine of innovation (Sitkin 1992; Cannon and Edmondson 2005). Organizations that "use failure prospectively and systematically" can be said to engage in "failure management" (Lee and Miesing 2017), encouraging intelligent, productive failure that is associated with the idea of "fast failure" (Matson 1991) and the mantra, "fail fast, fail often" (Draper 2017; see Chapter 13, Pearce).

In all these domains, *failure* in the sense of falling short of some expected or desired norm or ideal is understood to be a part of the process of success, and in some cases a critical part of it. Of course, the fact that success in these domains depends on failure doesn't make failure desirable – it is still something we seek to avoid because of the personal and professional havoc it can create (Sitkin 1992; McGrath 2011). By thematizing failure and approaching it explicitly and systematically, each of these disciplines harnesses failure and makes it a productive input into an epistemic process that enhances prospects for understanding. This book is our attempt to begin thematizing failure in the context of interdisciplinary and transdisciplinary research and practice, helping researchers and practitioners derive lessons from cautionary tales.

Learning from failure

Each of the disciplines canvassed in the previous section make it a point to *learn* from failure. Although failure can be a powerful motivator, it is not intrinsically valuable – at best it is only instrumentally valuable. Given the damage failure can cause and the difficulties it can create for individuals and organizations

(Dattner and Hogan 2011), one might think that it would be better to concentrate on learning from success, which has clear intrinsic value. Success, though, is limiting – it can lock one into a narrow range of options and reduce innovation and flexibility in a dynamic environment (Sitkin 1992; Baumard and Starbuck 2005). Furthermore, a blinkered commitment to success can make it harder to see flaws in one's approach which can manifest in the form of even bigger failure when circumstances change (Petroski 2018). Given how dynamic and *sui generis* the circumstances tend to be for interdisciplinary and transdisciplinary projects, it is very risky to assume that success in one context will translate into success in others.

Thus, there is reason to believe that failures can be better learning catalysts than successes, but this does not imply that all failures are equally informative. Failures due to inattention, carelessness, or incompetence are rarely informative for anyone other than the person or organization who should have been more careful, but failures due to a surprising or unforeseen complication can reveal important information about systems and contexts (Cannon and Edmondson 2005; Lee and Miesing 2017). In cases where failure catalyzes learning, an inability to perform in the short term gives way to an ability to perform in the longer term. This transition is facilitated by the application of existing knowledge to the experience, generating new and potentially innovative understanding (Kapur 2016).

If one wishes to manage failure proactively, one should create conditions for *intelligent* failure. (See Chapter 13 by Pearce on the concept of "failing forward" as an example.) Intelligent failure results from well-planned, modest actions with uncertain outcomes that quickly generate insights into the relevant domains or phenomena (Matson 1991; Sitkin 1992). Intelligent failure can motivate inquiry that changes how an individual or organization thinks about the problem space by moving from identification of the problem to causal analysis, evaluation and reflection and self-regulation (Tawfik et al. 2015). Because smaller failures, such as "micro-failures," can serve to elucidate "misconceptions" or "errors in causal reasoning" (Tawfik et al. 2015, p. 986), it can be especially helpful to proactively identify and learn from them (Cannon and Edmondson 2005).

Two points are worth emphasizing here, since as we have noted, it is not a given that individuals or organizations will actually learn from failures. First, it is important to facilitate the transition from experiencing failure to learning from it (Kapur 2016), perhaps with experts who have skill in analyzing the data it generates (Cannon and Edmondson 2005). Also, it is crucial that people are incentivized and rewarded for identifying failures; without a culture that is congenial to learning from failure, people will likely recoil from it and work hard to pretend it never happened.

How failure manifests in interdisciplinary and transdisciplinary projects – results from an international survey

As there is a shortage of comprehensive literature and case studies of interdisciplinary and transdisciplinary failures, we undertook an initial exploration into

8 *Michael O'Rourke and Dena Fam*

failure in complex integrative projects through an online survey. In designing and delivering a brief survey focusing on things that *don't work*, the aim was to gather preliminary data to compare the amount of failure experienced in collaborative, interdisciplinary and transdisciplinary projects to the amount of failure experienced in collaborative disciplinary projects. In addition, the brief nine-question survey incorporated open-ended questions to gain insight into the details of how failure had manifested in such projects. Reflecting what was discussed above, failure was characterized broadly as ranging from potentially major and catastrophic failure resulting in the end of a project, to potentially minor failures which could be experienced at any point in a project, and which forced the revision of project plans.

Invitations to participate in the survey were sent to international networks supporting collaborative research and practice. These networks included TDNet (Network for Transdisciplinary Research), the Science of Team Science network and the Integration and Implementation Sciences network, to name a few. Between March and November 2019, a total of 149 survey participants responded with a rich array of examples of what constituted failure and how failure had manifested in their own interdisciplinary and transdisciplinary initiatives.

Initial survey questions sought to determine whether participants had been involved in collaborative, interdisciplinary or transdisciplinary projects (95% responding in the positive) and the number of such projects conducted, which ranged from 2 to 50 projects per participant. This result provided evidence of the range of participants in the survey, from highly experienced to relatively new practitioners experiencing failure. From the 95% of participants who had previously been involved in interdisciplinary and transdisciplinary projects, 93% had experienced project failure.

In this section, we provide a brief overview of three key themes emerging from open-ended questions concerning how participants felt failure manifested in their projects. In analyzing and collating results to present within this short introductory chapter, key themes were categorized under three main headings: (1) *institutional failures*, (2) *praxis failures* and (3) *individual failures*.

Institutional failures

> "I feel failure [exists] between the lofty idealism and nearly utopic ambitions of projects and the actual messy reality of trying to get practical results from diverse stakeholders … with different disciplinary (and even different ontological foundations …). There are successes in the mix, but certainly a lot of compromises, anxieties, disjunctures and misses" (survey participant).

There is no lack of literature on the institutional challenges facing academics working in interdisciplinary and transdisciplinary environments (Yarime, Trencher et al. 2012; Bammer 2013; Evans 2015; Lyall 2019). This literature is concerned not only with institutional support of academics working in such environments from a departmental perspective but also, as Klein et al. (2017, p. 1055) note, with the "challenges across the entire academic system, from administrative policies and budget formulas to disciplinary cultures of research and education" which are all implicated in and contribute to these challenges. The lack of institutional support for, and the low value associated with, collaborative work was a strong theme in the survey results, with participants noting the "lack of commitment because of [a] lack of support from their departments or organizations which don't value interdisciplinary work." More disturbing from a professional perspective was a participant's comment that some "senior academics [even] fear being shunned in their departments and deprived of resources if they are working outside their discipline where the department's ability to evaluate their work is limited."

Praxis failures

In discussing praxis failures, we follow Evans (2015) in defining praxis as a unity and a nonlinear and non-hierarchical relationship between the domains of theory, practice and reflection. In the survey responses, results which were seen as having arisen from praxis failure generally related to team members having insufficient skills to work in collaborative, integrative ways, or to a disconnection between the theory and practice of collaborative, integrative work. One survey participant highlighted praxis failures that arose in teams due to a lack of consensus on methods and practice: "Most projects had a meta-analytical orientation and virtually all of them 'failed' in that they fell short of establishing consensus on the definition of the categories and methods under discussion." Other participants provided insight into failures related to adequately providing students with the skills needed to work in interdisciplinary and transdisciplinary ways: "Failure happened at [the] front end because … the knowledge relationships and practices of the students weren't properly taught before they started working on the project."

Individual failures

When individuals were implicated in the failure of interdisciplinary and transdisciplinary projects, survey results tended to emphasize inadequate management of projects, unrealistic expectations of team members and a failure to effectively work collaboratively. As one survey participant highlighted, failed projects emerged as a "very broad range [of failures] and was partly self-induced [through] mismanagement or failure of expectation management." These failures included those related to a lack of clearly defined objectives and operating relationships, illustrated by another survey participant who suggested, "when a loosely connected group comes together with vague objectives and poorly defined operating relationships (that, of course, spells trouble for any group)."

Finally, survey participants noted that while critical for dealing with complex problems, interdisciplinary and transdisciplinary approaches have the potential to be "high risk and low reward" endeavors. This was clearly evidenced by survey data: 51% of participants suggested that failure was more likely for these projects than for disciplinary projects. One participant lamented that "the success rate of these endeavors in most institutions remains small. So, high risk, low rewards and low probability of success. Who could resist such a deal?"

10   *Michael O'Rourke and Dena Fam*

How to think about failure in this volume

Building on what we can learn from the previous two sections, we offer in this section a more focused set of reflections on failure in interdisciplinary and transdisciplinary research and practice. We begin by offering a general definition of *failure* that is related to the idea of falling short of a desired or expected norm or ideal. In the context of interdisciplinary or transdisciplinary projects, we frame this way of thinking about failure in terms of substantive *plans*. Researchers and practitioners construct these plans as they pursue project objectives and are committed to them as a consequence. If we fall short of meeting them, we have failed to achieve something that is part of our project. (These plans are more than just "let's meet on Wednesday at noon," which would not count as a substantive project plan.)

For our purposes in this volume, we interpret the phrase "X failed" as "X didn't work as planned." Plans can fail to come off at any point in a project, from the initial discussion stage to the final dissemination stage. Project failure could be major and catastrophic, resulting in project collapse, or it could be more minor, forcing a revision of project plans. Of course, all projects require adjustments on the fly, and not all adjustments should be understood as failures. Modification in response to a failure, as opposed to a normal adjustment, means that the project team attempted to execute a substantive project plan (e.g., write a proposal together, collect data together, collaboratively write a paper) and failed to execute it, resulting in a fundamental change to the plan. And as we observed in the last section, these failures can be due to institutional, praxis, or individual considerations, among others.

Interdisciplinary and transdisciplinary projects as sites of failure

The projects described in this volume are one and all complex, as befits their interdisciplinary and transdisciplinary character. These projects address problems that are complex, and in many cases *wicked*. To call a problem "wicked" is to emphasize that its complexity resists formulation, and that it is a moving target that resists solution. In their classic formulation of wicked problems, Rittel and Webber (1973) emphasize that they are unique problems that are open to explanation from many angles and resist univocal formulation or best solutions; further, as "symptoms" of other problems, they change under investigation into new problems, leaving the investigator to conclude their work when they run out of resources rather than when they have solved the problem. When confronted by problems like these, we are well advised to marshal as many different perspectives as we can and work towards better responses.

Interdisciplinary and transdisciplinary projects respond to complex problems with complex responses out of respect for the nature of the problems and a desire to find sustainable responses. Their complexity resides along a number of dimensions:

- Epistemically, they seek to integrate potentially incommensurable ways of knowing that are responsive to different types of evidence, and that embed different norms of confirmation (Eigenbrode et al. 2007).

Perspectives on failure 11

- Socially, they combine different cultures, both within the academy and outside of it, and as a consequence create occasionally volatile mixtures of attitudes towards leadership, accountability and collaboration (Morse et al. 2007; Lang et al. 2012).
- Politically, they often reflect uneven and asymmetric relationships that can privilege some participants at the expense of others, for example in the case of research involving local and Indigenous knowledges (Raymond et al. 2010).
- Economically, they depend on funding, but the funding can be hard to come by (Bromham et al. 2016) even though there is evidence that cross-disciplinary research has greater impact over time (van Noorden 2015).
- Finally, it can be challenging to determine how to communicate the results of interdisciplinary research when there are few high-impact venues that specialize in it (Campbell 2005), although there is some evidence that the changing media landscape may work to its advantage (Álvarez-Bornstein et al. 2019).

In aiming to meet complexity with complexity, the projects in this volume seek responses that integrate perspectives, creating complex wholes that exceed the sum of their parts. When the projects address concerns that are not merely academic, as is true in many cases, they also strive to have an impact that includes improving the lot of the stakeholders involved.

In light of the high ambition of these projects and their intrinsic and extrinsic complexity, they present many different potential sites for failure (Lang et al. 2012). Of course, the collapse of a project will be hard not to see as a failure, even though it may be for the better, but there are also smaller failures that can affect the character of a project in unforeseen ways without causing it to collapse. When a project begins, there are expectations about how things will go over its lifecycle (Hall and O'Rourke 2014), and if reality does not coincide with these expectations, you have what could count as a failure. Often, these failures are attributable to the complex, integrative character of cross-disciplinary work. Failures such as these manifest in a variety of ways, including:

- Projects that do not get off the ground (e.g., attempting to get funding but not succeeding, failing to communicate project vision to institutional sponsors). See Chapter 4, Bellotti and D'Agostino; Chapter 5, Beal et al.; Chapter 12, Fam et al.
- Projects that do not have the correct personnel for specified objectives (e.g., recognizing that you need participation by a range of stakeholders but failing to enlist them, losing personnel because the project takes too long to unfold). See Chapter 12, Fam et al.
- Projects that do not reach their original objectives but meet other objectives (e.g., changing course midstream upon realizing that the original objectives are not realistic given the timeframe). See Chapter 2, Neuhauser et al. and Chapter 9, De Santolo.
- Projects that fail to anticipate important differences among collaborators (e.g., attempting to integrate different disciplinary perspectives but not

12   *Michael O'Rourke and Dena Fam*

succeeding, not recognizing that different collaborators need different things from the project to justify their participation). See Chapter 3, Fletcher and Lyall; Chapter 6, O'Rourke et al.; Chapter 7, Connon; Chapter 8, Robson-Williams et al.; Chapter 10, Ukowitz; Chapter 11, Imbruce and Prazak.

*   Projects that fail to manage power differences among participants (e.g., framing a transdisciplinary research problem without input from the stakeholders, underappreciating the potential for conflict within a project). See Chapter 6, O'Rourke et al. and Chapter 7, Connon.

As we have noted above, though, an outcome that might look like a failure from one perspective may not look so bad from another. If a project is built to be adaptive by a team that expects to make changes on the fly, then an unmet expectation could just be a signal that it is time to adapt. But even in these projects there will be fixed aspects that represent pivot points for change in more provisional aspects, and this fixed/provisional distinction can be useful for determining when changes count as failures and when they count as acceptable adjustments.

How to use this volume

We close this section by describing how we intend readers to use this volume. As we have commented above, it can be difficult to learn from one's own failures – there are psychological reasons that militate against learning in the individual case (Dattner and Hogan 2011) and institutional reasons in the organizational case (Baumard and Starbuck 2005). By recounting the details of failure in the projects of others, though, the chapters in this volume support vicarious learning about failures that are not one's own. Attention to these details can help one to appreciate hazards that are hard to spot, and to recalculate risks that arise in the course of one's own project, enabling one to avoid the avoidable failures that might otherwise compromise one's efforts. By playing an instructional role, this volume can also help researchers to recover from failure. It can do this by facilitating project transition from a flawed condition to a stronger and more secure one (Kapur 2016).

Think of this volume, then, as a contribution to "failure management" for interdisciplinary and transdisciplinary researchers and practitioners (Lee and Miesing 2017). In describing 16 benefits for organizations that engage in proactive failure management, Lee and Miesing argue that failure can be a "test bed," highlighting "what does and what does not work" (2017, p. 159). In this book, the tests have been conducted by others and they are described for the reader's benefit, providing a "case library" of failures to serve as a resource (Tawfik et al. 2015).

Introducing the chapters

All chapters in this collection provide insights into failures in complex projects. Each of them also provides recommendations and highlights lessons learned to help the reader in their own responses to failure in interdisciplinary and transcdisciplinary initiatives. The second chapter in this book aptly provides an overview of the evolution of scientific inquiry, with subsequent chapters organized into four thematic parts. Part 1 provides insight into cases where institutional environments were associated with failure. Part 2 details failures and responses associated with collaboration and stakeholder engagement. Part 3 offers chapters with personal reflections on failure which use an autoethnographic lens to investigate failed initiatives. Part 4 highlights how failure has emerged in interdisciplinary and transdisciplinary educational programs, at both the undergraduate and postgraduate levels, with the final chapter synthesizing the collection. A brief overview of each chapter is provided below.

Neuhauser, **Brettler** and **Boyle** provide an insightful review of the evolution of scientific inquiry in regard to the role of failure. Reflecting on the past while looking towards the future, the authors present the design-thinking process and transdisciplinarity as aligned concepts critical for dealing with complex global challenges, and the design sciences paradigm as the most recent epistemological paradigm. Illustrated through two diverse case studies of a factory worker wellness project in China and the design of a breast pump system appropriate for working mothers, the value of failure and an iterative, participatory design process are demonstrated.

Part I: Institutional environments associated with failure

Fletcher and **Lyall** philosophically reflect on their experiences of working in interdisciplinary projects as social scientists on teams dominated by science, technology, engineering and mathematics (STEM). They reflect on the failure of integrative syntheses of arts, humanities, and social science (AHSS) perspectives and the unrealized value of the social sciences in interdisciplinary projects. The valuable lessons learned here go well beyond their case study analysis of a collaborative project on industrially generated red blood cells. Their broader discussion examines how institutions, funding structures and policy discourses perpetuate the relegation of AHSS disciplines to the role of subservient handmaiden of STEM disciplines in interdisciplinary projects. They ask us to think more critically about the difference between the ideal notion of interdisciplinarity and the reality.

Drawing on their professional experience at the University of Queensland, **Bellotti** and **D'Agostino** reflect on the challenges of founding a cross-faculty institute in the face of unstable leadership, a lack of resources and resistance from discipline-focused administrative units. Reflecting on a two-year period of changing leadership and institutional politics, their chapter offers a rare and detailed insight into the rise, decline and restructure of the Global Change Institute, a university-wide research institute focused on facilitating cross-disciplinary-based projects on global issues. By bringing to the fore specific challenges for cross-faculty collaboration, they offer important insights for overcoming these challenges.

In their chapter, **Beal**, **Fam** and **Clegg** address the challenges of introducing innovative technology into basic infrastructure for essential services. Their case

14 *Michael O'Rourke and Dena Fam*

study describes the introduction of urine diversion systems into a sustainability-focused community in Queensland, Australia. In the early days of this experiment, there were congenial regulatory and normative circumstances that supported the introduction of these systems into 20 households, but as time went by these circumstances changed and undermined completion of the trial. In the end, failure to fulfil all the research objectives of the trial revealed a number of important lessons about the socio-technical and institutional conditions in which the introduction of an innovative technology could be successful.

Part II: Failures and responses associated with collaboration and stakeholder engagement

O'Rourke, Crowley, Eigenbrode and **Vasko** offer four illustrative case studies of failed workshops that implemented the "Toolbox" dialogue method and how these failures have influenced the evolution of the workshop-based method over the last 15 years. Insights into the process of learning through failure and adapting to the lessons learned provide recommendations for working with collaborative, diverse groups, especially in a workshop context. Some of the lessons include understanding positionality and the relationships of participants to one another, responding to hierarchical dynamics in groups, and ensuring that participants have the opportunity for introductions if they are unfamiliar with each other, even at the expense of a reduction in workshop time.

Drawing on her involvement in what was to become an award-winning Scottish research project on "transforming responses to power outages in extreme weather events," **Connon** identifies the importance of understanding place-based politics and power relations prior to actively engaging in transdisciplinary projects. The initial failure to select research methods sensitive to the local political context threatened to derail the project before it had started. Adaptive planning, redesign of data collection tools and direct consultation with community members regarding preferred modes of engagement provide lessons learned for others, particularly those conducting research during politically charged periods.

In their contribution, **Robson-Williams**, **Small** and **Robson-Williams** focus on failures that occurred across two transdisciplinary water resource projects in New Zealand. The projects were related to one another, with one focused on providing technical, scientific information about water quality standards to a policymaking process in the Canterbury region of New Zealand, and the other focused on developing good management practices for farms in that region and identifying the quantities of nutrients lost to fresh water by farms using those practices. These complex, multi-year projects enjoyed many successes, but also experienced a number of instructive failures. The authors of this chapter describe six of those failures, diagnose them using the i2S framework from Bammer (2013), and then derive lessons from them for the transdisciplinary researcher.

Perspectives on failure   15

Part III: Personal reflection on failed initiatives through an autoethnographic lens

De Santolo (Garrwa and Barrungam) reflects on an experience of "failure" in an academic context and the impact it had on his own scholarly journey. He describes the experience of preparing an application to enrol in a doctoral program in law, only to withdraw the application after realizing that Western law held little meaning for him and that the law school was not prepared to understand an Indigenous perspective on the law. The chapter describes how this experience transformed him by reorienting him to the teachings of his ancestors and his Elders. Instead of a PhD in law, he pursued a creative doctorate that enabled him to pursue a "much more important meaning-making experience." Through reflection on this experience and its effects, De Santolo provides an important description of how we might begin to decolonize failure.

In her contribution, **Ukowitz** reflects on a complex transdisciplinary project that involved both failure and success. This project – "Carinthia International" – was a sustainable regional development effort predicated on the assumption that "transnational relationships are important for enterprises, as well as regions." The researchers worked with representatives of regional enterprises in two phases to understand the significance of transnational relationships and develop strategies for coping with them. During its lifecycle, the project had to confront difficult circumstances that undermined its ability to realize its objectives, leaving the project team with feelings of failure. Ukowitz concludes her detailed case study by offering a number of lessons about the conditions for both failure and success in transdisciplinary projects.

Part IV: Failure in interdisciplinary and transdisciplinary educational programs

Imbruce and **Prazak** detail the challenges of working across disciplines to deliver a sequence of interdisciplinary, community-engaged courses. They participated in a working group that won a US National Science Foundation grant to design a course that focused on the complex future of a New England mill town. The grant supported the development of two environmental science courses on place that synthesized perspectives from the biophysical sciences, social sciences and the humanities. Using the town as the integrating frame, the sequence prepared students by offering them an introductory course on interdisciplinary process followed by a project-based course. An attempt to impart to students a complex understanding of the place in which they resided, the course ultimately failed to become a regular offering for a host of institutional, intellectual and interpersonal reasons.

Fam, **Mellick Lopes** and **Mitchell** discuss the successes and failures of a transdisciplinary research/teaching project conducted on the campus of the University of Technology Sydney. A multi-disciplinary group of researchers (e.g., law, design, engineering) joined with a group of collaborators from multiple professions (e.g.,

16 *Michael O'Rourke and Dena Fam*

the water industry, regulators, university facilities management) to trial a urine diversion system in a university building. A cutting-edge sustainability project, it generated a great deal of commitment on the part of the participants and it took advantage of the university context to generate important opportunities to learn by doing. Ultimately, the project failed to achieve its principal objective of facilitating broader adoption in the urban environment, but it provided a number of important lessons for those interested in conducting innovative transdisciplinary projects involving a wide range of university and community partners.

In her chapter, **Pearce** discusses how the concept of *productive failure* has been integrated into a sustainable development course at ETH-Zürich. Pearce articulates how she and her colleagues developed a curriculum that supports students in taking the risks necessary to address complex sustainability problems. After describing the education for sustainable development context, she details the learning design that foregrounds failure as a desirable part of the learning process. Productive failure informs development of the key parts of the learning process: goals, environment, activities and assessment. Pearce concludes the chapter by summarizing five course outcomes of the course's emphasis on productive failure and identifying broader implications that productive failure could have for sustainable development education.

In their contribution, **Vilsmaier** and **Thalheimer** provide a detailed account of student perceptions of failure in student-driven transdisciplinary research projects. These projects were pursued in the context of a curricular module on transdisciplinary research delivered as part of a sustainability science master's program at Leuphana University. Relying on conceptualizations of "limit situations and limit-acts," introduced by Vieira Pinto and Paulo Freire, they argue that failure must be understood relative to frames of reference, and they introduce several frames of reference that have to do with the composition of the teams, that is, the frames adopted by the student team, the academic team (including the lecturers) and the transdisciplinary team (including the stakeholders). The authors analyze research reports and reflective essays from eight courses and present a number of important insights into the structure, composition and delivery of transdisciplinary education at the graduate level.

In the concluding chapter, **Klein** offers a rich synthesis of barriers and common reasons for failure in inter- and transdisciplinary work that intersects with the academy, government, industry and communities. Four case studies are drawn on, along with insights from the chapters in this book to reveal the importance of considering how the political economy of knowledge, learning and stakeholder engagement are implicated in complex projects. Finally, Klein presents six overarching principles for success in cross-disciplinary and cross sectoral work.

Conclusion

We close by sharing some of the return correspondence from invited authors to this book, which proved to be just as insightful in regard to their personal and professional responses to failure as the international survey described above. The replies to our invitations were overwhelmingly positive, even when the respondents did not accept the invitation. In a number of instances, the contributors needed time to think about the relative success of their experiences before they could decide whether to accept the invitation. For some, it was challenging to recall failed projects, with the invitation prompting a recall of how and when failure had occurred: "My one problem [in contributing to the book] is that my projects are successful! However, they often come on the heels of other projects which have not been" (personal communication, Linda Neuhauser, University of California, Berkeley). Others were delightfully forthcoming about their failures: "I agree we can learn from failures and too often they are not published. I have a richness of failures to choose from!!" (personal communication, Bill Bellotti, University of Queensland). And sometimes it was not so much the project failure that prompted consideration but rather a feeling of failure that triggered their interest and involvement: "Of course I also have experiences of failure ... especially the feeling of failure [in ID and TD projects]" (personal communication, Martina Ukowitz, University of Klagenfurt, Austria).

As many of the authors in this book have highlighted in writing about their own experiences of failure, there is often a positive story to emerge from failed projects that is critical for moving forward: "failure is all about the learning opportunity. If we are not failing somewhere, then we are playing it safe. Not only are we in a situation (the Anthropocene) where playing it safe is not enough because we need a different kind of change at a grand scale now, playing it safe feels like a less interesting way to live my life, I'm in!" (personal communication, Cynthia Mitchell, University of Technology Sydney).

We have aimed to be provocative in the using the term "failure" in this book, and we recognize that the perception of failure is subjective and depends on who is telling the story: "Others involved may disagree with such an assessment – they may apply different personal and professional metrics. Certainly, to write about these things as failures I either should include a coauthor with whom I failed, or at least inform these colleagues that I have decided to analyze our collaboration in such a light" (personal communication, Sanford Eigenbrode, University of Idaho).

One of the many common threads connecting this collection of chapters and failure analysis is the human dimension of failure. This has emerged, for example, through the inability of team members to collaborate effectively, value alternative contributions and adequately manage time and competing academic expectations. One respondent articulated these human-centered failures well: "The disappointments have been almost entirely due to individuals, including myself, simply running out of time and energy and even raw intelligence to do what we hoped to do. Many scientists are in the habit of overcommitting due to the incentive structures of the academy and this always has costs. ... Typically, these costs disproportionately affect the collaborative aspects of the work, again because of biased incentives and also because they can take much more time and energy than expected or adequately planned for" (personal communication, Sanford Eigenbrode, University of Idaho).

18　*Michael O'Rourke and Dena Fam*

It is important to remember that the experiences collated in this book represent failures captured at particular points in time, many of which have become critical learning experiences and preconditions for successful developments.

> One of the complexities inherent in the topic of collaborative failures is the multiple and alternative ways that cross-disciplinary program success or failure can be defined and measured; and the time scale over which a particular collaborative initiative is evaluated for its "return on investment," positive vs. negative outcomes and overall sustainability. For instance, some interdisciplinary and transdisciplinary research and training centers might be funded for a five-year period, but fail to receive continuation support for another five years when the team's competitive renewal proposal is denied funding. While that situation on the face of it looks like a "failure" (to be renewed), the team members may continue to collaborate and publish together (and in some cases work with non-academic partners to redress community problems) in subsequent years, even after they lose funding for the center after the initial five years of the project. (personal communication, Daniel Stokols, University of California, Irvine – cf. Chapter 4, Bellotti and D'Agostino)

It is with these thoughts on complexities of failure in mind that we offer this collection of personal and professional experiences, uncommon in their honesty, reflection and critical analysis. We would like to acknowledge all the contributing authors in this book, and the conversations and contributions of those who, over the last two years, have influenced the way we have perceived and written about failure in interdisciplinary and transdisciplinary projects, research and education.

References

Álvarez-Bornstein, B., Montesi, M. 2019. Interdisciplinary research and societal impact: Analysis of social media. *E-prints in Library & Information Science* [Preprint]. Available from: http://eprints.rclis.org/38631/.

Bammer, G. 2013. *Disciplining interdisciplinarity: Integration and implementation sciences for researching complex real-world problems*. Canberra: ANU E-Press.

Baumard, P., Starbuck, W. H. 2005. Learning from failures: Why it may not happen. *Long Range Planning*, 38, 281–298.

Bromham, L., Dinnage, R., Hua, X. 2016. Interdisciplinary research has consistently lower funding success. *Nature*, 534, 684–687.

Campbell, L. 2005. Overcoming obstacles to interdisciplinary research. *Conservation Biology*, 19(2), 574–577.

Cannon, M. D., Edmondson, A. C. 2005. Failing to learn and learning to fail (intelligently): How great organizations put failure to work to innovate and improve. *Long Range Planning*, 38, 299–319.

Carper, K. L. 1996. Construction pathology in the United States. *Structural Engineering International*, 6(1), 57–60.

Cyert, R. M., March, J. G. 1963. *A behavioral theory of the firm*. Englewood Cliffs, NJ: Prentice Hall.

Dattner, B., Hogan, R. 2011. Managing yourself: Can you handle failure? *Harvard Business Review*, 4. Available from: https://hbr.org/2011/04/managing-yourself-can -you-handle-failure.

Draper, N. 2017. Fail fast: The value of studying unsuccessful technology companies. *Media Industries*, 4(1). doi:10.3998/mij.15031809.0004.101.

Eigenbrode, S., O'Rourke, M., Wulfhorst, J. D., Althoff, D. M., Goldberg, C. S., Merrill, K., Morse, W., Nielsen-Pincus, M., Stephens, J., Winowiecki, L., Bosque-Pérez, N. A. 2007. Employing philosophical dialogue in collaborative science. *BioScience*, 57, 55–64.

Engineering Failure Analysis (EFA). 2020. Aims and scope. *Engineering Failure Analysis*. Available from: http://journals.elsevier.com/engineering-failure-analysis.

Evans, T. L. 2015. Transdisciplinary collaborations for sustainability education: Institutional and intragroup challenges and opportunities. *Policy Futures in Education* 13(1), 70–96.

Firestein, S. 2016. *Failure: Why science is so successful*. Oxford: Oxford University Press.

Hall, T. E., O'Rourke, M. 2014. Responding to communication challenges in transdisciplinary sustainability science. *In*: K. Huutoniemi & P. Tapio, eds. *Heuristics for transdisciplinary sustainability studies: Solution-oriented approaches to complex problems*. Oxford: Routledge, 119–139.

Irvine, A. D., Deutsch, H. 2016. Russell's paradox. *In:* E. N. Zalta, ed. *The Stanford encyclopedia of philosophy*. Available from: https://plato.stanford.edu/archives/win2 016/entries/russell-paradox/.

JNRBM. 2020. Home. *Journal of Negative Results in BioMedicine*. Available from: http:// jnrbm.biomedcentral.com/.

Kapur, M. 2016. Examining productive failure, productive success, unproductive failure, and unproductive success in learning. *Educational Psychologist*, 51(2), 289–299.

Klein, J. T., Falk-Krzesinski, H. J. 2017. Interdisciplinary and collaborative work: Framing promotion and tenure practices and policies. *Research Policy*, 46(6), 1055–1061.

Lam, R. 2019. What students do when encountering failure in collaborative science. *NPJ Science of Learning*, 4, 6. doi:10.1038/s41539-019-0045-1.

Lang, D. J., Wiek, A., Bergmann, M., Stauffacher, M., Martens, P., Moll, P., Swilling, M., Thomas, C. J. 2012. Transdisciplinary research in sustainability science: Practice, principles, and challenges. *Sustainability Science*, 7(S1), 25–43.

Lee, J., Miesing, P. 2017. How entrepreneurs can benefit from failure management. *Organizational Dynamics*, 46, 157–164.

Lyall, C. 2019. *Being an interdiscipinary academic: How institutions shape universoty careers*. Switzerland: Palgrave Macmillan.

Matson, J. V. 1991. *The art of innovation: Using intelligent fast failure*. State College: Pennsylvania State University Press.

McGrath, R. G. 2011. Failing by design. *Harvard Business Review*, 4. Available from: http://hbr.org/2011/04/failing-by-design.

Morse, W. C., Nielsen-Pincus, M., Force, J. E., Wulfhorst, J. D. 2007. Bridges and barriers to developing and conducting interdisciplinary graduate-student team research. *Ecology and Society*, 12(2), 8. Available from: http://www.ecologyandsociety.org/vol12/iss2/a rt8/.

Parkes, E. 2019. Scientific progress is built on failure. *Nature*, Career Column. doi:10.1038/ d41586-019-00107-y.

Petroski, H. 1992. *To engineer is human: The role of failure in successful design*. New York: Vintage Books.

20 *Michael O'Rourke and Dena Fam*

Petroski, H. 2012. *To forgive design: Understanding failure*. Cambridge, MA: Harvard University Press.

Petroski, H. 2018. *Success through failure: The paradox of design*. Princeton, NJ: Princeton University Press.

Popper, K. R. 1999. *The logic of scientific discovery*. London: Routledge.

Raymond, C. M., Fazey, I., Reed, M. S., Stringer, L. C., Robinson, G. M., Evely, A. C. 2010. Integrating local and scientific knowledge for environmental management. *Journal of Environmental Management*, 91, 1766–1777.

Rittel, H. W., Webber, M. M. 1973. Dilemmas in a general theory of planning. *Policy Sciences*, 4(2), 155–169.

Sitkin, S. B. 1992. Learning through failure: The strategy of small losses. *Research in Organizational Behavior*, 14, 231–266.

Tawfik, A. A., Rong, H., Choi, I. 2015. Failing to learn: Towards a unified design approach for failure-based learning. *Educational Technology Research and Development*, 63, 975–994.

Vanasupa, L., McCormick, K. E., Stefanco, C. J., Herter, R. J., McDonald, M. 2012. Challenges in transdisciplinary, integrated projects: Reflections on the case of faculty members' failure to collaborate. *Innovations in Higher Education*, 37, 171–184.

Van Noorden, R. 2015. Interdisciplinary research by the numbers. *Nature*, 525, 306–307.

Yarime, M., et al. 2012. Establishing sustainability science in higher education institutions: Towards an integration of academic development, institutionalization, and stakeholder collaborations. *Sustainability Science*, 7, 101–113.

2 Re-thinking failure

Using design science theory and methods, including design-thinking, for successful transdisciplinary health and social interventions

Linda Neuhauser, Talya Brettler and Dennis Boyle

Introduction

We are all conflicted about failure. From an evolutionary biological and psychological perspective, we are hard-wired to seek success and survival (Buss 2015). Beginning in our earliest years, society infuses messages of achieving success and avoiding failure into all aspects of our lives. We are told that "failure is not an option." Business books and the popular press have generated tomes of guidance about achieving success. Often, people are labelled as either "successful" or "losers/failures" – perceptions that can greatly advance or hinder their life trajectories at all stages. Although we are told to avoid failure, we are also told that failure is to be expected and that we are to persevere through it: "If at first you don't succeed, try, try again." We learn that highly successful people like Thomas Edison spent years on "failed" efforts – it took him 10,296 experiments before he finally created a storage battery. Such contradictory messages leave us in the uncomfortable position of trying to avoid the ubiquitous presence of failure, but with little guidance about how to do so.

Loscalzo (2014) points out that the process that instils in us our negative concept of failure starts during our first experiences at school, where anxiety about failing tests and falling behind initiates a lifelong fear of failure. This sets up the false dichotomy that there is only success or failure, and it leads us to assume that failure is to be avoided because we need to succeed, and that the two states cannot coexist. Studies about the "science of failure" provide insight into this misguided view of success versus failure. For example, Schultz (2010) comments that it's cognitively difficult for people to admit mistakes in the present because once a person realizes they are wrong, they are no longer wrong. Psychologists recognize that this subconscious distancing of ourselves from failure means that we tend to attribute our successes to our skills and actions but blame failures on external factors that we cannot control (Frieze and Weiner 1971).

This simplistic binary view of success/failure, innate fear of failure and systemic pressures to avoid failure have significant negative impacts on education, innovation and science. The emphasis on success (and avoiding failure) from

22 *Neuhauser, Brettler and Boyle*

elementary school through to higher education can encourage students to focus on grade point averages (a measure of success) rather than on taking risky, challenging courses. Having been schooled to avoid failure, students then enter a risk-averse workforce.

In the scientific arena, investigators are trained to focus on research that is likely to be successful, and that will not be viewed as a failure. Researchers examining the nature of research proposals submitted to the US National Institutes of Health, and those selected for grants, conclude that the highly competitive environment and fear of failure are limiting the number of truly innovative studies that address high-risk hypotheses (Ness 2010; Kolata 2009). Currently, investigators are expected to "predict success" in grant applications without an opportunity to make revisions once the work is underway. This precludes investigators from learning from and adapting to early failures, and ultimately weakens the research process. Rigid adherence to failure-averse traditional scientific methods is linked to the disappointing outcomes of many health and social programmes (Smedley and Syme 2000; Bammer 2013; Jensen 2003; Fam et al. 2018; Neuhauser 2018a). For example, fear of failure may be a key factor accounting for the modest level of success in reducing US adult cancer mortality since 1970, despite the outlay of over US$100 billion (Ness 2010; Kolata 2009).

A related problem is that studies that do not reject the null hypothesis (considered to be "failures") are much less likely to be reported in the scientific literature. As a result, these studies are less likely to influence future research efforts and consequently, the very areas with the greatest potential to yield significant innovations are the ones which are less likely to receive attention. A seminal study by Dickersin and colleagues (1987) found that statistically significant clinical trial results were three times more likely to be published than those supporting the null hypothesis.

Fortunately, despite the notable societal pressures to avoid even *acknowledging* failure, the past 50 years of research in many fields, including the emerging areas of "failure science," "complexity science," "design science" and "transdisciplinarity," provide compelling evidence that understanding and leveraging failure might actually be the *key* to success (Edmonson 2011; Waldrop 1993; Bammer 2013; Simon 1996; Hadorn et al. 2010; O'Rourke and Fam 2020). Fundamentally, we are learning that most problems in science and society are complex, and in many cases investigators are neither able to predict an outcome or solution, nor truly understand a problem before a study ends (Rittel and Webber 1973). This means that multiple phases of trial and error experimentation, which Edmonson (2011) calls "intelligent failure," are required to reveal the many facets of a problem and select the best interventions to address them. Although this finding is well understood in engineering, it runs directly counter to the traditional scientific process in health, social science, and other disciplines that require successful predictions at the outset. Therefore, it is not surprising that so many investigator-defined outcomes ultimately fail. What we *can* understand is how failure operates in research and interventions processes, and how it can gradually guide us to success.

The objectives of this chapter are to describe: (1) problems with the traditional view of failure in scientific inquiry and intervention development; (2) the evolution of scientific inquiry, including the value of transdisciplinarity as a unifying approach; (3) how methods of participatory design – especially design-thinking – leverage failure; and (4) example cases using iterative design and initial failures to achieve success.

Complex problems and weaknesses of traditional research and interventions

In the traditional research process, when planning their research and writing applications for funding, investigators define problems, formulate hypotheses, develop methods and predict outcomes before conducting their research (Guba and Lincoln 1994). As mentioned above, this approach requires that the investigators "predict success" a priori and does not usually accommodate revisions if early outcomes begin to deviate from those predicted. This constrains research to only "success" or "failure" outcomes. A further problem is that traditional interventions research often wrongly assumes that an intervention that was successful with one population or in one location will be successful when "translated" into other contexts (Midgley 2003; Green and Glasgow 2006; Jensen 2003; Neuhauser 2018a).

The past half-century of research about research theory and methods documents the traditional weaknesses of this approach (Bammer 2013; Fam et al. 2018; Neuhauser 2018a; Phelan 2010; Smedley and Syme 2000; Lubchenko 1998). One conclusion is that traditional theory and methods are not robust enough to address complex or "wicked" problems, which are typically heterogeneous, changeable, contextually localized, value-laden, sometimes caused by those charged with addressing them, and difficult to understand and solve (Rittel and Webber 1973; Buchanan 1992; Tapio and Huutoniemi 2014; March and Smith 1995). Another layer of difficulty, as mentioned earlier, is that these problems often cannot be well defined until *after* they have been studied. And, because of their complexity and changeability, such problems must be constantly restudied and redefined. Health, social, technological and environmental problems are almost always wicked problems. In fact, it is difficult to think of any significant health or social research endeavour that is "simple." A fruitful avenue of exploration in this area is "problem structuring methods" that attempt to model the nature of problems that people want to address (Rosenhead 2013). Such problems may run the gamut from relatively "tame" to "super-wicked" (Culmsee and Awati 2014). Similarly, it is useful to apply the methods of systems science to understand the boundaries between what is known or what is unknown, and how values influence problem definition and intervention selection (Midgely 2003).

Scholars have identified many reasons why traditional research theory and methods do not align well with understanding or addressing complex problems, and one of these reasons is a lack of attention to failure. Major gaps in traditional approaches include the lack of integration in implementation across scientific disciplines and

24 *Neuhauser, Brettler and Boyle*

societal sectors, resulting in an inadequate understanding of the many factors influencing a complex problem and the barriers and supports to addressing it (Bammer 2013; Fam et al. 2018; Neuhauser 2018a). A further problem is the lack of significant participation of the end-users and relevant stakeholders during problem identification and solution generation (Reason and Bradbury 2008; Neuhauser and Kreps 2014; Minkler and Wallerstein 2008; Marcus et al. 2002; Lopes et al. 2012). In addition, there is often no explicit process to identify the many categories of "unknowns" that affect the understanding of a problem and the selection of interventions (Piso et al. 2016). This latter issue is a key reason why complex problems cannot be well understood initially, because so many unknowns exist when a study or intervention is in its initial stages and throughout its implementation.

The evolution of scientific inquiry and the role of failure

In addition to the biological, psychological and societal pressures to avoid dealing with failure, the foundation of scientific inquiry and changes to it over time help explain the origin of traditional research approaches and why the importance of failure has been overlooked until more recently.

Changing views about reality

The scientific approach reflects both perceptions of reality (ontology) and also ways of seeking knowledge to understand it (epistemology). Until the middle of the twentieth century, the common view was that there is only one reality and that it is "knowable." This perspective reflects a binary view that something is either real or not real, true or false. However, thinking has shifted towards the view that reality is made up of multiple dimensions (or, "directions in motion"), with neither a beginning nor an end – like the Internet, and that reality is complex, contextual, and ever changing (Deleuze and Guattarti 1980; Cook 1985). This newer perspective is non-binary: it proposes that reality is constantly in flux.

Newer paradigms of scientific inquiry

As perspectives about the nature of reality change, so do perspectives about ways to study it. The currently predominant view is that knowledge is "collective," and cannot be found through any single discipline. Accessing these "knowledges" requires that diverse investigators and stakeholders study phenomena from as many different perspectives as possible, and that they draw on multiple theoretical frameworks, methods, contextual settings, and interpretations of evidence (Kahn and Prager 1994; Cook 1985). Such scientific inquiry is needed to investigate complex, changeable "wicked" problems. This radical transformation of scientific inquiry is referred to as a "scientific revolution" (Kuhn 1962).

Before the mid-twentieth century, scientific inquiry was dominated by the "natural science" paradigm, which assumed that the world is knowable and governed by universal laws, and that knowledge can be generalized broadly to apply to multiple settings. Natural science inquiry has a strong focus on controlled experimental methods with predefined hypotheses. Although it has been a fairly good fit for investigating the natural sciences such as chemistry and physics, it has not been as useful for studying phenomena affected by human behaviour, or those that change over time. This approach to scientific inquiry assumes that investigators will either "succeed" or "fail" at understanding reality – a view enshrined in the traditional experimental method in which a study either succeeds in disproving the null hypothesis, or fails to do so.

This paradigm was challenged by study outcomes that failed to support the existence of a predictable reality and catalyzed the emergence of the second major epistemological paradigm, the "human sciences" paradigm, in such fields as sociology, medicine and anthropology (Dilthey 1988). Human science inquiry takes into consideration that because human phenomena are not as predictable as those in the natural sciences, they must be studied using multiple methods in many settings (Cook 1985). In this approach to inquiry, scientists can no longer claim "success" or "failure" in their interpretations of reality. Rather, they can only "suggest" that study outcomes point to a likelihood of those outcomes reflecting reality, with the strong caveats that interpretation is limited by time, the groups studied, and their specific attributes and contexts. Sophisticated statistical analyses, such as "random forests" (Denisko and Hoffman 2018) support this kind of research. A random forest is an algorithm that consists of many individual decision trees derived from a dataset. Taken together, these decision trees form a "forest" that can be used to explore many combinations of variables reflecting possible alternative contexts ("realities") with the intention of comparing outcomes or associations among these contingent situations.

Natural and human science inquiries study existing or past phenomena. However, solving complex problems requires not only understanding what exists now, but also how changes might alter phenomena in the future. "Intervention" can be defined as "purposeful action by an agent to create change" and takes scientific inquiry beyond the limits of the observation of the present and the past to include consideration of phenomena that observers predict will occur in the future (Midgley 2003, p. 10). For example, how might an environmental intervention affect sea levels in the coming decades, or how will a new health system affect patient health? In the mid-1900s, a third epistemological paradigm emerged to address this gap: the "design sciences" paradigm. Simon (1996) describes the design sciences as being concerned, not with how things are, but with how they might be. In this form of scientific inquiry used in the design sciences, researchers and other stakeholders study human-created objects, activities, services and environments to solve problems and meet goals (Buchanan 1992) by carrying out interventions. Although design science theory and methods originated in sociotechnical fields such as architecture, engineering and computer science, they are being rapidly adopted in health, the social sciences, the natural sciences, business, policy and many other fields.

The design sciences focus on solving problems, rather than testing theories and hypotheses, and this approach provides us with an especially robust way to address complex problems in nearly every discipline. Design science methods are highly participatory, qualitative, inductive and iterative (March and Smith 1995; Cross 2006; Cross 2007). A core feature of this approach is the problem development and solution generation cycle in which problems are iteratively identified from data, and solutions to address them are generated and evaluated. This involves the use of "problem identification and solution loops" and "build and test loops" (Markus et al. 2002) in which solution prototypes are developed, tested with users, and revised over time until user needs are met (Rubin and Chisnell 2008; Neuhauser et al. 2013a). The design approach is illustrated in Figure 2.1 and can be used successfully to attain end goals as diverse as building a computer program, building an aircraft engine, improving hospital services or creating a waste recycling programme. It is strikingly different from the traditional approach in which investigators – not end-users – predefine problems, hypotheses and interventions before a study or intervention begins (Guba and Lincoln 1994).

Among the three paradigms of scientific inquiry discussed above, failure is most explicitly incorporated into the design sciences paradigm. Because design science methods focus on rapid cycles of building and iterative testing of prototypes, early "failures" are a key part of that process. Failures are indications that a prototype has not yet met the desired specifications of the end goal. In this respect, early failures are highly valued as the signposts to improvement.

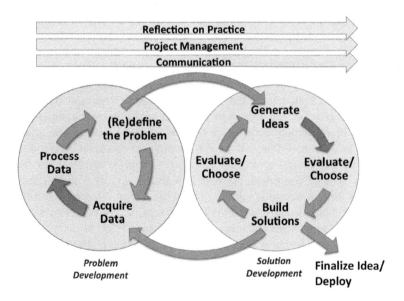

Figure 2.1 The general design process (Roschuni 2012). Courtesy of Celeste Nicole Roschuni

Re-thinking failure 27

Transdisciplinarity

Another powerful emerging trend in scientific inquiry is transdisciplinary (TD) research. This approach seeks to address the aforementioned weaknesses in traditional research and interventions when they are used to address complex problems. Developed over the past 30 years, TD is a concept and approach that is considered to have the best fit to unify research integration across disciplines and implementation across societal sectors with intense user/stakeholder participation and attention to unknowns. There are many TD definitions, theoretical frameworks and methods (see Bammer 2013; Nicolescu 2010; Hoffman-Reim et al. 2008; Hadorn et al. 2010; Fam et al. 2018). Pohl and Hirsch Hadorn's (2007, p. 20) description of TD describes its main concepts:

The starting point for transdisciplinary research is a socially relevant problem field. Within this field, transdisciplinary research identifies, structures, analyses, and deals with specific problems in such a way that it can:

a) grasp the complexity of problems
b) take into account the diversity of life-world and scientific perceptions of problems
c) link abstract and case-specific knowledge
d) develop knowledge and practices that promote what is perceived to be the common good.

Participatory research and collaboration between disciplines are the means of meeting requirements (a)–(d) in the research process.

TD is a comprehensive approach that reflects newer thinking about reality and scientific inquiry. It brings together all the above-mentioned theoretical frameworks and methods used in the natural, human and design sciences. TD work emphasizes highly participatory, mixed (quantitative and qualitative) methods that engage researchers, end-users, and stakeholders from multiple disciplines and societal sectors in real-world contexts from the initial stages and throughout the research. TD interventions are showing improved outcomes (Fam et al. 2018). Given the iterative nature of TD work (similar to that described for design science approaches), early, small failures are expected, incorporated into the processes, and valued.

However, to our knowledge the book in which this chapter is published (Fam and O'Rourke 2020) is the first in-depth, explicit discussion of failure as a key TD component. This book's deeper look at failure also identifies many past problems and potential future pitfalls of TD projects. Even seemingly well-designed TD projects may have hidden weaknesses. For example, in this book Fam and colleagues describe an ambitious project to create a better human waste disposal system at a university (Fam et al. 2020). Although the project was technically sound and highly transdisciplinary and participatory, the pilot effort did not meet expected outcomes. One reason was the lack of high-level stakeholders with decision-making power, needed to approve funding and advance the system. That

28 *Neuhauser, Brettler and Boyle*

chapter's dissection of specific failures, and plans to incorporate that learning into the next project, is exceptionally valuable, not only in the waste management area, but also for anyone interested in TD work.

Critique of TD projects, with attention given to potential failures and promising pathways for revision, is still at an early stage. International networks of TD collaborators provide a rich source of learning. The Integration and Implementation Sciences site (https://i2s.anu.edu.au/), hosted by the Australian National University, includes articles and blogs in which researchers and practitioners share their TD experiences, frameworks and methods.

TD and failure in the Changzhou Worker Wellness Project

The Changzhou Worker Wellness Project illustrates how TD can transform a failed traditional approach into success. In China, over 250 million people are moving from rural areas to work in urban zones, especially in factories. Although the new workers are critical to China's economy, the massive demographic shift has had negative impacts, including increases in infectious diseases, unplanned pregnancies, mental health problems, government policy issues, and family dislocation – issues that have also decreased worker productivity and retention (Lu and Xia 2016; Zhang 2010). Supporting the health of these vulnerable "migrant workers" is a key goal of China's economic and social plans, and many interventions have been tried. However, most of these efforts have defined "health" as physical health, and consequently generated solutions focused on health care access, without attention to the broad range of other areas that impact workers' holistic wellbeing. Furthermore, the programmes were typically designed by government officials and implemented without adequate input from workers and other stakeholders. Most of these programmes have failed to meet their goals and reflect the classic weaknesses of top-down and narrowly-defined health interventions.

In recognition of this problem, government leaders reached out to the Health Research for Action Center (HRA) at the University of California Berkeley School of Public Health (http://healthresearchforaction.org/), which uses highly participatory TD approaches to co-design, co-implement, and co-evaluate health interventions globally (Neuhauser et al. 2013b) to try a new approach. They also approached Pathfinder International, an international non-governmental organization focused on health interventions.

This collaborative effort between government leaders and the HRA created the Worker Wellness Project in Changzhou, China, a city of 5 million with over 1.5 million migrant workers (see Neuhauser et al. 2018b for details about the project). The project used a TD approach, setting up a cross-sector collaboration of governmental officials, health and social service professionals, factory workers and managers, and researchers who represented many disciplinary areas. After participants were trained in the new approach, highly participatory processes (focus groups, surveys, worker teams, design-thinking exercises, stakeholder committees, etc.) were used to get input from all stakeholders to do formative research, and to gradually identify problems and generate and iteratively test solutions.

Results showed that workers had many problems affecting their health and motivation to stay at their factories. These included their requirements for housing, education, job training, health information, communication with family members living far away, legal advice and opportunities to exercise and socialize – in addition to better health care access (Sun et al. 2011; Sun et al. 2012). These issues can be considered "unknowns" relative to the historic framing of migrant worker health in China.

Through the TD participatory processes, workers gained the skills and confidence needed to raise issues and propose solutions. They, with the help of other stakeholders, developed highly creative interventions. One of these was "wellness houses" – attractively designed factory spaces designed to be used for meetings, relaxation, exercise and computer and library resources. Other interventions included: a "Wellness Guide" with easy-to-use information about hundreds of issues the workers needed to manage in their daily lives; onsite health exams; and a buddy system in which experienced workers oriented new ones. Figure 2.2 shows a team of factory workers using the Wellness Guide to plan educational sessions for workers at the wellness house in their factory. Such worker teams also continuously review the guide and recommend revisions for the next edition.

Results are showing positive impacts of the project on worker knowledge, behaviours and satisfaction (Neuhauser et al. 2018b). An example is that in one factory, managers were distressed and confused by significant worker turnover in the summer. When that factory joined the project and workers identified their issues, it became clear that many workers left because their children did not have summer schools and could not be left alone while their parents worked. Workers and managers worked together to co-design and set up a quality summer school in the factory – resulting in high worker satisfaction and greatly reduced turnover. Likewise, managers have reported reductions in the incidence of worker health

Figure 2.2 Workers use the Changzhou Wellness Guide to plan worker educational activities in their factory wellness house. Source: Neuhauser

30   *Neuhauser, Brettler and Boyle*

issues, including unplanned pregnancies and abortions, after workers requested classes in reproductive health and the provision of contraceptives. The project has expanded to 31 factories, which are continuing to customize their programmes using TD methods. Other areas of China are considering adapting the approach to their local contexts.

Failure has been important in this project. The "epic failures" of past projects with poor outcomes catalyzed interest in trying this TD approach. And, although "failure" was not mentioned explicitly in the project techniques, it was carefully considered and planned for in the project. One early concern was that stakeholders were not used to participatory processes and time was needed for them to learn techniques, appreciate them and ultimately "buy-in" to these processes – or the project might not get off the ground. To avoid such a major failure, significant time (18 months) was invested in the early stages of project planning, in which stakeholders were trained to work across many disciplines and sectors using highly participatory processes, and stakeholder committees were established to oversee and continuously revise project plans as issues came up. Another approach was to ensure that workers and others were encouraged and allowed the time needed to experiment with and refine interventions.

An early failure occurred when the first version of the worker Wellness Guide was not understandable to the workers because it was overly influenced by medical professionals who preferred including medical jargon and college-level language. Fortunately, the project stakeholders included advisers on health literacy and plain language, and an iterative review and revision process was established that incorporated the input of the workers. This process was informed by participatory health communication approaches (Neuhauser 2017; Neuhauser and Kreps 2014). After issues were raised about the first version of the guide, workers and health professionals then produced a new version that both adhered to plain language principles and was professionally approved. Each succeeding edition of the guide has reflected iterative improvements. The extended planning phase was also key to thinking about long-term issues of sustainability and expansion of the project. In this project, stakeholders with budgetary decision-making responsibilities in the city decided on a realistic way to share future costs between the city and the factories. That budgetary formula has been successful, and long-term project activities are now incorporated into the city budget. This approach can help avoid high-level decision-making issues, as cited earlier in Fam et al. (2020: this book). See also Belotti and D'Agostino (2020: this book).

In addition, in follow-up interviews with factory managers, several commented that when they tried to cut corners with top-down decisions, they often failed, and they realized that success was only possible once they went back to the TD processes. In one notable example, a factory head was worried about the loss of 80% of workers each year, and tried to speed up the project by pre-designing a wellness house. This failed because workers wanted a wellness house with a different style and functions. The manager was willing to admit this early failure and workers redesigned the wellness house. Now, the factory is attracting new workers, retention is very high and its business is thriving. This has been a key lesson learned:

In TD, projects deviating from the central processes can lead to failure, but early, small failures are solvable by returning to those processes. Currently, representatives of each factory come together each year to discuss successes and challenges and the need to stick to TD processes.

Design-thinking and failure

As mentioned above, one highly popular design science and TD method is design-thinking; this design science method is perhaps the one that most explicitly values and integrates failure. Thomas Edison is often referenced as an inventor who understood this: "He [Edison] understood that an experiment ending in failure was not a failed experiment – as long as constructive learning is gained. He invented the incandescent lightbulb, but only after the lessons of a thousand unsuccessful attempts" (Kelley and Kelley 2013, p. 41). The authors go on to explain: "In fact, early failure can be crucial to success in innovation. Because the faster you find weaknesses during an innovation cycle, the faster you can improve what needs fixing. This approach is integrated into the design-thinking process by taking advantage of prototyping throughout."

It has been 140 years since Thomas Edison created the light bulb, and during that time, design was been dominated mainly by technical innovation. In the past few decades, however, there has been a shift in the potential applications of design via the design-thinking process. In 1992, with the publication of "Wicked Problems in Design-Thinking," Richard Buchanan promoted the utility of design to a diverse range of professions.

The design-thinking process begins with people: listening to, and observing, the end-user (see Figure 2.3).

The design-thinking process is best performed in situ, so that observers can ascertain the subtleties of the users' needs. Indeed, designing alongside end-users is mandatory for the design-thinking process. Let's consider a seemingly simple example of making a sandwich. When my friend tells me that she made a peanut butter and jam sandwich for lunch, I understand what she is eating. But when I stand next to her in her kitchen while she prepares her lunch, I observe that she struggles with where to place her sticky knife, and she goes on a rant about the environmental impact of the single-use plastic bag in which she wraps her sandwich. Often, the insights gained from watching can be magnified by observing those at the extremes, as opposed to the average user who is often sought in market or academic research. In our sandwich-making example, we might observe a five-year-old on her first attempt, or a teacher who has been making the same sandwich every day for 20 years. Starting with these people ensures that the product or service developed is one that is ultimately desirable.

After the research phase, team members begin the synthesis process, whereby they assemble the information they have gathered and organize it into insights. Crucial to the design-thinking process is transdisciplinarity, whereby team members are purposely selected from many different disciplines. Depending on the project, a team might include an anthropologist, an

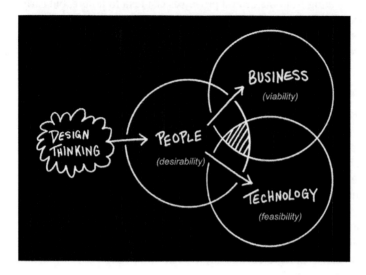

Figure 2.3 Design-thinking and innovation Venn diagram. Innovation occurs at the intersection of desirability, viability, and feasibility. Courtesy of IDEO

engineer, a physician, a designer, a computer scientist, a businessperson, a data scientist and so on. As demonstrated in Figure 2.4, synthesis of different perspectives of the problem is one of the first moments of attempted convergence. Assumptions are challenged, and discomfort and frustration can be common as team members try to discern patterns from interviews of individuals on opposite ends of a bell curve.

With insights in hand, designers are now able to work with the desirable characteristics and strategize around what is feasible (see Figure 2.3). As part of the prototyping process, designers may again tend to explore the extremes. Ideas generated at this point are not meant to strive for perfection. Rather, prototypes are designed to test how insights might be translated tangibly (Figure 2.4). A failed prototype at this stage can be enormously useful in triggering insights. As Tim Brown, former CEO and current Chair of IDEO stated: "Fail early to succeed sooner" (2009).

The design process continues with further testing and refining of prototypes, once again drawing on feedback from end-users. Ultimately, products and services are deemed ready for launch, but this does not dictate the end of the design-thinking process. With more users, further insights can be generated and new prototypes developed. As shown in Figure 2.5, the design-thinking process is circular. What is desirable can evolve, as can the feasibility and viability of new iterations as the product or service matures.

Embracing the circular nature of this approach allows companies and other groups creating interventions to stay nimble. While this process can be made most tangible when designing products, it applies equally to products and services with

Re-thinking failure 33

Figure 2.4 The phases of the design-thinking process. The design-thinking process occurs as a series of divergences and convergences. Courtesy of IDEO

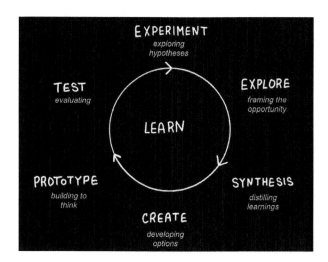

Figure 2.5 Iterative and cyclical design-thinking process. Progressive learning and innovation occur through repetitions of this cycle. Courtesy of IDEO

ambitions beyond profit, such as designing new school nutrition services, and health education or voting systems – as IDEO has done.

A willingness not only to tolerate, but also to value failure has been instrumental for IDEO in its ability to innovate with its clients. On their first day of work, all employees are given *The Little Book of IDEO*, which features "Learn from failure" as one of the seven values of the company, and this shows up in every project the company undertakes (IDEO 2013). Recently, IDEO collaborated with the company Willow to create the first all-in-one wearable breast pump. Historically, lactating women who wanted to provide their children with breastmilk but were unable to feed them directly would hook themselves up to a breast pump larger and heavier than a bowling ball, connected to a tangle of tubing and power cords (Figure 2.6).

Over the years, "innovations" of such pumps have resulted in slightly smaller and quieter models, but these versions would still seem very familiar to someone who used a breast pump 30 years ago. In the United States, where mothers with young infants generally return to the workplace, the burden of using a traditional breast pump likely contributes to the important problem of lower breastfeeding rates. A better breast pump could have significant public health implications, enabling more mothers to feed their children breastmilk in this way for a longer time. Making use of the design-thinking process, IDEO created a TD team comprising an industrial designer, a product designer, a mechanical engineer and a design researcher, that worked with Willow and end-users to explore the desirability, viability, and feasibility of a product that would create a new standard for breast pumps.

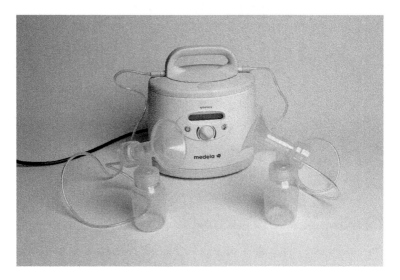

Figure 2.6 The Medela Symphony breast pump weighs 7.05 pounds (3.2 kilos) and is 10 ¼" × 8 ¼" × 12 ½" (26 cm × 21 cm × 32 cm). Photo credit: Thomas Wucherpfennig

Re-thinking failure 35

As mentioned previously, the design-thinking process is iterative. This is compactly visualized in the photograph of the Willow prototyping process in Figure 2.7.

Early in the process of developing the Willow breast pump, designers tested a more powerful mechanism, hoping to shorten an inconvenient and unpleasant activity via faster milk extraction. Early testers, however, prioritized comfort over efficiency, and found the powerful pump too painful. Design research also pointed to women preferring a leak-proof mechanism in order to prevent their "liquid gold" from spilling. Thus, the initial product incorporated a one-way valve which emptied into single-use plastic bags. Many environmentally minded (and frugal) users took matters into their own hands, and a "hack" that enabled multiple uses for the plastic bag was circulated among Willow users. As a company, Willow could have redesigned the bag to eliminate this work-around. Instead, they understood that they could capitalize on the desirability for reuse by creating a washable container as an alternative to the leak-proof bags. The option of using a bag or a container empowers users to decide whether they would like to prioritize reusability or minimizing leaks.

Other changes to the second-generation product have also been a result of adapting to user needs. Some mothers were having trouble with proper placement of the pump, a problem which was exacerbated by opaque materials. Willow 2.0 incorporated transparent casing for improved visibility. They also incorporated a smaller flange to better accommodate users who were only able to make the other sizes work with third party inserts. The Willow is no longer the only wireless breast pump on the market, demonstrating market validation for this product category. With integration of the design-thinking process, the Willow will likely continue to evolve to meet the needs of its users.

Figure 2.7 Willow breast pump prototyping process. Creating physical prototypes early in the design process allows users to see and feel an example product, generating guidance for designers. Courtesy of IDEO

Discussion

One of the greatest challenges in society is to solve complex problems, such as those related to climate change, poverty and disease. However, many of our efforts to understand and address such problems have not been successful. A root cause may be our ambivalent relationship to failure. On the one hand, we are evolutionarily predisposed to avoid failure and seek success. On the other hand, research increasingly shows that failure is necessary for success. Evolutionary psychologist Geher (2014) comments: "The most successful among us are, without exception, those who have failed the most – as a result of being those who have tried the most." An examination of nearly any successful important endeavour underscores the critical role of failure as a contributor to eventual success.

However, risk-averse attitudes towards acknowledging and experiencing failure are ingrained into us, starting with our earliest experiences. Hence, resistance to failure is a major obstacle to doing better in research and practice. Traditional scientific methods and funding criteria require that investigators and practitioners predefine problems and intervention designs before starting their work, with little leeway to make changes when outcomes deviate from expected positive results. This limits possible outcomes to the binary of either "success or failure," rather than a continuum of more nuanced results in between. For this reason, it is not surprising that many studies ultimately fail to gain a deep understanding of a problem, and many interventions have disappointing outcomes. How can we be successful if we are not allowed the necessary opportunities to fail during our efforts?

The so-called "scientific revolution" of the mid-twentieth century (Kuhn 1962) catalyzed a re-thinking of the nature of reality and scientific ways of understanding it. In this emergent view, reality is not considered static ("true" or "not true"), but rather constantly in motion, and therefore not definitively "knowable." Likewise, epistemological views of how to understand reality have changed from the earlier notion that reality is knowable and governed by laws that can be universally generalized, to one in which we can only "approach" an understanding of reality and must do this by drawing on multiple "knowledges" from many disciplines, in highly contextualized situations. Outcomes are limited by time, place, and many variables, given the dynamic nature of reality. These evolving views have generated two new major paradigms of scientific inquiry: the human sciences paradigm which focuses on the complexities of studying human behaviour, and design sciences paradigm which focuses on creating objects, environments, and services for a better future. These kinds of inquiry have developed many more methods, including qualitative and mixed methods in human sciences, and iterative cycles of problem identification and solution generation and testing in the design sciences.

Transdisciplinarity (TD) has emerged as a unifying concept and approach that reflects the newer thinking about reality and scientific inquiry. TD addresses the historic weaknesses of interventions research and interventions that do not adequately integrate knowledge from multiple disciplines or actively engage the end-users and stakeholders from relevant societal sectors in defining problems and co-creating and co-implementing solutions. Sophisticated TD processes draw on all paradigms of scientific inquiry and are especially informed by the futuristic, iterative and user-centred techniques of design science. TD work emphasizes the importance of gradual testing and refinement as a path to success. The Changzhou Worker Wellness Project describes how TD thinking and methods achieved success after many years of failure in non-TD projects. The TD approach in this project was grounded in the design science paradigm and was informed by theory and methods from many disciplines, such as systems science, complexity science, action research, failure science, integration and implementation sciences and others (Midgely 2003; Bammer 2013; Edmonson 2011; Reason and Bradbury 2008).

As described by other authors analyzing TD experiences and failures (Fam and O'Rourke 2020, this book), this work is highly complex, and overlooking *any* key processes or phases can jeopardize a project's success and sustainability. In the Changzhou Worker Wellness Project, it was important to have an early emphasis on workshops to train stakeholders in TD participatory processes (see guidance from O'Rourke et al. 2020, this book). Likewise, important decision-makers needed to have "buy-in" at the outset before the intervention could begin (see Fam et al. 2020, this book). Another recurring lesson in this project has been that even a promising TD project can be undone if the processes are not continuously followed. This requires constant attention to experimentation and processes of documenting small and large deviations from desired outcomes ("failures"). Because many people leading TD work are academics, a common frustration is that academic institutions are not set up to support this time-consuming work across disciplines, or to incorporate stakeholders from multiple sectors (see Belotti and D'Agostino 2020, this book). In this project, TD researchers took the role of "technical advisers" on TD processes and research methods, and ensured that the project itself was overseen by those who would need to head the effort in the long term. This resulted in early project ownership and later sustainability and expansion.

Design-thinking, developed over the past 50 years, beginning with work at the Stanford Institute of Design and now further embodied in the global work of IDEO, is a powerful design science and TD approach. Beginning with research into what is desirable, and understanding where desirability intersects with feasibility and viability, are critical to creating successful innovation. Early prototypes are often meant to fail, and in doing so, they lead to learning and achieving success sooner. Of all TD methods, design-thinking is perhaps the most explicit about the value of failure and sophisticated ways of learning from it. Design-thinking starts with adopting a confident mindset about failure ("embrace it") and incorporates specific steps to detect early "failures," and it continues iterative testing and revision ("fail early and often") via prototyping until the successful outcome is reached. Like any other TD process, design-thinking can be done poorly if it does not have a team of people from an adequate number of disciplines, or if it does not incorporate the intensive involvement of end-users, or enough prototyping. This

38 *Neuhauser, Brettler and Boyle*

is an important caveat for researchers or designers who may be tempted to short-cut the detailed processes described above. The Willow breast pump example, and IDEO's many other successes, illustrate how painstaking attention to processes and iterative failures can produce transformative change.

Although solving complex, intractable problems seems to be a daunting task, transdisciplinary approaches that integrate knowledge from many disciplines, and from stakeholders in multiple sectors, are improving outcomes. Identifying and valuing failures during TD processes, as informed by design sciences and design-thinking methods, is central to this success.

Conclusion

It will not be easy to change our historic visceral and organizational aversion to failure. The forward-looking, detailed and real-world methods by which TD and design-thinking embrace failure provide important guidance for researchers and practitioners, policymakers and the scientific community at large. Social linguists emphasize that language matters when an issue is reframed. More ways are needed to recast the word "failure" using concepts which have positive connotations (e.g., "intelligent failure" – Edmonson 2011) and which frame failures as opportunities for learning and improvement. We need to counter the binary view that the outcomes of initiatives are either "successes" or "failures." Finally, more research is needed into the nature of iterative failure and its central role in research and practice.

Take-home messages

- Traditional scientific approaches are failure-averse and limit intervention success.
- The design science paradigm is the approach best aligned with TD work.
- TD work integrates intensive collaboration with iterative design phases.
- Design-thinking is a powerful design science process in which people from diverse disciplines and end-users explicitly learn from failure to achieve success.

References

Bammer, G. 2013. *Disciplining interdisciplinarity: Integration and implementation sciences for researching complex real-world problems.* Canberra Australia: Australian National University Press. Available from: http://epress.anu.edu.au/titles/disciplining-interdisciplinarity/pdf-download.

Belotti, B., D'Agostino, F. 2020, this book. Initiating a transdisciplinary food systems research program in an Australian "sandstone" university. *In:* D. Fam and M. O'Rourke, eds. *Interdisciplinary and transdisciplinary "failures" as lessons learned: A cautionary tale.* Routledge, UK.

Brown, T. 2009. *Change by design: How design thinking transforms organizations and inspires innovation.* New York: HarperCollins.

Re-thinking failure 39

Buchanan, R. 1992. Wicked problems in design thinking. *Design Issues*, 8, 5–21.

Buss, D. M. 2015. *Evolutionary psychology: The new science of the mind.* 5th ed. Routledge, Chicago.

Cook, T. 1985. Postpositivist critical multiplism. *In:* R. Shotland and M. Mark, eds. *Social science and social policy.* Beverly Hills, CA: Sage, 25–62.

Culmsee, P., Awati, K. 2014. The map and the territory: A practitioner perspective on knowledge cartography. *In:* A. Okada, S. Buckingham, J. Simon and T. Sherborne, eds. *Knowledge cartography: Software tools and mapping techniques: Advanced information and knowledge processing.* 2nd ed. New York: Springer Verlag, 261–292. doi:10.1007/978-1-4471-6470-8_12. ISBN 9781447164692.

Cross, N. 2006. *Designerly ways of knowing.* London: Springer.

Cross, N. 2007. From a design science to a design discipline: Understanding designerly ways of knowing and thinking. *In:* R. Michel, ed. *Design research now.* Basel, Switzerland: Birkhäuser, Board of International Research in Design.

Deleuze, G., Guattari, F. 1980. A thousand plateaus. Trans. B. Massumi. London and New York: Continuum, 2004. Vol. 2 of Capitalism and Schizophrenia. 2 vols. 1972–1980. Trans. of Mille Plateaux. Paris: Les Editions de Minuit.

Denisko, D., Hoffman, M. M. 2018. Classification and interaction in random forests. Proceedings of the National Academy of Sciences of the United States of America, 115(8), 1690–1692. doi:10.1073/pnas.1800256115. PMC 5828645. PMID 29440440

Dickersin, K., Chan, S., Chalmers, T. C., Sacks, H. S., Smith Jr., H. 1987. Publication bias and clinical trials. *Controlled Clinical Trials*, 8(4), 343–353.

Dilthey, W. 1988. *Introduction to the human sciences.* Detroit, MI: Wayne State University Press.

Edmonson, A. C. 2011. Strategies for learning from failure. *Harvard Business Review*, April 2011. https://hbr.org/2011/04/strategies-for-learning-from-failure

Fam, D., Lopes, A. M., Mitchell, C. 2020, this book. Tertiary institutions and transdisciplinary living labs: A space to skin your knees. *In:* D. Fam, and M. O'Rourke, eds. *Interdisciplinary and transdisciplinary "failures" as lessons learned: a cautionary tale.* Routledge, UK.

Fam, D., Neuhauser, L. Gibbs, P., eds., 2018. *Transdisciplinary theory, practice and education: The art of collaborative research and collective learning.* Switzerland: Springer.

Fam, D., O'Rourke, M. 2020, in press: this book. *Interdisciplinary and transdisciplinary "failures" as lessons learned: A cautionary tale.* Routledge, UK.

Frieze, I. Weiner, B. 1971. Utilization and attributional judgments for success and failure. *Journal of Personality*, 39, 591–605.

Geher, G. 2014. Failure as the single best marker of human success. *Psychology Today.* Post 5 September 2014. Available from: https://www.psychologytoday.com/us/blog/darwins-subterranean-world/201409/failure-the-single-best-marker-human-success

Green, L. W., Glasgow, R. E. 2006. Evaluating the relevance, generalization, and applicability of research: Issues in external validation and translation methodology. *Evaluation and the Health Professions*, 29(1), 126–153.

Guba, E. G., Lincoln, Y. S. 1994. Competing paradigms in qualitative research. *In:* N. K. Denzin and Y. S. Lincoln, eds. *The handbook of qualitative research.* Thousand Oaks, CA: Sage, 105–117.

Hadorn, H. G., Pohl, C., Bammer, G. 2010. Solving problems through transdisciplinary research. *In:* R. Frodeman, J. Thompson Klein and C. Mitcham, eds. *The Oxford handbook of interdisciplinarity.* Oxford: Oxford University Press, 431–452.

40   *Neuhauser, Brettler and Boyle*

Hoffman-Reim H. et al. 2008. Idea for the handbook. *In:* G. Hadorn et al. eds. *Handbook of transdisciplinary research.* London: Springer, 3–18.

IDEO. 2013. *The little book of IDEO.* Available from: https://www.ideo.com/post/the-littl e-book-of-ideo.

Jensen, P. S. 2003. Commentary: The next generation is overdue. *Journal of the American Academy of Adolescent Psychiatry,* 42(5), 527–530.

Kahn, R. L., Prager, D. J. 1994, July 11. Interdisciplinary collaborations are a scientific and social imperative. *The Scientist,* 17, 11–12.

Kelley, T., Kelley, D. 2013. *Creative confidence: Unleashing the creative potential within us all.* London: William Collins.

Kolata, G. 2009. Grant system leads cancer researchers to play it safe. *The New York Times.* Available from: http://www.nytimes.com/2009/06/28/health/research/28cancer. html. [Accessed 3 December 2009].

Kuhn, T. S. 1962. *The structure of scientific revolutions.* 1st ed. Chicago: University of Chicago Press.

Lopes, A., Fam, D., Williams, J. 2012. Designing sustainable sanitation: Involving design in innovative, transdisciplinary research. *Design Studies,* 33(3), 298–317.

Loscalzo, J. 2014. A celebration of failure. *Circulation,* 129(9), 953–955. doi:10.1161/ CIRCULATIONAHA.114.009220.

Lu, M., Xia, Y. 2016. Migration in the People's Republic of China. Asian Development Bank Institute. ADBI Working Paper Series. Number 593, September.

Lubchenco, J. 1998. Entering the century of the environment: A new social contract for science. *Science* 279(5350): 491–497.

March, S. Smith, G. 1995. Design and natural science research on information technology. *Decision Support Systems,* 15(4), 251–266.

Markus, M. L., Majchrzak, A., Gasser, L. 2002. A design theory for systems that support emergent knowledge processes. *Management Information Systems Quarterly,* 26, 179–212.

Midgely, G. 2003. Science as systemic intervention: Some implications of systems thinking and complexity for the philosophy of science. *Systemic Practice and Action Research,* 12(2), 7–30.

Minkler, M., Wallerstein, N., eds., 2008. *Community based participatory research for health: Process to outcomes.* 2nd ed. San Francisco, CA: Jossey-Bass.

Ness, R. 2010. Fear of failure: Why American science is not winning the war on cancer. *AEP,* 20(2), 89–91. doi:10.1016/j.annepidem.2009.12.001

Neuhauser, L. 2017. Integrating participatory design and health literacy to improve research and interventions. *Information Services and Use,* 37, 153–176. Available from: http: //content.iospress.com/download/information-services-and-use/isu829?id=informati on-services-and-use%2Fisu829.

Neuhauser, L. 2018a. Practical and scientific foundations of transdisciplinary research and action. *In:* D. Fam, L. Neuhauser and P. Gibbs, eds. *Transdisciplinary theory, practice and education: The art of collaborative research and collective learning.* Switzerland: Springer.

Neuhauser, L., Kreps, G. L. 2014. Integrating design science theory and methods to improve the development and evaluation of health communication programs. *Journal of Health Communication: International Perspectives,* 19(12), 1460–1471. doi:10.1080/10810730.2014.954081.

Neuhauser, L., Kreps, G. L., Morrison, K., Athanasoulis, M., Kirienko, N., Van Brunt, D. 2013a. Using design science and artificial intelligence to improve health communication: ChronologyMD case example. *Patient Education and Counseling,* 92(2), 211–217.

Neuhauser, L. Kreps, G. L., Syme, S. L. 2013b. Community participatory design of health communication programs: Methods and case examples from Australia, China, Switzerland and the United States. *In:* D. K. Kim, A. Singhal, and G. L. Kreps, eds. *Global health communications strategies in the 21st century: Design, implementation and evaluation.* New York: Peter Lang Publishing.

Neuhauser, L., Wang, X., Hong, Y., Sun, X., Zong, Z., Shu, X., Mao, J., Lee, E. W., Aibe, S. 2018b. Collaborative research and action: The China Worker Wellness Project. *In:* D. Fam, L. Neuhauser and P. Gibbs, eds. *Transdisciplinary theory, practice and education: The art of collaborative research and collective learning.* Switzerland: Springer

Nicolescu, B. 2010. Methodology of transdisciplinarity – levels of reality, logic of the included middle and complexity. *Transdisciplinary Journal of Engineering and Science*, 1(1), 19–38.

O'Rourke, M., Crowley, S., Eigenbrode, S. D., Vasko, S. E. 2020, this book. Failure and what to do next: lessons from the Toolbox Dialogue Initiative. *In:* D. Fam and M. O'Rourke, eds. *Interdisciplinary and transdisciplinary "failures" as lessons learned: A cautionary tale.* Routledge, UK.

O'Rourke, M., Fam, D. 2020, this book. Theoretical and empirical perspectives on failure: an introduction. *In:* D. Fam and M. O'Rourke, eds. *Interdisciplinary and transdisciplinary "failures" as lessons learned: A cautionary tale.* Routledge, UK.

Phelan, J. C., Link, B. G., Tehranifar, P. 2010Social conditions as fundamental causes of health inequalities. *Journal of Health and Social Behavior.* 51(1 suppl), S28–S40.

Piso, Z., Sertler, E., Malavisi, A., Marable, K., Jensen, E., Gonnerman, C., O'Rourke, M. 2016. The production and reinforcement of ignorance in collaborative interdisciplinary research, *Social Epistemology*, 30:5–6, 643–664. doi:10.1080/02691728.2016.1213328.

Pohl, C., Hadorn, G. H. 2007. *Principles for designing transdisciplinary research.* Trans. A. B. Zimmerman. Munich, Germany: OEKOM.

Reason, P., Bradbury, H., eds., 2008. *The Sage handbook of action research: Participative inquiry and practice.* London and Thousand Oaks, CA: Sage.

Rittel, H. W. J., Webber, M. M. 1973. Dilemmas in a general theory of planning. *Policy Sciences*, 4(2), 155–169.

Roschuni, C. N. 2012. Communicating design research effectively. PhD dissertation. Available from: http://escholarship.org/uc/item/75f0z49v?query=roschuni.

Rosenhead, J. 2013. Problem structuring methods. *In:* S. Gass and M. Fu, eds., *Encyclopedia of operations research and management science.* 3rd ed. New York, London: Springer Verlag, 1162–1172. doi:10.1007/978-1-4419-1153-7_806. ISBN 9781441911377. OCLC 751832290

Rubin, J., Chisnell, D. 2008. *Handbook of usability testing.* Indianapolis, IN: Wiley Publishing.

Schultz, K. 2010. *Being wrong: Adventures in the margin of error.* Ecco/HarperCollins, New York.

Simon, H. 1996. *The sciences of the artificial.* 3rd ed. Cambridge, MA: MIT Press.

Smedley, B. D., Syme, S. L. 2000. *Promoting health: Intervention strategies from socialand behavioral research.* Institute of Medicine. Washington, DC: National Academies Press.

Sun, X. M., Shu, X. Y., Zong, Z. H., Mao, J. S. 2012. A focus group report of Changzhou Wellness Project, Nanjing College for Population Program Management.

Sun, X. M., Zong, Z. H., Shu, X., Mao, J..S, Hong, Y., Wang, X. 2011. Baseline survey results with 1114 migrant workers in Changzhou City. Nanjing University of Posts and

Telecommunication and Changzhou Family Planning Commission. Report: October 2011.

Tapio, P., Huutoniemi, K., eds., 2014. *Transdisciplinary sustainability studies: A heuristic approach*. New York: Routledge.

Waldrop, M. M. 1993. *Complexity: The emerging science at the edge of order and chaos*. New York: Simon and Schuster.

Zhang, H. 2010. The Hukou System's constraints on migrant workers' job mobility in Chinese cities. *China Economic Review*, 21, 51–64.

Part I

Institutional environments associated with failure

3 Stem cells and serendipity

Unburdening social scientists' feelings of failure

Isabel Fletcher and Catherine Lyall

Introduction

Interdisciplinary research often takes place without "deep thought to the specificities, advantages and limitations of such an approach" (LERU 2016, p.15). As a writing team, we draw on our shared knowledge of, and experience of working in, a number of current and past interdisciplinary research projects spanning the social and natural sciences[1] in order to explore this lack of "specificity." We consider, in particular, the case of one research collaboration[2] that sought to produce industrially-generated red blood cells (RBCs) for transfusion and the role that the social sciences played within this science-led team. The team was led by stem cell researchers (whose role was to create the RBCs) and also involved, inter alia, bioengineers (to grow the RBCs at scale) and physicists (to work out a way of separating the mature RBCs from their growing medium). This project was also "transdisciplinary" as the Scottish National Blood Transfusion Service (part of the National Health Service) was a key partner, although, as we have discussed elsewhere (Lyall et al. 2015a), this term is not widely used in the United Kingdom.

In what follows, we describe why this was a rather unsatisfactory project for the social researchers involved, who were brought in post hoc by the science team to assess what public reactions might be to such a blood product were it ever to be manufactured. As we shall discuss, our "failure" most closely resembles the notion of a "process failure" rather than a "product failure" (see editors' introduction to this volume). It involved a process of "falling short" – at least in terms of our own expectations – rather than an inability to produce a successful product. Other, more goal- or product-driven and less reflexive disciplines may indeed not see what we describe as a failure in any sense. Reflecting further on the editors' introduction to this book, we draw comfort from their statement that "where failure catalyzes learning, an inability to perform in the short term gives way to ability to perform in the longer term." We thus argue that our negative experiences with this particular project, and indeed our experiences elsewhere in our wider research careers, have made us more reflexive interdisciplinary researchers, and we are now attempting to apply this learning in a new study that reaches out beyond our experiences of research spanning the natural and social sciences to encompass the arts and humanities.[3]

46 *Isabel Fletcher and Catherine Lyall*

This chapter draws on interviews with members of the RBC project team[4] and uses an auto-ethnographically-informed approach (e.g., Denshire 2014) to reflect on our experiences and expectations of interdisciplinary research collaboration more broadly. This reflection was partly achieved through two separate interviews with the authors, conducted by a doctoral student in our department who encouraged us to reflect on our own experiences as interdisciplinary researchers. Auto-ethnography has been defined as "writing about one's own experiences for specific academic purposes" (Richards 2008, cited by Greenhalgh 2017). As a method, auto-ethnography falls somewhere between anthropology and literary studies (Denshire 2014) and auto-ethnographic writing is often highly personal, drawing, for example, on the researcher's own experience of illness. While our writing in this chapter does not share these features, it is nevertheless introspective, and as a result, undoubtedly "subjective" (Denshire 2014).

A significant theme in our story of how we seek to avoid notions of failure rests on the encouragement we had received to exploit serendipitous moments in order to produce "good" social science outputs from rather routine empirical research, illustrating how the thinking can go on beyond the end of a grant-funded project.

We begin by discussing the policy context in which the exemplar RBC project took place before briefly outlining the research project, the intention behind the social science "work-package" (and we will return to this freighted term in due course), and the project outcomes. Next, we draw on evidence from both the literature and data gathered through interviews to try to make sense of the role that social scientists (as well as those from the arts and humanities) play within collaborative research, and we reflect on how (and indeed, whether) this could be improved, in an attempt to offer more generalizable lessons in how to conduct social research successfully in a multi-partner, multidiscipline environment.

We will argue that few research collaborations across disciplines are currently capable of achieving the "integrative-synthesis mode" (Barry et al. 2008) of interdisciplinary research (IDR) routinely promoted by research funders. Structural factors – including disciplinary training, the ways in which research is presently funded and the reward structures of academic careers – still do not adequately support working between and/or across disciplines (see, for example, Lyall 2019; Klein and Falk-Krzesinski 2017). We therefore discuss the need to reorient research training so that it equips researchers with improved collaborative skills and enables them to better address the potential for feelings of failure. As we demonstrate below, failure to achieve success according to an idealized model of IDR does not mean that such research lacks value; rather, it means that we need to develop more realistic models of what can be achieved in the light of the structural constraints associated with IDR.

A powerful policy discourse

Increasingly, within the United Kingdom, Europe and internationally, a "big research" policy narrative prevails, leading to larger, publicly funded consortia tasked with undertaking research that is societally relevant and that has impact beyond the bounds of academia (Lyall et al. 2015a). This discourse engenders

Stem cells and serendipity 47

public pronouncements that favour cross-disciplinary research and associates this mode of research determinedly with "innovation" from leading policy figures:

[M]ost exciting and ground-breaking innovations are happening at the intersection of disciplines.

(Moedas 2017)

However, we also know that this same research policy agenda favours certain disciplines over others within such interdisciplinary engagements. Despite a push to integrate the social sciences and humanities within the European Union's predominantly science-led Horizon 2020 program,[5] analyses show that social science disciplines that are more likely to favour quantitative research methods such as economics and political science predominate to the almost total exclusion of a discipline such as history (EC 2017; EC 2018a; EC 2018b). We have to acknowledge, in the discussion that follows, that our experience as social researchers located within a science policy/science studies tradition may have been very different from that of a researcher coming from, say, anthropology or a fortiori a humanities discipline.

Myriad reports and assessments (for example, Bruce et al. 2004; LERU 2016; Hetel et al. 2015; Birnbaum et al. 2017; British Academy 2016) have made recommendations on how best to encourage such research. But despite this accumulated wisdom there remains, on the part of many stakeholders in both research and policy arenas, an absence of shared understanding of what "IDR" actually is.[6]

The term "IDR" can be used to describe a broad spectrum of activities, from the lone researcher reaching beyond her discipline-based training to access publications from a different area of research, to a group of humanists, scientists and policy makers working together to address a major societal issue, to multidiscipline projects in a new and emerging area such as neuro-humanities. IDR has thus become "a catch-all term, used loosely by a wide range of researchers to cover an array of very different research practices" (Bammer 2015). Notwithstanding many years of debate (Lyall et al. 2015a; Pohl et al. 2011), there remains a lack of consensus on the definitions of terms related to IDR, which leads to inconsistency, ambiguity and confusion. But despite these terminological issues, IDR has become a cornerstone of international research policy (NSF 2006; National Academies 2005; Bammer 2012).

The concepts underpinning IDR are, in general terms, communication between different disciplines, learning from each other and developing together new research questions, perspectives, methodologies and results. This can occur on small and large scales, at the level of the individual interdisciplinarian and, increasingly, it can involve large teams of researchers. Yet, the term IDR is often misappropriated and used in tokenistic ways, illustrated for example by researchers' concerns that their institutions promote IDR for the "wrong" reasons:

I think they're just pressured by money; they're influenced by where they can get the money from, it's not necessarily a belief in the good that interdisciplinary research can do.

(Respondent, cited in Lyall 2019, p. 40)

48   *Isabel Fletcher and Catherine Lyall*

Moreover, a lack of awareness about the institutional contexts that encourage or discourage successful IDR activity persists, leading to a glaring mismatch between the policy rhetoric and the reality of academic research lives (Lyall 2019). The experience for many arts, humanities and social science (AHSS) scholars, in particular, who embark on research collaborations with colleagues from STEM[7] subjects, is not the holy grail of the "integrative-synthesis mode" (Barry et al. 2008) where interdisciplinarity might be conceived of in terms of the integration of all the contributing disciplines in a relatively symmetrical and equal form. More commonly, the experiences echo the "subordination-service mode" (Barry et al. 2008) where the AHSS disciplines find themselves working in a support role for STEM. This unequal partnership is further confirmed by the roles frequently taken by (or assigned to) AHSS scholars, who find themselves required to "do the public engagement" (Lyall and King 2016; Balmer et al. 2015) in order to break down barriers between science and society (the "logic of accountability") or connect businesses to customer demand (the "logic of innovation") (Barry et al. 2008).

Consequently, a discussion of what interdisciplinary "success" or "failure" might look like in these situations is not straightforward and warrants some quite context-specific reflections. Not least, we have to engage with the troublesome prospect that an inevitable power imbalance dominates many interdisciplinary interactions (Callard and Fitzgerald 2015) and we need to consider how AHSS researchers might sometimes have to reconcile themselves to these "states of sub-jugation" (Callard and Fitzgerald 2015, p. 99) without succumbing to a sense of "failure."

This was nowhere more evident than in the experiences of the social science team in the Novosang project described below. However, before describing this research project we need to state unequivocally that what follows is not a criti-cism of any member of the Novosang research team but rather a critique of the research policy system in which these collaborators were being asked to operate, somewhat analogous to Bellotti and D'Agostino's analysis (in Chapter 4 in this volume) of the institutional factors that inhibit effective interdisciplinary engage-ment. Although we have interviewed some members of the team in order to gain broader perspectives, what we are presenting in this discussion is our interpreta-tion of the views of others, filtered through our own experiences as collaborators in a number of "interdisciplinary" research projects. Indeed, it must be stated that Novosang was perceived as an interdisciplinary success by other members of the team and, as we go on to describe, also achieved many worthwhile outcomes for the social scientists involved.

The Novosang project

Novosang[8] was a multi-partner research project involving four Scottish universi-ties, a small biotechnology company, the Scottish blood transfusion service and others. Working as part of this research collaboration, which spanned several dis-ciplines (including regenerative medicine, biology, bio-engineering, chemistry, physics and social science), the intention of the social scientists' role was to elicit

Stem cells and serendipity 49

the views of a wide variety of publics towards the potential use of laboratory-cultured red blood cells (derived from stem cells) for transfusion. The main aim of this workstream was to provide an in-depth assessment of perceived risks and benefits associated with conventional and novel ways of acquiring blood, blood substitutes and blood products. Four research questions were addressed:[9]

1. What types of perceived risks and benefits (to both conventional and novel blood-based technologies) are articulated by respondents?
2. How does the general public identify with their dual role as both blood donors and potential users of conventional and novel technologies?
3. How do particular groups of current blood users self-identify as future users of novel technologies, and in what ways do they attempt to engage with the development of these novel products?
4. What is the range of opposition to new sources of blood, and how do different groups mobilize their beliefs on these issues?

At the end of the project, the social scientists provided a report of their results to the principal investigator of the consortium and subsequently produced several academic publications and a short briefing document outlining their findings.

At the time, this was one of the first social science research studies to address cultured blood, although other research groups had studied attitudes to synthetic blood and other blood alternatives. This part of the project was funded by a Scottish government agency, the Scottish Funding Council (SFC),[10] whose funding interest lay in the potential commercialization of Scottish university research, and was nested within a larger, externally funded research consortium.

The role of serendipity

While some believe that serendipity is an important feature of all academic life (Merton 2004), it seems to feature predominantly in the lives of interdisciplinary researchers (Lyall 2019, ch. 5). The Novosang project was a particular example of this in at least two significant ways.

First, unlike the majority of hard-won, grant-funded research projects, the Novosang project arrived in the social researchers' portfolio as, essentially, a gift. (Although what might be construed as serendipity was also a recognition of the expertise developed by the ESRC Innogen Centre[11] and of the researchers' ability to adapt to unexpected opportunities.)

The aim of the Novosang project was to "use pluripotent stem cells to create a supply of red blood cells equivalent to those found in the body … scaling up and improving the efficiency of red blood cell production [in the laboratory] to develop a commercially viable product" (Novosang 2019). Some consortium researchers initially began working together in response to a DARPA[12] funding call for research into creating battlefield supplies of red blood cells. This application was unsuccessful, but a larger consortium – by now including researchers from the University of Edinburgh, Roslin Cells and NHS Blood and Transplant – later successfully applied to the Wellcome Trust's Translational Award program

50   Isabel Fletcher and Catherine Lyall

and received two rounds of funding. During the second round of funding, one of the consortium's lead researchers also successfully applied to the Scottish Funding Council (SFC) for further funding to support the potential commercialization of this basic biological research. A condition of this funding, stipulated by the SFC, was that before the research grant could be awarded, the consortium had to be extended to include a social science element that would test the public acceptability of such a laboratory-cultured blood product.

One of the two social scientists subsequently appointed to the team was a post-doctoral research fellow who had recently completed a PhD (King 2013) co-supervised by a Novosang researcher. Despite links between her PhD research topic and the consortium's research, she had not previously been officially part of the Novosang project (which at that stage had been known as BloodPharma). The second author of this chapter, who was then a senior researcher in a research centre set up to study the social and policy implications of the life sciences, was approached to take on the role of co-investigator on the grant.

Having received this gift, the social scientists were then presented with the challenge of how to ensure that a service deliverable (in the form of a final report to the consortium leader based on a relatively routine piece of social research) might also be transmuted into something that their peers would recognize as "good social science." Specifically, this meant publishing at least one paper that would be suitable for submission to the UK Research Evaluation Framework (REF).[13] In the REF, despite public statements to the contrary (Stern and Sweeney 2020), the view persists that the only strong submissions are discipline-focused and contribute to theoretical development of that discipline. Structured around a series of peer review panels (termed "Units of Assessment"), this mechanism has always presented those whose work does not fall neatly within a single discipline domain with problems. In the case of the social scientists involved in the Novosang team who worked in a department of science, technology and innovation studies, this was problematic because their outputs would be assessed by a panel of sociologists that had not previously been particularly receptive to interdisciplinary research.

The first attempt at publication was a methodology paper that examined the use of focus groups in determining public attitudes to new technology, and that presented this qualitative research method to clinicians and medical researchers (Lyall and King 2016). This type of "material and methods article" is described by Lindvig and Hillersdal (2019) as a well-established format, traditional in the natural and life sciences. However, the paper was variously described by sociology colleagues as "less innovative" in sociological research terms and "a meat and potatoes paper" (i.e., routine and businesslike). The social researchers understood from this reception that, in attempting to communicate sociological methodology to a non-sociological audience, they were unable to evidence "good" sociological research as required for REF purposes, and would need to take a different approach.

This is where the second serendipitous moment was grasped. The social researchers knew of another British social scientist who was conducting research

Stem cells and serendipity 51

on the social acceptability of laboratory-cultured meat, and they invited him to share his findings at one of the regular Novosang project meetings. This interaction led to the development of a joint publication drawing parallels between the two projects (Stephens et al. 2018) and this, in turn, prompted the Novosang social researchers to explore in greater depth what was meant by "naturalness" in the context of cultured blood. This finally led to the publication of a paper (King and Lyall 2018) quite far removed from the original purpose of their Novosang work-package. The authors were able to have this paper published in what sociologists consider a "good" journal.

So, given this apparent run of good fortune, why has the Novosang project been selected as a potential exemplar of interdisciplinary failure?

What counts as failure?

Looked at through the world-weary eyes of the social researcher brought in yet again to "do the public engagement" (Balmer et al. 2015), the Novosang project could indeed be viewed as another case where the social sciences were entirely subordinate to (Barry et al. 2008), and quite separate from, the rest of the consortium, and where the reasons for the social scientists being there at all were driven by external logics of innovation and accountability (Barry et al. 2008), in a role that required them to represent the public and "foretell" how a technology should develop and how the public would react (Balmer et al. 2015).

Certainly, given the circumstances of the funding described above, the social sciences had not been part of the initial problem-framing and could – rightly – be perceived as an afterthought (Webster 2016; Fam and Sofoulis 2017). Yet the consequence of this was that they were free to design their own research study within the larger project goals, which doubtless gave the social scientists a degree of freedom. However, it also meant that, while other parts of the collaboration (between the biologists, physicists and engineers) may have been interdisciplinary, the engagement between the STEM disciplines and the social scientists could, at best, be described as multidisciplinary: the social scientists were a separate "work-package" associated with but rather distanced from the core activities (see also Figure 3.1, Lindvig and Hillersdal 2019). There was, for example, no suggestion that the natural and social scientists might co-author any joint outputs. This led to a certain feeling of dissatisfaction about the project – or, in Fitzgerald et al.'s (2014) terms, feelings of ambivalence and equivocation – and a sense of being, if not exactly an outsider or an interloper, then most certainly a "guest" within the team, at least on the part of one of the social researchers. Ironically, we have written extensively on interdisciplinary research (e.g., Lyall and Fletcher 2013; Lyall et al. 2011) and this experience was a salutary lesson, demonstrating how difficult it was to influence an existing collaboration where there was no scope for joint publications and little feedback on whether our work was useful to the rest of the team.

This equivocation was perhaps intensified by the fact that the post-doctoral social researcher had been embedded with the wider team during her PhD study.

52 *Isabel Fletcher and Catherine Lyall*

During that time, she had helped the team with several high-profile outreach and public engagement activities, including working alongside Novosang researchers on a ten-day interactive educational stall at the Royal Society's 350th anniversary Festival of Science and Arts in 2010. This was a high-profile and popular event that became one of the project's largest public engagement initiatives, resulting in a significant amount of press coverage and more than 10,000 interactions with individual members of the public.

Participation in such work turned out to be a mixed blessing for her – it made it socially easy for her to work in a new group of researchers on this related Novosang project, but it also meant that she had to explain the difference between this new role and her previous public engagement activities, a difference that did not seem to be obvious to the non-social science researchers in the project. In particular, she:

> did have to be quite specific about what social scientists or social researchers do, because I think there was a bit of an expectation that … I would be booking all their hotels and going down to science festivals and that kind of thing because that's what their outreach people do (Interview 1).

Inevitably, this raises questions about the transition from graduate student to independent researcher[14] and about whether her earlier involvement had informed thinking within the wider team about the role of the social sciences, or whether her continuation on this new phase of the project merely reinforced the view that she was there "to do the public engagement."

Despite these misgivings, the Novosang project resulted in a number of academic publications in what are generally regarded as good quality social science journals, as well as the core project deliverable of a final report to the consortium and its funder.

The project developed the skills of the junior social scientist who learned about the practicalities of conducting social science "for real" rather than as part of the more constrained context of PhD research, and this experience led to her acquiring another academic research position. For the more senior social researcher, the experience enabled her to develop her mentoring and line management skills and prompted some valuable self-reflection on her role as an interdisciplinary scholar and commentator.

Two of the project's co-investigators said that they had been unfamiliar with social science research and had learned a lot from working with their social science colleagues on the Novosang project. One described a changing understanding of social science methods and the data they produce:

> [at the beginning I thought] it was all a bit woollier, because, of course, you're just asking people's opinions, and it's all like putting opinions together, and you're left thinking, well, can't you do some statistics on that, but you can't for that type of thing … at first I thought how valuable is it, and then I realised it was because it was a different way of … collecting data and putting

it together, it was a different way of doing it … yeah I learnt a lot from that (Interview 2).

For another, it profoundly altered their opinion of the value of social science:

> I frankly couldn't get the point of the social sciences at the beginning but we did it, but by the end of it, it's one of my favourite bits, you know, it, it means a lot and we have to do that (Interview 3).

This investigator described how they now thought of social science – by which they meant education, outreach and public engagement – as an "absolutely essential" component of publicly funded research.

So, in this example, what counts as "failure" when the social scientists achieved a number of conventional academic outcomes, rated by their social science peers, and the natural scientists stated that they learned a lot about social science as a result of working with the social scientists on the project? Powerful forces were at play in this project, as in so many supposed "interdisciplinary" engagements between the AHSS and STEM disciplines,[15] which means that defying potential feelings of failure required a high degree of pragmatism on the part of the social researchers involved, as we now go on to discuss.

Reflections on imperfection

Academic researchers in general, and interdisciplinary researchers in particular, work within an imperfect system where there exist at least two systemic failures that confound interdisciplinarity.

First, in the United Kingdom and elsewhere, government funding is a powerful driver for interdisciplinary research (Lowe and Phillipson 2006). Yet these resources are invariably unevenly distributed between AHSS and STEM disciplines (Soufoulis 2011). Moreover, this habitually short-term funding, coupled with the seemingly ubiquitous complaints about "time poverty" (Berg and Seeber 2016), are antithetical to the type of slow research that characterizes interdisciplinarity (Lyall 2019, pp. 84–86). Moreover, the funding focus within national and international research policy reinforces the prevailing logics of innovation and acceptability and continues to anticipate the "integrative-synthesis" mode, even though this has proved unrealistic in the context of many AHSS-STEM interactions.[16]

This misalignment may lead to a sense of failure on the part of the partners from the AHSS disciplines that may be wholly unjustified. Indeed, it has been argued that we expect too much from these encounters across disciplines where the "asymmetries of power" inherent in IDR mean that parity between the social and natural sciences remains an elusive goal (Callard and Fitzgerald 2015, p. 97).

Furthermore, the current funding landscape often requires research leaders to piece together a complex mosaic of funding in order to finance long-term work, for example in areas of the life sciences such as the Novosang project. This can lead to turnover of personnel, resulting in uncertainty, in particular among early stage researchers, about who is part of their project (Interview 1). It also results in a patchwork of potentially loosely interrelated projects where co-investigators/ work-package leaders may be more invested in their own aspects of the research and less committed to an overarching, interdisciplinary goal (see also Rhoten 2004). In the case of the Novosang project, from the perspective of the social scientists, the research represented a multidisciplinary engagement rather than a truly integrated interdisciplinary one.

This meant that the social researchers had to be flexible and adaptable in order to both deliver on the project goals and satisfy broader (more discipline-focused) research demands, but in doing so do they risked feeling as if they were selling themselves out and not trying hard enough. Science and technology studies scholars (e.g., Balmer et al. 2015; Marris and Calvert 2019) have long reflected on their role within science-led, and in particular life-science-led, collaborations. These "interdisciplinary" interactions have typically been modulated through ELSI (ethical, legal and social implications), which casts social scientists variously as advocates, translators, critics, activists, or reformers (Calvert and Martin 2009). This approach may, however, have set high ideals that other AHSS researchers may feel they fail to attain in similar cross-disciplinary interactions.

In the context of perceived interdisciplinary successes and failures, the management of expectations is indeed essential (LERU 2016, p. 14). We need to inject a dose of realism into the aspirational rhetoric that surrounds interdisciplinarity and admit that what is more often being funded is actually multidisciplinary and not interdisciplinary (or transdisciplinary),[17] and that interdisciplinarity requires much deeper commitments, not least in terms of project funding, researcher capacity building and career opportunities. At present, the subordinate service role is just too ingrained from the outset by current funding drivers – a factor recognized by all of our Novosang interviewees who acknowledged that there would not have been a social science element had the funding not been conditional on its inclusion. We are sympathetic to Callard and Fitzgerald's (2015, p. 109) suggestion that AHSS and STEM researchers may need to reconcile themselves to learning "different ways of being unsettled together," but it takes time to build such trust and, as noted below, this is often not a luxury afforded to interdisciplinary researchers on short-term contracts. Perhaps we need to accept that, in many cases, a multidisciplinary approach may have to be good enough because otherwise we are being set up to fail (see also Mennes 2020).

Do we therefore need to be more honest and acknowledge that true interdisciplinarity and parity of all disciplines may, in some instances, be an unachievable ideal? This would entail research funders and applicants being more careful about the language they use and curbing the current tendency to indiscriminately brand every form of cross-disciplinary research as "interdisciplinary."[18]

The second systemic failing is the failure to acknowledge the distinctive skills needs of interdisciplinary collaborations, as noted in the editors' introduction to this volume. Indeed, as Szostack (2013) indicates, one of the key challenges comes from "disciplinarians who claim that anyone can be (or indeed is) interdisciplinary."[19] Inherent in this claim is a misunderstanding of what IDR is, what it takes to be an interdisciplinary researcher, and the negative implications that this can have for university careers (Lyall 2019, passim.). The situation is exacerbated for post-doctoral researchers whose frequently fragmented careers do not allow them sufficient time to build enduring research relationships in a situation where successful interdisciplinary research is acknowledged to require extra time in order to develop trust and hence profitable research engagements.

The corollary of this is that many academic researchers are not well equipped to participate in successful collaborations (interdisciplinary or otherwise) because too much of the university education system focuses on "disciplinary excellence" (Lyall 2019, pp. 91–95) to the detriment of other essential academic life-skills (often unhelpfully termed "soft skills"). Yet, increasingly, we are beginning to question the value of discipline specialists and call for education that encompasses broader skills, not simply the finer points of a narrow discipline (Epstein 2019, passim.). This compels institutions to think about the more tacit, integrative skills (sometimes termed "meta-skills," Skills Development Scotland 2018) such as leadership, communication, negotiation and so on[20] that facilitate interdisciplinary collaboration, as discussed elsewhere in this volume by Pearce (at ETH Zurich) and Vilsmaier (at Leuphana University of Lüneburg) in the context of student experiences of sustainability education. As trends for interdisciplinary research increase, this must also have an impact on teaching and training in order to inculcate these "soft skills" or "meta-skills," yet activities to date are often regarded as "extra-curricular" rather than as core elements of degree programs.[21] This points to the need for a more far-reaching discussion about how such training might be achieved and embedded through educational practices, and at which step in a student's or academic's learning career it might take place. Interviews with research leaders in the United Kingdom have revealed that this question of when to develop interdisciplinary skills is a significant and contested issue (Lyall 2019). University leaders disagree on this question of timing, and this reveals some fundamental misunderstandings about the nature of interdisciplinary knowledge, how it is acquired and the skills that interdisciplinary researchers offer. While we are seeing an increase in trends towards more interdisciplinary teaching in the United Kingdom (e.g., Lyall et al. 2015b) and elsewhere in Europe (e.g., Lindvig et al. 2017; Pearce and Vilsmaier, both in this volume) at both the undergraduate and postgraduate levels, these developments are often ad hoc and insufficiently institutionalized to secure lasting futures.

At present, the overriding logics that steer much current IDR, and that shape the training that early career researchers receive, mean that even experienced interdisciplinary researchers may struggle to counter the powerful forces in play. In order to frustrate what may sometimes feel like an inevitable sense of failure, we have encouraged social scientists to be pragmatic. It follows that, given the project constraints, the social researchers in the Novosang project had to tread a careful path so as not to alienate the other partners, even if this meant casting themselves as the "acceptable face of social sciences." Donna Haraway describes this as "strategic essentialism":

56 *Isabel Fletcher and Catherine Lyall*

There is a strategic use to speaking the same idiom as the people that you are sharing the room with. You craft a good-enough idiom so you can work on something together. I go with what we can make happen in the room together. And then we go further tomorrow.

(Weigel 2019)

If we want to go further tomorrow, we need to empower change, both by enabling the AHSS disciplines to take more appropriate roles in research agenda-setting and by better equipping future generations with the tools and skills they need in order to become successful collaborators.

Conclusion

This book chapter was born out of a paradoxical experience where one of us was part of a project that was seen by many as an interdisciplinary success, yet the project felt unsatisfactory as it achieved neither full integration within a large and complex research project nor a synthesis of social and natural scientific approaches to the research topic. This "integrative-synthesis" mode of IDR is heavily promoted by universities and research funders as a way for academics to address global societal problems. However, we argue that it is problematic for two key reasons. First, it ignores the realities of funding, training and academic career structures that most researchers must work within. Second, it is particularly weighted against AHSS researchers, both in the framing of the research topics that are funded under such initiatives, and in the terms under which they are expected to collaborate with STEM colleagues. Our suggestion is therefore that universities and research funders should develop more realistic models of interdisciplinary research. This would allow researchers to collaborate across disciplines in a variety of ways without feeling that they have somehow "failed" if they do not achieve an often impossible ideal. Furthermore, power imbalances between disciplines should be overtly addressed by funders by giving AHSS researchers working within collaborations with STEM greater autonomy to define the topics for specific interdisciplinary projects and to stipulate the methods that are used to investigate these topics.

Take-home messages

- Be honest: Recognize that IDR may not be for you if you can't make it work in a way that satisfies your intellectual needs.
- Be realistic: Manage expectations from the outset. A multidisciplinary collaboration may be "good enough" and still generate successful outcomes.
- Be creative: Exploit serendipitous moments so that the thinking (and the research outputs) go on beyond the end of the collaboration.
- Be resourceful: Seek out opportunities to develop your collaboration skills if these are not part of your formal training.

Acknowledgements

Catherine Lyall acknowledges funding from the Scottish Funding Council (SFC Grant Number 227208694). Isabel Fletcher and Catherine Lyall have received funding from the European Union's Horizon 2020 research and innovation program under grant agreement No. 822705 and would particularly like to thank their partners in this SHAPE-ID project for helpful discussions about the nature of interdisciplinary collaborations involving AHSS disciplines. We would also like to acknowledge the contributions of the interviewees who shared their reflections on the Novosang project and of Nathalie Dupin for encouraging us to participate in self-reflection on our own roles in IDR.

Notes

1 Predominantly in the life sciences; see, for example, Lyall and Fletcher (2013).
2 In which the second author was a co-investigator.
3 See www.shapeid.eu (accessed 29 February 2020).
4 Conducted by the first author.
5 See, for example, Regulation (EU) no 1291/2013 of 11.12.2013 of the European Parliament and of the Council establishing Horizon 2020.
6 For helpful definitions see, for example, Figures 3.1 and 3.2 in European Science Foundation (2011).
7 STEM = science, technology, engineering and medicine.
8 http://novosang.co.uk (accessed 19 July 2019).
9 See Lyall and King (2016) for a more detailed account of the research design which involved 27 qualitative data collection opportunities, including one-to-one interviews with key informants, focus groups, mini-focus groups and discussions.
10 www.sfc.ac.uk (accessed 19 July 2019).
11 www.innogen.ac.uk (accessed 29 February 2020)
12 The US government's Defense Advanced Research Projects Agency.
13 Taking place on a roughly six-yearly cycle, the Research Evaluation Framework (REF) (https://www.ref.ac.uk, accessed 19 July 2019) is a national assessment of research quality across all UK universities which decides institutions' core funding allocations from central government.
14 The second author acted as principal investigator (PI) to this postdoctoral researcher and this revealed another asymmetry, not between the social researchers but in the more hierarchical nature of the line management relationships that existed between the natural science postdoctoral researchers and their PIs.
15 Experiences of interdisciplinary research can, of course, be very different depending on whether it takes place between proximate disciplines (i.e., within the social sciences, the natural sciences, the medical sciences, or the arts and humanities) or involves much more distant disciplines, for example, spanning the social sciences and natural sciences as in the case of the Novosang project described here.
16 This is recognized by the European Commission who have recently funded a Horizon2020 project, SHAPE-ID, in which the authors are participating, to address the challenge of improving interdisciplinary cooperation between AHSS and STEM disciplines and make recommendations to guide European policymakers, funders, universities and researchers in achieving successful pathways to interdisciplinary integration between AHSS and other sciences, as well as within AHSS disciplines. www.shapeid. eu (accessed 19 July 2019).
17 See footnote 3.

58 *Isabel Fletcher and Catherine Lyall*

18 In interviews with career interdisciplinarians that explored the issue of scholarly identity, one well-established researcher described how she typically eschewed the term "interdisciplinary" to describe herself, "unless writing a grant application in which case I say it 20,000 times" (Julia, quoted in Lyall 2019, p. 35).

19 None more so, we would argue, than the government funding agencies and university leaders who embrace this à la mode approach to research.

20 The key factors required to achieve successful collaborations include, for example, trust, vision, communication, mutual benefits, management and team dynamics (e.g., Dowling 2015; Bennett et al. n.d.; LERU Doctoral Summer School 2019).

21 See for example the 2019 LERU Doctoral Summer School "Building Research Capacity and a Collaborative Global Community" https://www.leru.org/calendar/leru-summer-school-2019 (accessed 19 July 2019).

References

Balmer, A. S., Calvert, J., Marris, C., Molyneux-Hodgson, S., Frow, E., Kearnes M., Bulpin, K., Schyfter, P., MacKenzie, A., Martin. P. 2015. Taking roles in interdisciplinary collaborations: Reflections on working in post-ELSI spaces in the UK synthetic biology community. *Science and Technology Studies*, 28(3), 3–25.

Bammer, G. 2012. Strengthening interdisciplinary research: What it is, what it does, how it does it and how it is supported. The Australian Council of Learned Academies. Available from: https://acola.org/wp-content/uploads/2018/08/strengthening-interd isciplinary-research.pdf.

Bammer, G. 2015. Distinguishing between multi-, inter- and trans-disciplinarity – 'theological' hairsplitting or essential categorisation? *Integration and Implementation Insights*. Available from: https://i2insights.org.

Barry, A., Born, G., Weszkalnys, G. 2008. Logics of interdisciplinarity. *Economy and Society*, 37(1), 20–49. doi:10.1080/03085140701760841.

Bennett, L., Gadlin, H., Marchand, C. n.d. *Collaboration team science field guide*. US National Institutes of Health. Available from: https://www.cancer.gov/about-nci/or ganization/crs/research-initiatives/team-science-field-guide/collaboration-team-scien ce-guide.pdf.

Berg, M., Seeber, B. 2016. *The slow professor: Challenging the culture of speed in the academy*. Toronto: University of Toronto Press.

Birnbaum, B. et al. 2015. Integration of social sciences and humanities in Horizon 2020: Participants, budget and disciplines. *2nd monitoring report on SSH-flagged projects funded in 2015 under the societal challenges and industrial leadership*. Brussels: European Union.

British Academy. 2016. *Crossing paths: Interdisciplinary institutions, careers, education and applications*. London: British Academy.

Bruce, A., Lyall, C., Tait, J., Williams, R. 2004. Interdisciplinary integration in the Fifth Framework Programme. *Futures*, 36(4), 457–470.

Callard, F., Fitzgerald D. 2015. *Rethinking interdisciplinarity across the social sciences and neurosciences*. Basingstoke, UK: Palgrave.

Calvert, J., Martin, P. 2009. The role of social scientists in synthetic biology. EMBO Rep.10/3, 201–204.

Denshire, S. 2014. On auto-ethnography. *Current Sociology Review*, 62(6), 831–850.

Dowling, A. 2015. *The Dowling review of business-university research collaborations*. London: Department for Business, Innovation & Skills.

Epstein, D. 2019. *Range: How generalists triumph in a specialized world.* London: Macmillan.

European Commission. 2017. Integration of social sciences and humanities in Horizon 2020: Participants, budget and disciplines. *2nd Monitoring report on SSH-flagged projects funded in 2015 under the Societal Challenges and Industrial Leadership priorities.* Brussels: Directorate-General for Research and Innovation.

European Commission. 2018a. Integration of social sciences and humanities in Horizon 2020: Participants, budget and disciplines. *3rd Monitoring report on SSH-flagged projects funded in 2016 under the Societal Challenges and Industrial Leadership priorities.* Brussels: Directorate-General for Research and Innovation.

European Commission. 2018b. Integration of social sciences and humanities in Horizon 2020: Participants, Budget and Disciplines. *4th Monitoring report on SSH-flagged projects funded in 2017 under the Societal Challenges and Industrial Leadership priorities.* Brussels: Directorate-General for Research and Innovation.

European Science Foundation. 2011. *European peer review guide. Integrating policies and practices into coherent procedures.* Strasbourg, France: European Science Foundation.

Fam, D., Sofoulis, Z. 2017. A knowledge ecologies analysis of co-designing water and sanitation services in Alaska. *Journal of Science and Engineering Ethics*, 23(4), 1059–1083.

Fitzgerald, D., Littlefield, M. M., Knudsen, K. J., Tonks, J., Dietz, M. 2014. Ambivalence, equivocation and the politics of experimental knowledge: A transdisciplinary neuroscience encounter. *Social Studies of Science*, 44(5), 701–721. doi:10.1177/0306312714531473.

Greenhalgh, T. 2017. Adjuvant chemotherapy: An autoethnography. *Subjectivity*, 10(4), 340–357. doi:10.1057/s41286-017-0033-y.

Hetel, L. et al. 2015. Integration of social sciences and humanities in Horizon 2020: participants, budget and disciplines. *Monitoring report on SSH-flagged projects funded in 2014 under the Societal Challenges and Industrial Leadership.* Brussels: European Union.

King, E. 2013. *Blood, sweat and tears: A case study of the development of cultured red blood cells for transfusion.* PhD thesis, University of Edinburgh.

King, E., Lyall, C. 2018. What's in a name: Are cultured red blood cells "natural"? *Sociology of Health Illness*, 40(4), 687–701. doi:10.1111/1467-9566.12717.

Klein, J. T., Falk-Krzesinski, H. J. 2017. Interdisciplinary and collaborative work: Framing promotion and tenure practices and policies. *Research Policy*, 46(6), 1055–1061.

League of European Research Universities. 2016. *Interdisciplinarity and the 21st century research-intensive university.* Leuven, Belgium: LERU.

LERU Doctoral Summer School. 2019. Research collaborations: A guide for early career researchers by early career researchers (Abou-Ali and 52 others), University of Edinburgh. Available from: https://edglobal.egnyte.com/dl/aepwc64quL/ [Accessed 1 August 2019].

Lindvig, K., Hillersdal, L. 2019. Strategically unclear? Organising interdisciplinarity in an excellence programme of interdisciplinary research in Denmark. *Minerva*, 57(1), 23–46. doi:10.1007/s11024-018-9361-5.

Lindvig, K., Lyall, C., Meagher, L. 2017. Creating interdisciplinary education within monodisciplinary structures: The art of managing interstitiality. *Studies in Higher Education*, 44(2), 347–360.

Lowe, P., Phillipson, J. 2006. Reflexive interdisciplinary research: The making of a research programme on the rural economy and land use. *Journal of Agricultural Economics*, 57(2), 165–184.

Lyall, C. 2019. *Being an interdisciplinary academic: How institutions shape university careers*. London: Palgrave Pivot.

Lyall, C., Bruce, A., Tait, J., Meagher, L. 2011. *Interdisciplinary research journeys: Practical strategies for capturing creativity*. London: Bloomsbury Academic.

Lyall, C., Fletcher, I. 2013. Experiments in interdisciplinary capacity building: The successes and challenges of large-scale interdisciplinary investments. *Science and Public Policy*, 40(1), 1–7.

Lyall, C., Meagher, L., Bandola, J., Kettle, A. 2015b. Interdisciplinary provision in higher education: Current and future challenges. *Report to Higher Education Academy*, August 2015.

Lyall, C., Meagher, L., Bruce, A. 2015a. A rose by any other name? Transdisciplinarity in the context of UK research policy. *Futures*, 65, 150–162. doi:10.1016/j.futures.2014.08.009.

Lyall, C., King, E. 2016. Using qualitative research methods in biomedical innovation: The case of cultured red blood cells for transfusion. *BMC Research Notes*, 9(1). doi:10.1186/s13104-016-2077-4.

Marris, C., Calvert, J. 2019. Science and technology studies in policy: The UK Synthetic Biology Roadmap. *Science, Technology and Human Values*, 45(1), 34–61.

Mennes, J. 2020. Putting multidisciplinarity (back) on the map. European Journal for Philosophy of Science, 10, 18 https://doi.org/10.1007/s13194-020-00283-z.

Merton, R. K. 2004. Afterword. Autobiographical reflections on the travels and adventures of serendipity. *In:* R. K. Merton and E. Barber, eds. *The travels and adventures of serendipity: a study in sociological semantics and the sociology of science*. Princeton, NJ: Princeton University Press.

Moedas, C. 2017. The European open science cloud: The new republic of letters. *Speech given at the European Open Science Cloud (EOSC): summit*.

National Academy of Sciences. 2005. *Facilitating interdisciplinary research*. Washington, DC: National Academies Press.

National Science Foundation. 2006. *Investing in America's future strategic plan FY 2006–2011*. Washington, DC: National Science Foundation.

Novosang. 2019. Approach. Available from: http://novosang.co.uk/ [Accessed 1 August 2019].

Pohl, C. et al. 2011. *Questions to evaluate inter- and transdisciplinary research proposals*. Bern: Working paper, td- net for Transdisciplinary Research.

Rhoten, D. 2004. Interdisciplinary research: Trend or transition. *Items and Issues*, 5(1–2), 6–11.

Richards, R. 2008. Writing the othered self: Autoethnography and the problem of objectification in writing about illness and disability. *Qualitative Health Research*, 18(12), 1717–1728.

Skills Development Scotland. 2018. Skills 4.0. A Skills Model to Drive Scotland's Future. Glasgow: Skills Development Scotland.

Sofoulis, Z. 2011. Cross-connections: Linking urban water managers with humanities, arts and social sciences researchers. Waterlines Report 60 (October 2011), Canberra: NWC. Available from: https://researchdirect.westernsydney.edu.au/islandora/object/uws:11648. [Accessed 24 February 2020].

Stephens, N., King, E., Lyall, C. 2018. Blood, meat, and upscaling tissue engineering: Promises, anticipated markets, and performativity in the biomedical and agri-food sectors. *Biosocieties*, 13(2), 368–388.

Stern, N., Sweeney, D. 2020. Institutions must be bold with impact in REF 2021 (Times Higher). 22 January. Available from: https://www.ref.ac.uk/about/blogs/institutions-must-be-bold-with-impact-in-ref-2021/.

Szostak, Rick. 2013. The state of the field: Interdisciplinary research. *Issues in Interdisciplinary Studies*, 31, 44–65.

Webster, A. 2016. Recognize the value of social science. *Nature*, 532, 7.

Weigel, M. 2019. Feminist cyborg scholar Donna Haraway: The disorder of our era isn't necessary. *The Guardian*, 20 June.

4 A fragile existence

A transdisciplinary food systems research program cut short

Bill Bellotti and Fred D'Agostino

Introduction

Along with many Australian and international universities (Lyall and Fletcher 2013), the University of Queensland (UQ) established an interdisciplinary research center, the Global Change Institute (GCI, https://gci.uq.edu.au/), in 2010 to focus UQ disciplinary research on complex global challenges such as climate change, renewable energy, sustainable water and food security. One of the authors of this chapter (Bellotti) was appointed the inaugural director of the Food Systems Program in early 2016. By the end of 2018, after just under three years, the Food Systems Program was disbanded, the direct result of a major restructuring of the GCI. The demise of the GCI Food Systems Program is one example of a wider phenomenon of universities failing to adequately support and promote interdisciplinary research institutions. According to Barry (2007, quoted in Lyall and Fletcher 2013):

> **Interdisciplinary research institutions**
> *often have a fragile existence, dependent on political circumstances, or on the patronage and energies of key individuals.*

This chapter tells the story of the GCI Food Systems Program. It begins with a brief background on the challenge of food and nutrition security and the promise of a food systems approach to address this challenge. It then describes the GCI Food Systems Program, emphasizing outputs from the program, including some ongoing research and teaching activities. The story then moves on to describe a 2016 external review of the GCI. This was a normal five-year review that made eight largely supportive recommendations to senior UQ management. The key recommendation was to change the GCI so that it focused on integration and synthesis research. A year after the review, a separate "future directions paper" was released by UQ Senior Executive, prescribing a radical reduction in budget and staff numbers. The university's vision for the GCI is for a university-wide virtual institute with a focus on integration, synthesis and stakeholder engagement relevant to the major global change challenges.

Despite the short life of the GCI Food Systems Program, and acknowledging that the short duration was directly related to changes to the scope and scale of the GCI, some useful observations can still be made regarding the experience. Six key challenges to implementing the Food Systems Program are identified. These challenges operate individually, but more commonly they interact with each other to create barriers and opportunities for implementation. Finally, possible responses to these challenges are discussed.

The aim of this reflection is to identify as honestly as possible why the Food Systems Program existed for just under three years, what the challenges were and what lessons we can draw from the experience. Although the Global Change Institute Food Systems Program is a specific case which occurred under specific circumstances, it is situated within the broader enterprise of developing transdisciplinary research in a research-intensive university. While acknowledging the limits of individual case studies (see the chapter by Klein, this volume), it is hoped that this story and the lessons it entails will have some utility for future interdisciplinary, transdisciplinary and systems approaches to complex challenges like climate change, food security and sustainable development, to name a few.

Food systems as a transdisciplinary research initiative

The study of food systems is a relatively new research endeavor requiring a transdisciplinary approach to studying the intractable and complex challenges of food and nutrition security. Two main observations are behind the rise in interest in food systems. First, malnutrition is the largest single contributor to the global burden of death and disease and, second, food and agriculture are responsible for a large proportion of our environmental footprint. It is apparent from this framing that the study of food systems requires contributions from food and agriculture, business and logistics, public health and environmental sciences. In turn, each of these topics involves an interplay between biophysical and socioeconomic factors, locating the study of food systems as a prime example of a socioenvironmental issue.

The 2017 Global Nutrition Report (Development Initiatives 2017) highlighted the central role of progressing food and nutrition security (Sustainable Development Goal 2) as a prerequisite for progress on many of the other SDGs. To this end, the report called for "double duty actions" to address multiple forms of malnutrition concurrently, and "triple duty actions" to address malnutrition and related SDGs through integrated interventions. The 2019 EAT-Lancet Commission report (Willett and Rockstrom 2019) called for systems research to develop healthy diets from sustainable food systems to address the twin challenges of severe environmental degradation and increasing malnutrition and preventable disease. The common theme, from a research perspective, in these and other international synthesis reports is the need for a food systems approach supported by interdisciplinary and transdisciplinary research methodologies.

64   Bill Bellotti and Fred D'Agostino

Prominent contributions to food systems approaches include the Global Environmental Change and Food Systems (GECAFS) project that developed a comprehensive food systems framework (Ericksen 2008; Ingram 2011) that explicitly linked food system *activities* (producing, processing, distributing and consuming food) with food system *outcomes* (food and nutrition security, economic outcomes and environmental outcomes). Subsequent papers have developed a catalogue of metrics and indicators to support implementation of the food systems framework (Gustafson et al. 2016; Melesse et al. 2019). The framework and related indicators both require researchers to work across disciplines and traditional departmental boundaries.

Universities have responded to the challenge of food and nutrition security, and the SDGs more generally, by establishing university-wide, interdisciplinary research institutes. Weingart (2000) highlights an interesting paradox in the development of interdisciplinarity in universities, pointing out that the rise in interest in interdisciplinarity coincides with increasing disciplinary specialization and fragmentation. He argues that interdisciplinarity and specialization are parallel and reinforcing phenomena in the production of knowledge. The outdated view of interdisciplinary and transdisciplinary research as a search for unity of scientific perspectives has been replaced with a more pragmatic notion of interdisciplinarity as a way to harness diverse and heterogeneous research activities under the broad social activity of science. Aligned with this logic, the GCI Food Systems Program was positioned to complement traditional agriculture disciplinary research activity.

The University of Queensland (UQ) established the Global Change Institute (GCI) in 2010 to provide a focus and catalyst for UQ research into global change issues. The stated mission of the GCI was:

> To advance discovery, create solutions and influence decision-makers in order to position the University of Queensland as a global leader in addressing the challenges of a changing world.

The GCI represented the entire university community, and it was positioned outside the traditional discipline-based faculties from an administrative perspective. This was important in addressing the problem of discipline-based approaches to global change issues that require interdisciplinary and transdisciplinary research philosophies and methodologies. The GCI was structured around four themes: Healthy Oceans and Coasts, Renewable Energy, Sustainable Water and Food Systems. In early 2016, one of the authors of this book chapter (Bellotti) was appointed the inaugural Director and Professor in Food Systems to lead the GCI Food Systems Program. The position was supported by a full-time Food Systems Program Manager in addition to other GCI administration support staff.

Initial progress

The GCI Food Systems Program (FSP) facilitated interdisciplinary meetings of academic staff from across the university. Global challenges are often framed as

A fragile existence   65

socioenvironmental issues, and consequently they require disciplinary input from across the "sacred divide" between the arts and sciences. The challenge of food security, as described in SDG2, illustrates this requirement clearly. The initial GCI FSP strategy was to develop position papers in four key initiatives and then engage with external stakeholders in government, the private sector and civil society in order to develop transdisciplinary research programs. The topics of the four initial Food Systems Discussion Papers (https://gci.uq.edu.au/food-systems) were:

A. a research agenda for food systems;
B. urban food systems – a renewed role for local governments in Australia;
C. food system governance in Australia: co-creating the recipe for change;
D. the challenge of characterizing food waste at a national level – an Australian example.

The FSP facilitated interdisciplinary working groups of UQ academics from a wide diversity of disciplines to focus on specific food systems challenges: resilience of food systems, governance of food systems, and food and nutrition security in developing countries. These working groups were modeled along the lines of the University of Maryland National Socio-Environmental Synthesis Center (SESYNC) pursuits model (M. Palmer, Kramer, Boyd, and Hawthorne 2016). In essence the "pursuits" model assembles groups of researchers and practitioners to focus on a specific challenge over a defined period of time. The pursuits produce targeted outputs such as review papers, policy briefs and research proposals. The SESYNC model is well regarded internationally as a successful model for conducting interdisciplinary and transdisciplinary research. The SESYNC receives significant multiyear funding from the US National Science Foundation, whereas the GCI FSP operated on a very modest budget.

In the three years of its existence (2016–2018), the GCI FSP facilitated several research, educational and outreach initiatives, some of which continue in various guises:

- Facilitating a food systems community of practice at UQ. This was a foundation objective of the FSP, for although UQ is strong across nearly all major disciplines related to food systems (agriculture, environment, public health, business, sociology, engineering, etc.), there is still no clear focus on food systems. An informal UQ academic network continues as the Food, Agriculture and Nutrition (FAN) forum.
- Hosting key international food systems and soft systems methodology thinkers at the GCI. These visitors made significant contributions to the profile of food systems, inspired postgraduate students, and supported early career academics. They also raised the profile of food systems with the senior executive.
- Progressing several research initiatives in relation to external funding: some of them are already funded (ARC food system governance; and CRC food waste reduction) and others are currently under consideration for funding (ACIAR transforming nutrition systems to reduce stunting in Indonesia).

66 Bill Bellotti and Fred D'Agostino

- Operating and developing teaching initiatives. The Asia-Pacific Network for Global Change Research funded a project, "Enhancing Food System Resilience in Indonesia and Pacific Island States" (2018–2020). And FSP staff have contributed to a UQEdX MOOC (University of Queensland free online course) on the Sustainable Development Goals, specifically "SDG2 End Hunger, Enhance Food and Nutrition Security and Promote Sustainable Agriculture."
- Promoting food systems to the public through public lectures and popular media, and supporting the local UQ community by initiating a process that culminated in a new community garden located on the UQ St Lucia campus for students, staff and the wider community.

However, despite the Food Systems Program's promising and fruitful beginning, the GCI was struggling under growing pressure from UQ's senior executive to radically change its mode of operation. This pressure is described in the following section and was particularly detrimental to the Food Systems Program, as it was only in its second year of operation when forced reductions in staff and budgets began to be felt.

External review of the GCI and subsequent UQ administration of the GCI

The GCI was reviewed in May 2016 as part of the normal UQ policy of periodically reviewing all major organizational units. The GCI Review Committee comprised three external and three internal reviewers. The reviewers were all well-established and highly regarded scholars representing a range of disciplines and subject matters, including climate change, energy economics, food systems, psychology, mining and social science. The Review Committee interviewed external stakeholders from government, the private sector and civil society, along with UQ academic and professional staff and students. Those interviewed included GCI staff members.

The review committee made eight recommendations covering purpose, methods and approaches, engagement, setting and delivering the agenda, structure, diversity, learning and performance indicators. The key recommendations can be summarized as shifting the GCI focus to be the "UQ center for integrating and synthesizing disciplinary knowledge on global change issues," and in support of this, that it should "shift the core capability of GCI staff to focus on integrative methods and approaches." This shift in function would also require greater focus on "internal engagement strategy" and building "a strong and effective two-way external engagement strategy."

This significant shift in purpose and function was to be supported by a new leadership structure which provided top-level positions in "Engagement and Agenda" and "Knowledge Integration." It also involved the formation of an Agenda Setting team (which was to decide what the GCI would focus on) and an Integration Methods team (which would decide how the GCI would operate). The clear intention of the proposed restructure, as illustrated by the two new Co-Director positions, was to emphasize stakeholder engagement and knowledge integration and synthesis. It is no coincidence that these two roles are central to the transdisciplinary research enterprise. It is also striking that some of the matters identified by the review panel (e.g., internal and external engagement) turned out to be, and indeed were already known to be, key success factors for the Food Systems Program.

Whether this proposed new leadership structure (and the implementation of other key recommendations) would have provided a supportive or indeed more supportive context for the development of the Food Systems Program is an interesting question, as there are other important variables (such as resources and financial support) that are also crucial in this respect. But it is not a question that we have any basis for answering because, in particular, this structure was not implemented, and nor were most of the recommendations. The Review Report was, in due course, overwritten by a "Future Directions Paper" that focused on GCI's relations with other university organizational units and was a harbinger of budgetary and staffing reductions.

Coming as they did before the Food Systems Program had been fully bedded down, these changes played a significant, and indeed perhaps the most significant, role in the subsequent history of the Food Systems Program, in effect multiplying the impact of other factors, many of which are common across the range of interdisciplinary initiatives wherever they are undertaken. They are therefore the context for understanding the impact at the GCI of these other, more widely observed challenges.

Challenges to implementing a food systems research program at the University of Queensland

Six key challenges were experienced and are discussed separately here. However, it is apparent that each challenge is interconnected to a greater or lesser extent with one or more of other challenges (Figure 4.1). For example, the challenge of stable long-term resourcing of the FSP was linked to the internal politics of budget allocation for scarce resources, competition from discipline-based schools and faculties for "ownership" of a particular issue and the accepted disciplinary approach to that issue, and the success or failure in attracting funding from primarily discipline-based, external research funding schemes. These points are expanded in the following sections.

Leadership knowledge of interdisciplinary and transdisciplinary research philosophy and methodology

It would seem obvious that leaders of interdisciplinary or transdisciplinary research institutes should possess a good understanding and knowledge of interdisciplinary and transdisciplinary research philosophy, methodology, and practice. But, unfortunately, this is not always the case. One reason for this is that the interdisciplinary and transdisciplinary research enterprise is in its relative infancy compared to traditional, disciplinary research and consequently there is a relatively

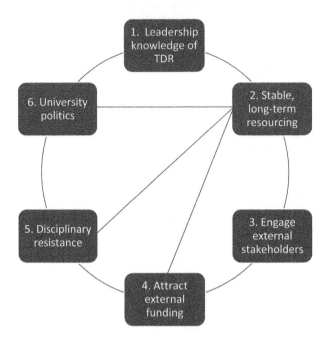

Figure 4.1 Interconnectedness of key challenges. Each of the separate challenges is potentially influenced by the other. For illustrative purposes, and to avoid overcomplicating the figure, only one example of interconnectedness is shown.

small pool of potential interdisciplinary and transdisciplinary research leaders. Insofar as kudos for research leadership traditionally and currently accumulate on a largely disciplinary basis (e.g., citations, grants, etc.), the pool becomes smaller still if it is required, as it may be at a high-prestige, research-intensive university that the institute director must also have this kind of standing.

A further complicating factor is the lack of a single widely accepted definition of what actually constitutes transdisciplinary research. This is often portrayed as a weakness, and it can result in academics "talking past each other," but in reality this plurality of definitions should be viewed as a defining characteristic of interdisciplinary and transdisciplinary research (Weingart 2000; Woelert and Millar 2013). Klein (2013) identifies five major clusters of meaning around the term transdisciplinary:

A. integration, synthesis, boundary critique;
B. complexity, uncertainty, diversity, interdependence;
C. participation, collaboration, partnering, networking;
D. system knowledge, transformation knowledge, local knowledge;
E. interrogation, critique, reformulating.

Given this diversity of meaning, it is no wonder that leadership of transdisciplinary research is challenging.

Exacerbating the leadership challenge is the complexity of leading an interdisciplinary research institute within a university that fundamentally remains a research and education institution based firmly in disciplinary structures such as faculties and departments. Interdisciplinary research leadership requires a greater emphasis on working across disciplinary boundaries to secure stakeholder engagement, facilitate collaboration and communicate effectively to interested parties whose own orientation is primarily to their disciplines. It also requires being able to stimulate reflection on the part of potential collaborators who are new to interdisciplinary research work (L. Palmer 2018). This is, patently, a skillset that is different from that commonly associated with high-performing disciplinary scientists who are neither instructed in, nor required to have as a success condition, knowledge or empathy for interdisciplinary and transdisciplinary research philosophy, an appreciation for the need for a plurality of research methodologies or an openness to other perspectives when framing complex global challenges.

Stable and long-term funding and resourcing from the host institution

No university research center, whether it is discipline-based or interdisciplinary, can survive without a secure funding base for staff and operations. For interdisciplinary or transdisciplinary synthesis centers, such as the Global Change Institute, this problem has been exacerbated by the unfortunate timing which meant that the Institute needed significant new investment during a time of general tightening of public funds for university research and education. One novel perspective to address this challenge is to view university synthesis centers as critical research infrastructure (Baron et al. 2017). The traditional view of infrastructure is that it comprises physical facilities and equipment such as DNA sequencers, medical clinics, research farms, and marine research vessels. However, with increasing opportunities for synthesizing existing data rather than continually generating new data, and with a growing societal demand for science-based solutions to global challenges, there is a strong argument for viewing socioenvironmental synthesis centers as a special category of research infrastructure with a legitimate case for increased government and private sector investment.

Interdisciplinary research on complex global challenges is by its very nature long-term. First, there is the task of listening and adequately representing the diversity of relevant stakeholder perspectives. Second, there is the challenge of assembling willing academic and non-academic research teams with relevant disciplinary and practical expertise and motivation to collaborate outside of their normal professional boundaries on a specific challenge. Third, the expectation that interdisciplinary research should have impact, and that it should improve a specific situation, requires greater attention to the adoption and uptake of research outputs by intended users and society more generally. In combination, these three considerations result in longer time requirements for interdisciplinary and transdisciplinary research relative to simpler, more tightly defined, disciplinary research questions.

70 Bill Bellotti and Fred D'Agostino

Strong focus on needs and views of external stakeholders

The plan for the GCI Food Systems Program was initially to understand the capacity and willingness of UQ academics to participate in FSP projects, and only then go to external stakeholders to further refine research opportunities. The aim was to first develop a capability statement in several areas (e.g., governance, resilience, agricultural research for rural development) before going to government, the private sector and civil society stakeholders to invite their perspectives and participation. This approach was necessitated in part by the Director of the Food Systems Program being a new appointment at the University of Queensland. In hindsight, this strategy was ill-conceived; it would have been more strategic and effective to first engage external stakeholders and then enlist relevant UQ disciplinary expertise.

As it transpired, the initial scanning and team building of UQ capacity and willingness took closer to 18 than 12 months. Unfortunately, by this time, GCI operating budgets and staff numbers were already being cut back as a result of general financial stringencies and in the wake of the complex review process. In effect, there was inadequate internal capacity to engage with external stakeholders in a meaningful and professional manner. Early stakeholder engagement has several advantages including:

- making sense of complexity using well-established soft systems methodology;
- providing a forum and process for marginalized and disadvantaged stakeholders to voice their concerns and aspirations;
- developing mutual understanding of an issue when actors may hold very different perspectives;
- supporting stakeholders to move toward accommodations and therefore facilitating implementation;
- developing research questions that reflect the needs of stakeholders;
- securing greater buy-in from intended users of research outputs to support transformational change;
- setting the research agenda, including protecting the research agenda from powerful vested interests;
- protecting the research agenda from narrowly conceived disciplinary perspectives by making underlying assumptions and worldviews more transparent (after Midgley 2000; Midgley 2003).

Successful attraction of significant external research funding

A key metric for individual university research staff and university research centers is external research funding. Successful proposals often attract significant matching university funding in addition to formal mechanisms for additional core government funding, ostensibly to support fixed overheads of research including facilities such as libraries and computing, legal and other essential services. A less tangible but important consequence of external funding is the credibility it confers on individual researchers and the research philosophy and methodology proposed. In traditional disciplinary research, a successfully funded project indicates the researchers and associated methodology have been endorsed by a discipline-based peer review. Herein lies a problem for interdisciplinary, transdisciplinary and systems research proposals, as the appropriate and necessary peer review panels have not yet been conceived or institutionalized. It is hardly surprising that the success rate of interdisciplinary, transdisciplinary and systems research proposals is low when they are evaluated against disciplinary criteria. In a rare evaluation of the process of funding interdisciplinary research by the Australian Research Council, the key finding was unambiguous: "the greater the degree of interdisciplinarity, the lower the probability of being funded" (Bromham, Dinnage and Hua 2016). The authors made several recommendations, including the need for reviewers with research experience spanning multiple disciplines.

Two main sources of funding in Australian universities are the Australian Research Council (ARC) and the Rural Industry Research and Development Corporations (RIRDCs). Unfortunately for food systems research, the ARC is strongly based on disciplinary categories and themes, and the RIRDCs are based on agricultural commodities. Neither ARC nor the RIRDCs is naturally inclined toward supporting interdisciplinary or systems research. The GCI Food Systems Program submitted an ARC Discovery proposal on "Resilient Food Systems," but the proposal was rejected by expert reviewers using inappropriate agricultural production disciplinary criteria.

In Australian university research funding, there is a particular "paradox of interdisciplinarity" (Woelert and Millar 2013). On the one hand, there is rhetoric regarding the need for interdisciplinary research, yet on the other hand, modes of governance and research evaluation rely almost exclusively on discipline-based classification systems. It need not be this way. In the United Kingdom, several government research funding schemes, for example the Global Challenges Research Fund (GCRF, https://www.ukri.org/research/global-challenges-research-fund/) are calling for interdisciplinary and systems approaches to address complex global challenges in food systems, public health, rural development and climate change. Ideally, Australian research funding schemes will follow this trend and allocate a proportion of funds to new schemes prioritizing interdisciplinary and transdisciplinary research and systems thinking to complement traditional disciplinary funding models.

Resistance and inertia from disciplinary-based schools and faculties

Discipline-based structures (faculties, departments, schools, etc.) have been the basis of university administration from their inception. In general, the disciplinary model has served society well, providing great advances in understanding, technology and well-being. However, in the era of the Anthropocene (Steffen et al. 2015), the limitations of the disciplinary approach for addressing complex global challenges are increasingly recognized. D'Agostino (2012) points out that disciplines are sustained by both institutional elements (research classification

72   Bill Bellotti and Fred D'Agostino

systems, e.g., Fields of Research (FoR) and Socio-Economic Objective (SEO) codes, professional associations, publishers, undergraduate curricula, academic departments) and intellectual elements (a body of accumulated knowledge, an accepted narrative, styles of subjectivity, a discursive community, etc.). These disciplinary elements support the continuation of disciplinary paradigms, including acceptable processes for paradigm change. In a very real sense, academic faculties and departments are the gatekeepers of disciplinary worldviews.

The University of Queensland is very highly ranked in the discipline of agriculture. It has two administrative units, the School of Agriculture and Food Sciences (SAFS, https://agriculture.uq.edu.au/) and the Queensland Alliance for Agriculture and Food Innovation (QAAFI, https://qaafi.uq.edu.au/). The traditional agriculture disciplinary view of the term "food security" is centered around the notion of increasing food production as the key strategy. This is in sharp contrast to the food systems perspective that sees food production as just one of several activities contributing to food security, which in turn is only one of several key outcomes from the food system (Ingram 2011). This is an example of a discipline "owning" a particular issue (food security), and in the case of the GCI Food Systems Program it was paradoxically easier to forge interdisciplinary links with academics from the disciplines of social science, economics, public health, environment and engineering than with SAFS or QAAFI academics.

In addition to the potential disciplinary obstacles outlined above, Lowe and Phillipson (2009) highlight the importance of institutional structures and relationships for bridging divides between disciplinary expertise. While the GCI more generally, and Food Systems Program specifically, can be viewed as an internal (The University of Queensland) attempt to facilitate interdisciplinary and transdisciplinary research, this attempt required supporting institutional reform with external stakeholders, including external research funding organisations.

Internal university politics

A crucial success factor for any academic organizational unit is its budgetary position. In any contemporary university, this is a complex matter that takes in executive and senior management decision-making and strategic priorities at several levels.

A key element, in the contemporary Australian context, is that stand-alone research institutes and/or centers are to varying degrees reliant on so-called "strategic funding" which is typically generated from the surpluses associated with teaching international fee-paying students. Since surpluses available for strategic allocation are typically generated in organizational units other than those that will spend them, they are typically allocated at relatively senior levels of university management and are thus unavoidably subject to the sorts of political contestation that is associated with limited means and a variety of worthy ends.

While the Global Change Institute initially enjoyed strong support from UQ senior management in the form of budget, support staff and physical space, this support was not sustained: the original GCI was discontinued, and a new "virtual" GCI has been proposed.

In relation to the "politics" of strategic funding allocations, one element was, precisely, the success of the GCI in attracting research that could have been conducted in the traditional disciplinary schools. Competition between the GCI and disciplinary administrative units for external and internal research income contributed to the GCI's demise. This was an unfortunate development that could have been avoided. The role of the GCI should not be to compete with disciplinary units; rather, the role of the GCI should be to add value to their core research capacity (see the following section for suggestions on how this might be achieved). For this reason, the GCI Food Systems Program was careful not to encroach on food production research that was properly the domain of SAFS and QAAFI.

A second contribution to the demise of the original GCI was a lack of common purpose from senior university staff over the future of the institute following the formal review in 2016. This was most clearly evident with the release in 2017 of the "Future Directions" paper. This paper made no mention of the recommendations from the 2016 formal external review of the GCI and was at odds with the inaugural director's vision for the future of the GCI. The decision to transition the GCI to a new mode of operation was not ill-conceived or unreasonable in any way. However, the process for implementing this transition diminished the GCI's capacity for delivering on its original stated mission and hence clouded the opportunities for the Food Systems Program to succeed. On an optimistic note, with new leadership and structures in place, the new GCI has every opportunity to succeed.

Responding to the six identified challenges

In hindsight, it is evident that the GCI Food Systems Program did not have the time or resources to succeed. The Food Systems Program was collateral damage in the confusion occasioned by the extended process of organizational review and, crucially, by the associated withdrawal of strategic funding support. Putting this reality aside, there are some important lessons to be gained from the Food Systems Program experience, and these are discussed here. It is hoped that this reflection may help future initiatives avoid repeating some of the mistakes and/or challenges described earlier.

An essential prerequisite for success of the new center is a common purpose supported by senior leadership. In the case of the Global Change Institute, a shared vision along the following lines could work:

To be the UQ centre for integrating and synthesizing disciplinary knowledge on global change issues.

The strength of this vision is that it is clear and concise, and it distinguishes the GCI from the faculties and schools. It also locates the GCI in a position of strength relative to similar synthesis centers in other universities by emphasizing

74 *Bill Bellotti and Fred D'Agostino*

its UQ-wide role. Under this vision, the disciplinary content remains in the faculties, while the approach and methodology of the GCI are focused on integration and synthesis across faculties. The vision communicates a GCI purpose and role that is intended to add value to the academic business of the faculties and schools while avoiding internal competition. Importantly, the internal consultation process can facilitate institutional ownership and support.

In line with this vision, the future GCI would place high priority on stakeholder engagement, both internally within UQ and with a wide and diverse range of external stakeholders. Internal engagement would focus on positioning the GCI as a friend and ally of the disciplinary schools and faculties, rather than as a competitor for research funds. The GCI would add value to the disciplinary expertise in schools by making available integration, synthesis and stakeholder engagement expertise not available in the schools. External engagement would include wide consultation to shape the research agenda, establishing UQ as a thought leader on global change issues and earning a reputation for being a trusted friend on these complex challenges. The GCI would also facilitate formation of project teams from across the faculties, and also with external partners. The formation of interdisciplinary project teams could be modeled on the SESYNC pursuits model (see earlier).

Although the new GCI would not accommodate academics who are naturally aligned with existing disciplinary schools, there would still be a place in the GCI for academics whose special expertise aligned with the core GCI functions of integration, synthesis, systems thinking, stakeholder engagement and policy advice. There would also be a need for specialist professional staff like innovation brokers, communication specialists, engagement facilitators, special events organizers and community outreach officers. The new GCI would require a significant budget for facilitating "pursuits" involving international collaborators, visiting fellowships for international experts on integration, synthesis and stakeholder engagement, and for hosting high-profile international and national forums on key global challenges.

Commensurate with the unique and distinct role of the GCI, performance metrics for individual staff and for the Institute as a whole would differ from those applied to disciplinary units. There would be greater emphasis on collaboration and on rewarding interdisciplinary, multi-authored papers and proposals, greater emphasis on outcomes and impacts, including policy influence and behavior change, and a greater emphasis on outreach, engagement and communication. There also needs to be a more appropriate approach to monitoring metrics that integrates discovery, learning and improving the situation that aligns more closely with transdisciplinary research (Mitchell, Cordell and Fam 2015).

Conclusions

Food and nutrition security is one of the defining challenges of the Anthropocene. It is a prime example of a socioenvironmental challenge requiring integration across a wide and diverse array of disciplines, sectors, actors, and scales. The term "food systems" refers to a specific approach to addressing food and nutrition security, and it is gaining considerable support in international literature. At the

University of Queensland, a Food Systems Program was established within the Global Change Institute to address this important opportunity.

Despite initial progress and some ongoing food systems research and teaching activities, the Food Systems Program was disbanded after less than three years of operation. The Food Systems Program was collateral damage in the wider demise of the GCI, brought about by a failure to negotiate an agreed future purpose of the GCI. While the immediate cause of the termination of the Food Systems Program was unrelated to the program itself, there are many lessons to be gained from the Food Systems Program experience.

Six interconnected challenges in implementing the Food Systems Program were identified (Figure 4.1). Leadership for success in interdisciplinary research requires a deep understanding and experience of doing interdisciplinary and transdisciplinary research and systemic intervention. Stable, long-term funding is required, particularly in the case of integration and synthesis centers, as the research that they undertake is often complex and there is an expectation for research impact. Stakeholder engagement is central to transdisciplinary research and early stakeholder engagement can be an aid to attracting wider internal university support for an externally supported proposal. Related to this is the desirability of attracting external research funding, not just for the immediate resources brought to bear, but also to demonstrate credibility among academic peers. One significant characteristic of the dominant disciplinary culture of universities is the notion of particular disciplines "owning" specific issues. A relevant example is the issue of "food security" owned by agricultural science and framed as a food production challenge. Lastly, university politics is subject to the discipline of opportunity costs in relation to strategic surpluses and their allocation, and the old GCI, and consequently the Food Systems Program, did not survive debates about these matters.

Important lessons include the need to engage key external stakeholders early and often. This has the effect of heading off internal resistance, particularly if engagement leads to external research funding. In promoting interdisciplinary, transdisciplinary and systems approaches to a specific challenge it is critical not to alienate disciplinary approaches to the same problem. There are various ways to achieve this, but general qualities of respect, humility, agility, vision, and communication are required. The aim must be to add value to and complement the disciplinary approach, not directly compete with it. Above all, effective ongoing leadership is required to constantly build consensus and accommodations, head off dissent and allay fears, and create an atmosphere of innovation and collegiality in the transdisciplinary research enterprise.

Take-home messages

- **Vision and purpose:** Leadership of transdisciplinary institutes and the overall university leadership require a shared vision of the future.
- **Adequate resources:** Transdisciplinary research institutes in research-intensive universities require long-term, stable funding.

76 Bill Bellotti and Fred D'Agostino

- **Stakeholder engagement:** Early engagement with a diverse range of external stakeholders can build internal academic peer support and shape the research agenda, as well as being good transdisciplinary research practice.
- **Academic disciplines:** Transdisciplinary and interdisciplinary approaches and traditional disciplinary approaches are complementary and mutually reinforcing. This reality needs to be communicated and synergies exploited.
- **Institutional support:** Organizations and procedures need to support and incentivize transdisciplinary research, for example by using more appropriate criteria for evaluating research and by applying relevant criteria for staff tenure and promotion.

References

Baron, J. S. et al. 2017. Synthesis centers as critical research infrastructure. *BioScience*. doi:10.1093/biosci/bix053.

Bromham, L., Dinnage, R., Hua, X. 2016. Interdisciplinary research has consistently lower funding success. *Nature*, 534(7609), 684–687. doi:10.1038/nature18315.

D'Agostino, F. 2012. Disciplinarity and the growth of knowledge. *Social Epistemology*, 26(3–4), 331–350. doi:10.1080/02691728.2012.727192.

Development Initiatives. (2017). *Global nutrition report 2017: Nourishing the SDGs*. Global Nutrition report. Available from: https://globalnutritionreport.org/reports/201 7-global-nutrition-report/.

Ericksen, P. J. 2008. Conceptualizing food systems for global environmental change research. *Global Environmental Change*, 18(1), 234–245. doi:10.1016/j.gloenvcha.2007.09.002.

Gustafson, D., Gutman, A., Leet, W., Drewnowski, A., Fanzo, J., Ingram, J. 2016. Seven food system metrics of sustainable nutrition security. *Sustainability*, 8(3), 196. doi:10.3390/su8030196.

Ingram, J. 2011. A food systems approach to researching food security and its interactions with global environmental change. *Food Security*, 3(4), 417–431. doi:10.1007/s12571-011-0149-9.

Klein, J. 2013. The transdisciplinary moment(um). *Integral Review*, 9, 189–199.

Lowe, P., Phillipson, J. 2009. Barriers to research collaboration across disciplines: Scientific paradigms and institutional practices. *Environment and Planning A: Economy and Space*, 41(5), 1171–1184. doi:10.1068/a4175.

Lyall, C., Fletcher, I. 2013. Experiments in interdisciplinary capacity-building: The successes and challenges of large-scale interdisciplinary investments. *Science and Public Policy*, 40(1), 1–7. doi:10.1093/scipol/scs113.

Melesse, M., van den Berg, M., Bene, C., Brouwer, I., de Brauw, A. 2019. *Improving diets through food systems in low- and middle-income countries: Metrics for analysis*. International Food Policy Research Institute, Washington, USA.

Midgley, G. 2000. *Systemic intervention: Philosophy, methodology and practice*. Springer, New York, USA.

Midgley, G. 2003. Science as systemic intervention: Some implications of systems thinking and complexity for the philosophy of science. *Systemic Practice and Action Research*, 16(2), 77–97. doi:10.1023/A:1022833409353.

A fragile existence 77

Mitchell, C., Cordell, D., Fam, D. 2015. Beginning at the end: The outcome spaces framework to guide purposive transdisciplinary research. *Futures*, 65, 86–96. doi:10.1016/j.futures.2014.10.007.

Palmer, L. 2018. Meeting the leadership challenges for interdisciplinary environmental research. *Nature Sustainability*, 1(7), 330–333. doi:10.1038/s41893-018-0103-3.

Palmer, M., Kramer, J., Boyd, J., Hawthorne, D. 2016. Practices for facilitating interdisciplinary synthetic research: The National Socio-Environmental Synthesis Center (SESYNC). *Current Opinion in Environmental Sustainability*, 19, 111–122. doi:10.1016/j.cosust.2016.01.002.

Steffen, W. et al. 2015. Planetary boundaries: Guiding human development on a changing planet. *Science*, 347(6223), 1259855. doi:10.1126/science.1259855.

Weingart, P. 2000. Interdisciplinarity: The paradoxical discourse. In P. Weingart and N. Stehr, eds. *Practising interdisciplinarity*. Toronto: University of Toronto Press, 25–41.

Willett, W., Rockstrom, J. 2019. *Healthy diets from sustainable food systems*. European Commission, Brussels. Available from: https://ec.europa.eu/knowledge4policy/sites/k now4pol/files/eat-lancet_commission_summary_report.pdf.

Woelert, P., Millar, V. 2013. The "paradox of interdisciplinarity" in Australian research governance. *Higher Education*, 66(6), 755–767. doi:10.1007/s10734-013-9634-8.

5 Over-promising and under-delivering

Institutional and social networks influencing the emergence of urine diversion systems in Queensland, Australia

Cara Beal, Dena Fam and Stewart Clegg

Introduction

Urine diversion (UD) systems present a way of recovering and reusing urine for its nutrient content, and they have been used in many European, African and Asian countries in both modern and ancient times (Simha and Ganesapillai 2017). The purpose of UD systems is to collect nutrients (e.g., nitrogen, potassium, phosphorus) at the source, through the use of UD toilets and waterless urinals, while minimizing contamination of the urine from faecal matter (Figure 5.1). By separating faeces from urine, nutrients can be captured and used as fertilizer without the intensive, expensive (economically and energetically) and time-consuming process of conventional wastewater treatment. UD systems require less water to operate and thus have the potential to reduce water use by 90% compared to traditional toilets (Beal et al. 2008). Furthermore, UD systems offer a method of closing the "nutrient loop" by storing, dehydrating and recycling urine as an alternative fertilizer in agriculture (Harder, Wielemaker, Larsen, Zeeman and Öberg 2019)

As the concept of sustainability becomes more prominent in an increasingly water-constrained environment in Australia, there is growing pressure on the water and wastewater sectors for sewage infrastructure to respond to these new challenges. Increasing awareness of the value of closed-loop water cycles in Australia has led to a national focus on recycling and reuse of water from sewage within most Australian cities (Department of Sustainability and Environment 2004). Attitudinal shifts towards thinking of sewage as a valuable resource to be recycled, rather than a pollutant to be disposed of, has led to interest in resource recovery and reuse projects both Australia-wide and internationally (Larsen, Udert and Lienert 2013; Lopes, Fam and Williams 2012). These projects have been focused on recovery and reuse, not only of water, but also of phosphorus, through the use of UD systems (Hood, Gardner and Beal 2009).

Fostering emerging technological innovation, such as UD, is considered an important element in any large-scale transition towards sustainability (Abeysuriya et al. 2013; Ziegler 2019). The challenge resides not only in the introduction of new technologies but also in the development of an assemblage of new markets, user practices, rules and regulations, associated infrastructures and the emergence

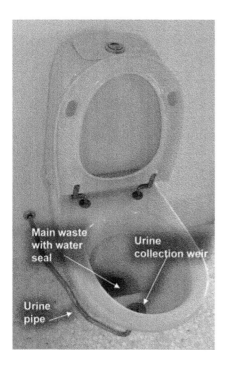

Figure 5.1 Urine-diverting toilet installed at the Ecovillage at Currumbin, Queensland, Australia.

of new cultural meanings and habits of practice (Uddin, Muhandiki, Sakai, Mamun and Hridi 2014). This suggests a need for participatory, collaborative arrangements with stakeholders across the water, waste, planning and agricultural sectors as well as a need for local communities to adopt such systems to ensure their long-term success. Furthermore, prior identification of institutional roadblocks through approaches such as social mapping or political economy analyses would greatly benefit a fulsome understanding of what is required for the successful use of innovative technologies. These complex, intertwined requirements suggest that successful introduction of socio-technical systems such as UD, which are radically different from mainstream sanitation systems, may depend on a co-evolution of emerging technologies with enabling institutional and socio-cultural structures (Uddin et al. 2014). Drawing on an applied research project in South East Queensland, Australia, this chapter will analyze the institutional environment and social networks which both supported and ultimately hindered the UD research trial and ongoing system uptake.

The peri-urban community known as the Ecovillage at Currumbin was the first of its kind in Australia to trial UD systems in 20 households over a period of two years (Hood et al. 2009; Beal et al. 2008). The aim of the trial was to (i) test a UD

80　*Cara Beal, Dena Fam and Stewart Clegg*

system in an Australian context, (ii) explore the feasibility of urine as a fertilizer and (iii) evaluate the social acceptance of the UD system. Although the trial was not completed, as discussed in this chapter, valuable insights regarding the institutional environment and social networks that both enabled and hindered the trial's success were identified.

We first analyze UD as an emerging system of innovation before addressing the institutional environment influencing the relative success of UD in Australia. We follow this with a description of the dynamic context in which UD emerged in Australia, using the Ecovillage at Currumbin trial as a relevant case study. The chapter concludes with a discussion of the need to manage the politics of innovation in basic infrastructure for essential services by considering multiple institutional factors and actors supporting and facilitating the emergence of innovative technologies in practice.

Before we begin, it is important to define what is considered "failure" in this chapter. As it suggests in the term "research trial," the UD project in Queensland was a finite initiative that had a tight budget and small human resource pool. There was agreement from regulatory agencies that this trial would not result in a wider roll-out of UD technology but would seek to understand some of the barriers and benefits of installing and using a UD toilet, and also the storage, treatment and reuse of urine. These objectives were not fully realized, and the trial was not complete by the end of the project lifetime. In this context, the project "failed' to fulfil all of its objectives. This failure was a consequence of a number of converging factors that are discussed below.

Urine diversion and institutional framing

Increasing interest in UD systems, both nationally and internationally, has in part been driven by growing awareness of global phosphorus scarcity (Gondhalekar, Al-Azzawi and Drewes 2019; Neset and Cordell 2011). Phosphorus rock, a non-renewable resource and critical ingredient in agricultural fertilizers, will be depleted within two generations on current projections (Cordell, Drangert and White 2009). While there is no substitute for phosphorus rock, wastewater streams such as urine present a potential renewable source of phosphorus for agricultural production. UD systems, therefore, are technologies that generate considerable interest among international water utilities and research institutes (Larsen 2020). UD technologies can be used to determine the viability of recovering and reusing urine to help manage nutrient flows sustainably.

Innovative technological systems that diverge from the mainstream are typically confronted with significant barriers to development and implementation (Berndtsson 2006; Hughes 1987; McConville, Kvarnström, Jönsson, Kärrman and Johansson 2017). They must overcome embedded standards and compete against established technologies or systems of service provision. Large technical systems (Hughes 1987), such as water and sanitation systems, are characterized not only by technologies and associated infrastructure but also by conglomerates of organizations, institutions, social and technical habits of practice and patterns

Over-promising and under-delivering 81

of actor-based interactions (Geels, Hekkert and Jacobsson 2008). These technological systems are embedded in institutional environments that, in the past, have been highly centralized public sector bureaucracies. Management was largely a matter of following rules and mastering basic engineering knowledge. In introducing novel and distributed socio-technical systems such as UD, the challenge resides in the technological, social and regulatory "mismatch" that decentralized UD systems represent compared with a centralized system of service provision. For bureaucracies accomplished in centralized and rule-guided control, decentralization is, in itself, innovative, and therefore challenging. Moreover, decentralized systems such as UD are typically delivered in technologically and socially "non-conforming" ways.

In the face of factors supporting and reinforcing established technologies, radical innovations may only become competitive if they have the opportunity to develop and improve within a protected niche (Smith and Raven 2010). Such a niche would be one in which the new product or technology is temporarily protected from the traditional standards and regulations in the field (Rip and Kemp 1998). These niche environments can be created by well-resourced economic actors, as well as by policy makers who are supportive of the innovation. Market niches can emerge from the demand of specific customer segments, or from particular contexts of application in which a novel technology might be seen as superior or more appropriate to the established system of service provision.

From an institutional perspective, the maturing of a niche innovation such as UD entails the development of a new set of institutions. Such institutions could either co-exist with, or undermine, those of the established regime. An innovation that was fully institutionalized would be characterized by a mature suite of mutually supportive institutional settings that collectively provide rules for reinforcing the innovative technological system.

The case study and the methods of inquiry

The research context of the Ecovillage at Currumbin ("the Ecovillage"), was a 144-lot development on a former 110 ha grazing property in the Currumbin Valley, in South East Queensland, Australia (http://www.theecovillage.com.au). The Ecovillage is based on a concept of sustainable living in which environmental conservation and recycling of resources are key goals (Beal, Gardner, Ahmed, Walton and Hamlyn-Harris 2008). The concept of sustainable living extends to the management of water and nutrients, infrastructure design and the use of recycled materials and housing thermal standards. The Ecovillage was originally conceived as a role model for the property development industry. A UD demonstration project managed by the then Queensland Department of Environment and Resource Management (DERM) was incorporated into the design. UD toilets were installed as part of a sustainable system of sewage management. The DERM managed the project in liaison with the developers, Landmatters Currumbin Valley Pty Ltd and the design engineers, Bligh Tanner Pty Ltd.

82 *Cara Beal, Dena Fam and Stewart Clegg*

The research project involved focusing on the two stages of the trial: Stage 1 – Demonstrating the UD system in practice and Stage 2 – Beneficial reuse of urine on-site. (Stage 2 did not proceed due to funding cuts to the project and the long lead times required to develop knowledge and safely test the reuse of urine on allotments). In analyzing the trial of UD systems at the Ecovillage, primary and secondary data were collected. Five key actors involved in instigating, managing and maintaining the trial, and six residents involved in the everyday use of UD systems, participated in face-to-face, in-depth, semi-structured interviews. In addition to interview data, two years of meeting notes, pre- and post-installation surveys and previous interviews with participating residents provided multiple perspectives on, and knowledge of, the institutional challenges that UD presented in practice. In conjunction with field data gained from interviews, policy analysis was used to determine the multiple levels of governance that influence nutrient recovery and reuse policy and practice in Australia.

Data was coded in terms of the institutional factors influencing the case. We sought to bring to the fore the opportunities and barriers to implementing UD systems, and in order to do this we identified both formal and informal institutions that would influence successful uptake of UD systems. Coding sought to identify institutional elements and the degree to which they emerged throughout the trial period. Interview questions were based around two predominant themes: (1) challenges and opportunities of UD in the trial, and (2) the institutional environment influencing the successful uptake of the innovation. Before expanding on the prevalence of these institutions, an overview and background to the Ecovillage is provided.

Formal institutional environment: Regulatory frameworks, policies and guidelines

UD systems are a relatively new and unfamiliar technology in Australia. Hence, substantial knowledge gaps exist for regulatory bodies governing the safe installation, transportation and use of UD systems and the application of urine to land. After consultation with government agencies in the planning stages of the Ecovillage trial (Queensland Health, the Queensland Environmental Protection Agency, the Local Government Department of Planning, Recreation and Sport, Gold Coast City Council and Gold Coast Water), a ministerial exemption was granted on the grounds that it was only for a pilot research project involving the temporary installation of UD at the Ecovillage under the Queensland Plumbing and Drainage Act (2002) (Beal et al. 2008). Regulatory frameworks regarding the safe use of urine in Australia are yet to be developed, as guidelines have not been established for applying treated urine to land, and nor is there clarity on the classification of urine. It can be classified as either faecal-contaminated grey water or as sewage effluent (Queensland Government 2002). The classifications are crucial: urine-diverted water that is free of faecal contamination is *not classified* in the existing regulatory frameworks. The lack of formal guidelines for the application of urine presents a strong limiting factor for the development of legitimately regulated UD installations in Australia (see Mitchell et al. 2013 for further discussion on regulating UD projects in Australia).

Interview participants raised concerns about the need for further research on the impact of urine on land as a critical precursor to the development of regulatory guidelines for applying it to land in Australia. One project team member of the Ecovillage trial noted:

> There [are] some issues that need to be sorted out and that's something we wanted to do if the project continued – jumping over regulatory hoops in one way shape and form ... the intention to study die-off strategies [of pathogens in urine] as part of usage ... would then lead [to] dealing with the regulatory issues [of using urine], there's no issue in collection and storage [of urine] as long as you do it according to the code. (Australian Standard 3500 and Australian and New Zealand Standards 1546/1547)

While regulatory arrangements for the application of urine to land presented barriers to the legitimacy of UD systems over the long term, the development of regulatory guidelines for grey water reuse in Australia presented a timely window of opportunity in the early stages of the UD project (e.g., NRMMC and EPHC 2006). For instance, the Ecovillage trial occurred during the early years of the Millennium Drought (from the early 2000s to 2009) when funding opportunities were made available for water efficiency and water recycling projects in Australia. As a result of the drought, the use of grey water (from showers, bathrooms, laundries and kitchen sinks) became a more acceptable practice in many Australian cities, with new regulations developed during this period to classify conditions of usage. Each state now has its own compliance regulations regarding grey water treatment and diversion systems (see Power 2010). Two interviewees perceived the development of guidelines for the application of grey water as influential in the acceptability of UD; increasing acceptance of grey water recycling was perceived as a factor contributing to the reduction of political barriers to the Ecovillage trial. As the project manager of the trial noted:

> Getting ... change (in grey water regulations) was a big deal ... the UD project piggy backed on that, without that [regulatory change] I don't think the UD project would have got up, it wouldn't have got through the regulatory process. ... Reusing urine and grey water is just a matter of degrees so the political barriers of reusing alternative sources of water [for outdoor household use] had [been overcome] with changes in grey water regulations.

Resource mobilization and changing political climates

The Millennium Drought presented a window of opportunity for funding for innovative projects, which in this instance came from a Queensland government department rather than a research and development corporation. Early funding

84 Cara Beal, Dena Fam and Stewart Clegg

opportunities for trialling UD in the Ecovillage was linked to the state government's need to manage water scarcity through investment in both incremental upgrading of centralized infrastructure and more innovative forms of water management, such as rainwater tanks and experimentation, as in the UD trial. With the end of the drought in late 2009, which occurred in conjunction with an incoming federal government that viewed many of the previous government's sustainability initiatives as "wasteful," funding sources diminished. In describing the interrelated events a project team member recalled:

> once the drought broke ... there was an institutional change in the mindset about innovation, they [the Australian government] spent billions of dollars on the interconnection of pipes between dams ... they were innovated out by ... 2008–2009. ... There was no support for the [UD] project ... and certainly the department was moving away from all this airy fairy sustainability stuff back into mainstream, so tolerance for innovative ideas had evaporated by then.

Availability of resources after the drought was linked to changing investment priorities in the water sector; these changing priorities had a significant impact on the ongoing governance arrangements of the Ecovillage trial. For instance, funding cuts limited the progression of the project from Stage 1 (Demonstrating the UD system in practice) to Stage 2 (Beneficial reuse of urine on-site). As government resources became limited, there was concomitant reduction in support among participants for continuing the trial in Stage 2, which would have extended the management and application of urine to land. As one project team member commented:

> Everyone who was involved in the project had disappeared from the department, all the people [that the household residents] knew on a daily basis ... [the person installing the toilets] left before the project finished. There was nobody left that the community knew on a face-to-face basis.

The premature ending of the UD trial meant that the inability to move on to the application of urine to land and the goal of trialling an on-site closed-loop nutrient cycle was not achieved. Therefore, the tangible benefits of the trial were left unrealized. All interviewees perceived this as the primary reason UD toilets were decommissioned and the vast majority of participants in the trial reverted to conventional flushing toilets. Commenting on funding cuts and declining support for the project during this time, one project team member noted:

> participants didn't actually see those promised benefits and outcomes, they didn't see great rice fields [fertilized] from urine, they didn't have anything tangible to see from their efforts ... because the project died ... so maybe one of the reasons why [participants opted for decommissioning and installing] a standard toilet was because there was never any clear benefits.

Informal institutions: Social networks, commitment and cultural knowledge

The project needed regulatory approval and support. In addition, however, human-centred factors emerged as important, including the establishment of mutually beneficial relationships between researchers and government departments as well as with established social networks that were critical for enabling the trial in the early stages of planning. In particular, the creation of a supportive social network, and commitment and buy-in from users and champions within government departments, created momentum for the UD trials and helped to overcome barriers. These networks sustained a normative environment favourable to the UD trial in the early days of the project.

The normative dimension of institutions emphasizes the "prescriptive, evaluative, and obligatory dimensions" of social life (Scott 2001, p. 54). Values of preferred or desirable outcomes and norms, specifying how things *should* be done, constitute normative institutions. Defining how things should be done in a trial requires more than following standards: it requires discussion between relevant actors negotiating the use, management and regulation of innovation. Overall, the formation of supportive social networks, and a commitment and buy-in from stakeholders, was a significant contributor to the legitimization of the trial. Conversely, the eventual deterioration of this support system and consequent lack of participant commitment ultimately led to the trial's failure.

Social networks: Building on existing relationships with strategic stakeholders

There are a multitude of factors that have the potential to affect the success of collaborative initiatives in innovative projects. In particular, this research identified the role of social capital in the shape of networks, norms and trust that enabled participants to act more effectively together to pursue shared objectives. More specifically, the importance of trust, built upon existing relationships with government departments, overcame many of the "grey areas" of regulation associated with installing and operating UD systems as a novel system of sanitation. All members of the project team referred to the importance of existing relationships with government departments and public servants within city councils in the planning and development of the trial. One project team member recalled:

> [government departments didn't] throw up any road blocks … they could have just said this isn't within regulations so we're not going to support it and could have been very bureaucratic … the reason that didn't happen is because we did actually have a good relationship [with them] … we got public servants approval [for the plumbing] and they contacted the plumbing inspector and that was enough. A lot of the process was built on trust. There was a lot of trust there … [and] a previous [working] relationship.

86 Cara Beal, Dena Fam and Stewart Clegg

Trust was translated into commitment and buy-in from government departments in planning the Ecovillage trial, and was identified not only as a means of negotiating regulatory barriers but also as a way of recruiting other critical stakeholders and organizations into the project. As one project team member of the trial recalls:

> Once we had their [the Department of Health and Environmental Protection Agency's] in-principle approval, it was very easy to get the rest on board … Once we had a consenting site, we could talk to people, design the fliers, we could say "this has approval by the government and Department of Health" and that endorsed the project and led to its legitimacy.

Particularly for innovative trials of technologies that are radically different from the mainstream, engagement of a range of actors from industry and government has the potential to legitimize the system and set a precedent for the trial and installation of future systems. The Ecovillage became a role model for other UD trials within Australia, where learning was centred, not only around technological aspects of the system but also the social and institutional lessons involved in trialling UD innovation in practice (Mitchell et al. 2013). It was evident that the technology was not implementable without supportive social capital, particularly networks connecting industry and government but also at the community and household scale where there was a willingness to participate in the project and connect with, and provide feedback on, the innovative technology.

Commitment and buy-in: Green motivations and investment in innovation

The most enduring UD systems internationally are those that have been collaboratively organized and/or managed by end-users, such as co-operative housing estates and eco-villages (Fam and Mitchell 2013). Lessons learned from these "early adopters" of UD system trials have contributed to knowledge development and feedback to manufacturers in developing iterative UD toilet models (Kvarnstrom et al. 2006). The social driver for these communities was not in trialling UD as an isolated technology but rather in situating it in relation to a broader vision of what sustainable development means for community living (Krantz 2005). Such ideas resonated with the philosophical views of the Ecovillage residents where the adoption of UD systems aligned with broad beliefs about sustainable living.

Participants in the UD trial constituted a "non-average" group of household residents. Preliminary assessment using Dunlap's (2008) New Environmental Paradigm tool revealed all residents scored above average on the scale of "green" commitments to sustainable living. Residents invested in ecological living by purchasing properties with clear commitments to sustainability in the Ecovillage. This was evident through their personal practices and intrinsic motivations to support sustainability initiatives, such as using rainwater tanks, composting green waste, recycling, building energy-efficient homes with recycled materials, prohibiting domestic carnivores as pets and growing food locally. Residents were willing to accommodate the inconvenience of adopting UD systems and the challenges associated with first generation technology because of strongly held beliefs about the necessity of reducing their environmental impact. By contrast, trialling a novel of system of sanitation in an unprotected, uncontrolled and public environment in which participants were not committed to the philosophy of sustainable living would have been much more challenging in terms of gaining commitment and buy-in to the project. One project team member, commenting on the level of commitment by residents, mentioned that:

> The community took to it, it was received well, they were a forgiving audience [and] a very deep shade of green, the way it was received and the way it was engaged once they were on board … they didn't change their mind.

While the commitment to the project by household residents was driven by a strong belief that recovery and reuse of nutrients from wastewater was of environmental benefit, there was a lack of investment by residents in the infrastructural (i.e., UD toilets and their installation), operational (i.e., urine collection, storage and pump out) and/or technological (i.e., UD toilets) components of the system. This lack of financial buy-in was perceived by all members of the project team as one of the factors that contributed to the project not lasting beyond the trial period:

> There wasn't sufficient "pay for buy-in." If someone gives you an Alfa Romeo to drive and at the end of two years they ask you to pay for it, they'd probably say, "Oh no, I don't think so." (Project Team Member)

> When push came to shove we were subsidizing everything [during the trial, including pump out costs] and at the end of the day they decided not to continue the trial because they had to pay … between \$200–500/year each to continue the pump outs – I don't think I would go down that road again. There wasn't sufficient … buy-in. (Project Team Member)

While issues contributing to the early end of the trial have been clearly identified, including funding cuts, there was also a lack of normative institutionalization. Green sympathies did not necessarily translate into normative support for a long-term financial commitment. Embedded experiential, disciplinary and cultural knowledge amongst both the end-users and tradespeople installing the system was also lacking in the Ecovillage trial. There is an evident difference between being "guinea pigs" in a trial and being stakeholders in an ongoing project. While the end-users were happy to be recruited to a project that felt good and cost nothing, they were less enamoured of sustaining the project when the costs of doing so were noticeably greater for them personally than being connected into the normal sewer line. The formal regulatory environment was only a part of the institutional framing; in addition, there had to be strong stakeholder commitment, a normative as well as a regulatory pillar.

88 *Cara Beal, Dena Fam and Stewart Clegg*

Experiential, disciplinary and cultural knowledge

While experiential knowledge of UD systems in the Australian context was clearly lacking at the time the Ecovillage trial was installed, international expertise was abundant and sought after by project team members who engaged leading research institutes in Sweden, Switzerland, and Germany. As a result significant learning across multiple dimensions of the system had been documented and published from a range of international perspectives (Blom 2009; Blume 2008; Drangert 1998; Peter-Fröhlich, Pawlowski, Bonhomme and Oldenburg 2007) before the Ecovillage trial was planned and installed. The main difference in international experiences of UD in comparison to Australia was that most installations overseas were conducted in apartment blocks with centralized urine storage rather than individual homes, as was the case in the Ecovillage trial. While there is a substantial body of international research on UD from elsewhere (e.g., Larsen 2020; Udert, Larsen and Gujer 2003) that provides a valuable foundation, this is not a substitute for complementary local knowledge developed under specific local conditions which differ in regard to climate, plumbing practices, regulatory codes and other features. Australian trials of UD systems in Sydney and Victoria that were informed by the Ecovillage trial have subsequently contributed to expanding the international knowledge base by installing UD systems in different Australian geographical and planning contexts. These include a multi-story public institutional setting (Mitchell et al. 2013) and residential households (Fam et al. 2013). Different types of users have been engaged in these trials including staff and visitors at a sustainability research institute within a university setting and residents in a rural residential suburb in Kinglake, Victoria (Fernando et al. 2014). The value of reproducing UD trials in different geographic and state-wide contexts is that a depth of knowledge is gained on how UD systems function under different regulatory frames, climatic conditions, cultural sensibilities and management contexts while contributing to aggregated learning of UD systems in practice.

The lack of local experience by a range of stakeholders installing (i.e., tradespeople), using (i.e., household residents) and managing, maintaining and regulating (i.e., government regulators) UD systems meant unexpected lessons were learned locally. In particular, lack of disciplinary knowledge in installing UD systems by plumbers and builders was identified as a significant barrier to overcome. The challenge for tradespeople was in adapting prescriptive plumbing and building routines normalized on more centralized and bureaucratically regulated solutions; this difficulty has been noted in all three UD trials in Australia (Mitchell et al. 2013; Fam et al. 2013; Beal et al. 2008). Unfamiliar specifications for plumbing fixtures for UD toilets and collection tanks required tradespeople to work outside conventional norms, practices and guidelines. Recalling the challenge of changing norms and practices of tradespeople, one project team member noted:

> The plumbers put them in the wrong way, they'd tile over something or didn't leave an access hole, trying to bend the brass urine pipe, they broke a few [toilet pans] … the biggest problem was changing the mindset of plumbers.

Over-promising and under-delivering 89

... It's more work for plumbers and [you need to] make sure that they got the [pipe gradients] right to stop blockages.

Subsequent trials of UD systems in Sydney (Abeysuriya et al. 2013) and Victoria (Fam et al. 2013) reflected similar experiences as the Ecovillage trial, with tradespeople failing to follow installation instructions that required them to work outside conventional disciplinary guidelines. In the Sydney trial, for example, the plumber did not follow the manufacturer's instructions but rather defaulted to conventional plumbing practices. The s-bend odour trap in the pipework of the UD toilet was therefore incorrectly installed, causing poor urine drainage and subsequent odour issues. Such failures exemplify a valuable lesson on the need for the institutional entrepreneurs of innovative projects to engage closely with local tradespeople, such as plumbers, whose training might be compliant with paramount local plumbing codes yet be incompatible with installing UD systems in Australia (Abeysuriya et al. 2013). Local, practice-based research is required to further develop detailed technical guidelines for the installation of UD at scale in Australia.

The scientists involved always conceived of the Ecovillage trial as a short-term research project. They expected to learn about the technical and social dimensions of successfully implementing UD in practice. The scientists, however, did not consider the long-term viability of the systems in regard to educating and empowering the community to take on the responsibility of self-managing the system after the research period ended. Doing so was essential to long-term sustainability, but it was not part of the scope of the trial; rather, the focus was more on proof-of-concept relating to the technical side of the trial (e.g., extracting data from the trials) rather than ensuring that the system would be sustainably embedded for the long term in the local community.

Interviews with household residents involved in the Ecovillage trial highlighted (unsurprisingly) the lack of experiential knowledge of using urine on-site, even though interest in knowing how to close the nutrient cycle and reuse urine in horticultural settings in the community was identified:

It would have been our (the community's) responsibility to reuse the urine [when the trial ended] and it was just going to be hard work for just a few people who might have been interested in following it through without the knowledge and without the history ... or the understanding (Ecovillage resident).

As one enthusiastic resident mentioned:

It's a shame [the collected urine wasn't used], because we all do a lot ... in a place like this by voluntarily contributing to the community – that's just the way a place like this operates and a lot of people already do a lot ... voluntarily ... using urine could have been something we did.

Discussion

If research is to contribute to the institutionalization of innovative technologies in practice, there is a need to facilitate the transfer of knowledge beyond the project team to other relevant stakeholders – ideally, an interdisciplinary range of stakeholders – as highlighted in this chapter. An important lesson is that scientific research must be interdisciplinary; social researchers, skilled in action research, are required. Stakeholders involved in using, managing, maintaining and regulating the system need to be collaboratively involved in developing sustainable management systems. One challenge for researchers is the availability of funding and constraints on its use. Often, funds are restricted to technological research only, with applied social research not being considered as appropriate for funding. Decisions about funding research projects that are narrowly technical with respect to what can be charged and supported do not always allow for the necessary involvement of skilled researchers with relevant cross-sectoral and industry stakeholders, such as the end-users, plumbers, regulators and water utilities. The benefit of knowledge transfer and collaboration with these stakeholders is that it allows actors to participate meaningfully, gain experience and develop new practices, all of which are necessary in the process of creating new institutions and securing the long-term viability of innovative technologies in practice.

There is increasing acknowledgement by sustainability scholars that long-term engagement and participation of relevant stakeholders in the design, planning and management of innovative systems contribute to facilitating large-scale sociotechnical change (Guest et al. 2009). Social research involvement, particularly for interdisciplinary approaches, is essential to securing these outcomes. Through inclusion of stakeholders in the planning and decision-making process, project managers have the potential to facilitate social learning, minimize and resolve conflicts, elicit and adopt local knowledge, achieve greater public and stakeholder acceptance of innovative systems of service provision over the long-term (Giupponi, Jakeman, Karssenberg and Hare 2006), and see innovations better supported and used in practice. While there is no way of knowing whether residents would in fact have contributed to the application of urine as fertilizer in practice, had there been enabling regulations and resources to support adequate knowledge transfer, there are indications that the organizational structure of the Ecovillage had the potential to facilitate community participation in voluntarily managing the system after the trial had ceased.

What this research has highlighted in analyzing the emergence of UD systems as a novel system of sanitation, from an institutional perspective, is that the UD trial provided insight into the potential impact of changing political preferences and the investment in, and ongoing support for, innovative projects. Regulatory dynamics acted in two ways in the trial: as a positive enabler of funding where UD was philosophically linked to the emergence of grey water regulations, and as a negative influence on the maturation of UD where a lack of guidelines for urine application limited its development.

Positive social networks and existing working relationships between project team members and strategic government and industry stakeholders proved to be an important factor in overriding potential regulatory barriers to innovation. The value of social capital in the innovation process emerged not only with regard to the importance of existing working relationships but also in developing new working relationships to support the emergence of innovative technologies. In particular, the transfer of knowledge to those using, managing and maintaining innovative systems is critical, as is working closely with tradespeople needing to perform tasks outside established guidelines and norms. Often-overlooked social and participatory features of the institutional environment, barely visible from the test bench or technology assemblages, can make or break innovation. Local plumbing and building knowledge embedded in a set of standards designed for far more centralized and standardized systems are a case in point. It would be easy to assume that the installers of the system would play a relatively minor role in the project, but in fact they were capable of inadvertently undermining the institutionalization of sophisticated UD systems through their routine actions. Additionally, opportunities for higher-status contributions to scientific knowledge were limited by the very different patterns of urban settlement between a European urban space shaped by apartment dwelling, and an Australian urban space shaped by individual and self-contained houses. Existing cultural norms such as "volunteerism" were an underutilized form of social capital that could have had the potential to contribute to the ongoing use and self-management of UD systems in the community over the long term, as knowledgeable participants could lead socialization of others not so well-versed.

Conclusion

Innovation processes may be facilitated or hindered by events occurring outside of the system, including new political preferences, such as for more sustainable solutions in the midst of a major drought, or technological breakthroughs such as urine capture. The institutional framing of emergent innovative projects is constantly evolving, and is responsive to environmental, economic and political triggers. As a result, windows of opportunity facilitating the emergence of innovation may close (or indeed open) as institutional preferences change. Managing the politics of major innovations in basic infrastructure, such as sanitation systems, means attending to both the formal and informal institutional settings in which they exist. In the future, it would be advisable to explicitly audit institutional infrastructure prior to initiating similar innovation projects.

Investing in technological innovation without consideration of the complex institutional dynamics in which it must function has the potential to relegate promising technological solutions to failure. This chapter has explored a specific case of emerging innovation – decentralized UD systems in a peri-urban setting – whose institutional context played identifiable roles both in securing its initial success and subsequently in hindering successful development of the complete stages of the Ecovillage trial.

92 *Cara Beal, Dena Fam and Stewart Clegg*

Take-home messages

Think beyond a project lifecycle (and technology) and consider interdisciplinarity to prompt longevity of a project beyond its budgeted lifecycle. The lack of foresight resulting in the failure to build on the existing social capital for long-term success of the UD system was an oversight. In this project the scientists were focused more on fulfilling the research goals for the life of the project than on supporting the key elements (i.e., the people) of the project who would actually ensure longevity beyond the project lifecycle.

Never undervalue the power of social mapping and political economy analysis prior to commencing an interdisciplinary project that is technically-driven but relies on community participation. Such an analysis will enable a thorough understanding of the political and socio-cultural context surrounding the project and the potential barriers and enablers for success (or failure!). For example, at the community scale, the project participants (and non-participants) were initially activated, engaged and motivated to support the UD project beyond the life of the project, but this support did not eventuate due to a number of poorly understood barriers. Better social mapping of the Currumbin residents could have informed a more resilient "exit" strategy for the UD project. At the government scale, the appetite for long-term engagement with the UD technology was clearly not there from the outset, and the interrelated reasons for this lack of interest have been described in this chapter. Again, a thorough understanding of the political climate and institutional dynamics at the time would have perhaps reshaped and/ or reframed long-term expectations of the longevity of the project (i.e., it was hoped that people would continue to use UDs and would be self-motivated to seek permission for urine reuse).

The maxim of "under-promise and over-deliver" needed to be a stronger fundamental principle of this project. In reality, the goals were too ambitious, given the novelty of the technology that required approval and ongoing support from an inherently conservative public health regulator.

References

Abeysuriya, K., Fam, D., Mitchell, C. 2013. Trialling urine diversion in Australia: Technical and social learnings. *Water Science and Technology*, 68(10), 2186–2194.

Beal, C., Gardner, T., Ahmed, W., Walton, C., Hamlyn-Harris, D. 2008. Urine separation and reuse trial. *Water*, 35(1), 66–69.

Berndtsson, J. C. 2006. Experiences from the implementation of a urine separation system: Goals, planning, reality. *Building Environment*, 41, 427–437.

Blom, L. 2009. Acceptability of urine diversion toilets at Mondalstad primary school (Personal Communication).

Blume, S. 2008. Two years of experiences from a urine diversion project in GTZ Headquarters, Eschborn, Germany. *Paper presented at the IWA World Congress and Exhibition*, Vienna, Austria.

Cordell, D., Drangert, J.-O., White, S. 2009. The story of phosphorus: Global food security and food for thought. *Global Environmental Change Journal*, 19, 292–304.

Over-promising and under-delivering 93

Department of Sustainability and Environment. 2004. *Our water, our future: The next stage of the government's water plan.* Available from: http://images.theage.com.au/fi le/2011/12/09/2828453/water_policy.pdf.

Drangert, J.-O. 1998. Fighting the urine blindness to provide more sanitation options. *Water SA*, 24(2), 157–164.

Dunlap, R. E. 2008. The new environmental paradigm scale: From marginality to worldwide use. *The Journal of Environmental Education*, 40(1), 3–18.

Fam, D., Mitchell, C. 2013. Sustainable innovation in wastewater management: Lessons for nutrient recovery and reuse. *Local Environment*, 18(7), 769–780.

Fernando, R., Cook, S., Narangala, R., Pamminger, F., Gellie, A., Sharma, A., Wrigley, R. 2014. Decentralised sewage servicing – evaluation of a yellow water, grey water and black water trial: Review of the Kinglake West sewage project by Yarra Valley Water in Victoria *Water*, November 2014, 41 (7), 41–53.

Geels, F., Hekkert, M. P., Jacobsson, S. 2008. The dynamics of sustainable innovation journeys. *Technology Analysis and Strategic Management*, 20(5), 521–536.

Giupponi, C., Jakeman, A. J., Karssenberg, D., Hare, M. P. 2006. *Sustainable management of water resources: An integrated approach.* Northampton, MA: Edward Elgar Publishing.

Gondhalekar, D., Al-Azzawi, M., Drewes, J. E. 2019. Urban Water reclamation with resource recovery as a cornerstone of urban climate change resilience. *In:* W. L. Filho, ed., *Handbook of climate change resilience.* Cham, Switzerland: Springer International Publishing, 1–22.

Guest, J. S. et al. 2009. A new planning and design paradigm to achieve sustainable resource recovery. *Environmental Science and Technology*, 43(16), 6126–6130.

Harder, R., Wielemaker, R., Larsen, T. A., Zeeman, G., Öberg, G. 2019. Recycling nutrients contained in human excreta to agriculture: Pathways, processes, and products. *Critical Review of Environmental Science and Technology*, 49, 695–743.

Hood, B., Gardner, E., Beal, C. 2009. Domestic urine separation captures plant macronutrients. *Water – Journal of the Australia Water Association*, 367, 94–99.

Hughes, T. P. 1987. The evolution of large technical systems. *In:* W. K. Bijker, T. P. Hughes, T. Pinch, eds. *The social construction of technological systems: New directions in the sociology and history of technology.* MA: MIT Press, Vancouver.

Krantz, H. 2005. *Matter that matters: A study of household routines in a process of changing water and sanitation arrangements.* (PhD), Linkoping; Linkoping University.

Kvarnstrom, E. et al. 2006. *Urine diversion: One step towards sustainable sanitation.* Stockholm Environment Institute. Available from: https://www.sei.org/publications/ur ine-diversion-one-step-towards-sustainable-sanitation/.

Larsen, T. A. 2020. Urine source separation for global nutrient management. *In:* D. J. O'Bannon, ed. *Women in water quality: Investigations by prominent female engineers.* Cham, Switzerland: Springer International Publishing, 99–111.

Larsen, T. A., Udert, K. M., Lienert, J. 2013. *Source separation and decentralization of wastewater management.* London: International Water Association (IWA) Publishing.

Lopes, A., Fam, D. M., Williams, J. 2012. Designing sustainable sanitation: Involving design in innovative, transdisciplinary research. *Design Studies*, 33(3), 298–317.

McConville, J. R., Kvarnström, E., Jönsson, H., Kärrman, E., Johansson, M. 2017. Source separation: Challenges and opportunities for transition in the Swedish wastewater sector. *Resource Conservation and Recycling*, 120, 144–156.

Mitchell, C. A., Fam, D. M., Abeysuriya, K. Institute for Sustainable Futures, UTS 2013, *Transitioning to sustainable sanitation: a transdisciplinary pilot project of urine diversion,* pp. 1–137. Sydney.

94 *Cara Beal, Dena Fam and Stewart Clegg*

Natural Resource Management Ministerial Council, Environment Protection and Heritage Council, Australian Health Ministers' Conference. 2006. National guidelines for water recycling: Managing health and environmental risks. URL: https://www.awa.asn.au/Do cuments/water-recycling-guidelines-health-environmental-21.pdf. Accessed Jan. 10th, 2019

Neset, T., Cordell, D. 2011. Global phosphorus scarcity: Identifying synergies for a sustainable future. *Journal of the Science of Food and Agriculture*, 92(1), 2–6.

Peter-Fröhlich, A., Pawlowski, L., Bonhomme, A., Oldenburg, M. 2007. EU demonstration project for separate discharge and treatment of urine, faeces and greywater – part I: Results. *Water Science & Technology*, 56(5), 239–249.

Power, K. 2010. Recycled water use in Australia: Regulations, guidelines and validation requirements for a national approach. Available from: http://www.geo-processors.com/_downloads/Power-2010-Recycled_Water_Use_Aust.pdf.

Queensland Plumbing and Drainage Act. 2002. Available from: https://www.legislation.q ld.gov.au/view/pdf/repealed/current/act-2002-077.

Rip, A., Kemp, R. 1998. Technological change. *In*: E. Malone and S. Rayner, eds. *Human choice and climate change*, vol. 2. Colombus, OH: Batelle Press, 327–399.

Scott, R. 2001. *Institutions and organisations*. 2nd ed. Thousand Oaks, CA: Sage Publications.

Simha, P., Ganesapillai, M. 2017. Ecological sanitation and nutrient recovery from human urine: How far have we come? A review. *Sustainable Environment Research*, 27, 107–116.

Smith, A., Raven, R. 2010. Niche protection in transitions to sustainability. Paper presented at the EASST conference: Practicing science and technology, performing the social, Trento, Italy.

Uddin, S. M. N., Muhandiki, V. S., Sakai, A., Mamun, A. A., Hridi, S. M. 2014. Socio-cultural acceptance of appropriate technology: Identifying and prioritizing barriers for widespread use of the urine diversion toilets in rural Muslim communities of Bangladesh. *Technology in Society*, 38, 32–39.

Udert, K. M., Larsen, T. A., Gujer, W. 2003. Estimating the precipitation potential in urine-collecting systems. *Water Research*, 31(11), 2667–2677.

Ziegler, R. 2019. Viewpoint – water innovation for a circular economy: The contribution of grassroots actors. *Water Alternatives*, 12(2), 774.

Part II

Failures and responses associated with collaboration and stakeholder engagement

6 Failure and what to do next

Lessons from the Toolbox Dialogue Initiative

Michael O'Rourke, Stephen Crowley, Sanford D. Eigenbrode and Stephanie E. Vasko

Introduction

In this chapter, we identify lessons about cross-disciplinary practice from our experience in the Toolbox Dialogue Initiative (TDI). These include (1) the rich variety of ways failure can manifest in projects, (2) the need to learn from failure, especially in the context of cross-disciplinary research and (3) the need for project flexibility (cf. Morton et al. 2015).

TDI is a 15-year-old effort that aims to understand and enhance collaboration within interdisciplinary and transdisciplinary projects. TDI has developed an approach to capacity-building – the "Toolbox dialogue method" – that is both an intervention designed to facilitate collaboration and a foundation for research on collaborative processes. Implemented in a workshop setting, the Toolbox dialogue method is built around dialogue structured by prompts that derive from philosophical analysis and illuminate the implicit beliefs and values which influence deliberation and decision-making (O'Rourke and Crowley 2013). The small-group research literature tells us that group reflection and perspective-taking can benefit teams (Salazar et al. 2019). By strengthening a team's ability to engage in these behaviours, the Toolbox dialogue method can have salutary effects for teams, such as increased mutual understanding (WMUEC 2017; Rinkus and O'Rourke 2020).

At this point (early 2020), TDI has conducted more than 330 Toolbox workshops around the world. While most of these workshops have benefited participating teams (WMUEC 2017), some workshops have failed to achieve the objectives we set for them. (See Table 6.1 for a comprehensive list of workshop objectives pursued in the various types of workshops TDI has conducted.) What counts as a workshop "failure" is open to interpretation – workshop failures tend not to be failures for everyone who participates in them, and workshop successes can be failures for some. Prior to running a workshop, we collaborate with the leadership of the participating team to design an experience valuable to each participant, in part by contributing to their understanding of how their research perspective compares to that of their colleagues. There are many ways in which workshops can fail to clear this high bar.

98 O'Rourke, Crowley, Eigenbrode and Vasko

Table 6.1 A representation of how success conditions vary across four Toolbox contexts. Toolbox workshops in each category draw their purposes from the set of purposes marked with a checkmark. "(ind)" indicates that the individual but not the group purpose is pursued

PURPOSE \ CONTEXT	Research Team	Other Team	Affiliated Group	Ad Hoc Group
Build capacity	✓	✓	✓	
Define mission/vision/goals	✓	✓		
Identify group and individual values	✓	✓	✓	✓ (ind)
Identify group and individual priorities	✓	✓	✓	✓ (ind)
Develop next steps for group action	✓	✓	✓	
Identify relevant stakeholders	✓	✓	✓	
Reflect on previous process	✓	✓		
Foster new research collaborations		✓	✓	✓
Explore group power dynamics	✓	✓	✓	
Be introduced to the Toolbox	✓	✓	✓	✓

In the next section, we provide a general account of the Toolbox dialogue method before describing in more detail what we consider to be "failure" for our purposes in this chapter. We then focus on four workshops that failed to achieve the objectives we set for them, but were nonetheless instructive, yielding insight into the Toolbox dialogue method and also informing improvements in the method. These improvements include working more closely with our partners to design each workshop and acknowledging power differences among workshop participants.

The Toolbox dialogue method

The Toolbox dialogue method is an approach to capacity-building in complex research environments that has been developed by the Toolbox Dialogue Initiative (TDI 2019; Hubbs et al. 2020). TDI originated in a US National Science Foundation (NSF)-sponsored Integrative Graduate Education and Research Traineeship (IGERT) project at the University of Idaho (UI) that focused on biodiversity conservation and sustainable agriculture in fragmented landscapes (Bosque-Pérez et al. 2016). Doctoral students in this project worked on interdisciplinary teams, developing their dissertations on aspects of a common research problem they identified together. This required them to work collaboratively, integrating their different disciplinary perspectives. This, however,

Failure and what to do next 99

proved difficult, and the students requested a seminar to provide guidance for conducting integrative research.

Heeding this call, two of the authors of this chapter, Eigenbrode and O'Rourke, offered a seminar that examined whether philosophy could help students identify common aspects of their disciplinary practices that might support integration. As the seminar unfolded, participants became interested in developing a tool that could facilitate cross-disciplinary integration, work that gave rise to the original Toolbox dialogue method and a published report of it in *BioScience* (Eigenbrode et al. 2007). Subsequently, the NSF funded what was then called the "Toolbox Project" to explore, develop and evaluate the approach with other IGERT teams (NSF 2019). In 2012, the Toolbox Project relocated from the UI to Michigan State University (MSU). In subsequent years, we adopted the new name "Toolbox Dialogue Initiative," and have offered national and international workshops with continued support from NSF as well as funding from a fee-based consulting practice. TDI as a whole engages in research informed by its facilitation efforts, and facilitation informed by its research results.

The Toolbox dialogue method was originally conceived as a workshop-based dialogue structured by a "Toolbox" instrument consisting of a set of questions (Eigenbrode et al. 2007). Once the authors of the original paper began running more workshops, it became clear that these questions were not effective at prompting dialogue about implicit research commitments. An early failed workshop highlighted the difficulty in generating productive dialogue when the participants responded to most of the questions by saying, "it depends," forcing the facilitator to explicitly request follow-up detail. For us, successful dialogue involves participants talking to one another and delineating differences and similarities, which can enhance their collective ability to communicate and collaborate; however, the "it depends" response and follow-up requests for clarification from the facilitator diluted participant exchanges. This experience led us to modify the instrument, replacing the questions with statements, each associated with a rating-response scale, which encouraged stance-taking among the participants (Looney et al. 2014). Stance-taking in these dialogues is helpful behaviour because it involves participants defending their positions and offering explanations for their views that can help increase mutual understanding within the team. (See Table 6.2 to compare the Values module from the original Toolbox instrument and the Values module from the revised instrument.)

In a typical Toolbox workshop conducted at that time (around 2008), we would use the following protocol. First, participants would listen to a brief preamble by the workshop facilitator that described the Toolbox dialogue method and then score the Toolbox statements, which expressed approaches to scientific research. Variations in these scores could reveal unacknowledged differences in belief and value among collaborators. After completing the Toolbox instrument, participants in the workshop engaged in a 90-minute to two-hour, lightly facilitated dialogue about the issues raised by the prompts (which included both more general core questions and more focused probing statements). The dialogue was followed by a debrief discussion. These dialogues were audio-recorded to enable evaluation of

100 O'Rourke, Crowley, Eigenbrode and Vasko

Table 6.2 The Values module from Eigenbrode et al. (2007), with questions, is above the bar, while the Values module from Looney et al. (2014), with statements, is below it

Principal Philosophical Domain (Entry Point)	Specific Philosophical Issue	Core Question	Probing Questions
Metaphysics	Values	Is value-neutral scientific research possible?	If it is possible to conduct scientific research without values, how is that accomplished?
			Do you consider questions about when hypotheses count as knowledge to be value questions?
			If you regard values as an ineliminable part of scientific research, how can they be managed to avoid biasing research results and interpretations?
			Does the introduction of values into the research process amount to advocacy?

Values

Core Question: Do values negatively influence scientific research?

1. Objectivity implies an absence of values by the researcher.

   Disagree   *Agree*

   1   2   3   4   5   I don't know   N/A

2. Incorporating one's personal perspective in framing a research question is never valid.

   Disagree   *Agree*

   1   2   3   4   5   I don't know   N/A

3. Value-neutral scientific research is possible.

   Disagree   *Agree*

   1   2   3   4   5   I don't know   N/A

4. Determining what constitutes acceptable validation of research data is a value issue.

   Disagree   *Agree*

   1   2   3   4   5   I don't know   N/A

5. Allowing values to influence scientific research is advocacy.

   Disagree   *Agree*

   1   2   3   4   5   I don't know   N/A

6. The members of this team have similar views concerning the values core question.

   Disagree   *Agree*

   1   2   3   4   5   I don't know   N/A

Failure and what to do next   101

the sessions, and a session recorder kept track of which speaker was responsible for each speaking turn so that transcripts would be accurate. Within ten days of the workshop, participants were asked to complete the instrument a second time and respond to a post-workshop questionnaire that focused on the nature of their experience.

This was the beginning of the period in the history of TDI that we refer to as "Toolbox 1.0." Throughout this period, Toolbox workshops were structured by updated versions of the Toolbox instrument originally adumbrated in Eigenbrode et al. (2007). This instrument was developed from the "top-down" in the sense that we began with categories and issues that were drawn from the philosophy of science rather than from the experiences of our partner teams. Typical workshops were also focused exclusively on dialogue, ending with a debrief conversation that took place shortly after the dialogue concluded. This period is our primary focus in this chapter since most of the failures we highlight are failures that helped us transition from Toolbox 1.0 into Toolbox 2.0, which is the current period in the history of TDI (see Hubbs 2020).

Failure in the Toolbox context

In his book *Failure*, Stuart Firestein declines to define "failure" because "like so many important words," it "is much too simple for the class of things it represents. Failure comes in many flavors, and strengths, and contexts, and values, and innumerable other variables" (Firestein 2016, p. 7). Although we are inclined to accept the general idea that failure manifests when things *don't work out* in some sense, we agree with Firestein that a real definition identifying all and only those things that qualify as *failures* would be nearly impossible to provide. This is reinforced by recognizing that failure, like beauty, is in the eye of the beholder.

Fortunately, for our purposes in this chapter, rather than *define* it, we only need to specify what form of failure most interests us, acknowledging that failure has a broader meaning. We are interested in endogenous failures – that is, workshops where the failure to meet intended objectives can be attributed to the Toolbox dialogue method itself – that teach us something new about the approach. These are failures that highlight a fundamental flaw or weakness in the design of Toolbox workshops, rather than just poor execution or a bad day.

There are a number of ways in which Toolbox workshops can be successful – that is, ways in which they *work out* by meeting intended objectives. These vary in character depending on the context and purpose of each specific workshop. We run workshops primarily for interdisciplinary or transdisciplinary research teams, but we also run them for administrative teams, groups of affiliated researchers (e.g., research centres) and ad hoc groups of participants who are interested in the approach. The purposes of workshops also vary, from enhancing communicative efficiency within teams to introducing individuals to the Toolbox dialogue method and demonstrating for them how it could be useful in their own projects. Table 6.2 indicates the set of purposes pursued in four main types of Toolbox workshops we conduct. A specific workshop from one of these categories will typically only pursue a subset of these purposes.

102 O'Rourke, Crowley, Eigenbrode and Vasko

Whether or not a workshop achieves its purpose in context is typically determined from two different perspectives – the perspective of the participants and the perspective of TDI. Groups interested in Toolbox workshops approach us and then become partners in developing them; since we work with these groups to identify workshop purposes and then design workshop experiences to achieve them, both the partners and TDI have a stake in how things go. Further, TDI will often have its own method-specific goals, such as determining the value of a new set of prompts or assessing a different facilitation technique.

We can characterize these perspectives in terms of two general objectives: (A) what the participants want to get out of a Toolbox workshop, and (B) what TDI as a research and facilitation initiative wants to get out of it. Under (B), there are both (B1) what we want to get out of the workshop for ourselves, and (B2) what we want the participants to get out of the workshop. Given that we are working closely with the partner, we want (A) and (B2) to significantly overlap. For any given workshop, though, the idea is that it can *work out* in the sense of providing the participants with what they wanted out of the experience and/or it can work out by providing TDI with what it wanted.

A complete workshop failure would be a workshop that failed to meet all of these objectives, whereas a partial failure would be one that failed to meet some of them. In what follows, we describe case studies of workshops that were partial failures from the perspective of (B1) – that is, workshops where we failed to get what we wanted for ourselves. These workshops could also have been failures or successes, at least in part, from other perspectives (e.g., from the perspective of at least some of the participants), which underscores the point that failure is in the eye of the beholder.

Case studies in Toolbox failure

This section provides four case studies that mark important turning points in the development of the Toolbox dialogue method. These case studies focus on specific workshops that did not go as planned from the perspective of TDI. The failures involved were taken to indicate that various fundamental aspects of the dialogue method were flawed, and these failures were important because they led us to make substantial changes to the approach. The first three workshops are from the Toolbox 1.0 period. The fourth is a more recent one that revealed inadequacies with the emerging Toolbox 2.0. The first three involved use of the Scientific Research Toolbox instrument (Looney et al. 2014; Hubbs et al. 2020), while the fourth involved use of an instrument designed for the partner group. Each of the authors of this chapter was involved in running at least one of these workshops. We structure these case studies by presenting details of the workshops, specifying what failed in them and discussing how we might have operated differently given the protocol we had in place at the time. In the next section, we will address how these workshops helped us make substantive changes to the Toolbox approach.

Failure and what to do next 103

Ad hoc groups – creating a temporary community

The first workshop we discuss came soon after the project received its initial NSF award. This particular workshop was the first we ran with participants who were not teammates. This type of workshop – what we call an "ad hoc workshop" – can be challenging because there is no independent reason for a participant to share their research perspective with the other participants, who are in some cases complete strangers.

The setting for this workshop was a major research university in 2009 as part of a series of workshops and presentations to members of an active IGERT project and a research centre focused on sustainability. This specific workshop was conducted for a group of department chairs and faculty members in an agriculture and life sciences college that was undergoing a restructuring to promote interdisciplinary collaboration. As such, this was an ad hoc group of participants who were not working together on a project and just convened for the purpose of participating in this workshop. The goal of the workshop was to help the participants understand the Toolbox approach and its potential value for collaborative teams involving their faculties and students. We decided the best way to achieve this was to lead them in a formal Toolbox workshop, following the protocol described previously and using the Scientific Research Toolbox instrument, to allow them to experience and understand its effectiveness. TDI was represented by two of the authors of this chapter serving as facilitator and recorder. There were six participants, and the preamble, workshop and discussion took place over two hours.

The workshop was deemed a failure by the facilitator and recorder because it did not appear to achieve its goal. Rather than engaging fully in the dialogue, the participants engaged in "meta-discussion" about the design of the instrument, the wording of the prompts and how the instrument might be applied. The level of spontaneous engagement by participants was low. Of the six participants, two contributed relatively little (together 12% of participant words in the dialogue transcript and 10% of participant contributions), while three dominated the discussion (together contributing 60% of the dialogue and 50% of the contributions). Strikingly, the facilitator was called upon much more often than is typical, making 76 remarks, sometimes speaking at length, either to address questions pertaining to the meta-discussion or to move the reluctant participants to explore different modules and prompts. Only once did a participant initiate such an exploration. This created a stilted atmosphere that was frustrating for the facilitator and recorder who had anticipated much more spontaneous engagement with the instrument. Both were relieved when the scheduled time to close the discussion finally arrived.

Based on a review of the transcript, and despite the feelings of the organizers and the subdued energy of the workshop, the substance of the discussion was of high quality and, in retrospect, potentially very useful to the participants. Many astute comments were made about the collaborative process, the sources of communication difficulties, the constraints of the academy, the subtleties of some of the core questions and the potential application of Toolbox dialogue. In retrospect, this workshop was a lost opportunity. The participants were keenly interested in

104   *O'Rourke, Crowley, Eigenbrode and Vasko*

the topics they broached, but the determined effort by the facilitator to stick to the instrument created unproductive tension in the room. By the end of the discussion, there was little energy left to debrief, resulting in weak closure without recapping what was learned.

Cultural differences across the sciences

The second workshop we consider was conducted in early 2011 with a research team at a large, research-intensive university working on a project that combined biophysical research at the bench with clinical research involving patients. Twelve members of the research team participated in the workshop, ranging over specialties in the physical and biological sciences, engineering and clinical health sciences. There were a number of experienced, later-career scientists alongside early-career scientists. The goal of the workshop was to help build collaborative capacity and team cohesion in a team that involved participants from several different research cultures (Foster-Fishman et al. 2001). TDI was represented by a facilitator, a recorder and an observer (two of whom are authors of this chapter), and there were 12 participants in a 2.5-hour workshop.

Although the TDI representatives knew going into this workshop that the participants would represent different scientific research cultures, we were not prepared for the number and depth of these differences. In the end, while the workshop did illuminate some divides between team members, it generated little engaged, *dialogical* interaction in which participants built on each other's contributions, and it did not facilitate much integration across disciplinary lines. Setting aside the 21 facilitator turns, there were 131 total speaking turns involving the participants, with a mean of 10.9 comments and a median of four comments per participant during the 60-minute session. In our experience, a disparity of this size between mean and median is unusual, with the low median indicating low involvement by a large number of participants. One striking observation concerns the number of words per turn in this workshop. In the transcript, there is an average of 75.4 words per turn, which is more than double the words per turn in a typical Toolbox workshop. Furthermore, few turns were direct responses to the previous turn. In most cases, contributions to the conversation were in the form of stand-alone expressions of opinion or experience.

Other indicators of low dialogical engagement were the limited number of clarificatory questions, little overlap in speaking turns and many long pauses. In our view, these observations are explained by the hierarchical nature of the team and the episodic nature of its interactions. Senior members spoke freely, but junior members usually did so only at the behest of a senior member, discouraging more vigorous interaction. Individuals tended to "have their say" on a topic in long, definitive comments and then wait for the next topic to be raised rather than create a team-level understanding of the topic by building on or challenging statements of others. Participants were very articulate and had interesting things to say, but unlike other Toolbox workshop groups with high collaborative capacity, they seemed relatively uninterested in each other's contributions. While this may have been a result of a limited sense of the team as a team, it may also have been due to diffidence in a hierarchical environment.

In general, this group seemed to be less a *team* (i.e., an interdependent group that requires the mutual understanding Toolbox workshops aim to produce) than a well-coordinated set of professionals sharing the output of their relevant expertise. As such, the group appeared more multidisciplinary than interdisciplinary in its composition and function. It is important to note that participants did have insightful things to say in response to the prompts, and a few of the participants did derive value from the experience based on feedback. The group touched on all the modules in the Scientific Research Toolbox instrument, and devoted substantial time to discussing differences between basic and applied research, the process and products of research and the nature of confirmation, in particular.

Building the workshop for the participants

The previous case study emphasized attending to the needs of the participants when conducting a workshop for a team of scientists from different domains. This case study reinforces the importance of building the workshop for the participants and, in particular, not assuming that a Toolbox instrument built for scientists will work to structure a valuable dialogue for humanists and other non-scientists.

Two months after the workshop described in the second case study, TDI travelled to another research-intensive university to conduct an ad hoc workshop for a professional development programme for faculty. We utilized the Scientific Research Toolbox instrument with a group that included an administrator and researchers from the humanities, social sciences, and science, technology, engineering and mathematics (STEM) disciplines. As with the first case described above, this was an ad hoc group that gathered simply for the purpose of participating in the Toolbox workshop. The goals of the workshop were to introduce participants to the Toolbox dialogue method and to discuss differences in philosophical assumptions that separated the humanities and the sciences. TDI was represented by a facilitator and a recorder, one of whom was an author of this chapter, and there were nine participants in a three-hour workshop.

This workshop failed to achieve its goals, as participants did not have a positive experience learning about their own views and the views of the other participants. Rather, they had a stressful conversation with the workshop facilitator about the limitations of the workshop itself. The discussion in this workshop was less engaged than most, with long pauses, little overlap, more long turns than usual, little laughter and few challenges or questions between participants. Much of the discussion focused on the Toolbox instrument and how the prompts "framed" the issues. Discussion tended to focus on core questions rather than probing statements, with concern mainly for what the questions revealed about the Toolbox developers' biases and assumptions. In fact, much of the conversation was explicitly addressed to the facilitator rather than to the other participants. This is not typical in our experience and resulted in a higher degree of involvement by the

106   *O'Rourke, Crowley, Eigenbrode and Vasko*

facilitator, both in the number of speaking turns and the degree to which those turns were substantive rather than facilitative.

This workshop also failed to create the kind of environment or generate the kind of discussion we prize in Toolbox workshops. As with the first case study, the bulk of the conversation was meta-discussion that focused on concerns the participants had with the instrument. The humanists in the group emphasized that it felt inappropriate to focus on science when their background was in the humanities; they even suggested that if they had answered honestly, they would have responded "not applicable" to every statement. For some, the experience seemed like push polling, that is, steering participants to certain answers rather than allowing them to answer freely. Participants referred to the answers they felt were being pushed as "fantasies." As a result, participants felt either disengaged – some people barely spoke at all – or "attacked," with some stating they were hesitant to express their real views given that their responses were being recorded.

The dialogue in this session was one of the most unusual we have experienced. While almost all participants had cross-disciplinary experience, there did not seem to be much interest in examining how philosophical differences separating the humanities and the sciences might be reconciled. Rather, most participants seemed to view the Toolbox with scepticism, taking the explicit focus on science to be exclusionary rather than an invitation to explore different disciplinary worldviews. In fact, participants used the term "paranoia" on several occasions to describe their reaction to the instrument. Nevertheless, even though it did not generate the intended conceptual and philosophical dialogue, exploration of affective issues that may interfere with collaboration across the science-humanities divide was enlightening.

The importance of dialogue and expectation management

Our last case study is one that occurred in the time period we internally refer to as "Toolbox 2.0." In this evolution of the Toolbox dialogue method, the workshop protocol combines the usual preamble with a set of prompts customized for the partner, an instrument which is online instead of on paper and "co-creation" activities designed to capitalize on the dialogue. Many of the practices in Toolbox 2.0 were developed in response to lessons like those learned in the workshops reported in the first three case studies. This case study demonstrated for us that while these changes were proving useful, we needed to remain sensitive to other ways the method could still be improved.

This specific workshop was our first in a multiyear partnership with an international transdisciplinary project involving the arts, sciences and humanities. The workshop took place in 2016 and occurred at the end of a larger kick-off event that featured presentations from key project stakeholders. We envisioned a workshop dialogue structured by a custom 41-prompt Toolbox instrument assembled by TDI for this community. As is standard practice in Toolbox 2.0, we sought to develop this instrument collaboratively with the partner. The objectives for this initial workshop were to inform partner leadership about stakeholder perspectives, values, ideas and needs, to evaluate and enhance communication and collaboration within the partnership, and to enable stakeholders to be agents of change in the project. TDI was represented by one of the authors, who served as both facilitator and recorder, and seven members of the project participated in a four-hour workshop.

This workshop was a failure from our perspective for multiple reasons. First, power structures within the team and messaging about our role in the collaboration negatively influenced the dialogue. This particular team had a deeper hierarchy than many we work with, in part due to some of the disciplines involved and the prestige of the project leader. Recognizing this, we relied on an influential member of the collaboration to help us navigate the potentially complex power structure and build trust and buy-in within the community. However, we failed to communicate the Toolbox process and our role within their project prior to the workshop. As a result, the preamble was prolonged significantly when the facilitator was asked many questions by the participants, which resulted in the need to reorganize parts of the workshop on the fly, including eliminating the planned co-creation activity.

The second failure relates to the role of the prompts in a successful dialogue. Our ability to generate information about stakeholder perspectives depends on stakeholders moving through much of the instrument; however, these participants engaged with very few of the prompts. While participants did have a lively discussion, they did not seem interested in using the Toolbox process to examine their working methods, which was an organizing theme of the Toolbox instrument and the motivation for involving TDI in the partnership in the first place. This could have been due to the inclusion of too many prompts, the timing of this session during the kick-off event or a misalignment of prompts with the interests of the partner, a possibility in this case since we did not receive much feedback from the partner while developing the instrument.

This workshop did not engage the participants in the dialogue we were expecting based on the structure of the instrument or the co-creation activity we had designed, and thus the workshop did not achieve the goals we had set for it. This was partially due to mistaken assumptions by TDI about the workshop and how the dialogue would unfold. Recognition of those missteps illuminated a path forward. While this initial workshop was a failure, reflection on those aspects of it that did not meet our own expectations and dialogue involving both parties about alternative modes of partnership resulted in a fruitful relationship.

Lessons learned and changes made

The four case studies in the previous section highlight four prominent failures in the life of TDI. Although most of our workshops have been successful, at least in part, there are of course additional workshops we could describe as "failures." These four workshops stand out, though, because they were especially instructive failures. We learned valuable lessons from them about the Toolbox dialogue method, the workshop protocol we use in delivering particular workshops, and

108 *O'Rourke, Crowley, Eigenbrode and Vasko*

our own assumptions about working with partner groups. In this section we consider the most important of these lessons, beginning with those that pertain to the method in general before turning to those that concern the workshop protocol.

General lessons about the Toolbox dialogue method

The first lesson learned from these failed workshops concerns how we should understand the role of meta-discussion in Toolbox dialogue, that is, discussion about the prompts themselves rather than the issues they raise. Meta-discussion could be a sign that a prompt is not well written – that it is confusing, ambiguous or vague in a way that does not help reveal multiple interpretations in a group. That would be an indication of Toolbox failure at the level of the prompt. However, it is not uncommon for workshops to open with meta-discussion, allowing participants to move slowly into dialogue by making it about TDI at first before engaging with the issues raised by the prompts. This creates a sense of psychological safety by way of a generally amiable "us" against "them" positioning that enables participants to grow more comfortable in the workshop setting before articulating and discussing their own deeply felt research views (cf. Edmondson 1999).

Meta-discussion can also be a way of *avoiding* discussion of one's research perspective. These dialogues are opportunities to reflect on one's core beliefs and values as a researcher, being honest with oneself and other participants about key aspects of one's professional identity. However, if a participant is in a dialogue with people they don't trust or just don't know, there are disincentives to being open about their own views. This likely contributed to the failure in Case 1 above. Rather than sit in silence or have the workshop become a soliloquy by the facilitator, people focused the discussion on the instrument and not on themselves. The workshop in Case 3 also involved meta-discussion, although it was less about lack of trust for each other than it was about lack of trust in TDI. In this case, the "us" against "them" positioning wasn't an amiable, temporary posture occupied by the participants, but rather an adversarial, hostile posture that remained in place for the duration of the workshop.

The second lesson also concerns *positionality*, that is, how those involved in the workshop – participants and Toolbox representatives – relate to one another. The key lesson is that the more we anticipate the implications of different positions in the workshop, the better we facilitate dialogue that reveals implicit commitments and enhances mutual understanding.

One key relationship is that of workshop participants to one another. We saw in both Case 1 and Case 2 the importance of acknowledging how participants relate to one another and planning the workshop instrument and protocol accordingly. We didn't fully appreciate the stultifying effect that lack of cohesion and unfamiliarity would have on participants in the first case. In the second, the participants were familiar with one another, but the cultures represented in the room – bench research and clinical research – were different enough that we should have utilized a more inclusive Toolbox instrument that better represented the clinical perspective.

Failure and what to do next 109

The other key relationship involves the workshop participants with the Toolbox representatives. Case 3 is similar to Case 1 in that it involved a substantial amount of meta-discussion, and to Case 2 in that it involved people (e.g., humanists) who were not the target audience of the instrument that structured the dialogue. Unlike those cases, though, Case 3 became adversarial, foregrounding TDI's role in designing the experience and emphasizing our responsibility for structuring a discussion that was not suited to the participants. We became the focus of that workshop, which was at odds with our desire to create dialogue that focuses on the issues and interests of the participants.

Although we were working in advance to develop an experience that suited the participants by the time the workshop in Case 4 took place, this workshop demonstrated for us how much we still had to learn about our positionality vis-à-vis the participants. As with Case 3, Case 4 involved challenges rooted in the relationships among the participants (e.g., differences in power), but much of the difficulty encountered in the workshop derived from TDI's failure to communicate to the community both our general approach and the value of the workshop experience. Failure to appreciate the power structures in this project led to faulty decisions on our part prior to the workshop, which reinforced for us the need to be more explicit about buy-in in advance of a workshop.

General lessons about the Toolbox protocol

In addition to learning important lessons about how the Toolbox dialogue method functions in the complex contexts we encounter when working with our partners, we have also learned much about the protocol we use in delivering the workshops. In response to the failed ad hoc workshops in Case 1 and Case 3, for example, we decided to approach this type of workshop differently. Because ad hoc workshops bring together participants who are not teammates to discuss aspects of their knowledge-making practices, it is important not to assume that they will readily engage with one another; instead of moving into the workshop directly, we began to allow the participants to introduce themselves and share stories about their interdisciplinary work. "Thick" introductions of this sort build a temporary community among the participants, creating a relational context in which it is easier to be more candid about one's own views (cf. Keyton 1999; Thompson 2009). We won't start the dialogue until we feel the group is ready, but we also want to reserve enough time together to explore the issues as deeply as possible. The trade-off in ad hoc workshops conducted this way is that there isn't as much time for dialogue, but allowing more time for dialogue is problematic when it is of suspect quality.

A second lesson concerns the Toolbox instrument used in the workshops. As noted above, Toolbox 1.0 was focused primarily on running workshops with the Scientific Research Toolbox instrument. This was partly to build a data set of workshops that relied on a single instrument. However, workshops like those in Cases 2 and 3 highlighted the trade-off we were making by operating in that fashion. During that phase, we chose to reduce variability so that our data were

110 O'Rourke, Crowley, Eigenbrode and Vasko

comparable across workshops rather than respond to the specific needs of each group and thereby increase variability. We came to realize through workshops like these, though, that so long as we were running workshops expressly to enhance communication and collaboration in cross-disciplinary research projects, we needed to develop the instrument in a more bottom-up way. Initially we did this in small steps, adding prompts to the Scientific Research Toolbox instrument that reflected the specific interests of the partner; however, as we moved into Toolbox 2.0, we began developing tailor-made Toolbox instruments designed for the partner in their entirety. Thus, we now trade-off our ability to conduct an empirical evaluation of team science communication across workshops in favour of providing effective interventions for our partners.

The final lesson we'll consider concerns power differences in workshop groups. While we have always been aware of power differences, this awareness has not always influenced the way we deliver Toolbox workshops. Because of the workshops described in Cases 2, 3 and 4, though, that has changed. Case 2 illuminated the need to anticipate how power is distributed among members of a team so that we could facilitate an open, engaged dialogue. Case 3 was undermined by power differences among representatives of different disciplines, with the humanists feeling attacked by the emphasis on scientific research. Case 4 highlighted the importance of acknowledging and actively managing the power differences that might exist between the partner group and TDI.

In Cases 2 and 3, power differences existed among workshop participants. Power is often distributed hierarchically in a research group, with a Principal Investigator (PI) having the most authority, followed by co-PIs, associated researchers, postdoctoral researchers and graduate students. Whether this has implications for project communication will depend on the research culture – some cultures are flat, with everyone having an equal voice, while others are more vertical, where people lower in the hierarchy speak only when given permission. Vertical power distribution is exhibited in Case 2. Power can also be distributed in cross-disciplinary groups according to discipline, as exhibited by Case 3. In a research project, certain disciplines may be foregrounded and others backgrounded, with predictable implications for deliberation and decision-making. In other cases, there is a differential distribution of power related to the pre-eminence of certain disciplines in the academy (e.g., biophysical sciences, health sciences, engineering) over other disciplines (e.g., social sciences, humanities) (cf. Campbell 2005).

The power differences in Case 4, by contrast, obtained between TDI and the partner group. TDI designs and delivers the workshops and so has influence over their structure and the nature of the experience. The participants, though, can make or break a workshop depending on their buy-in or the buy-in communicated by team leadership for the prompts and process.

Several adjustments have been made to address the concerns about power dynamics in Toolbox workshops raised by these three cases. First, we spend more time communicating with the partner and the participants before the workshop about our involvement and about workshop goals and expectations. We are also explicit about goals and expectations in the workshop preamble. Second, we make

Failure and what to do next 111

sure that the workshop facilitator develops a relationship with the partner before the workshop itself. Finally, we begin every workshop by explicitly negotiating ground rules with the participants, gaining their approval before the dialogue commences. These highlight the need to share the floor and respect the perspectives of other workshop participants.

Conclusion

In this chapter, we have described four workshops that failed to meet the objectives we set for them. As should be evident from the previous two sections, none of them can aptly be described as a *complete* failure. In each case valuable learning took place. We've described some of what TDI learned in Section 5, but we're confident that participants learned too, given that our approach centres the interests and commitments of the participants; because these are centred, there will typically be things said during the discussion that are illuminating or are at least worth thinking about. This is especially true if the participants are teammates who will continue to work together after the workshop – they will be independently motivated to find value in the contributions of their collaborators.

Because so much of their success relies on the participants, Toolbox workshops require buy-in, and this can be undermined by a host of factors, only some of which are within our control. If someone was cut off in traffic before arriving at the workshop or is just having a bad day, that can adversely affect the experience for them and for the other participants. The four workshops we have discussed, though, failed primarily because of policies in place at the time we delivered them. We made no allowances for differences between research teams and ad hoc groups, unrealistically assuming the latter would find common ground on their own. We used the same Scientific Research Toolbox instrument for differently constituted groups, even if they included humanists. And later on, after making changes to reflect differences among groups, we still failed to appreciate the complex ways dialogue could be inflected by power differences.

Like many of the groups we partner with, TDI is a work in progress. Failure is an important engine for change in our project, as it is in any project, and while the experience of failure within a specific workshop can be very uncomfortable for us as facilitators, we have come to value the lessons it generates that can help us move forward. We recognize that it is challenging to run process-oriented workshops for product-oriented academics, and there are always new things to learn from our participants. Furthermore, as we expand the reach of our workshop interventions into different communities and augment the set of objectives we aim to achieve in them, there will be unanticipated difficulties that force us to react by changing how we operate. A little epistemic humility goes a long way in these contexts – we *won't* be able to anticipate everything in advance, and so we should expect failure and be flexible in the face of it. The key to remaining valuable and viable in the face of failure is to treat it as instructive and continue to use it as a vehicle for improving the Toolbox dialogue method.

112 *O'Rourke, Crowley, Eigenbrode and Vasko*

Take-home messages

General recommendations from TDI's experience with failure:

- The emotional impact of a failed effort can make it difficult to appreciate that, in many cases, the effort will also have successful aspects.
- Treat failure not as a reason to quit but as an opportunity to innovate.

Recommendations for those running capacity-building interventions:

- Design the intervention to ensure psychological safety for the participants.
- Be explicit about expectations concerning how the intervention might unfold.
- In designing and delivering the intervention, consider the positionality of all participants, including the facilitators.
- Collaborate with the participants when designing the intervention, as this will increase buy-in by communicating how it is relevant to their experience.
- Make sure that power dynamics inform the design and delivery of the intervention, both within the participant group and between the participants and the facilitators.

Acknowledgements

The authors thank the members of TDI who have helped develop Toolbox 2.0 in response to the failures described in this chapter (and others!). We are also grateful to previous TDI members who contributed to the development of the dialogue method, especially Liela Rotschy, who was involved in running the workshops described in the second and third case studies above. We also thank BinBin Pearce and Dena Fam for helpful comments on this chapter.

References

Bosque-Pérez, N. A. et al. 2016. A pedagogical model for team-based, problem-focused interdisciplinary doctoral education. *BioScience*, 66(6), 477–488.

Campbell, L. M. 2005. Overcoming obstacles to interdisciplinary research. *Conservation Biology*, 9, 574–577.

Edmondson, A. 1999. Psychological safety and learning behavior in work teams. *Administrative Science Quarterly*, 44, 350–383.

Eigenbrode, S. et al. 2007. Employing philosophical dialogue in collaborative science. *BioScience*, 57, 55–64.

Firestein, S. 2016. *Failure: Why science is so successful*. Oxford: Oxford University Press.

Foster-Fishman, P. G., Berkowitz, S. L., Lounsbury, D. W., Jacobson, S., Allen, N. A. 2001. Building collaborative capacity in community coalitions: A review and integrative framework. *American Journal of Community Psychology*, 29, 241–261.

Hubbs, G. 2020. A narrative history of the Toolbox Dialogue Initiative. *In:* G. Hubbs, M. O'Rourke, and S. H. Orzack, eds. *The Toolbox Dialogue Initiative: The power of cross-disciplinary practice*. Boca Raton, FL: CRC Press, 37–47.

Hubbs, G., O'Rourke, M., Orzack, S. H. (Eds.). 2020. *The Toolbox Dialogue Initiative: The power of cross-disciplinary practice*. Boca Raton, FL: CRC Press.

Keyton, J. 1999. Relational communication in groups. *In:* L. R. Frey, D. Gouran and M. S. Poole, eds. *The handbook of group communication theory and research*. Thousand Oaks, CA: Sage, 192–222.

Looney, C., Donovan, S., O'Rourke, M., Crowley, S., Eigenbrode, S. D., Rotschy, L., Bosque-Pérez, N., Wulfhorst, J. D. 2014. Seeing through the eyes of collaborators: Using Toolbox workshops to enhance cross-disciplinary communication. *In:* M. O'Rourke, S. Crowley, S. D. Eigenbrode and J. D. Wulfhorst, eds. *Enhancing communication and collaboration in interdisciplinary research*. Thousand Oaks, CA: Sage Publications, 220–243.

Morton, L. W., Eigenbrode, S. D., Martin, T. A. 2015. Architectures of adaptive integration in large collaborative projects. *Ecology and Society*, 20(4), 5. doi:10.5751/ES-07788-200405.

NSF. 2019. *Improving communication in cross-disciplinary collaboration 2008–2012, SES-0823058*. Alexandria, VA: National Science Foundation.

O'Rourke, M., Crowley, S. 2013. Philosophical intervention and cross-disciplinary science: The story of the Toolbox Project. *Synthese*, 190, 1937–1954.

Rinkus, M. A., O'Rourke, M. 2020. Qualitative analyses of the effectiveness of Toolbox dialogues. *In:* G. Hubbs, M. O'Rourke, and S. H. Orzack, eds. *The Toolbox Dialogue Initiative: The power of cross-disciplinary practice*. Boca Raton, FL: CRC Press, 142–161.

Salazar, M. R., Widmer, K., Doiron, K., Lant, T. 2019. Leader integrative capabilities: A catalyst for effective interdisciplinary teams. *In:* K. L. Hall, A. L. Vogel and R. T. Croyle, eds. *Advancing social and behavioral health research through cross-disciplinary team science: principles for success*. New York: Springer, 313–328.

Thompson, J. L. 2009. Building collective communication competence in interdisciplinary research teams. *Journal of Applied Communication Research*, 37, 278–297.

Toolbox Dialogue Initiative (TDI). 2019. *Toolbox dialogue initiative*. Available from: http://tdi.msu.edu/.

Western Michigan University Evaluation Center (WMUEC). 2017. MSU Toolbox Dialogue Initiative: 2017 evaluation report. Available from TDI, toolbox@msu.edu.

7 Failure to consider local political processes and power relations in the development of a transdisciplinary research project plan

Learning lessons from a stormy start

Irena Leisbet Ceridwen Connon

Introduction

Managing power relations presents a challenge in transdisciplinary research (Siebenhuner 2018). While no unanimously agreed definition of transdisciplinary research exists, it can be defined as an "integrative, method-driven scientific principle aiming at the solution or transition of societal problems by differentiating and integrating knowledge from various scientific and societal bodies of knowledge" (Jahn et al. 2012, p. 6). Most significantly, it seeks to ensure that solutions to these societal problems acknowledge and address their complex root causes, which ultimately transcend individual scientific disciplines and societal institutions (Pohl 2011). Unlike positivist forms of scientific inquiry, transdisciplinary research is characterized by its use of integrative methodologies and collaboration between scientific and non-scientific communities, including industry, governments, civil society and local communities (Brown et al. 2010, p. 4).

Owing to the integration with society that this form of research affords, transdisciplinary researchers inevitably encounter the power relations and political processes that shape society (Jasanoff 2004; Jeong 2008). Transdisciplinary research is, therefore, by its very nature, heavily politicized. This results in one of the greatest challenges within transdisciplinary research – that of managing political contestations and conflicts rooted in societal power relations (Siebenhuner 2018). The existing transdisciplinary research scholarship contains numerous examples of how political contestations and uneven power relations present challenges for researchers (See Siebenhuner 2018). These examples include contestations resulting from conflicting economic motivations (Hirch-Hadorn et al. 2006) and contestations rooted in conflicting claims to legitimacy in participation (Pohl et al. 2010). Most significantly, these examples highlight that the specific forms of conflict that occur within each project are particular to the politics and power-based relations embedded within each local research context (Adler et al. 2018; Lohr et al. 2017).

However, the scholarship examining ways of managing power relations within transdisciplinary research remains limited (Siebenhuner 2018). In addition, almost all the current scholarship focuses upon the different forms of

Failure to consider local political processes 115

power-related conflicts that manifest during the *active* phase of a research project, such as during knowledge integration and solution development activities (see Lohr et al. 2017 and Siebenhuner 2018 for examples). This means that they focus predominantly on conflicts that emerge once the data collection phase is already complete. In addition, the limited number of suggestions offered for overcoming contestations are also focused on conflicts that emerge during the active research phase, which takes place *after* research plans have been successfully launched (see Leventon et al. 2016 and Pohl 2010 et al., for examples). What is missing from this scholarship are case studies that illustrate why conflicts rooted in place-based politics and power relations need to be considered within the research planning stage, *prior* to the active phase. This is because if a research project seeks to transform a complex societal problem, it must address existing inequities in participation in research by successfully engaging all relevant stakeholder groups. For example, in order to find solutions that address existing inequities in adaptations to extreme weather amongst different social groups, a research project must engage with both members of vulnerable groups, such as people with disabilities, and with members of the societal institutions that ultimately create the conditions of enhanced vulnerability amongst these groups through policies and practices that shape their social marginalization (Connon 2017, 2019). This requires ensuring that research activities do not risk perpetuating existing inequities by failing to secure the participation of all relevant groups in solution development. At present, the existing transdisciplinary research scholarship lacks examples that reveal why place-based power relations need to be managed at the planning stage of the research in order to address issues of societal inequity in solution development.

Another branch of transdisciplinary research scholarship has examined the concept of progress in transdisciplinary research (Lang et al. 2012; Pohl et al. 2010). For example, Pohl et al. (2010) explain that progress can be evaluated in terms of the lessons that can be learnt from the experience of undertaking transdisciplinary research. This is because these lessons can then be elaborated upon through tools and case studies that help guide researchers in managing future transdisciplinary research projects and practices (Pohl et al. 2010). However, although a plethora of examples exist that demonstrate progress in transdisciplinary research practice (see Palmer 2013 and Ruppert-Winkel et al. 2014), these examples predominantly focus on lessons learnt from the successes of research rather than from failures to achieve intended research aims and outcomes. It can be argued that this limits the scope of lessons that can be learnt from the experience of undertaking transdisciplinary research, as not all projects are successful, some are only partially successful and some are successful in different ways to what was originally intended (Hruschka et al. 2018). Failure also represents a crucial part of the scientific method, as every failed experiment helps to refine approaches to problem solving (Loscalzo 2014). In addition, failure can be regarded as an especially important part of the learning experience in transdisciplinary research, owing to the emphasis on interaction with wider society that this form of research involves. This is because the analysis of failure in cross-cultural research has shown that learning from failure can help ensure that future research questions and methodologies are

116 *Irena Leisbet Ceridwen Connon*

consistent with local realities (Faas et al. 2019; Hruschka et al. 2018). Several other chapters within this edited collection (see chapters by O'Rourke et al. and Robson-William et al.) highlight how a failure to successfully manage stakeholder dynamics can contribute to failure in transdisciplinary research. However, these chapters focus on failure that occurs during the active phase of the research, rather than at the very start of the project.

This chapter addresses the above shortcomings in the existing transdisciplinary research scholarship and complements the other chapters in this edited collection that focus on failure in managing stakeholder dynamics. It does so by contributing a case study that shows how a project that eventually proved to be a highly successful and award-winning transdisciplinary research effort emerged from a major failure that occurred at the very start. The failure was that the project did not secure the willingness of a fundamental group of participants to participate. A retrospective failure analysis was conducted that drew upon in-depth qualitative research data obtained from activities undertaken as part of the revised project plan. The analysis found that the failure to secure willingness to participate resulted from a major shortcoming in the initial research design. This was a failure to adequately consider, when selecting research methods for conducting the project, the political processes and power relations that characterized the research context, and which shaped participant willingness to participate in the proposed project activities. The chapter begins with an overview of the project in question, a description of initial reactions to the proposed project plan, and details of how failure to obtain the willingness of key stakeholders to participate led to revisions being made to the research plan in order to steer the project towards a successful outcome. This is followed by an outline of the approach used to analyze the failure in the original research design and an in-depth discussion of the findings. The chapter concludes by presenting the key lessons learnt and by highlighting how the case study presents an important contribution to the existing transdisciplinary research scholarship. In addition, a series of recommendations and take-home messages are provided to help inform future transdisciplinary research practice.

A turbulent tale in chasing storm trails: Overview of a transdisciplinary knowledge transfer partnership project

Research problem and context

Extreme weather can seriously disrupt daily life. Studies within the environmental hazards scholarship emphasize that human vulnerability to extreme weather, defined as the conditions that make up a person's capacity to prevent, withstand and cope with the effects of hazardous weather, is associated with demographic, environmental, social, cultural and economic determinants (Fadigas 2017). As such, the impact of extreme weather is a complex problem which affects, and is affected by, all aspects of society.

Over the past decade, the United Kingdom has witnessed increasing severity and frequency of seasonal weather patterns, including flooding, heavy snow and

Failure to consider local political processes 117

unpredictable seasonal weather patterns (Scottish Government 2012). This severity is predicted to further increase over the next 50 years (IPCC 2013). Power disruption during extreme weather results in disruption to livelihoods and produces significant levels of fear and stress (see Connon 2017; 2019).

Between 2013 and 2014, discussions with personnel from Scottish and Southern Energy Networks (SSEN), a private sector energy company responsible for delivering power supplies to Scotland and the south-east region of England, revealed that during periods of extreme winter weather between 2011 and 2013, certain groups of community members, including people with disabilities, were deemed more likely to have had significant difficulties coping with power disruption than others. This was further supported by discussions with members of emergency responder public service groups (local and national government, police, ambulance and fire and rescue services), who stated they had observed that community members, particularly those who had experienced difficulties coping during power outages and extreme weather, wished to receive more information and support to enable them to better prepare for and respond to future weather-related events. Similarly, SSEN recognized that it needed to develop new forms of support for communities so that the "well-being gap" between electricity disruption and restoration for its customers could be effectively addressed. Members of the emergency services also expressed concerns that their resources were becoming less able to meet the demand for emergency support during winter storms. Concerned about increasing pressures being placed upon official emergency response organizations, both the UK and Scottish governments recognized the need to focus on increasing the ability of communities to withstand the impacts of extreme weather. In particular, the governments looked at how a participatory approach, involving community-led action aimed at enabling communities to be able to plan for and respond during periods of extreme weather, would help build community resilience, with resilience being defined as, "that which maintains the continuity of our way of life or returning to relatively normality after a disruptive event" (Scottish Government 2012, p. 3).

Development of a transdisciplinary research project to address vulnerability to power outages in extreme weather in the United Kingdom

As a result of identifying a shared need for improving community-level responses to power outages, a 36-month Knowledge Transfer Partnership (KTP) project between the University of Dundee (UoD) and Scottish and Southern Electricity Networks (SSEN) was developed in 2014. The aims of the project were four-fold:

- *Understand* how a sample of communities and individuals in urban and rural areas has responded to recent natural hazard events (e.g., flooding, snow) and electricity supply disruption.
- *Develop* effective solutions to prepare for and respond to the challenges of hazard events and electricity supply disruption by drawing on these insights

118 *Irena Leisbet Ceridwen Connon*

and working with sample communities, local authorities, emergency services and voluntary groups.

- *Mobilize* the solutions generated throughout society and institutions.
- *Embed* knowledge at all scales and levels.

As the project aimed to integrate knowledge from a range of stakeholders to co-develop solutions to help transform responses to extreme weather, an initial research plan was drawn up to mobilize the project aims. Six case study sites were identified after discussions with the government and emergency response personnel on the basis of being either "exceptionally outstanding" (all rural areas) or "relatively poor" (urban areas) by these organizations, in terms of community coping ability during extreme winter weather between 2011 and 2014. The six case study sites included: three villages and a town in Scotland, and a village and a larger town in England. Each of the six sites had been affected by prolonged power outages (lasting 24 hours or more) in the previous four years as a result of extreme weather, including snow, rain and gale-force winds, which damaged overhead power lines and flooded electricity substations.

Knowledge of each community's strengths and limitations in responding to extreme weather was obtained through researcher consultation with local government and SSEN representatives. The knowledge offered by these representatives was further supported by SSEN data on the number of complaints made by community members about the loss of power during the storm events. This was then used to select appropriate research methods. As the project sought to identify and mobilize the knowledge required to ensure successful coping ability during extreme weather, an emancipatory approach was chosen that aimed to recognize local communities as key participants, rather than passive recipients of the outcomes of scientific research (Mauser et al. 2013). The project plan therefore aimed to utilize participatory methods of engagement that focused to a greater extent upon knowledge integration, synthesis and the provision of co-learning opportunities than what is normally afforded by traditional exploratory research methods (Davidson et al. 2007).

The charrette method was chosen as the means to facilitate the integrative, democratic co-learning process. The charrette method is defined as "a time-limited, multi-party design environment organized to generate a collectively [produced]" outcome (Condon 2008) and one which "involve[es] all associated stakeholders in critical decision-making points" (Lennertz and Lutzenhise 2006). The plan was to implement three charrettes in each of the case study sites through a series of meetings held within each site. The first would facilitate team building, opportunities to hear different understandings of the research problem and collaborative reframing of the research problem. The second would focus on determining the possibilities for change and the co-production of solution development. The third aimed to refine the solution through the dissemination of the results among different stakeholder groups and to develop the project toolkit to mobilize the solution throughout communities, institutions and society. The decision to conduct charrettes within each of the sites was made on the basis of findings from the existing

Failure to consider local political processes 119

transdisciplinary scholarship that emphasized the importance of acknowledging context in solution development (Mauser et al. 2013, pp. 426–428).

The plan was to select a broad range of participants who would represent each of the stakeholder groups. This approach to participant selection was influenced by systems approaches to societal transformation (Fazey et al. 2007; Reed et al. 2010), with the idea being that each charrette would represent a microcosm of society. Each charrette would therefore include members of SSEN, members of official emergency response organizations including fire and rescue services, ambulance services, police, members of transport providers, local and regional government, local voluntary organizations and members of the local communities. The plan was to seek community members whose experiences of coping during extreme weather ranged from highly successful to extremely problematic. Plans were put in place for the lead researcher to visit each site with project information sheets to source out potential participants and introduce them to the project. This was to be facilitated through one-week visits made by the lead researcher to local SSEN outreach depots within each of the sites to shadow the work of the power outage response staff and to meet with local residents during the course of these activities. The first two visits to each of the case study sites took place in two rural Scottish communities in April 2014.

Reception to the project plan: A failure from the start

Despite efforts made by staff from the local SSEN depots to introduce the researcher to local community members who had previously coped well or who had experienced difficulty coping during previous storm encounters, initial attempts to engage community members in the proposed project activities failed. Although community members expressed interest in the researcher's visit, listened to details about the project aims and read the project information sheet, all participants said the same thing – that they did not wish to participate in the proposed meetings. This was despite the fact that they assured the researcher that the project sounded interesting and that they believed that local residents like themselves could make an important and beneficial contribution to the project. Without their agreement to participate in the proposed activities, the project plan could not be mobilized. The reasons as to why participants refused to participate were not made explicitly clear until the project was later mobilized with a revised research plan. However, these reasons, which are detailed and analyzed in depth in the following sections of the chapter, are key to understanding why the original project plan failed.

Transitioning from failure towards success

This failure to secure participant willingness meant the original research plan had to be revised. The revised plan took into consideration the brief insights offered by community members during initial discussions about the weather, including information about the vulnerabilities of certain groups of community

120 *Irena Leisbet Ceridwen Connon*

members that were hidden from official accounts about the coping abilities of residents. Most importantly, however, the revised plan drew on what a number of residents had explained to the researcher – that understanding local people's responses to severe weather required visiting the area for a number of weeks to experience it for themselves. Therefore, instead of undertaking a charrette-based approach to simultaneously engage all participants, the revised plan utilized a qualitative, multi-tiered approach. This involved undertaking 12 weeks of ethnographic research and conducting semi-structured interviews with participants in each case study site in order to better understand the nature of the research problem and to enable participants to offer inputs for solution development (see Palmer 2017 about the benefits of ethnographic and deep qualitative research methods in transdisciplinary research). Focus-group meetings using the charrette method were later utilized to integrate the knowledge gathered from the ethnographic and semi-structured interview research in the development of solutions with members of official institutions. Permission was sought from each participant for the researcher to share their insights at these meetings. The outcomes of these meetings were then fed back to participants for further input. While this meant community participants were not involved in face-to-face interactions with other stakeholders, it still allowed for knowledge integration and collaborative generation of solutions. Community approval of the revised plan was checked in advance by contacting a number of potential participants from the initial site visits, who said that they would be much happier with the ethnographic approach and agreed to offer their contributions via qualitative interviews. Formal ethical clearance by the University of Dundee was obtained in advance of commencing the revised plan in the summer of 2014.

The project successfully followed the revised project plan through to completion. In March 2017, the research team achieved an award from Innovate UK for "Outstanding Contribution to Knowledge Exchange," for the project's eventual success in helping to transform responses to power outages during extreme weather.

Analyzing the failure of the original research plan

The failure to secure the participation of community members in the originally proposed project activities was analyzed by conducting a forensic (retrospective) failure analysis through an analysis of qualitative interview data obtained from interviews with community members conducted during the active phase of the revised project plan. Failure analysis refers to the process of collecting and analyzing data to determine the cause of a failure (McDanels 2002).

During the ethnographic phase of the revised project, semi-structured interviews were undertaken with community members in each case study site. However, only the 29 interviews conducted at the two case study sites where the initial field visits took place have been included in this analysis. This is because, during these interviews, participants from these sites either proactively offered reasons why they had previously been reluctant to engage in the research, or directly referred

Failure to consider local political processes 121

to this matter when answering a question about preferred methods of community engagement. These interviews lasted between 60 and 90 minutes and were conducted between September 2014 and December 2015. All interview responses were recorded and transcribed.

These responses were used to develop a failure analysis framework between February and May 2019 to uncover the reasons why the initial plan failed. Data were analyzed by identifying key themes and reasons as to why participants were unwilling to take part in the proposed activities. Predominant themes were used to develop conceptual headings. Data were then assigned to each of the headings as appropriate. Findings were cross-checked using NVivo software.

Direct quotations from the interview transcripts have been included in the reporting of the findings. This is to ensure that the voices and insights from participants help guide the development of recommendations from the findings. Owing to the politically sensitive nature of the research context, all responses have been anonymized.

Findings: Understanding the failure to mobilize the original project plan

The analysis revealed that the political processes and uneven power relations that shape rural Scottish society influenced the willingness of potential participants to take part in the proposed research activities. It also revealed the failure of the researcher to consider these political processes and power relations in the original project design.

Failure to consider how political processes influenced local views on the representation of local knowledge

The failure to secure community members' interest in participating in the charrettes was exposed as being due to the failure of the initial research design to fully acknowledge: (a) the extent to which local conceptualizations of identity were bound up with local weather-related knowledge, and (b) how political processes that shaped Scottish society heightened resident consciousness of this symbolic link and perspectives on local representation.

This is because the interviews revealed the presence of a symbolic connection between local weather-related knowledge and the extent to which a person viewed themselves or others as being "local." For example, one participant explained that having the knowledge to be able to forecast weather and to be prepared in anticipation of a storm were regarded as core skills associated with having a local identity. This is because these skills could only be learnt through long-term experience of local weather conditions:

> We grew up with how things were round here. How to get by during storms, well it is something you know if you've seen it; it is something we all grew up with. It's how things are round here ... you get used to what the storms

122 *Irena Leisbet Ceridwen Connon*

round here look like and you come to know what parts flood round here and what's normal. You've got to really grow up with it. (Participant, Case Study Site (CCS) 2)

Another participant explained how possession of weather-related knowledge was used to demark those born and raised in the area from other residents:

All of us round here. You have to know the place to get by … weather, protecting from high winds. It sort of all came natural to us. We were brought up like that. We'd say a real local knows all this like the back of their hand. For others, it's not the same. They live here but don't think quite the same way as a local local. (Participant CCS1)

This connection between weather-related knowledge and local identity was deeply embedded in local society but could not be fully accessed by the researcher on the basis of the secondary information available about the project sites, which was used to design the initial project plan.

Analysis of interview data also revealed how the failure to appreciate the extent to which weather-related knowledge was bound up with local identity conceptualizations resulted in an inappropriate selection of research methods for the local context in question. This is because the interviews highlighted that although residents were proud to be in possession of knowledge that enabled them to cope during extreme weather, they were unwilling to share this in focus-group meetings with other participants. This unwillingness was due to the heightened awareness of the link between local weather-related knowledge and identity politics that arose in the case study sites as a result of ongoing political processes in the lead-up to the Scottish Independence Referendum of 2014. In the United Kingdom, Knowledge Transfer Partnership projects are jointly funded by the UK government and a private sector organization, in this case, SSEN. UK government funding was not in itself seen as problematic from the perspective of Scottish participants, including those in favour of Scottish Independence. However, as initial sourcing of participants took place during the months immediately preceding the referendum, when political debate and discussions of identity politics dominated both national media and local conversations and invoked critical questioning about who should represent local views, and with whom local knowledge should be shared, people were concerned about the potential implications of what the project was asking them to do.

As the project interviews continued for over one year after the referendum, they captured the extent to which enhanced thinking about identity politics influenced residents' perceptions regarding communication of the issues associated with extreme weather. For example, the Independence Referendum was often alluded to when answering direct questions about preferred methods of engagement and reasons for refusing to take part in the originally proposed charrette-based activity:

Failure to consider local political processes   123

It's not we had anything against what you wanted to find out. But it's where this would all go; that was the worry. I suppose we wanted that control over it and we didn't know you then like now. It's with everything, what we are now saying to outsiders is this is our knowledge, we decide what we do with it. The referendum and all that, whatever you make of it, it's brought all that out in the open. We're all thinking about all that now. (Participant CCS2)

As revealed in this statement, residents were particularly conscious about maintaining control over what their knowledge would be used for. This affected their willingness to share knowledge, particularly in the public space, for the purposes of the project.

The interviews also revealed that enhanced consciousness of identity politics resulted in those who had struggled to cope during the periods of bad weather refusing to share their experiences within the public space. This was due to concerns about the risk of exacerbating existing tensions between long-term residents and recent in-migrants at a time of heightened local tensions:

Everyone was talking and I didn't want people to hear me say that I would prefer better arrangements during the storms or anything really as your adding fuel to the fire. You're basically saying we [incomers] are different and things were tense enough then. I didn't want to sway people one way or another over things like this. (Participant CCS2)

In addition, enhanced consciousness of identity politics also affected the willingness of lifelong residents who had struggled to cope during periods of severe weather to share their experiences via participation in the proposed project activities. In particular, the enhanced pride attributed to being able to cope during storms resulted in generating feelings of shame and low self-worth amongst those who had encountered difficulties:

It was sort of a sense that I had somehow failed. I'm born and bred here so I should know what I am doing. To sit down at a table and say to people from in front of local leaders who I felt will be thinking I should know better that I struggled with the bad weather, you know I'm like standing up and saying I'm a failure. (Participant CCS2)

The interviews also exposed how increased consciousness of issues concerning local representation led to a situation whereby residents who had struggled to cope believed that by publicly exposing local variations in the coping abilities of long-term residents, they risked undermining public images of cohesive rural community identities that each village sought to portray. They believed that undermining these images through public discussion of failures to cope during the storms risked harming local political campaigns calling for increased political

124   *Irena Leisbet Ceridwen Connon*

recognition of rural affairs and for the transfer of decision-making power from the central to local government:

> If you say not all cope well, you are talking about division and that gives the government a way not to give more control to us. It will be used against us. You say that, then you get problems because locals will say your siding against them. So you start problems. ... No-one would dare do that in those meetings you were wanting. (Participant CCS1)

This shows that the proposed charrette activities were highly insensitive to the political dynamics of the local context. It reveals clear failure on behalf of the researcher to adequately understand and address underlying power relations and political processes that impacted upon residents' lives when constructing the original project plan.

Failure to acknowledge pre-existing tensions between local communities and national-level governments

The interviews revealed that long-term tensions between the central government and rural communities also impacted upon willingness to participate in charrette-based project activities. This also exposed how the original plan failed to consider the presence of tensions between official governments, institutions and communities, as a result of researcher reliance on secondary information from "known-contacts."

In particular, the interviews exposed that participants were concerned about "hidden agendas" by national government institutions. Comments were frequently uttered about how, since the 1980s, the interests of the central UK government were believed to have been heavily geared towards the financial capital of London and south-east England, at the expense of local economies and communities. Rural regions of Scotland were also described as having been given limited and unequal attention by the devolved Scottish government. As a result, participants had specific concerns about the extent to which the project aims would benefit central government agendas over the needs of local residents:

> I know you wanted it to be equal, but when big governments are involved it's never going to be equal. The fact they were in on it means they want something out of it. They are only interested in it for themselves. (Participant CCS1)

Other participants raised concerns that the project initiatives would be used to justify central government financial cutbacks to the emergency services. This, they argued, would place an unfair amount of responsibility for safeguarding human well-being during periods of extreme weather upon local communities. While participants viewed the transfer of formal political decision-making power

Failure to consider local political processes 125

to local communities as a positive move, they did not feel comfortable with the transfer of responsibility for human safety and well-being:

> Political decisions, that sort of thing, yes. That's what we want. But to say we are in charge of filling the hole of the emergency services, that's not right. Dangerous when you think about it. And it's worse when you think that this is only so they can shrink down the emergency services. (Participant CCS2)

Because of this widespread lack of trust over the motives of central government institutions, residents were particularly suspicious about participating in project activities that involved face-to-face interaction with institutional representatives. In particular, interacting on a face-to-face basis with government representatives raised concerns over loyalty to local communities and inducing local-level tensions:

> I suppose it's a matter of take part to stop the government trying to have things all their way, but to be seen to be sitting down with them, it feels wrong. Defending local rights against big government doesn't usually involve working with them. I wanted to be involved, to keep check on the government, but not out in the open like that. Folk would have been thinking I'm on their side and even if I said no, I'm not sure they'd trust me. Being there would be the problem. (Participant CCS2)

This reveals the extent to which the charrette method was highly unsuitable for the project context, owing to the public exposure that this form of participation would result in for those taking part.

Failure to acknowledge long-standing differences in motivational values between local communities and large corporate industries

The interviews also revealed that residents were often even more distrustful about the motivations of private industry, including SSEN, which is a private utility company. Participants expressed concerns about the incompatibility of the financial profit-generating agendas of the corporate industry with local understandings of "the greater good." A significant number believed that the corporate industry would not support the project unless it had a strong economic reason to do so – a reason which they believed would override the needs of society in the interests of economic benefit. Furthermore, this lack of trust in the motivations of corporate organizations led to a reluctance to have discussions with, and work together with, members of these organizations to develop solutions. This was often justified in terms of an ethical duty to protect local interests in the face of interests of large economically powerful organizations. This is because large nationwide industries were associated with past failures of local businesses and downturns in local economies during the previous three decades:

126 *Irena Leisbet Ceridwen Connon*

I've known these companies. They are interested in one thing and one thing only – money. Yes, they are interested in people, but that boils down to one reason –money. These companies, they harmed people round here. It would be immoral to agree to sit down and say we're doing this together. Goes against what the done thing should be. (Participant CCS1)

Residents also expressed concern that the project risked commodifying experientially based local knowledge to serve the economic interests of private industry. Concerns were highlighted about whether SSEN, being a private company, would measure the success of the project outcomes in terms of financial savings made because of reduced complaints during periods of extreme weather as a result of the development of community resilience activities. As a result, participants were concerned that the project risked "putting a price on local knowledge" and "investing off the back of human misery," for the purpose of greater returns on the company "profit margins." This, participants believed, was irreconcilable with their beliefs about what it meant to serve the collective interests of society:

Businesses are about money however you look at it. What to me they are doing here is wanting to take that knowledge to benefit them. People become a by-product of a business success. They are expecting us to provide it and they are benefitting. And those who suffered during the storms, they are saying you follow the instructions and we take credit for it. Think about it. What they're doing is investing in people's misery. They've thought, how can we make money on the back of that. (Participant CCS1)

This led to concerns among potential participants that by refusing to participate in the proposed face-to-face activities, they risked undermining local voices in the development of strategies that would affect the lives of local members of society. This was because they feared that local ideas would be inadequately represented in solution development if very few local residents participated in the project. This, they believed, could risk harming community members in the event of a future weather-related emergency. However, at the same time, participants believed that if they were to sit down and collaboratively work with members of these organizations, they would be perceived by others as betraying the local community:

I can see the point for the community, but to work with them and openly say I'm working with them, I'd be seen as selling out the place, our knowledge, selling us to big players and it wouldn't go down well, I tell you. You have to say something to make sure they don't make money out of us and to keep them in line by saying it's our knowledge, we call the shots, but at the same time, you can't be seen to do it. (Participant, CCS1)

Failure to consider local political processes 127

This reveals how the original project plan risked creating a moral "paradox of participation" for these local residents, which stemmed from the need to reduce harm to local people, while, at the same time, the very act of working with members of corporate organizations risked participants being perceived by other members of the community as acting against local interests. The original project activities therefore risked creating upset in the communities, again due to the lack of anonymity afforded by participation via the charrette method:

> It was a case of damned if you do, damned if you don't. Catch 22. On one hand you don't want to leave it all to them. But then you don't want to be disloyal to folk here by saying we'll work with them. You have to take part, but then you also can't take part at the same time. Then I chose not to. But when you then said it wouldn't be face to face now, well that was much better because I'm not going to be seen as a traitor anymore. I'm doing it for them so I'm not being a traitor, but not all will see it that way. (Participant CCS1)

Concluding discussion: A cautionary tale and learning lessons from chasing storm trails

Learning lessons from failure to mobilize intended project activities

The study reveals how failure to consider how political processes and uneven power relations between stakeholders in the original research design led to a failure to secure the willingness of community members to participate in the proposed project activities. It shows how the charrette method of engagement was clearly unsuitable for the research context, owing to the need to utilize anonymous methods of community engagement to show sensitivity to the political situation and power dynamics that shape Scottish society. This failure also highlights the need for researchers to be fully informed about the political processes and power dynamics embedded within society *prior* to the development of the research activity plan. From this, four recommendations can be made for informing future transdisciplinary research practices.

Recommendation 1: Undertake a deep primary scoping study prior to developing the project plan

The failure to consider power relations when designing the project activities reveals the need for researchers to undertake deep primary scoping research activities in advance of constructing the research plan. This is to ensure that the methods selected are sensitive to contextual power dynamics that ultimately shape willingness to take part. In addition, the discrepancy between the depth of information provided about political tensions in the interviews and the researcher's lack of knowledge about these tensions during the construction of the original project plan illustrates that these scoping

128 *Irena Leisbet Ceridwen Connon*

activities need to avoid over-reliance on "known" sources of secondary information. This is because information about divergences in local opinions is unlikely to be volunteered in contexts where there exists a perceived need to present a united public image.

Recommendation 2: Select research methods that are sensitive to local political contexts

The insights offered reveal the importance of selecting research methods that are sensitive to the particular local context in question. The delicate task of balancing intentions to reduce existing social inequalities of representation, and selecting methods that are suitable for navigating the power dynamics that influence relationships between participants, requires in-depth knowledge of participant preferences and consideration of potential consequences of adopting particular methods. Collaborative charrette-based workshops aimed at providing opportunities for participants to share experiences and to contribute on an equal basis to the project outcomes can be regarded as an inappropriate strategy for situations where high levels of distrust amongst participants exist. This is because interactional group settings may risk enhancing participant discomfort, feelings of disloyalty, perceptions of moral transgressions and local-level tensions. In these instances, participants require the use of less public and more anonymous forms of engagement.

Recommendation 3: Consult directly with community participants to obtain views on preferred methods of engagement prior to constructing the project plan

The failure encountered at the start of the project could have been avoided if the researcher had spoken directly with community members about preferred methods of engagement before devising the original activity plan. Early consultation not only ensures that activities are suitable for politically sensitive local contexts but also provides community members with greater agency in devising the project plan.

Recommendation 4: Be adaptable when managing the research project

The case study shows that project failure can be overcome. However, it also shows the need for researchers to be able to adapt to the changing political context and to be flexible in managing the development, as well as the implementation, of project plans.

Enhancing knowledge in transdisciplinary research practice

This case study addresses a limitation in the existing transdisciplinary research scholarship focusing on power dynamics and ways of managing power relations in transdisciplinary research practice by showing why conflicts rooted in place-based politics and power relations need to be considered within the research planning stage, *prior* to the active stage of the research. It also contributes to discussions about progress in transdisciplinary research practice by showing the importance of learning from failure in order to develop recommendations aimed

Failure to consider local political processes 129

at improving transdisciplinary research practice. Only by understanding the reasons for failure can recommendations be made to avoid the same problems emerging during future research endeavours.

Take-home messages

- **Be knowledgeable** about place-based power dynamics prior to constructing the research plan.
- **Be mindful** of political issues and power relationships when choosing research methods.
- **Be proactive** by asking stakeholders how they would prefer to participate.
- **Be flexible**: If your plan fails to mobilize, revise it and try again.

References

Adler, C., Hirsch-Hadorn, G., Breu, T., Wiesmann, U., Pohl, C. 2018. Conceptualizing the transfer of knowledge across cases in transdisciplinary research. *Sustainability Science*, 13(1), 179–190.

Brown, V., Harris, J., Russell, J. 2010. *Tackling wicked problems through the transdisciplinary imagination*. London: Earthscan.

Condon, P. 2008. *Design charrettes for sustainable communities*. London: Island Press.

Connon, I. L. C. 2017 Extreme weather, complex spaces and diverse rural places: An intra-community scale analysis of responses to storm events in rural Scotland, UK. *Journal of Rural Studies*, 54, 111–125.

Connon, I. L. C. 2019. Young, mobile, but alone in the cold and dark: Experiences of young urban in-migrants during extreme weather events in the UK. *In:* F. Rivera, ed. *Emerging voices in natural hazards research*. Oxford, UK: Elsevier Butterworth-Heinemann, 367–392.

Davidson, C., Johnson, C., Lizarralde, G., Dikmen, N., Sliwinski, A. 2007. Truths and myths about community participation in post-disaster housing projects. *Habitat International*, 31, 100–115.

Faas, A. J., Velez, A-L., Nowell, B., Steelman, T. 2019. Methodological considerations in pre- and post-emergency network identification and data collection for disaster risk reduction: Lessons from wildfire response networks in the American Northwest. *International Journal of Disaster Risk Reduction*, 40, 101260.

Fadigas, A. 2017. Vulnerability factors of shellfisherwomen in the face of oil spill events: An analysis of the Prestige case. *International Journal of Disaster Risk Reduction*, 24, 560–567.

Fazey, I., Fazey, J., Fischer, J., Sherren, K., Warren, J., Noss, R., Dovers, S. 2007. Adaptive capacity and learning to learn as leverage for social–ecological resilience. *Frontiers in Ecology and the Environment*, 5(7), 375–380.

Hirsch-Hadorn, G., Bradley, D., Pohl, C., Rist, S., Wiesmann, U. 2006. Implications of transdisciplinarity for sustainable research. *Ecological Economics*, 60, 119–128.

Hruschka, D., Munira, S., Jesmin, K., Hackman, J., Tiokhin, L. 2018. Learning from failures of protocol in cross-cultural research. *PNAS*, 115(45), 11428–11434.

IPCC. 2013. *Fifth assessment report: climate change 2013*. Available from: www.ipcc.ch/publications_and_data/publications_and_data reports.shtml. [Accessed 15 August 2019.]

130 *Irena Leisbet Ceridwen Connon*

Jahn, T., Bergmann, M., Keil, F. 2012. Transdisciplinarity: Between mainstreaming and marginalization. *Ecological Economics*, 79, 1–10.

Jasanoff, S. 2004. *States of knowledge: the co-production of science and social order.* London: Routledge.

Jeong, H. 2008. *Understanding conflict and conflict analysis.* London: Sage.

Lang, D., Wiek, A., Bergmann, M., Stauffacher, M., Martens, P., Mol, P., Swilling M., Thomas, C. 2012. Transdisciplinary research in sustainable science: Practices, principles, and challenges. *Sustainability Science*, 7, 25–43.

Lennertz, B., Lutzenhiser, A. 2006. *The charrette handbook: The essential guide for accelerated collaborative community planning.* Chicago: The American Planning Association.

Leventon, J., Fleskens, L., Claringbould, H., Schwilch, G., Hessel, R. 2016. An applied methodology for stakeholder identification in transdisciplinary research. *Sustainability Science*, 11, 763–775.

Lohr, J., Hochmuth, C., Graef, F., Wambura, J., Sieber S. 2017. Conflict management programs in trans-disciplinary research projects: The case of a food security project in Tanzania. *Food Security*, 9, 1189–1201.

Loscalzo, J. 2014. A celebration of failure. *Circulation*, 129(9), 952–955.

Mauser, W., Klepper, G., Rice, M., Schmalbauer, B-S., Hackmann, H., Leemans, R., Moore, H. 2013. Transdisciplinary global change research: The co-creation of knowledge for sustainability. *Current Opinion in Environmental Sustainability*, 5(3–4), 420–431.

McDanels, S. 2002. Preparing and writing a failure analysis report. *Practical Failure Analysis*, 2(5), 20.

Palmer, J. 2017. Ethnography as transdisciplinary inquiry: Two stories of adaptation and resilience from Aceh, Indonesia. *In:* D. Fam, J. Palmer, C. Riedy and C. Mitchell, eds. *Transdisciplinary research and practice for sustainability outcomes.* Oxford, UK: Routledge, 190–203.

Palmer, J., Chiveralls, K., Pullen, S., Zuo, J., Wilson, L., Zillante, G. (2013). Transdisciplinary charrettes: A research method for sustainable design. *The International Journal of Architectonic, Spatial, and Environmental Design*, 7(1), 95–106.

Pohl, C. 2011. What is progress in transdisciplinary research? *Futures*, 43, 618–628.

Pohl, C. et al. 2010. Researchers' roles in knowledge co-production: Experience from sustainability research in Kenya, Switzerland, Bolivia and Nepal. *Science and Public Policy*, 37, 267.

Reed, M. et al. 2010. What is social learning? *Ecology and Society*, 15(4). [online]. Available from: http://www.ecologyandsociety.org/vol15/iss4/resp1/.

Ruppert-Winkel, C., Hauber, J., Stablo, J., Kress, M. 2014. Das World Café als Integrationsinstrument in der transdisziplinaren Nachhaltigkeitsforschung. *GAIA: Ecological Perspectives for Science and Society*, 23, 3, 243–252.

Scottish Government. 2012. *Preparing Scotland: Scottish guidance on resilience.* Edinburgh: Scottish Government.

Siebenhuner, B. 2018. Conflicts in transdisciplinary research: Reviewing literature and analysing a case of climate adaptation in northwestern Germany. *Ecological Economics*, 154, 117–127.

8 A week in the life of a transdisciplinary researcher

Failures in research to support policy for water-quality management in New Zealand's South Island

Melissa Robson-Williams, Bruce Small and Roger Robson-Williams

Introduction

> Monday's failure: forgot research's place
> Tuesday's failure: just wanted a face
> Wednesday's failure: a product of pressure
> Thursday's failure: a boundary by Escher
> Friday's failure: was too loving and giving
> Saturday's failure: worked too hard for a living
> And the project conceived on the 7th day was happy and faultless and without a delay.

Water management is one of the most pressing issues in the Canterbury region of New Zealand's South Island (Figure 8.1). The way water has been managed in Canterbury over the past 20 years has influenced national policy and resulted in a new act of parliament to improve the management of this precious resource in the region. New Zealand's identity is closely associated with its freshwater resources, and the aquifers, rivers and lakes in Canterbury are highly valued for cultural, economic and recreational purposes. Potentially conflicting uses have led to tensions between farmers, water sports enthusiasts, environmentalists and Māori, the country's indigenous people, for whom water has important cultural significance. Declining water quality and increasing conflict over water resources among these and many other groups have become increasingly apparent (Weber et al. 2011).

After about a decade of increasing concerns about effective water management (Kirk 2015), in 2009 the regional council, Environment Canterbury, embarked on a journey of collaborative water management and policy-making, guided by the recently published *Canterbury Water Management Strategy* (CWMS) (CMF 2009). The implementation of this collaborative approach to addressing water management was influenced by a temporary act of parliament, the *Environment Canterbury (Temporary Commissioners and Improved Water Management) Act (2010)*. This act reduced the democratic rights of citizens by removing elected

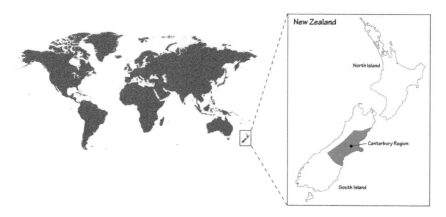

Figure 8.1 New Zealand, with the Canterbury region highlighted.

councillors but gave special weight to the principles of the CWMS. The act removed the right to appeal decisions to a higher court, but this also meant that water management decisions could not be held up in court for years, and it encouraged those with an interest to become involved in the collaborative process.

This shift in context and in the way water policy was being made gave rise to the two interrelated projects discussed in this chapter. The projects were considered transdisciplinary because they sought to bring together not only different scientific disciplines, but also stakeholders and end-user perspectives in order to share responsibility for formulating issues, developing research processes and synthesizing and interpreting findings, while simultaneously trying to address valid science questions, create socially robust knowledge and bring about change in a real-world societal issue (e.g., Mauser et al. 2013; Pohl and Hirsch Hadorn 2008; Polk 2014).

Case study #1: The Selwyn Waihora Project

Between 2011 and 2015 New Zealand's first collaborative policy-making process to set freshwater quality limits was undertaken. Its aim was to understand the cultural, economic, social and environmental values in the Selwyn Waihora water catchment, and to set water-quality limits to protect the waterways and a lake called Te Waihora, as well as provide other benefits. The collaborative policy-making was centred on a committee consisting of representatives from the important social units (regional and district councils, local rūnanga (Māori tribal representatives) and community representatives). A technical team was formed to support the committee. The Selwyn Waihora Project case study focuses on the work of this technical team.

The technical team began by using community aspirations for social, economic, cultural and environmental wellbeing, established through community consultation, to define the project's research scope and identify key knowledge sources and possible future land-use scenarios, as well as indicators to evaluate the scenarios. For each scenario the technical team went on to evaluate the likely impact on environmental, social, cultural and economic values. Using these scenario evaluations, it was possible to assess the degree to which a community's aspirations for economic growth, healthy rivers and cultural and social wellbeing could be met.

Although the committee was working at the level of community values, each scenario was also associated with a nutrient limit for water quality. In general terms, the lower the nutrient limits, the greater the potential adverse economic impact via constraints on agricultural intensification in a district where farming contributes significantly to prosperity.

The evaluations of each of the scenarios were widely tested with community groups and then presented to the committee, all over approximately 18 months. After this, the committee developed a package of solutions for the catchment, made up of elements of the scenarios. Once a recommended solutions package had been agreed to, the technical team worked with resource management planning staff at Environment Canterbury to convert it into statutory and non-statutory provisions, including catchment water-quality limits. These provisions went through a statutory resource management process during 2014/2015. The technical team was required to give evidence on the technical work they had undertaken. New regulations governing the maximum levels of nutrients in lake Te Waihora and associated rivers came into effect in 2015 and reflected many of the recommendations from the collaborative process that was informed by the Selwyn Waihora Project.

Case study #2: The Matrix of Good Management

Shortly after the Selwyn Waihora Project began (see Figure 8.2), agricultural industry groups operating in Canterbury expressed concern about the quality of the information on nutrient losses from farming operations that was being used in the development of nutrient management policy. The same concern was raised by the committee in the Selwyn Waihora Project. The term "good management practice" (GMP) in relation to agriculture had begun to be used in national and regional documents (e.g., CMF 2009; LAWF 2010), but there was neither a nationally agreed definition of what constituted on-farm GMP nor a credible assessment of the nutrient losses associated with farms using GMP.

These concerns gave rise to the second project analyzed in this chapter, which became known as the Matrix of Good Management, or MGM Project. It was a collaboration between six primary sector organizations (Foundation for Arable Research, HorticultureNZ, Beef and Lamb NZ, Deer Industry NZ, Dairy NZ and NZPork), three Crown Research Institutes (Plant and Food Research, AgResearch, Landcare Research) and Environment Canterbury.

The purpose of the MGM Project was to define industry-agreed GMP and to estimate the nutrient loss from farms using GMP. The project took a co-design and co-production approach, which was intended to increase the relevance, credibility and legitimacy of both the agreed GMP definitions and the nutrient loss estimates; increase trust between the primary sector industries and Environment Canterbury; and foster a sense of project ownership (Cash et al. 2003). The choice of approach was also a practical response because there was no recipe for a project like this; political, technical and policy challenges

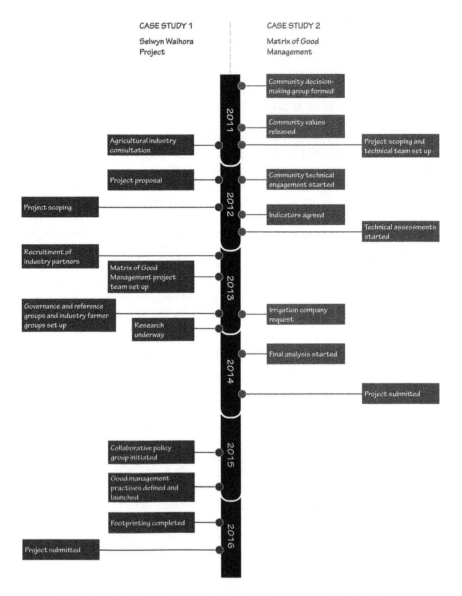

Figure 8.2 Selwyn Waihora and Matrix of Good Management project timelines.

emerged over the course of the project, and, crucially, there were no unequivocally right answers to the project's goals of defining and modelling GMP (Robson et al. 2015, pp. 5–9).

A number of groups were formed during the project to ensure effective governance and delivery, including a pan-stakeholder governance group, farmer reference groups and an industry, council and research operational group, called the

MGM Project team. The MGM Project case study focuses on the work of the MGM Project team. The project took approximately two-and-a-half years to complete – significantly less than the four years originally proposed. The reason for the curtailing of time was to take advantage of the limited appeal rights under the Environment Canterbury Act of 2010. However, due in part to the limited time allowed for the project, the approach taken did not produce complete consensus on all the project decisions (Robson et al. 2015, p. 9).

The methodology and information generated by the MGM Project were picked up and used in policy and subsequent statutory resource management processes between 2016 and 2017, with project team members required to give evidence on the technical work they had undertaken.

The integration and implementation sciences framework

The integration and implementation sciences (i2S) framework has been proposed as a way of improving the methodological soundness of transdisciplinary research (Bammer 2013). The framework is structured around three domains – synthesizing science and stakeholder knowledge, understanding and managing unknowns and supporting policy and practice change – and poses five questions for each domain (summarized in Figure 8.3). The framework provides a systematic way to document and reflect on transdisciplinary research. Accordingly, examination through the i2S framework can help identify weaknesses or failures in such projects. Specifically, the three i2S domains and five questions were found to be useful for identifying the root causes of failures in the two projects, and for moving beyond a superficial – and potentially misleading – diagnosis.

The failures are presented in the following sections as six days in the week of a transdisciplinary researcher. The failures for each day are described and then diagnosed using the i2S framework; lessons for future transdisciplinary projects are subsequently based on these analyses.

Monday's failure: Forgot research's place

The role of the Selwyn Waihora Project technical team was to develop science to inform – not lead – the policy-making process (Robson-Williams et al. 2018). This was a significant change for many members of the team, who were familiar with operating in an environment where science drove policy development. Moreover, the community-led collaborative process meant that the technical team needed to produce knowledge that was credible, salient and legitimate (after Cash et al. 2003), not just to scientists and policy makers but also to the committee representing the community.

Eager to reflect this new approach, the technical team used the community's environmental, social, economic and cultural aspirations to shape the project. An example of a community aspiration was that lake Te Waihora be "healthy." The work of the technical team was then to inform discussion about the trade-offs with other community aspirations, such as "healthy communities," associated with achieving such an outcome. To do this required more detail on what was

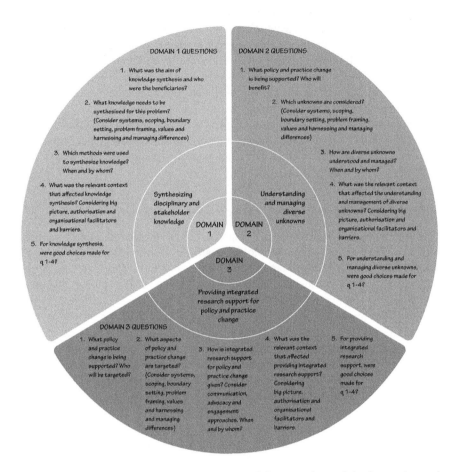

Figure 8.3 A summary of the three domains and five questions of the integration and implementation sciences (i2S) framework.

meant by, for example, a "healthy lake." It also required some specific, measurable, modellable and agreed-to indicators that would reflect progress towards the outcomes the community aspired to.

Determined to avoid a science-led policy-making process, the technical team asked the committee to provide descriptions (narratives) of the desired future state as a way of embedding the community values and knowledge in the technical work. For example, part of the committee's narrative relating to a healthy lake referred to the water being of a certain (albeit unspecified) clarity that had been experienced by an ancestor of one of the rūnanga members. The technical team adopted these narratives somewhat uncritically and sought to identify a suite of measurable indicators that could be used to determine whether the committee's narrative descriptions – and, by extension, the aspirations of the community – could be delivered and with what trade-offs.

A week of a transdisciplinary researcher   137

The reasons this proved to be problematic can be illustrated by examining the "healthy lake" aspiration and the associated "clear lake water" narrative. Due to the shallowness of the lake and the windy nature of the region, even in pre-agricultural times, the lake would have been prone to turbidity, with sediment from the lake bottom re-suspended in the water by wind action. While it was generally accepted that the accumulation in the lake of excess nutrients from agricultural intensification around the lake margins in recent years had made matters worse, it was very difficult to establish a historical benchmark of water clarity and, furthermore, to judge what depth of clarity is now acceptable. How clear was clear enough to meet the community aspiration of a healthy lake, and over what time period should the improvement in water clarity be achieved?

Had the technical team engaged more critically with the committee on the development of the narratives intended to describe the community's aspirations, it is likely that a more robust and appropriate description of what constituted a healthy lake might have been identified. Rather than adopting water clarity as an indicator of health, a number of other metrics – such as lake biodiversity or the absence of nutrients above certain thresholds – might have taken precedence. Instead, with good intentions, the technical team adopted the committee's narratives and was then faced with the need to make value judgements to assess when these indicators reached acceptable standards. Put another way, while the aspirations for the Selwyn Waihora water catchment were set by the community, the technical team ended up having to make judgement calls on the best indicators and whether results met the aspirations.

Diagnosis

Using the i2S framework, we are able to diagnose a failure of managing values on Monday. The values held by the technical team caused them to privilege community knowledge over scientific knowledge at this stage in the research. This was because the technical team's values were strongly influenced by the project's context: the historical privileging of scientific knowledge in New Zealand's environmental policy-making. These two factors led the technical team to uncritically accept the narratives from the committee. We consider there was a failure to recognize the impact of the values of the technical team (Domain1, Q3 – see Figure 8.3) and this policy-making context and (Domain 1, Q4) on the way that different sources of knowledge were synthesized. If the technical team had reflected more objectively on their keenness to avoid some of the past pitfalls of science-led policy-making, they may have been more willing to constructively challenge the committee and co-create better indicators for the community's aspirations.

Lessons

The overarching lesson learned from Monday's failures was that acute awareness of context – in this case, the historical privileging of scientific knowledge in New Zealand's environmental policy-making – can per se influence what is in or out of scope for a project in a deleterious way. Superficially, this may seem counter-intuitive. Surely it is not possible to pay too much attention to the context of a transdisciplinary project? In this case study, however, the technical team over-compensated for the historical context by disproportionately privileging the per-spectives of the community in the early stages of the research. The missing factor here was to pay explicit attention to the role of different knowledge sources in the project. Instead, mindful of the context, the Selwyn Waihora Project technical team were reticent about questioning the committee's narratives for water quality from a scientific perspective, to the detriment of the overall project.

Tuesday's failure: Just wanted a face

The MGM Project appeared to be ripe for collaboration among Environment Canterbury, farming organizations and a number of research organizations. Environment Canterbury was in urgent need of a definition of "good management practice" in relation to on-farm management practices and an estimate of how much of these nutrients might leave the farm and pollute freshwater resources. Meanwhile, the farming community was anxious for Environment Canterbury's nutrient management policy, in response to new national legislation, to be based on the best possible information. Here was a shared problem, and due to the nature of the problem, a co-development approach was used, and consensus decision-making within the MGM Project was the agreed modus operandi. Moreover, the council hoped to build credibility and legitimacy among farmers and buy-in among those who would be involved in the future implementation of the Environment Canterbury policy by inviting industry groups to be part of the MGM Project team to generate science for policy. Industry groups and science were the "faces" that Environment Canterbury wanted to co-develop with.

However, as the project progressed in parallel with the development of Environment Canterbury's nutrient management policy, it became increasingly dif-ficult to reach a consensus within the MGM Project team on what constituted appro-priate science for policy. This was attributed to concerns regarding the way in which the project findings would be implemented in the policy. Consequently, some team members found themselves in the difficult position where their presence in the pro-ject was lending legitimacy to an overall policy approach they neither agreed with nor recognized as aligning with their organization's theories of change (Taplin and Clark 2012), which included using voluntary approaches to achieve GMP on farms, rather than Environment Canterbury's regulatory approach.

Following the completion of the project, several of the organizations that were part of the MGM Project team challenged its methodology and findings during the statutory process for Environment Canterbury's land and water management plan, thus reducing the overall legitimacy of the project.

Diagnosis

Tuesday's failures are in Domain 3 of the i2S framework. Domain 3, Q2, asks what efforts have been made to understand the system that is being targeted, and what efforts have been made to scope the ways the desired change could be accomplished. In this case, although Environment Canterbury had orchestrated a co-production process, its purpose in doing so was to produce science to support the production of policy for improving water quality and regulation of farm nutrient losses based on good management practice. The utility of a regulatory approach to managing farm nutrient losses for improved water quality was not universally acknowledged among the team members, and nor was it explicitly discussed, with the result that the "scoping of the ways that change could be achieved" was very limited.

In many ways the MGM Project was a genuine attempt at co-development of science for policy. Environment Canterbury wanted the right faces at the table, but they wanted them there to lend robustness, credibility and legitimacy to their policy approach, not to draw on the diverse expertise in the team on achieving on-farm change. This seems at odds with undertaking a transdisciplinary approach to the research. Critical aspects of the context surrounding the project were already decided or decided beyond the scope of the MGM Project (in the parallel policy development project), such as the farm-level, numeric, regulatory approach adopted. If the policy approach had been established before the MGM Project, it would likely have discouraged some industry involvement.

Lessons

There are two main lessons derived from Tuesday's failure. First, where projects have some predetermined, non-negotiable aspects (in this case, that information is intended for use in policy for regulation), those non-negotiable aspects need to be transparently discussed and their consequences explored. The second lesson is that agreeing on project outcomes is not enough. How the project expects to achieve those outcomes needs to be made explicit (for example by supporting regulatory or voluntary measures), and the approaches taken need to be accepted within the project team. The upshot of both of these lessons is that if the non-negotiable aspects are unacceptable for some, there may need to be a turnover of people within the project, and this should be addressed early.

Wednesday's failure: A product of pressure

During a sustained period of intense work for the Selwyn Waihora Project on modelling the flow of nutrients and water in the Selwyn Waihora catchment, a request was made by an irrigation company for a specific, absolute nutrient allocation. The company needed this information to support its marketing campaign, which sought to recruit farmers to buy irrigation shares. Faced with an already tight deadline to deliver the project, the technical team worked late into the night over the course of a week to meet this new, unanticipated but apparently reasonable request to provide a nutrient load allocation figure.

Within weeks it came to light that a simple transposition of numbers in that late-night calculation meant that the share offer had been issued with an allocation greater than was available. Environment Canterbury immediately went to the

140 *Robson-Williams, Small and Robson-Williams*

interested parties with the error. The irrigation company's share offer to farmers had to be re-issued, the credibility of the science from the project was diminished and stress levels for members of the technical team soared.

Diagnosis

A superficial analysis would suggest this was a straightforward error in the technical work of the project, and on one level that is unarguably the case. However, more context is needed to fully understand the issues surrounding Wednesday's failure, and in the context of the i2S framework, we diagnose a failure to stick to the research purpose and beneficiaries (Domain 1, Q1). In particular, as the technical team developed scenarios for trade-offs between different community aspirations for the Selwyn Waihora water catchment community, the committee agreed with the technical team that these should be understood on the basis of relative changes rather than absolutes. So, for example, a scenario of improved lake health resulting from reductions in nutrient losses from surrounding farms would be described in terms of a percentage improvement rather than an absolute value for a given indicator. This was the agreed approach due to the scale of the uncertainty of so many dimensions of the work. It was only towards the end of the project that the technical team needed to settle on absolute values for the policy process.

Wednesday's failure was not recognizing that the way unknowns were being managed in the midst of an emergent process was inconsistent with the timing of the request for absolute and final results. The project lost sight of the focus of the research, which was to support and inform policy-making, and diverted time and attention to service requests from one stakeholder group. This behaviour was consistent with the "service-oriented" nature of the team and, as identified in Monday's failure, an overly heightened responsiveness to context.

Lessons

The first lesson from Wednesday's failure is that it is important to maintain clarity of project purpose and project beneficiaries and to ensure that the project has the authorization and confidence to keep to the project boundaries. Disciplinary experts often rely on intuition and tacit knowledge acquired through years of experience to spot mistakes and system inconsistencies (after Schon 1983). In a transdisciplinary project, where data and information are produced across sources of knowledge, the intuition and tacit knowledge of individuals may be insufficient to detect errors and inconsistencies. Thus, the second lesson is, before time pressure mounts, design systems-level sense checks on the data and information being produced.

Thursday's failure: A boundary by Escher

The MGM Project always had issues with boundaries. Like the Escher picture with impossible staircases, the lines were clearly drawn, but they are not so simple to use.

At the beginning of the project the MGM Project team acquiesced to making a start without knowing the full policy approach that would be used to implement the project findings. There was a clear boundary set which stipulated that the project was about seeking scientific results to supported policy rather than policy development itself. However, as the MGM Project got underway, some members started to contest this boundary, arguing that "you can't do science to support policy development until you know exactly how the policy is going to be used." However, any discussion on altering project boundaries tended to be closed down by the project lead. Although this created tension in the project team, the work continued.

As the project progressed and the policy approach started to become clearer, concerns grew among some members of the MGM Project team about the level of uncertainty in some of the project results. This situation was exacerbated by the constrained time frame of the project, with less time available for extensive ground-truthing. Some team members found they were in an untenable position, being asked to support results they were concerned would be problematic for their farmers due to their high level of uncertainty. This issue made it increasingly difficult for the project team to achieve consensus on project decisions and resulted in a degree of marginalization of some concerns in order to get the project finished within the restricted timeline.

In the end, consensus was not achieved on two important outputs of the MGM Project: the details of the modelling of irrigation GMP, and fertilizer GMP. This reduced the legitimacy of the project results, and the eventual outcome was that these two aspects were litigated during the statutory process by some organizations that had been involved in the MGM Project team.

Diagnosis

Paradoxically, although the recurring issue was about boundaries, the failure was not predominantly a failure in boundary setting. We diagnose two failures on Thursday. First, there was a failure to understand and respond to the growing anxiety about acceptable levels of uncertainty as the policy context emerged. Although constrained by time frames, the project did not adequately manage the differences in the project partners' range of acceptable strategies for dealing with unknowns (Domain 2, Q3 and Q4). The second failure was related to boundary setting across all three domains (Domains 1, 2, 3, Q2); it was a failure to understand that the boundaries between science and policy are not hard and fast but are co-produced by the individuals and/or organizations who work on them (e.g., Wehrens 2014), and the relevant unknowns can change through a project as other contextual factors emerge.

Lessons

There are three lessons from Thursday's failures. The first is about "referred pain." In the MGM Project a problem repeatedly manifested as a boundary issue,

142 *Robson-Williams, Small and Robson-Williams*

and the project team dealt with the issue by clarifying the project boundary decision and getting increasingly senior people to confirm the boundary. Our diagnosis indicated that the failure was, in fact, referred from a problem elsewhere – one of managing uncertainty. Therefore, the first lesson is to consider that recurring issues in transdisciplinary projects may have their roots elsewhere.

The second lesson is that even if the boundary decisions have already been made, there still needs to be an open discussion to clarify the consequences of drawing the boundary in a certain place.

In Monday's failure we saw the Selwyn Waihora Project technical team being overly responsive to context or over-compensating for contextual factors. For the MGM Project team the response to context also provides insight, but in this case, it was a lack of response to changes in context that had an impact on the project. Lesson three is that if the context is emergent, then the project needs to design mechanisms to identify and then adapt to changes in the project context.

Friday's failure: Too loving and giving

The Selwyn Waihora Project technical team adopted a rigorous regime of getting as much information as possible into the public domain as quickly as they could. This was born out of a genuine intent to embrace their role of informing and not leading policy processes, and their willingness to open the "black box" of science. This was manifested in a gruelling programme of community engagement sessions, alongside publishing content on a dedicated website and providing the technical work at three levels of detail and complexity. Open communication was a cornerstone of the project, and the team believed that through this openness they were providing support for decision-makers and achieving transparency.

However, an unexpected criticism arose during the statutory process on Environment Canterbury's proposed plan. The criticism was that some interested parties (industries and environmental groups) had found it very hard to engage with the project (for reasons not specified) and perceived a lack of transparency in the process. This puzzled the team until a colleague involved in the process (but no longer working for the council) observed that in a similar process, the sheer quantity of information made available to them was analogous to an impenetrable thicket. In other words, the well-intentioned effort to be open did not result in transparency.

Diagnosis

The decision made by the project team to maximize openness paradoxically led to reduced transparency. The failure here was poor communication of the research findings (Domain 3, Q3), "making accurate information easy to access when needed is an important aspect of communication" (Bammer 2013). The large amount of information was not sufficiently translated and curated to be easily accessed and understood, and there was not anyone dedicated to that task.

Lessons

Data and information needs may be viewed differently by different groups. Therefore, it is important to identify the groups that have an interest in the project, their information needs based on their varying degrees of participation and the most appropriate means of communicating information to them in a meaningful and accessible way. It is also important to seek, and act on, feedback from those groups on the success or otherwise of the communication strategy (Mitchell et al. 2015).

Due to the project team's desire to be open about the work, the project communication strategy curated the project findings for maximum openness – but not for maximum comprehension. Curating project findings to maximize accessibility and, where communication is important, dedicating resources to this specific task are valuable lessons.

Saturday's failure: Worked too hard for a living

In both the Selwyn Waihora and the MGM projects, policy makers and stakeholders frequently expressed the need for minimal uncertainty in order to make decisions. This was not surprising given the high stakes of managing water quality. Both projects recognized the inevitability of uncertainty and to a degree understood the challenge before them. Nevertheless, the pressure to provide as much certainty as possible weighed heavily on scientists in both teams. This pressure was especially acute as both projects were conducted under high degrees of public visibility.

This pressure often found expression in one of two ways. Some would work exceedingly hard in pursuit of an often-undefined accuracy target, producing significant additional work to support project deliverables. Excellence was sometimes pursued at considerable personal expense, with scientists working well beyond reasonable hours and to the exclusion of other responsibilities such as family and other work. Other scientists, feeling acutely responsible for the uncertainty associated with their findings, would present these findings surrounded by so many caveats that non-experts would struggle to comprehend the significance of the results. A consequence of both of these tendencies was that the project leads shouldered much of the responsibility for managing and then communicating uncertainty. These conditions resulted in an unhelpful feedback loop, whereby the teams worked harder to produce more information to reduce and communicate uncertainties, which fed into Friday's failure of producing an overwhelming thicket of data, which reduced overall transparency and comprehensibility, driving calls for more certainty.

Diagnosis

Saturday's failures are located throughout Domain 2 of the i2S framework. While the overall intent of managing unknowns was relatively well defined, team members had different concerns and goals. The failure began with not clearly identifying those impacted by the approach to managing unknowns (Domain 2, Q1), not iteratively defining acceptable uncertainty for team members, and failing to adequately manage differences between the projects' stakeholders in terms of their tolerance of uncertainties and unknowns (Domain 2, Q2). These shortcomings were exacerbated by an imperfect response to imperfection by some team members who tried to tackle the issue of uncertainties and unknowns simply by working harder and producing more data (Domain 2, Q3).

Lessons

There are two lessons we can derive from Saturday's failure. The first lesson is that team members need to be explicit about what they want to achieve in the project and articulate the acceptable uncertainties: how good is good enough to achieve the project outcomes? The acknowledgement of the inevitability of unknowns (Bammer 2013, p. 68) is an approach to sharing the burden of uncertainty across the project team and stakeholders (Robson-Williams et al. 2018). Lesson two is that reflection and flexibility are important. What is considered good enough to deliver project outcomes may change over time, and projects need space for reflection and the ability to adapt in order to keep pace with those changes.

Summary

The chapter began with a description of a week in the life of a transdisciplinary researcher and the failures experienced in two related case studies. For each day, the failures were described and diagnosed, and lessons derived. To support a

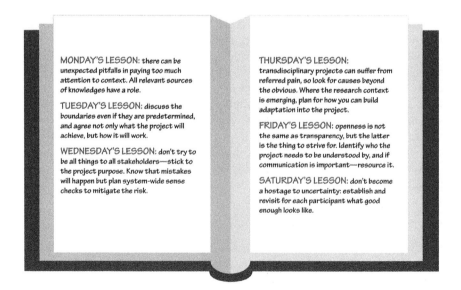

Figure 8.4 A week of salutary lessons for transdisciplinary researchers.

A week of a transdisciplinary researcher   145

healthy life for the transdisciplinary researcher, here is a week of salutary lessons (Figure 8.4).

In reality there are no perfect projects conceived on the seventh day. Despite the failures we have reflected on here, both the Selwyn Waihora Project and the MGM Project have contributed to the overall programme of managing water quality in Canterbury. However, in order to learn and increase both capability and capacity for undertaking transdisciplinary research, we need to be able to examine successes and learn from failures, as individuals and projects, and as a community of transdisciplinary researchers. Roux et al. (2010) called endeavours to build the practice of transdisciplinary research "experiments." However, we can only call them experiments if we actively learn from reflection. For this reflection, the i2S framework proved highly valuable as a means of identifying important lessons to be learned.

References

Bammer, G. 2013. *Disciplining interdisciplinarity: Integration and implementation sciences for researching complex real-world problems*. Canberra, Australia: ANU E Press. doi:10.22459/DI.01.2013.

Cash, D. W., Clark, W. C., Alcock, F., Dickson, N. M., Eckley, N., Guston, D. H., Jäger, J., Mitchell, R. B. 2003. Knowledge systems for sustainable development. *Proceedings of the National Academy of Sciences of the United States of America*, 100, 8086–8091.

CMF 2009. *Canterbury water management strategy: Strategic framework–November 2009 with updated targets, provisional July 2010*. Christchurch, NZ: Canterbury Mayoral Forum.

Environment Canterbury (Temporary Commissioners and Improved Water Management) Act 2010. Wellington, NZ: Ministry for the Environment.

Kirk, N. 2015. *Local government authority and autonomy in Canterbury's freshwater politics between 1989 and 2010*. Doctoral dissertation, Lincoln University.

Land and Water Forum (LAWF). 2010. *Report of the land and water forum: A fresh start for freshwater*. Wellington, NZ: Land and Water Forum.

Mauser, W., Klepper, G., Rice, M., Schmalzbauer, B. S., Hackmann, H., Leemans, R. Moore, H. 2013. Transdisciplinary global change research: The co-creation of knowledge for sustainability. *Current Opinion in Environmental Sustainability*, 5, 420–431.

Mitchell, C., Cordell, D., Fam, D. 2015. Beginning at the end: The outcome spaces framework to guide purposive transdisciplinary research. *Futures*, 65, 86–96.

Pohl, C., Hirsch Hadorn, G. 2008. Methodological challenges of transdisciplinary research. *Natures Sciences Sociétés* 16, 111–121.

Polk, M. 2014. Achieving the promise of transdisciplinarity: A critical exploration of the relationship between transdisciplinary research and societal problem solving. *Sustainability Science*, 9, 439–451.

Robson-Williams, M., Norton, N., Davie, T., Taylor, K., Kirk, N. 2018. The changing role of scientists in supporting collaborative land and water policy in Canterbury, New Zealand. *Case Studies in the Environment*, 2018, 1–5.

Robson, M.C., Brown H.E., Hume, E., Lilburne, L., Pinxterhuis, I.J.B., Snow, V.O., Williams, R.H., B+LNZ, DevelopmentMatters, DINZ, ECan, HortNZ, NZPork. 2015.

Overview report – Canterbury Matrix of Good Management Project. Christchurch, NZ: Environment Canterbury. Report No. R15/104.

Roux, D. J., Stirzaker, R. J., Breen, C. M., Lefroy, E. C., Cresswell, H. P. 2010. Framework for participative reflection on the accomplishment of transdisciplinary research programs. *Environmental Science and Policy*, 13, 733–741.

Schon, D. A. 1983. *The reflective practitioner: How professionals think in action*, London: Temple Smith.

Taplin, D., Clark, H. 2012. *Theory of change basics: A primer on theory of change*. New York: Acknowledge.

Weber, E. P., Memon, A., Painter, B. 2011. Science, society, and water resources in New Zealand: Recognizing and overcoming a societal impasse. *Journal of Environmental Policy and Planning*, 13, 49–69.

Wehrens, R. 2014. Beyond two communities – from research utilization and knowledge translation to co-production? *Public Health*, 128(6), 545–551. doi:10.1016/j.puhe.2014.02.004

Part III

Personal reflection on failed initiatives through an autoethnographic lens

9 Reframing failure and the Indigenous doctoral journey

Jason De Santolo (Garrwa and Barunggam)

Introduction

We all experience failure at some stage in our professional lives. One of my biggest experiences of "failure" occurred within the process of applying for a PhD in law. It took me years to work through the mixed emotions of not submitting the PhD application. The emotional impact of failure is something we tend to hold close to our hearts, especially in the context of academia where perceptions can influence the way we are received. To overcome this setback, I was forced to reflect on my perceptions of failure in an academy where knowledge frameworks are predominantly disciplined and subject to colonial logic (Behrendt 2019). This moment of reorientation would transform my doctoral concept into a creative and sensory knowledge-making journey back in my Gulf Country homelands in the Northern Territory of Australia. This chapter reflects on the emotional resonance of failure and champions' interrelatedness as a sensory Indigenous storywork principle for decolonizing creative Indigenous doctoral journeys in the academy (Archibald 2008).

Doctoral applications are complex, and there are added layers to this knowledge journey for Indigenous candidates. These layers of influence move beyond the usual realms of institutionalized education and into real-world knowledge systems and the everyday reality of living on unceded Country/homelands. As Indigenous scholars we must traverse the often hidden and always complex territory of knowledge and storytelling protocols. In my experience the personal commitment involved in this process carries with it significant teachings in themselves. Without personal and collective experiences, we would find it difficult to describe ways of understanding and the nature of being on Country. We are responsible to the knowledge journey we are on, in our own homelands and as visitors on other people's homelands. As I continue to learn and grow, I see more meaning in the processes and relationships than in the prescribed outcome. These are deeper conversations that I continue to have with my Elders Nancy McDinny and Stewart Hoosan and other senior knowledge holders for our clans. Cherished Elder storywork scholar Jo-ann Archibald has mentored me in the storywork space, where she describes the importance of preparation and "being prepared" as being "story

150   *Jason De Santolo (Garrwa and Barunggam)*

ready" (Archibald 2019). How do we become ready? This becoming is part of the constant cycle of earning respect, building trust and going through experiences in order to carry responsibility, to hold and then to learn and share Indigenous story and knowledge. Sharing knowledge down the generations is considered part of responsibility in community, and it is also considered part of the privilege of gaining a higher education. In the past few decades many of us have been activating doctoral pathways through the Indigenous research paradigm as a way to complement community responsibilities and cultural resurgences in our homelands (Wilson 2008). Indigenous doctoral applications are transdisciplinary in nature, for our knowledge systems are relational and cannot be constrained by outdated disciplinary boundaries. Conceptualization of the doctoral project often involves deep relational experiences with Elders, on Country, in Indigenous communities where meaning is made (Smith 1999; Behrendt 2019), where the land is everything (Hoosan 2014), where we seek united understanding in contested spaces (Van Leeuwen 2016, Gibbs 2018). There is much to learn from experiences of failure in the higher education realm as it is still a deeply contested institutional space. So why are Indigenous scholars so hesitant to write about these experiences of failure? Some of these reflections will help others negotiate the application process and offer some markers as they conceptualize meaningful new doctoral projects for new and emerging contexts.

So what happens when we fail to meet the mark, get rejected by the "faculty" or "university," or even worse we find the process so contested and emotional that we fail to reach the doctoral "submission" moment? Despite all the support in the world, there is also a critical personal responsibility to frame a doctoral project that is transformative for our communities, meaningful within the academy, and personally fulfilling. With 20 years as a researcher behind me, I can now see my moments of "failure" much more clearly as moments of empowered reorientation and transformation. On reflection, these challenging moments have occurred when I was not grounded in myself, when the work did not relate meaningfully to the world I aspire to live in, and when it was not transformative. There is a need to constantly check myself and re-orientate what I am trying to achieve in this privileged space of academia. This was what I was forced to undertake when I withdrew from a PhD in law application. Only now do I realize that this personal experience of failure was projected into my professional life from a vastly different academic worldview and a limited understanding of the interrelated nature of our knowledge systems. Eualeyai and Gamilaroi scholar Larissa Behrendt understands this as a question of worldview and standpoint where Indigenous scholarship deeply challenges Western assertions of sovereignty and the Eurocentric notions of objectivity:

> Storytelling also plays a key role in our resilience as the world's oldest living culture and in our assertion of sovereignty and in the countering of colonial narratives, the colonial stories, which have spread across our lands. Reasserting our stories on our land is a way of reasserting ownership. This is an important role within the academy, in spaces that have been unwelcoming

The Indigenous doctoral journey 151

and alienating for Indigenous people and in disciplines that have privileged colonial perspectives over Indigenous ones.

(Behrendt 2019, p. 177)

One of the resonances of failure is this "unwelcoming" feeling, that instinct that the educational system we are operating in is not made for us or our knowledge systems. Of interest are other contexts which explore personal failure as a refusal of modern power in a narrative therapy context where "power relations engage people in the fashioning of their own lives and in the fabrication of their own identities according to norms that have been constructed through modern disciplines and disciplines of the self" (White 2002, p. 24). This power dynamic is an important dimension for Indigenous scholars and practitioners who are embarking on the first phase of the doctoral journey: the dreaded application. There are unique cultural, personal and political nuances within the Indigenous research paradigm, with all of our related historical power trajectories and cumulative lived experiences. How do we navigate these institutional complexities from within an Indigenous research paradigm? Moving through the process requires sensitivity, respect and fluidity and the enigmatic energy to thread them all together (Archibald 2008; Pihama 2015; Wilson 2008). For Indigenous support units, faculties and potential supervisors, these challenges continue to arise. For many educational institutions it marks new territory in the decolonial project and new exposure to the instrumental, fluid, and organic forces that Indigenous theories of transformation pose (Behrendt 2019; Pihama 2015).

In this chapter, I unpack the limitations of transdisciplinary collaboration from the standpoint of an Indigenous researcher with conflicted experiences of the doctoral application process. The paper may inspire the use of Indigenous storywork and creative methodologies as a way to reassert intellectual sovereignty beyond disciplinary silos, or what Behrendt describes as assertive self-determination (Behrendt 2019). Storywork as a decolonizing methodology helps us to reimagine doctoral projects as journeys that transcend disciplines, institutional limitations, and bias. Storywork also reveals emergent forms of scholarship like social semiotics where we are posing new decolonizing meaning-making projects through the Indigenous sensorium: "Storywork, a term coined by Professor Jo-ann Archibald, tells us that this is not a book of short stories but a book that works with story making and is as much about the principles of making stories to the art of telling stories and to the cultural understanding of making sense of stories" (Smith in Archibald et al. 2019). Sense-making is deeply tied to the experience of gaining knowledge in relational living environments through sovereign bodies, on sovereign lands. These are contexts that challenge systems thinking through decolonial theories and liberational methodologies that challenge and sit outside the Western canon.

I also place another marker for those of us in transdisciplinary studies who are exploring deep teaching experiences and collaborations within the critical climate justice space where "epistemological pluralism is the commitment to open and deliberative discussion and negotiation of disciplinary values and

152   *Jason De Santolo (Garrwa and Barunggam)*

knowledge perspectives" (Fam et al. 2018, p. 89). In particular, I reflect on the role of Indigenous storywork as an allied theory and decolonizing methodology for storying moments of failure into meaningful, transformational experiences. For now, I write with renewed vigour from here in a School of Design, where I am beginning to take on exciting new doctoral supervision roles. In writing this openly, I hope to shift that uneasy feeling of failure into something meaningful for me to share with others as a way to support that leap of faith into the Indigenous doctoral space.

The emotional resonance of failure

> *Our songlines show us all the way forward, they hold the key to protecting Country. Culture is stronger than contamination. Songlines before Treaty. Trees before Treaty. Land before Treaty. Water Before Treaty. Country before Treaty. Why would we want to Treaty with a govt that wants to destroy our Country. A Govt that lifted the moratorium on Fracking, a govt that tortures our young people.*

(Hoosan 2019)

In 2011, I had been studying and working in the Indigenous research space for ten years. I had taken my foundational studies in a treaty and Indigenous and international environmental law and applied it in a new creatively inspired direction. This was, in part, a response to the drastic situation of our people in Australia and in particular the draconian Northern Territory (NT) intervention laws that were oppressing Indigenous peoples in the Northern Territory. It seemed that the only way to transform these experiences was to be part of a creative resurgence and begin reimagining self-determination through our own cultural modalities. The shift also occurred as a reflection of my own decolonizing journey and my own transformations that were taking place as I connected more with my Garrwa homelands (in the South West Gulf of Carpentaria, NT), culture, language, and lived experience. In many ways I was experiencing deep shifts in thinking, and over time this began to resonate in my everyday lived experience as a form of emotional resonance.

In a way my work had become more practice-led research, but at that time I was still unsure of what that entailed, as the creative practice space was still specifically framed in academia (De Santolo and Ypinizar 2008). My gut feeling was saying this is important work – I was emotionally engaged, and people were engaging emotionally with the work I was doing. Despite this, the main recognition derived from using video and new media practices to disseminate the more distinct intellectual work of writing and researching. We were not shifting the old-fashioned entrenched perceptions of what was academic rigour. At that time, non-traditional outputs were always going to be the poorer cousin. With a young son growing up fast, I realized it was time to take heed of trusted colleagues – a doctorate would ensure a permanent job down the track. I was invited to apply for a PhD in law that was attached to a specifically funded project and an Indigenous

The Indigenous doctoral journey 153

scholarship. It would look prestigious and give me some contractual stability. Little did I know that this would not shape up to serve any of those needs.

Two things happened in the process that shook me up. First, it was harder now to find motivated meaning in the prescribed legal language of Western human rights frameworks (Cavino 2019; Behrendt 2019; De Santolo 2019). Things were not translating across, and while my Elders and family understood the broader rights issues, they were not excited about the Western legal paradigm since it held so much colonial baggage. It became apparent that this was not just about worldview or the fluid modalities of the Indigenous research paradigm. It was about the legal paradigm that I was trying so very hard to reform and change; it was about the language, terms and definitions I was using in order for my argument to have validity. This was a genuine moment of reorientation, and as Linda Tuhiwai Smith notes, these moments of reflection are rare and important for us as we grow to respond to the dynamic nature of the communities and knowledge systems we work in:

> What are the paradigms we are bringing to our understanding of the communities we describe? What are the forms of knowledge that we are using that begin to put language and terms and definitions around what we see and what we describe and how good is our language? … as a writer who struggles you know who struggles for words sometimes … because often I feel it is inadequate to describe something dynamic and deep and relational. And part of our journey is finding the language … to talk about what we can see, what we experience and what we feel.
>
> (Smith 2015)

The practice of researching and writing was simply not resonating with the family and with our belief systems. It held epistemological, ontological, and pedagogical implications at a time where Elders deeply wanted cultural revitalization to drive the protection of our homelands from extractive industries. The cosmological and spiritual dimensions of our creation stories were beginning to have more significance for me, and I was not comfortable in how my work was being framed and critiqued. This personal reaction was at odds with the machinations of the research culture in Australia, for "Indigenous storytelling is the counter-narrative of colonization" (Behrendt 2019, p. 183). By removing creative practice from my academic work, I had started to affect its relational dimensions. The storywork had returned to a centring around text and left little trace of what had excited me, the dynamic inter-relational storytelling that spoke of cultural resurgence, Country, and family. That was okay in the short term, but there was a momentous shift in my orientation, and I felt it in my heart, body, mind, and spirit. I began to ponder what had been so important in these teachings with Elders and being on Country.

It was certainly something deeper than what I could immediately render into text. I was searching for a language that was more emotional, sensory, and inter-relational. What emerged was a greater awareness of the importance for our

154   *Jason De Santolo (Garrwa and Barunggam)*

people of the artistic, creative dimensions of shared knowledge practices. This knowledge translation space was demanding greater recognition in an academy that was failing to articulate complex, deep, relational moments of understanding. If Indigenous people were to feel comfortable with our work in an era of contamination and climate crisis, we needed to reject the Cartesian divide. Indeed, this is reflected in emergent responses to climate justice such as in Randerson's meteorological art where she emphasizes: "In Indigenous cosmologies, the sense of interconnectedness 'discovered' in late modern meteorological science merely described what many cultures already sensed and encoded in social and environmental lore" (Randerson 2018, p. 2). Randerson highlights some fantastic transdisciplinary examples of projects that reach new audiences in profound new ways. Participatory art projects like *O-Tu-Kapua* explored internal senses and external weather through a shifted perspective from the clouds down, connecting children's life experiences with Māori-centred cosmologies. As an indication of situational depth, the research can be framed as a redistributor of knowledge for children "that reveals Indigenous, scientific, and children's weathers are never mutually exclusive," according to Randerson (Randerson 2018, p. 66). It is the dynamic, unseen and invisible influences that prickle and spark sensory responses that challenge our perceptions and understandings across different cultural paradigms and shifting ecological landscapes of meaning.

As I reflect more deeply now, I realize that it was my thinking that had significantly shifted towards a state of mind that was free from the invisible shackles of my Western legal training. With my spirit strengthened through cultural ways on Country, I had started healing that deep sense of loss. A sense of loss and disconnection that comes from being taken from family and a fractured sense of belonging. For others around me this was not a new thing; rather, it was one of the determining reasons why they continued to focus on doing things that were sourced outside of the academy and were therefore without the need for validation. For Victor Steffensen, this involved significant courage and a compassionate commitment to shared knowledge principles developed through a grassroots revitalization of traditional fire practices across the continent in a colonized context:

> There is a fine line when you are working with communities on the subject of traditional knowledge. There are cultural protocols and lores that need to be considered that come from the people and the landscape. Even in contemporary times these traditional lores and protocols must always be the foundation for progress. It is important to understand that natural lore never changes, unlike Western law, which changes all the time.
>
> (Steffensen 2019, p. 232)

The uneasy feeling had stemmed from a crossroads – I was choosing to take a different pathway. A pathway where I would commit my energy and spirit to things that were important in a reform context (e.g., systemic and iterative self-determination) but not directly seen as a personal responsibility by my Elders and family.

The Indigenous doctoral journey   155

Secondly, I received very negative feedback on my application by a law school that did not have the necessary Indigenous law or lore expertise. The law school was bound by its own hegemony, driven by its own colonial fantasy and constrained by its own extractive logic. The response to the application was part of an imposed systemic ecology where "success or failure of these processes remains to be seen, and for many Indigenous people evaluation will rest on the capacity of state and territory governments to genuinely recognize Indigenous self-determination" (Maddison 2019, p. 25). The Western legal tradition has always been threatened by framings of authority and self-determination that are sourced well beyond what Western law could see or feel or relate to, for the Indigenous jurisdiction (e.g., visual sovereignty) is in constant flux and sits beyond the reach of the Western legal paradigm, beyond mere definition (Raheja 2010). At the time, of course, it hit me more like a rejection, a failure to meet the agreed standards of academic rigour. But now I know this reaction was formed in part from my legal training as conditioning, and the weakening of my standpoint as a Garrwa man, a member of a nation with its own sources of validation and ontological creational practices of law/lore.

Two points are emphasized here. We need to remain vigilant and not be complacent as we decolonize our training, as we decolonize the institutions we work in. There are important conditions to understand and unpack when we attempt to make meaning in disciplined silos such as law. First, what cannot be seen or heard cannot be acknowledged or understood without significant paradigm shifts, shifts that require deeper engagement than previously experienced. Esteemed Māori lawyer and activist Moana Jackson has articulated this in his work on Māori constitutional transformation, which is quite distinct in intent and form from limited self-determination propositions in constitutional recognition or voice-to-parliament models in Australia. Jackson helped lead a robust independent Māori-led national consultation report *Matike Mai* which emphasizes: "For the constitutional imperative is to work towards a new constitutional order that is based on Te Tiriti rather than one which merely tries to assimilate it into the existing Westminster system" (Matike Mai 2016, p. 102). For Jackson, transformation is held up as a dynamic model that ties in with broader and much more ancient Māori conceptualizations of authority, expressions of power and dynamic living jurisprudence as guided by Tino Rangatiratanga, Mana Motuhake and other broader international rights concepts. Margaret Mutu also led this constitutional transformation moment, which exposed the limitations of domestic nation-state legal systems. What becomes clear is that there is very little sovereign stability for colonizing nation-states when viewed from an international historical rights trajectory:

> Governments then instigated the "treaty claims settlement" process to extinguish all Māori claims, remove Māori rights and entrench colonisation. Research undertaken has shown that Māori loathe this process and do not accept that settlements are full and final. Research on constitutional transformation has identified a possible solution. The first step towards that goal

156 *Jason De Santolo (Garrwa and Barunggam)*

involves implementing the United Nations Declaration on the Rights of Indigenous Peoples.

(Mutu 2019)

There are very clear overlapping inquiries and strategies here with the push by the Victoria and Northern Territory governments for treaties in their jurisdictions. This is happening at a time when Australian First Nations have significantly limited negotiating power, and this calls into question the motives behind efforts to reach a full and final settlement. It seems like a common-sense strategy to hold various Australian governments to account first in their obligations to uphold Indigenous rights as reflected in the United Nations Declaration on the Rights of Indigenous Peoples 2007 (UNDRIP 2007). Jackson errs on the side of caution in these ongoing discussions:

> There is promise and peril in the treaty process, and history shows the governments are not very good at honouring treaties with Indigenous people. The great Native American leader Sitting Bull once said in the late 19th century the United States government has signed hundreds of treaties with Indigenous peoples and the only thing they have in common is they have broken every one.
>
> (Jackson 2018)

In Australia treaty making is still a beacon of hope for many. But for some Indigenous researchers these government-led treaty processes are revealed in a new light, especially in the context of treaty discussions that will cede sovereignty and encapsulate the full and final settlement in detail. We are strategically stronger when we articulate our rights, demands and conceptualizations from both our own cultural land-based paradigms of authority and power and broader Indigenous rights at international levels of influence. At one level this involves our own questioning of why we are doing this research, what language we are using, what shared meaning-making experiences we are creating and how is this work dynamic and related to the communities we are working with (Smith 1999).

Secondly, how do we legitimately assert our own unique tribal cultural rights paradigms in colonial projects? Through growing engagement with Indigenous storywork in Australia, we see reassertions of "Indigenous story as law" (Behrendt 2019) where "lore comes from the land and unlike Western law it never changes" (Steffensen 2019). In creative fields of study (in particular, Indigenous film and design studies), I believe we can assert our cultural rights through a Two Laws (1981) meaning-making framework. In my tribal context we are incredibly mindful of how these legal systems affect us and our ability to live healthy, unfettered lives on healthy lands in the context of living under two laws. We are in a dynamic rights movement that stories our experiences through our own standpoints, through our own lineage of resurgence and the voices of Elders and the rightful guardians of the land (Two Laws 1981; Warburdar Bununu 2019). Through our own storywork methodology, Yarnbar Jungkurr (De Santolo 2018),

The Indigenous doctoral journey   157

we are continuing to find meaning in our own conceptualizations of authority and self-determination as exemplified in the statement (quoted above) by one of our leaders and brother Gadrian Hoosan: "Songlines before treaty." As a story-based communication strategy, we see its effectiveness take shape in spaces where our assertions are seen, heard, and felt. These significant alignments bolster understandings of our right to self-determination in a way that is expressive and creative, and as such can strategically inform broader political and social campaigns.

Global campaigns like the student-led climate strikes of 2019 are also critiquing the Western systems of power and control over land and resources. After months of consultation and solidarity work, Indigenous speakers were appointed as leaders of the climate strike on Gadigal lands. Aunty Rhonda Grovenor Dixon and Nadeena Dixon welcomed 80,000 people to their Gadigal lands through their Gadigal protocol. Gadrian Hoosan followed, framing his speech as a moment of unity for a #ClimateJusticeFamily that challenges both government and extractive industries in their failure to look after the environment. Hoosan asserted our own understanding and canons of law that emerge from our homelands. The Two Laws worldview sits alongside and surrounds more recent Western legal constructs of native title and land rights through the everyday ancient practices of talk, story, song, dance and art. The ethical implications of these moments can provide markers for ongoing legal reform and community development (Burrows 2019).

What I experienced in the process of applying for a PhD in law is really a fraction of what others have experienced historically in the colonization of our lands through war, and within the academy's ongoing research culture as framed by disciplines and faculties. As I write this chapter, I wonder if this experience translates into a meaningful reflection for others? Steffensen sees this assimilationist approach (2019) as also a violation of ancient knowledge-sharing principles:

> This form of colonization is happening to our knowledge today, which continues to be dispossessed, separated, and made dependent on Western management and leadership. The good will of Aboriginal people trying to repair their knowledge and country through shared knowledge is violated. It is not only Aboriginal people who need to decolonize but non-Aboriginal people as well. Non-Indigenous people will never learn from Indigenous knowledge systems and landscapes if they do not decolonize from control and power.
>
> (Steffenson 2019, p. 233)

Decolonization is a deeply personal journey as well as systemic intervention; there is a lineage and whole corpora of knowledge that align with this as liberation movements, as Indigenous theories of transformation (Pihama 2015).

I acknowledge that I wouldn't be here in academia without all of those strong Elders and Indigenous scholars who have created and held this space for us to move into/through. For me, the experience solidified my resolve to continue to decolonize my research practice, and in order to do that I would maintain my passion for creative methodologies and storywork. This shift harnessed my creative potential and revealed alignments in other fields such as Indigenous cinema,

158   *Jason De Santolo (Garrwa and Barunggam)*

video art and design activism. Drawing out these values in practice was not hard at a personal level as it marked an important shift in my conceptual understanding of the intent behind my work and the ways I could act on it in a research context. This shift allowed me to move from a place of rejection into a place of meaningful transformation, of self-determining intent. I chose to free myself of this tension by valuing my own specific cultural paradigm as part of my own practice-led research that is deeply tied to our homeland resurgence.

Even today I feel strongly that we do not need to be overly anxious about Western-based intellectual critiques as long as we hold and respond with rigour through our own pursuits and carry our own knowledge journeys with a clear, compassionate heart; an open mind; a strong body; and with good spirit (Archibald 2008). Even if this is perceived as naïve, I am committed to moving forward with compassion at the very least, for it respects emotional responses and validates the relational nature of the work we do in the Indigenous research paradigm.

Compassionate action within the Indigenous research paradigm

> *Decolonizing research methodologies do not totally dismiss Western methodological approaches; they encourage us as Indigenous researchers to connect research to our own worldview and to theorise based on our own cultural notions in order to engage in more meaningful and useful research for our people.*
>
> *(*Archibald et al. 2019, p. 6)

I often find when first people spend time with our Elders, they come away feeling really good and empowered. Elders have that ability to hold compassion and see the best in people and are able to often bring the best out in us all. For example, there were plenty of tears in the audience when Elders spoke on a panel at the Institute for Sustainable Futures at UTS. Having emotional responses to our work is a recognition of its potency in today's climate. When I was offered a job in the School of Design at UTS, it was the Elders that I went to first. Moving into a mainstream faculty was a big thing for me after working within Indigenous research centres for so many years. Having their support and blessing meant I was not going into this space on my own; the responsibility was shared, and I could feel it was the right move. This is part of how I view compassionate action: in the Indigenous world we support each other because we are respectfully connected to each other and because responsibility is guided by wisdom when it comes to knowledge.

Much like taking on a new job, to consider the PhD venture is a big thing. It takes three to eight years to complete a PhD. It takes huge amounts of personal energy and commitment to develop a substantial and original research proposal with all the required rigour. In terms of preparing for the knowledge journey, there are significant demands on you as an individual. This is despite the fact that as Indigenous scholars and researchers, we work in shared knowledge realms where collective responsibilities often guide and hold us in dynamic teaching and

The Indigenous doctoral journey   159

learning spaces. So from the outset, we are navigating complexities in scope and the application of stories, practices and knowledge paradigms. Our own Elders and knowledge holders are guides for us here as they hold us compassionately in a space that is contested and historically problematic. What is exceptional here is the ability of Elders (and Indigenous knowledge holders/practitioners) to synergize relationality to the core knowledge principles that are being forged in the doctoral space.

Supporting doctoral applications of this nature is highly challenging for higher education institutions. Indigenous support units have to deal with disciplinary borders that are entrenched in systems and categories that emerge from outdated modes of thinking (Page, Trugett and Andrews 2019). As a university, UTS is a world leader in developing Indigenous education and research. Many of us have grown and benefitted from Larissa Behrendt's research leadership, which has created space for transformative work. Susan Page, Michelle Trugett and Gawaian Bodkin Andrews have worked to roll out a multifaceted cross-campus Indigenous Graduate Attribute strategy. In particular, I have found the greatest potential for meaningful collaboration through personal resonance in working in the creative arts, transdisciplinary studies, and design activism fields. Collaboration takes on greater meaning when people work from a place of solidarity and compassion. There is a sense that our actions are driven by a deeper mission that translates beyond the institution, beyond the life of the project.

If we are committed to holding compassionate actions within the Indigenous research paradigm, then cultural conceptualization of the research concept is a fundamentally important aspect of this in transdisciplinary contexts. In my practice-led research, I have attempted to link "the importance of seeking to harmonize knowledge pathways with localized lores, protocols and big-picture principles for research media" (De Santolo 2015, p. 16). We are literally writing and researching about lived experiences of individuals, families, clans, tribes, and nations living in fourth world conditions. From this super-privileged position, I know that there must be deep emotional engagement and compassion if this work is to be meaningful for our families, clans, tribes and nations in community. Compassion helps in daily meditation and is fuel for deeper meaningful interactions in life when we are surrounded by the social and environmental crisis of colonization: "Compassion is one way to feel the Earth's pedagogy, a songline logic, a form of relational, emotional resonance" (De Santolo 2019).

Compassionate actions help us to manifest wisdom, spirit and the unseen forces that interact and drive life cycles and natural systems of law/lore. So how do we weave this into meaningful research studies that earn trust and gather respect for this responsibility of holding and sharing Indigenous story and knowledge? Esteemed Indigenous scholar Jo-ann Archibald embodies this in her work as a highly respected Elder in this space, describing this so eloquently though the idea of being "story ready," or ready for the ceremony of knowledge-sharing (Archibald 2019). This is very much part of the doctoral journey I ended up taking after failing to submit my law application. Meeting and yarning and working with Jo-ann Archibald has had such a profound impact on my research practice and

160 *Jason De Santolo (Garrwa and Barunggam)*

decolonizing research approach. As an Elder scholar her compassionate teaching and sharing of her transformative experiences helped me hold courage and centre our own ways of meaning-making, for: "To get away from this 'new act of colonization,' I had to read and hear the voices of First Nations/Indigenous peoples and find the theories embedded in their stories" (Archibald 2008, p. 16).

In subverting the hegemony of Western rights frameworks, storywork methodologies form a transformative praxis where talking emerges into culturally centred action. In some of my doctoral work the resurgence of storying offered a meaningful and open challenge to the norms of Western jurisprudence (De Santolo 2018). In my doctoral study we created two key videos, *Ngabaya* and *Darrbarrwarra*, as Garrwa and Yanyuwa expressions of Indigenous self-determination in the Gulf Country that transcends the Australian state's sphere of influence. The song videos continue to evoke authority and legitimacy via a profound creational mandate to protect Country for all future generations and living beings. In this way the dynamic song dance compositions spark new discourses that renew emotional engagement. It is this emotional resonance that activates meaning-making kinetic expressions of visual sovereignty within the videos and through the inter-relational dimensions of the Yarnbar Jungkurr as a Garrwa storywork methodology (De Santolo 2018).

Making sense of failure

The failure to submit a PhD in law has offered a great moment for me to reflect on the here and now, where I work in a School of Design leading the Indigenous Design Synergies (IDS) ecology. By "ecology" I mean fluid and organic, where IDS and the Indigenous Action Strategy that we are developing offer deeper engagement points for our Indigenous students, communities and communities of practice (i.e., our cohort of creative scholars, design activists and professionals). These rare reflexive moments help to activate meeting points across teaching innovation, meaningful working conditions and transformational research. In the longer term there is huge potential to forge new insights and set new directions for knowledge-making with new materials and new ways of iterative design thinking that are free of colonial logic. Undeniably, looking back (at this moment of failure) has provoked some huge shifts in my perception of self, for to realize my failure was framed by a systemic disciplined power of both the knowledge institution that I was "submitting" to and the self as Indigenous scholar.

Storywork methodologies offer intimate and inter-relational ways to engage with Indigenous knowledges, practices and sensory meaning-making (Wilson 2008; Smith 2019; Paris and Alim 2017, p. 213). It is through the principle of interrelatedness that we begin to see emotional resonances across Country, story and dynamic characters. Shared knowledge principles are deeply tied to kinship systems and aspects of relationality that tie in with story as law/lore. There is such a resonant beauty and strength in our storywork characters as living and eternal creator beings, humans and other entities. It is this sense of unfolding, of dynamic emergence, that has shaped the reframing of failure for me. Within

The Indigenous doctoral journey 161

this reorientation there was strong reconnection with the decolonizing notion that meaning can only be made within the community and not in institutions alone. The sources and practices that drive the meaning-making endeavour are profound in nature, not because we are dealing with secret, sacred material but because paying tribute to our own cultural knowledge journeys means we are healing both the land and the people (Steffensen 2019). But do we have to fail in order to shift personal perceptions, to re-orientate back to the source, to reestablish inter-relational dimensions in our doctoral research journeys? The quick answer is no.

So what are some of the ways we can slow down, re-orientate and connect with the unfolding world around us? There are intersectional dimensions to the Indigenous research paradigm; there are practice-led insights and new material cultures that we can draw upon as we reimagine self-determination and rebuild Indigenous societies. There are justice-driven pedagogical shifts that are taking place for our youth and new cohorts of people as they move into cultural-sustaining futures (Paris and Alim 2017). There is deep solidarity work being done in the climate justice space, in the rise of the Fire Sticks Alliance as a force for land management, and in the emergence of profound literary projects like Fire Country that share knowledge as experience and action (Steffensen 2020). For so many of us our Elders are the real guides for us as we journey through Country and knowledge and practices of renewal. We make meaning through actions, practices and being in the living world which is so richly described here by Elder scholar Rosalie Little Thunder:

> The value and discipline of slowness and deliberateness, where to go slowly means to go with care, perception, and discipline, where to go slowly encourages reflection, deliberation, and pause, in turn nurturing skills of critical thought, intuition, insight, and vision, which develop leadership and wisdom; deliberation cycles back into relationship, where to go slow and be thoughtful again encourages perception that looks more closely at the unfolding world; this is a practice very much embodied by Elders, a value that younger generations learn to understand by spending time watching how Elders approach doing.
>
> (Rosalie Little Thunder, quoted in Paris and Alim 2017, p. 213)

For so many of us, living on our homelands is far from easy. The vast majority of us in Australia live in cities and urban contexts. We must continue to hold fast and emphasize the importance of our own methodologies, our own stories, our own research agendas. The principle of interrelatedness offers so many of us the potential for relational collaboration in transdisciplinary contexts and in particular in Indigenous-led projects. The Institute for Sustainable Futures here at UTS champions this work in the areas of sustainability and contamination through deep, long-term collaboration with the Jumbunna Institute and the School of Design. For Jenny Lee-Morgan, a compassionate heart holds true to the idea that relationships are core to Purakau as a Māori-centred storywork methodology:

162   *Jason De Santolo (Garrwa and Barunggam)*

To this end, *purakau* methodology without strong relationships (to the kaupapa and the communities to which the *purakau* belong) and good heart may render the research fruitless and simply ignored. Worse still, it may continue to perpetrate the colonizing approaches that put or stories and ourselves at risk.

(Lee-Morgan 2019)

If we fail to explore our limits, then we are also placing our future generations at risk. As future ancestors, it is our mandate to take responsibility to learn, share, innovate and create new directions in knowledge, according to the challenges we face in the present moment.

Conclusion

In writing this chapter openly, I have shifted that uneasy feeling of failure into an experience that is transformative and meaningful for me. The doctoral journey I entered into was magnificently challenging, to say the least, but it was profoundly transformative for my family and my community. The failure to submit a law PhD application helped me to re-orientate my intent and actions back to the teachings of my ancestors and Elders.

We relate to each other's compassionate aspirations through our stories, actions, and inactions, and through the inter-relational modalities and sensory experiences that can follow in a dynamic world of education and research. As our children grow into this society they will begin to see and feel the impacts of the colonial project in much more profound ways through their educational experiences, especially in light of the climate crisis and social upheavals that are taking form. Looking back to make sense of failure is an important step in revealing our limitations as well as our abilities to challenge modern notions of institutional and disciplined power. We must all become story ready, so our children can be prepared for big planetary challenges. A return to Indigenous knowledge and leadership is key to our survival. As we witness the unfolding climate crisis, will society allow this to happen in time?

Storywork offers a point of connection and commitment and Indigenous ethics for transformative research practice, for "An Indigenous ethic of care is signalled in dadirri, a deep and attentive listening to the earth's biota, air, and winds and inward to ourselves" (Randerson 2018, p. 187). We must look inwards for a sensory understanding of the importance and role of Indigenous knowledges and practices that will play a key role in shifting perceptions in the institutions we all work in. Transdisciplinary studies should align with assertions of Indigenous sovereignty as part of a commitment to epistemological pluralism in an era of climate crisis (Fam et al. 2018, p. 89). As Steffensen sharply reminds us

The important thing about this is that looking after the country never stops. Managing the country with fire, for one, has to go on forever. Once the country is healthy, then we need to maintain it otherwise we end up back in our current circumstances.

(Steffenson 2019, p. 232)

By doing a creative doctorate I was able to engage with the vibrancy of Garrwa ontologies and epistemologies through talking and storying, through Yarnbar Jarngkurr. In this way the journey held the Ngabaya walaba (public songline) in a place of reverence for the relational nature of research is part of the ceremony of knowledge exchange (Wilson 2008; De Santolo 2018). I have validated a much more important meaning-making experience through the reframing of a historically projected moment of failure. I hope this inspires others to forge a creative doctoral knowledge journey through wise actions and with liberational intent to harmonize heart, mind, body and spirit.

Take-home messages

- Colonization has projected failure as a paradigm into Indigenous worlds and educational contexts.
- Reframing failure is an essential part of the decolonial project in academia.
- Indigenous theories and methodologies can contribute to greater Indigenous-led outcomes in transdisciplinary studies.

References

Archibald, J.A. 2008. *Indigenous storywork: Educating the heart, mind, body and spirit.* Vancouver, Canada: UBC Press.

Archibald, J. 2019. *Indigenous storytelling traditions: Performance, pedagogy, and research, congress 2019.* Vancouver, Canada: University of British Columbia.

Behrendt, L. 2019. Indigenous storytelling, decolonizing institutions and assertive self determination – implications for legal practice. *In:* J. Archibald, J. Lee-Morgan and J. De Santolo, eds. *Decolonising research, indigenous storywork as decolonizing research methodology,* London: Zed Books, 175–186.

Burrows, J. 2019. *Law's indigenous ethics.* Toronto: University of Toronto Press.

De Santolo, J., Ypinazar, J. 2008. Just push play: Where research meets video, online. *The Australian Journal of Indigenous Education,* 37(1), 73–80.

De Santolo, J. 2015. Conceptualising research and consultation within a creative doctorate. In: *International indigenous development research conference proceedings,* Nga Pae o Maramatanga, University of Auckland, Auckland, NZ.

De Santolo, J. 2018. Shielding Indigenous worlds from extraction and the transformative potential of collaborative research. *In:* D. Fam, L. Neuhauser and P. Gibbs, eds. *Transdisciplinary theory, practice and education: The art of collaborative research and collective learning.* London: Springer, 175–186.

De Santolo, J. 2019. A reflection on compassion. *In:* M. Özbilgin, F. Bartels-Ellis and P. Gibbs, eds. *Global diversity management, a fusion of ideas, stories and practice.* London: Springer.

Gibbs, P. 2018. Philosophical reflections: A coda. *In:* D. Fam, L. Neuhauser and P. Gibbs, eds. *The art of collaborative research and collective learning: Transdisciplinary research, practice and education.* London: Springer.

Hoosan, G. 2014. Gadrian Hoosan: The land is the most important thing for Indigenous people. *The Guardian.* Available from: https://www.theguardian.com/commentisfre e/2014/oct/10/gadrian-hoosan-the-land-is-the-most-important-thing-for-indigenous -people [Accessed 10 October 2016].

164   *Jason De Santolo (Garrwa and Barunggam)*

Hoosan, G. 2019. Songlines before treaty. Speech to Climate Strike September 20, Indigenous Design Synergies, UTS. Available from: https://www.facebook.com/indigenousDS/videos/vl.2847545328597426/2377276225712622/?type=1 [Accessed 25 October 2019].

Jackson, M. 2018. *What can Australia learn about Indigenous rights from New Zealand?* Sydney: RN Drive, ABC Radio National.

Maddison, S. 2019. *Colonial fantasy: Why white Australia can't solve black problems.* Crows Nest, NSW: Allen & Unwin.

Mutu, M. 2019. 'To honour the treaty, we must first settle colonisation' (Moana Jackson 2015): the long road from colonial devastation to balance, peace and harmony. *Journal of the Royal Society of New Zealand*, 49(sup1), 4–18. doi: 10.1080/03036758.2019.1669670

Page, S., Trudgett, M., Bodkin-Andrews, G. 2019. Creating a degree-focused pedagogical framework to guide Indigenous graduate attribute curriculum development, *Higher Education*, 78(1), 1–15.

Paris, D., Alim, H.S. 2017. *Culturally sustaining pedagogies: Teaching and learning for justice in a changing world.* Columbia, SC: Teachers College Press.

Pihama, L. 2015. *Kaupapa Maori theory, transforming theory in Aotearoa.* Hamilton, NZ: Te Kotahi Reader, University of Waikato.

Raheja, M. 2010. *Reservation reelism: Redfacing, visual sovereignty, and representations of Native Americans in film.* Lincoln: University of Nebraska Press.

Randerson, J. 2018. *Weather as medium, toward a meteorological art.* Cambridge, MA: MIT Press.

Smith, L. 1999. *Decolonising methodologies.* London: Zed Books.

Smith, L. 2015. Heritage and Knowledge: Decolonizing the research process. *President's Dream Colloquium on Protecting Indigenous Cultural Heritage, Spring, Simon Fraser University.* https://www.sfu.ca/dean-gradstudies/events/dreamcolloquium/DreamColloquium-Indigenous/LindaTuhiwaiSmith.html [Accessed 10 September 2018].

Steffensen, V. 2019. Putting the people back into the country. *In:* J. Archibald, J. Lee-Morgan and J. De Santolo, eds. *Decolonising research, indigenous storywork as decolonizing research methodology.* London: Zed Books, 224–238.

Steffensen, V. 2020. *Fire country.* Sydney: Hardie Grant.

United Nations Declaration on the rights of Indigenous peoples (UNDRIP 2007), General Assembly. New York: United Nations. Available from: https://www.un.org/development/desa/indigenouspeoples/wp-content/uploads/sites/19/2018/11/UNDRIP_E_web.pdf. [Accessed 15 October 2019].

Van Leeuwen, T. 2016. A social semiotic theory of synesthesia? – a discussion paper, *Hermes* 55, 105–119.

White, M. 2002. Addressing personal failure. *International Journal of Narrative Therapy & Community Work*, 2002(3), 33–76.

Wilson, S. 2008. *Research is ceremony, Indigenous research methods.* Black Point, Nova Scotia, Canada: Fernwood Publishing.

10 Transdisciplinary research – challenges, excessive demands and a story of disquiet

Martina Ukowitz

Introduction

In our everyday working life, between managing existing projects and simultaneously planning new projects, teaching, writing papers and fulfilling administrative duties, the question of a project's success or failure is hardly ever discussed explicitly and in-depth. While continuous reflection on the research process and reflection-based decision-making regarding further steps are integral parts of projects, there is frequently too little time and commitment for an ex post reflection. Final project workshops might end with an open round of feedback on "How was it?," but this is mostly a collection of impressions and thoughts, and not an in-depth consideration of research processes in general and of the relationship between the processes and their outcomes in particular. In order to reflect upon failure, it is necessary to switch to a meta level and to have a closer look at what happens in everyday project life.

This contribution starts by taking stock of experiences in various interdisciplinary and transdisciplinary projects, and then discusses one transdisciplinary project, "Carinthia International," in more detail. Some information on the project and its design is provided, and four topics are then discussed, which – in retrospect – seem to have been crucial to the project's success: (1) mediating between individual interests and cooperative project development, (2) stability and dynamics within the social system of research, (3) incremental processes and a major breakthrough – who is pushing the development? and (4) success, failure and the importance of having staying power. The reflection starts from concrete scenes experienced in the project, integrates methodological considerations and finally leads to what can be called "lessons learned."

Taking stock

Looking back at the last nine to ten years of my interdisciplinary and transdisciplinary project work, and taking stock of results and impacts, evokes feelings of success as well as failure. My assessment touches upon different dimensions, the most important of which seem to be academic reputation, success in publishing, the attention of my colleagues and the impact of the scientific work on society.

166   *Martina Ukowitz*

Interestingly, the question of interdisciplinary cooperation among researchers within project teams came to light only during a second glance. Interdisciplinary cooperation is an ingredient which is necessary for managing projects successfully, but it is not sufficiently necessary to be a criterion for success itself. I would like to mention three projects I remember well. Obviously, they have left a significant impression and show that conducting transdisciplinary research sometimes involves being torn between "what counts" in academia and what one is satisfied with apart from that.

First, a project dealing with institutional dynamics in nature conservation comes to mind. This project was successful even before it started. It succeeded in a very competitive funding programme, which led recognition among colleagues and the university board. The project, which finished recently, addressed both scientific goals and the improvement of practices in nature conservation. Regarding the latter, there were no expectations from the funding institution's side, whereas the transdisciplinary attitude of the team focused seriously on this aspect. Furthermore, the results of the research were interesting, and they provided a solid basis for publishing a book as well as for preparing a journal contribution (Ukowitz und Pichler-Koban 2018). In addition, the topic "decision-making in nature protection" also gained attention from the media. There were items about the project on regional television and in the regional and national press. However, the impact in practice, at least so far, could be greater. That's why, in addition to the feeling of having done good work, there is the feeling of not having finished yet, of there being more to do. Further discussions of possible impacts of the research are still on the agenda with local politicians. The feeling of success is based on the fact that the project was approved, and that the results merited publication.

The second project that comes to mind could also be described as a successful one, but in a different way. It was a small transdisciplinary project in the broader context of regional development. It was financed by an association which develops health-promoting projects on small farms. This kind of third-party-financed research, which in my view is characteristic of transdisciplinary research constellations, does not prioritize publishing in A-journals and gaining grants in a competitive way. The feeling of success in this project derived mainly from the impact on the field of practice involved. The results of the research proved to be important for the further development of the initiative as a whole and, what was even more impressive, they led to a better understanding of the initiative within local communities. The very spontaneous feedback of an influential farmer at a workshop, who said, "Now I can see what the initiative wants to achieve, it is a good thing, you did a good job!," left us with the really good feeling of having contributed to a promising development. Publishing the results, on the other hand, is a little bit problematic because the main results concern organizational matters which need to be handled confidentially.

Thinking of a third project in the area of sustainable regional development – which is described in more detail below – provokes ambivalences and some sort of feeling of failure, too, since we did not succeed in achieving project objectives.

An initiative for further education, developed in a participatory way, could not be implemented in practice. Now, more than two years after the formal conclusion of the project, from time to time I still think of restarting the whole thing. It seems to be some sort of insult, not having success with an idea which still seems to be a good one. It leaves me with feelings of disquiet.

Research and development within "Carinthia International"

Against the background of increased emigration of young people from rural regions, which leads to a lack of skilled employees, and economic changes due to ongoing globalization, the interdisciplinary and transdisciplinary project "Carinthia International" raised the question of how to find new ways of mediating between the local, regional and global spheres. The topic was embedded in the question of sustainable regional development (the project was funded by a regional development programme), and the focus of the project was on small and medium-sized enterprises in the manufacturing industry in two regions in Carinthia. These manufacturing companies are important regional actors that are able to contribute to sustainable development. The starting hypothesis was that in a globalized world, regions, organizations and people generally act in the field of tension between the local and the global. Local dynamics have to be handled by focusing on local strengths, and at the same time, a high awareness of global processes is needed. This requires people to continuously switch between perspectives, which ideally lead to integrating "the best" of different worlds. "Carinthia International" started with the assumptions that an international attitude and international activities are crucial for sustainable (regional) development, and that at the same time this development implies new challenges for organizations and people.

Finding ways to foster internationality was a major concern of the enterprises involved in this project. The managers realized that, over time, a culture of internationality may develop by itself under the pressure of circumstances, but that proactive handling of internationalization and its consequences in enterprises would increase the opportunity for coherent development. At the same time, we should not mask the challenges that derive from thinking and acting between different societal spaces, described by Dieter Läpple as the micro-, meso- and macro-spaces (Läpple 1991). Right from the beginning of a project, the necessity of mediation between these spaces should be considered. Accordingly, building bridges between the local and the global – i.e., the micro and the macro – can be understood as a process of institutionalization. This is in accordance with Douglas and Bischoff, who emphasize the habitualization and stabilization of social acting, and Heintel and Götz who focus strongly on collective reflection and a reflective "organization" of societally relevant topics in processes of institutionalization (Douglas und Bischoff 1991; Heintel und Götz 2000).

The project was organized in two stages. In the first exploratory and preliminary stage, semi-structured qualitative interviews were conducted with managers. Some of the questions addressed how enterprises experience emigration and the

168   *Martina Ukowitz*

lack of skilled workers, how they have reacted so far to the loss of skilled workers, the significance of international perspectives and activities and experiences with internationalization in their enterprises, with a particular focus on human resource management. At the end of stage I, the results were discussed with the managers and the funding agency and decisions were made regarding the aspects that should receive additional attention.

In stage II, internationalization of enterprises and associated questions concerning human resource management were selected for further examination. Workshops with managers were held, and interviews with employees of the involved enterprises and an online survey among the employees of the cooperating enterprises were conducted. From the perspective of the entrepreneurs, practical relevance and a focus on implementation were crucial. The entrepreneurs were interested in building cooperative relationships with foreign enterprises and in acquiring information about measures of personnel development.

Two tasks were defined for stage II: The first one was a qualitative study to gain deeper understanding of international relationships and mobility in a globalized working environment, of the fields of tension that may accompany international activities, and of collective strategies to cope with the challenges. The second task was conceptualizing measures of further professional development to foster internationality.

Under the name of *On the Move*, an interorganizational mobility programme for further professional development was created that focused on experience-based learning and inter-collegial exchange. *On the Move* organized temporary stays at partner enterprises for employees from enterprises in Carinthia and from abroad. It provided a platform for the announcement and placement of so called "guest positions" at Carinthia and in foreign enterprises. In addition to useful information about organizational matters (e.g., legal aspects), it offered a design for two types of stay, which differed in length, fields of learning and the roles taken by participants at the host enterprises.

To develop a customized programme in the qualitative empirical study, knowledge was collected about the expectations and needs of employees, their experiences abroad, and their motivation for further professional education and what hindered them in the pursuit of this training. The development of the mobility programme, which in the end unfortunately couldn't be started within the project, took place in a series of meetings with the group of entrepreneurs.

The project was concluded with a research report and two final meetings with the funding agency and the practice partners (i.e., non-academic practitioners who are project partners) and, socially, with an invitation to dinner for the whole group from one of the entrepreneurs. I had the impression that we all felt a little bit sorry that we didn't succeed in starting the mobility programme, but at the same time it was good to know that the project would come to an end with this last step. I personally still have a feeling of disquiet when I think about the end of the project, because it wasn't the desired one. In retrospect, there were several crucial scenes during the project – moments and constellations that were possibly decisive for success or failure. I will reflect upon these below.

Transdisciplinary research 169

Mediating between individual interests and cooperative project development

The decision to divide the project into two stages – a preliminary, exploratory one and a more focused, deeper one – was based on the premise that transdisciplinary projects should be developed together with the actors in the region, in this case entrepreneurs, and in consultation with the funding agency. The superordinate topic of internationalization in small and middle-sized enterprises was introduced by the research team, but the relevant questions and tasks were concretized on the basis of an initial series of interviews with managers, a series of exploratory talks with representatives of institutions dealing with the topic, and workshops with the two regional groups of participating entrepreneurs. The division into two stages was also reflected in the financial plan for the project. We, as researchers, suggested critically evaluating the first stage in an intermediate report and in a meeting with the funding body before deciding upon next steps. The elaboration of the research questions and tasks was done in a participatory way, but project administration, including contact with the funding institution, lay within the scope of the research team. The practice partners signalled their commitment to the project by signing a letter of intent in which they gave assurances that they would have time for the project and provide meeting rooms. We made it clear right from the start that the project should only be continued in a second stage if the actors involved saw potential in the topic and were willing to engage with it more deeply. The project design was intended to reflect participatory decision-making about the research content and the processes of collaboration.

Theoretically, the project was based on intervention research, a transdisciplinary research approach which goes back to the tradition of dialectic and transcendental philosophy, and to systemic organizational development (Heintel 2005; Ukowitz 2012). By focusing on the procedural aspects of (transdisciplinary) research, intervention research provides the precondition for the possibility of negotiating a topic. This approach is understood as a social-communicative process for dealing with frequently contradictory perspectives (Ukowitz 2014). Consequently, organizational development in the sense of establishing a "social body" of research, of introducing structures and adequate social processes, and of carefully moderating the processes is a core task in transdisciplinary intervention research. Due to its roots in process-oriented systemic counselling, the approach, well positioned in contract research, strongly focuses on the perspectives, interests and needs of the practice partners, while scientific interest, in the sense of major concentration on scientifically relevant questions and publishing in highly ranked journals, is not as high a priority.

From the perspective of intervention research, the question of how research processes are developed is crucial. In my role as a project leader I decided to adopt a slightly different approach by raising as a topic the question of globalization and related fields of tension, which had been shown to be important in earlier projects in the field of sustainable regional development and in the scientific discourse (Läpple 1991; Groß und Ukowitz 2009). I was theoretically basing this approach

170   *Martina Ukowitz*

on reflections in the philosophy of science suggesting that science has the duty to provide a mirror to society by confronting it with contextual and orientational knowledge, and by opening up discourses (Mittelstraß 1982; Knorr-Cetina 2008; Gibbons et al. 1994). Consequently, the way of dealing with the research questions subsequently was a participatory one. In transdisciplinary research, that means a step-by-step approach to the research goes along with organizing the social system, which sustains the research process (Ukowitz 2020).

In the first stage of the project, with a focus on internationalization in small and middle-sized enterprises, entrepreneurs were invited to contribute because they were interested in this topic and had a contribution to make to the research. In selecting potential practice partners, according to experiences from organizational development, it is useful, if possible, to address networks of actors, because then the social body of research can build on existing relationships and mutual interest among the actors. Trust fosters commitment to a new initiative. It was the aim of the first stage to elaborate a "thematic landscape" as a basis for decisions about possible tasks for stage two. The research team also expressed interest in specific contents. Besides methodological reflection on transdisciplinary processes (which lead to contributions like the present one), the team was interested in how people nowadays manage work in a globalized working environment, which competencies are required for this sort of work, and what chances and risks associated with it can be described from the perspectives of employees and entrepreneurs. These topics were pursued using a qualitative social research design.

The topic of internationalization proved to be relevant for the entrepreneurs, so with a group of five enterprises which had collaborated with one another, we decided to start stage two. The first step in stage two was to formulate two tasks: a qualitative study of the significance of international relationships and mobility in a globalized working environment, and secondly, the development (and implementation) of a mobility programme for employees that would foster international exchange between enterprises from different countries, experience-driven learning and the development of a culture of internationality.

Looking back, I think we navigated carefully through the process of developing the project. Since participatory development of the research process is one critical success factor, I think we were on the right track. The fact that I suggested introducing an explicit research focus, instead of working more openly on the content, caused a little irritation among the research team. My colleagues were used to strictly following the intervention research approach, which promotes the researchers' abstinence regarding content contributions, whereas I suggested integrating the entrepreneurs' and the researchers' scientific interests. The practice partners supported our suggestions without hesitation. (Admittedly that might be attributed to the fact that we researchers had already procured funding for the initiative.)

Right at the beginning of stage two we identified what we thought was one crucial aspect of the project. From earlier cooperation with the group of entrepreneurs we knew that the network of enterprises cooperated in settings that involved inquiries by researchers and in public events with presentations and contributions by experts from universities and other fields of practice. Developing a mobility programme across organizations (which in the end was an intervention into routines within enterprises) would have been a relatively new experience for this group of entrepreneurs. This kind of cooperative work on a concrete task followed a different logic than public events, which provide attractive networking possibilities but do not really concern the enterprises' daily routines.

In transdisciplinary research one knows that mediation between individual perspectives is not always achieved. In spite of participatory development, what is known about the significance and expected utility of transdisciplinary outcomes always remains incomplete. Sometimes, the actors involved in the first stage of transdisciplinary projects have not fully realized what motivates them to participate. Expectations are sometimes diffuse, and it is difficult to talk about them. Mediation between perspectives remains the path and the goal.

Stability and dynamics within the social system of research

In our experience, stable cooperative relationships are beneficial for collaboration between groups. Stability does not mean stagnation, though, since the dynamics deriving from synergies, and also from productive differences, are crucial for the lively development of social systems (Krainz und Ukowitz 2014). Stable relationships can be understood as balanced relationships that can withstand difficulties. The "Carinthia International" project had to experience more than one difficult situation. To illustrate that, two scenes will be discussed below.

Scene 1, project stage one:
> The project was initiated in two regions in Carinthia, more precisely in two regional networks, and we knew some of the actors from both groups due to earlier collaborations. After the analysis of the interviews and meetings, a feedback workshop was organized at the end of stage one in both regions. In one of the regions, entrepreneurs decided to continue with the project, while in the other the offer was rejected after a turbulent workshop in which we as researchers unexpectedly competed with a regional manager (a professional linked to regional governments in Austria) who also had particular ideas for the region. In a phone call shortly after the workshop, the informal leader of the group explained that the group was well positioned and would not need support in the form of projects. We felt misunderstood, but the actors obviously had their own plans, and our initiative came at an unfavourable moment. A specific role was taken by the leader, who was funding a new regional network at that time and he had invited the regional manager to the workshop without informing us. During the workshop it could be observed that the regional manager took the opportunity to get in contact with other entrepreneurs and develop projects in the region, and the leading entrepreneur (the CEO of the best-known enterprise in the region) supported her. Cooperation with us – which would have been possible – was not welcome.

172   *Martina Ukowitz*

Scene 2, project stage two:

> The second scene involved a major disturbance in the group after the qualitative inquiry had been conducted and the group was starting to conceptualize the mobility programme. At this point one of the enterprises left the project. At the beginning of one of the regular project meetings with the representatives of the five participating enterprises, the representative of one of the biggest enterprises informed us, the researchers and the group, that they were going to withdraw from the project because they had a conflict with another enterprise in the project group. This meeting was hosted by the other enterprise in the conflict and was embarrassing. The conflict had nothing to do with our initiative – as far as we know it was about the poaching/headhunting of one staff member and his customer stock – but it had an influence on the atmosphere in the group and on the project. The group was quite small after that, because the representative of the "accused" enterprise also didn't attend the meetings anymore and we all felt dispirited, and trust within the group seemed to be at risk. We researchers tried to clarify the situation with the group, but there was no further communication about it. Nevertheless, the group decided to go on with the project. Following this event, the group continued to suffer from the scars it left, and the disturbance remained present subliminally, even though some months later another enterprise, represented by a very active participant, joined the project.

Once again, our experiences showed that scientific work in transdisciplinary research projects is strongly influenced by social dynamics. Trust proves to be an important ingredient – trust not only between researchers and practice partners, but also between practice partners (Luhmann 2000/1968). In all constellations, we can observe trust in the sense of readiness to trust, which means trusting that a cooperative arrangement will be based on mutual respect and a common commitment to pursuing socially relevant questions. From the perspective of the practice partners, trust in the system is a relative factor – participants (mostly) have trust in the knowledge and competence of academic institutions. Finally, the familiarity and trust developed step by step during collaboration between individuals are important factors as well. Of course, trust can be easily threatened; it is a phenomenon which is strong and fragile at the same time. Prejudices and unexpected actions, but also competitive dynamics or differences in value patterns, can cause irritation and disrupt trust. It is one of the researchers' duties to keep an eye on social qualities like trust, but even if critical social situations are dealt with competently, it is sometimes not possible to improve the situation.

Incremental processes and a major breakthrough
– who is pushing the development?

During the qualitative inquiry the research team worked quite independently from the group of entrepreneurs. We just reported relevant observations regarding the research process and invited them to discuss the outcomes of our research with their employees. For the planning of the mobility programme, which was based on the results of the research, strong cooperation with the entrepreneurs was essential. The ideas of developing a plan that was ready for implementation, of starting a pilot stage, and of taking care of the long-term embedding of the plan in the organizations was ambitious – we were all aware of that. We could not predict whether the initiative would in the end really be of interest to employees in the participating enterprises in the region of Carinthia, whether the partner enterprises abroad would be interested in cooperating, or whether the programme would be feasible in terms of everyday work. After reflecting on possible risks, our project partners indicated that they liked the idea, and that we should try it out. With regard to commitment, we saw once again the effects of the group dynamic: one very engaged, dynamic and inspiring entrepreneur strongly supported the idea and fostered the commitment of the other group members.

For the research team it was important not to speed up the process; we just did what had been decided within the group and what was required by the actual situation. We acted in a cautious way, since participation of the practice partners was a fundamental priority. It was crucial not to "lose" the group, especially in the context of the possible institutional implementation of the mobility programme. In communicating the initiative to regional institutions and politicians –representatives of the two actor groups that had signalled their interest – and also to enterprises abroad, we were circumspect because we didn't want to make promises which couldn't be kept.

Looking back, I ask myself if a more proactive approach would have fostered and pushed the process. There were signs of commitment and support for the idea from institutions and relevant persons, but at the same time, step-by-step planning and multiple safeguards gave the whole process an atmosphere of hesitance, which may have impeded progress in the direction of implementation. On the other hand, we know that proactive decisions from researchers can lead to resistance from the practitioners, and these decisions can also put practitioner groups in an awkward position if the communication from the researchers is misleading.

How implementation is handled in transdisciplinary research constellations is a strategic question and also a question of research ethics, since all such projects will, to a certain degree, have a social impact. Remaining too hands-off increases the risk of not achieving implementation, while too much involvement on the part of the researchers increases the risk of losing sight of the practice partners and thus hindering the true role of research, which mainly lies in analyzing and not in taking action. This problem raises theoretical or conceptual questions: If we assume that transdisciplinary research focuses on "Gestaltung" (i.e., designs, following Gestalt theory and Gestalt therapy), which comprises cognition, design and implementation of results, and if implementation (i.e., realization and experience) is part of the process (Krohn et al. 2017), the roles of researchers and practice partners have to be discussed further, especially in regard to the legitimation for taking action and the question of how long-term activities beyond the life of the project can be sustained.

174 *Martina Ukowitz*

Experiences in other projects have shown that it is advantageous to set up a project structure which includes a person who plays the role of intermediary. Ideally, this is a trusted person from the relevant field of practice with leadership skills who is familiar with the social situation in the project and ideally is independent from the individual actors within the project group. It is important to decide on the specific role of this intermediary, especially as a multiplier and broker who commits to and supports project implementation. The focus of the intermediary role lies more in facilitating the processes of implementation in fields of practice, and not in facilitating interdisciplinary and transdisciplinary cooperation within a project, as described by Wehrden et al. (2019). In the "Carinthia International" project, such a role was not established, but there was one person who may have been interested in taking that role. And it may have been possible to arrange that with the funding agency. Unfortunately, we realized this too late.

Success, failure and the importance of having staying power

Within the project we achieved two major tangible results. First, the qualitative content analysis provided insight into the experiences and expectations of employees in the context of professional mobility. This result was interesting for the enterprises, and for personnel development and the management of projects abroad. From the researchers' point of view this result is a contribution to discourses in social anthropology, and it is also interesting in the context of regional development. It can be seen that even in a globalized world, internationalization and mobility involve ambivalences and that longer stays abroad or stays in more distant parts of the world are still an adventure and are often challenging, physically and mentally. Internationalization, particularly in smaller enterprises in rural regions, is not only a question of management; it also requires effort to develop an organizational culture congenial to international collaboration while maintaining a bond with the local region. The second result is a detailed mobility concept for temporary professional mobility and knowledge exchange. However, the pilot stage could not be started, and the future of the mobility concept we developed is unclear.

Scientific research is primarily interested in generating new knowledge. In transdisciplinary research, the practical application of knowledge and the implementation of measures that derive from scientific results are further issues, so researchers have to deal with the scientific realm and the interests of project partners at the same time. This characteristic influences the choice of methodology: Some authors distinguish between the field of knowledge production and practical intervention (Defila und Di Giulio 2019). A more integrative approach is offered by the outcome spaces framework (Mitchell et al. 2015) which proposes designing projects in such a way that the results lie on various levels (e.g., improving the situation, contributing to knowledge stocks and flows, mutual and transformational learning). The different types of results reflect the interests of those involved (e.g., researchers and project partners), and the responsibility for generating the results is a shared one.

Transdisciplinary research   175

Implementation of measures that derive from scientific results in fields of practice normally requires a strong commitment from practice partners, with greater responsibility for implementation lying on the side of practice. Participatory development of initiatives can increase the probability of success, but it doesn't provide a guarantee. Nevertheless, the following can be observed: The greater the commitment of the practice partners, the more robust the development process. But even if the probability of success can be increased by designing adequate participatory processes, all the actor groups involved should be aware that being interested in a project is only one side of the coin, and having the willingness and capacity to actively contribute is the other. Against the background of the project on internationalization, two other crucial considerations can be mentioned. First, it is good to have a critical mass of practice partners. It is a difficult decision for an enterprise to exempt an employee from work for three weeks for an educational stay abroad – even if it is in their own professional field and strongly linked to the enterprise's interest. In a bigger group, it is easier to find an enterprise and the employees who can participate in an educational stay abroad. Second, it is important to invest adequate time in the project. Researchers need to be patient in revising the research design and in catching up on the communication steps which have been missed, and in responding to setbacks. Due to a lack of time we terminated the "Carinthia International" project without making a second attempt to implement the mobility programme.

Lessons learned

Failure is an enigmatic term

Failure can appear in various forms. It can be a deviation from the ideal or a total breakdown, a mistake, an accident, or a misfortune. The type of failure also varies in its quality depending on how serious and how far-reaching it is, and what opportunities it leaves for continuing a project. Often, whether something is a failure or not depends on one's point of view. Failure is a question of interpretation. And we have to admit that failure may hurt – this can be experienced especially in German-speaking European countries with their culture of failure which tends to emphasize the negative aspects of failure and therefore strongly recommends avoiding it.

Success and failure in transdisciplinary projects lie close together

In transdisciplinary research constellations, the chances of success are quite high, since different goals can be pursued on different levels. Possible areas of impact include innovative scientific knowledge, knowledge to improve practice in broader society, shared perspectives regarding desirable futures, structures and routines to handle a socially important topic, or the mutual learning of the actors involved. Our recommendation is to think carefully about different outcome spaces (Mitchell et al. 2015) during the planning stage. At the same time, it is

176 *Martina Ukowitz*

important to be on the lookout for surprising developments while understanding that the impact of the research process sometimes is not recognizable in all its facets.

Failure is a relational phenomenon

In transdisciplinary projects, especially in regard to those tasks in which researchers are cooperating and sometimes closely working together with practice partners, the researchers are not in a position to make decisions on their own about content, results, or actions that derive from the research work. Researchers and practice partners depend on each other. In the end, success or failure is a shared result. Still, it seems to be the researchers' duty to ensure success. But how far does the responsibility of the researcher go? Is implementation of measures that derive from the research results, the major point in this case story, an indispensable criterion for judging the success or failure of transdisciplinary research, or it rather a regulatory idea in the sense of Immanuel Kant (Kant 2009)? These questions extend into the theory of transdisciplinary research (Krohn et al. 2017) and should be discussed further.

Social dynamics and prevailing system logics have a major influence on transdisciplinary projects

The case study shows that social processes and the prevailing logic of social systems strongly influence the outcome of a transdisciplinary research project. In more general terms, transdisciplinary research is not just a cognitive, neutral process of knowledge generation or problem solving. It is deeply immersed in the social sphere. Observing and moderating the social dynamics which are driven by the different needs and interests of the persons involved are important duties and competencies of transdisciplinary researchers. Failure might arise if we do not recognize conflicting attitudes to the project within the project group (Lackner 2018) or if an adequate response to these conflicting attitudes can't be found. Intervening in the social process is seldom a question of right or wrong, since each intervention makes different developments possible. We only know about the consequences of an intervention when we see how those affected react. In projects that involve social intervention, researchers play a facilitation role that they should perform with attentiveness for existing social processes and underlying values and norms. The problem is that transdisciplinary researchers steer a process in which they are themselves involved. (This is different, for instance, from process-oriented systemic consulting, where the experts have no stake of their own regarding the content.) This is a challenging role for researchers to assume in a project, and it is only one role among others they must assume (Wieser et al. 2014; Pielke 2010).

Summing up, from the perspective of the "Carinthia International" project and other transdisciplinary research experiences, it is important to find the right balance between having challenging expectations and imposing excessive demands. It is important to strive for success and calmly bear the occasional feeling of

Transdisciplinary research 177

failure. And finally, having a certain amount of humility towards constraints in practice is appropriate, and simultaneously the courage to follow good ideas.

Take-home messages

For a project that is transdisciplinary and aims to implement results in practice:

- Design the project so that there are achievable goals on several levels, increasing the likelihood of success given that there could be obstacles to implementation in the field of practice.
- Have an intermediary who acts as an effect multiplier and broker and commits to implementation of measures that derive from project results.
- Make sure that there are enough practice partners to implement measures that derive from project results.
- Be patient in revising the research design and in catching up on the communication steps which have been missed.
- Be patient in responding to setbacks.

References

Defila, R., Di Giulio, A. 2019. Eine Reflexion über Legitimation, Partizipation und Intervention im Kontext transdisziplinärer Forschung. *In:* M. Ukowitz and R. Hübner, eds. *Interventionsforschung, Band 3: Wege der Vermittlung. Intervention – Partizipation.* Wiesbaden, Germany: Springer, 85–108.

Douglas, M., Bischoff, M. 1991. *Wie Institutionen denken.* Frankfurt, Germany: Suhrkamp.

Gibbons, M., Limoges, C., Nowotny, H., Schwartzman, S., Scott, P., Trow, M. 1994. *The new production of knowledge: The dynamics of science and research in contemporary societies.* London, Thousand Oaks, CA, and New Delhi: Sage.

Groß, H.P., Ukowitz, M. 2009. Die Rolle der Wissenschaft im Zukunftsprozess. *In:* H.P. Groß, G. Strohmeier and M. Ukowitz, eds. *Zukunftsgestaltung als Prozess: Kulturell nachhaltige Wirtschafts- und Lebensraumentwicklung am Beispiel des Kärntner Lavanttales.* München, Germany: Oekom, 139–171.

Heintel, P. 2005. *Zur Grundaxiomatik der Interventionsforschung.* Klagenfurt, Germany: Alpen-Adria-Universität Klagenfurt.

Heintel, P., Götz, K. 2000. *Das Verhältnis von Institution und Organisation: Zur Dialektik von Abhängigkeit und Zwang.* 2nd ed. München, Germany: Hampp.

Kant, I. 2009, Beantwortung der Frage: Was ist Aufklärung? *In:* W. Weischedel, ed. *Schriften zur Anthropologie, Geschichtsphilosophie, Politik und Pädagogik.* 15th ed. Frankfurt, Germany: Suhrkamp, 53–61.

Knorr-Cetina, K. 2008. Die eine Vernunft und die vielen Rationalitäten. Der gemeinsame Boden der Wissenschaften?. *In:* G. Magerl and H. Schmiedinger, eds. *Einheit und Freiheit der Wissenschaft: Idee und Wirklichkeit.* Wien, Köln: Böhlau, 47–61.

Krainz, E.E., Ukowitz, M. 2014. Produktive Irritation. Differenzen in der transdisziplinären Forschung handhaben. *In:* G. Dressel, W. Berger, K.Heimerl and V. Winiwarter. Eds. *Interdisziplinär und transdisziplinär forschen: Praktiken und Methoden.* Bielefeld: Transcript, 91–101.

178 *Martina Ukowitz*

Krohn, W., Grunwald, A., Ukowitz, M. 2017. Transdisziplinäre Forschung revisited: Erkenntnisinteresse, Forschungsgegenstände, Wissensform und Methodologie. *GAIA – Ecological Perspectives for Science and Society*, 26(4), 341–347.

Lackner, K. 2018. Failure in consulting: Consultation cannot fail!. *In:* S. Kunert, ed. *Strategies in failure management: Scientific insights, case studies and tools.* Cham, Switzerland: Springer, 161–174.

Läpple, D. 1991. Essay über den Raum. *In:* H. Häußermann, ed. *Stadt und Raum: Soziologische Perspektiven.* Pfaffenweiler, Germany: Centaurus-Verl.-Ges, 157–207.

Luhmann, N. 2000/1968. *Vertrauen: Ein Mechanismus der Reduktion sozialer Komplexität.* 4th ed. Stuttgart, Germany: Lucius & Lucius.

Mitchell, C., Cordell, D., Fam, D. 2015. Beginning at the end: The outcome spaces framework to guide purposive transdisciplinary research. *Futures* doi:10.1016/j.futures.2014.10.007.

Mittelstraß, J. 1982. *Wissenschaft als Lebensform: Reden über philosophische Orientierungen in Wissenschaft und Universität.* Frankfurt, Germany: Suhrkamp.

Pielke, R.A. 2010. Expert advice and the vast sea of knowledge. *In:* A. Bogner, ed. *Inter- und Transdisziplinarität im Wandel?: Neue Perspektiven auf problemorientierte Forschung und Politikberatung.* Baden-Baden, Germany: Nomos, 169–187.

Ukowitz, M. 2012. Interventionsforschung im Kontext transdisziplinärer Wissenschaften. *In:* L. Krainer and R. Lerchster, eds. *Interventionsforschung, Band 1: Paradigmen, Methoden, Reflexionen.* Wiesbaden, Germany: Springer, 75–101.

Ukowitz, M. 2014. Auf dem Weg zu einer Theorie transdisziplinärer Forschung. *GAIA*, 23(1), 19–22.

Ukowitz, M. 2020. Prozessorganisation – ein methodisches Grundprinzip transdisziplinärer Forschung. *In:* M. Niederberger and E. Finne, eds. *Forschungsmethoden in der Gesundheitsförderung und Prävention.* Wiesbaden, Germany: Springer.

Ukowitz, M., Pichler-Koban, C. 2018. *Der Vertigo-Effekt: Institutionelle Dynamiken im Naturschutz* (Beiträge zur sozialwissenschaftlichen Nachhaltigkeitsforschung). Marburg: Metropolis.

Wehrden, H. von, Guimarães, M.H., Bina, O., Varanda, M., Lang, D.J., John, B., Gralla, F., Alexander, D., Raines, D., White, A., Lawrence, R.J. 2019. Interdisciplinary and transdisciplinary research: Finding the common ground of multi-faceted concepts. *Sustainability Science* 14(3), 875–888.

Wieser, B., Brechelmacher, A., Schendl, G. 2014. Identitäten und Rollen in inter- und transdisziplinärer Forschung und Lehre finden. *In:* G. Dressel, W. Berger, K. Heimerl and V. Winiwarter, eds. *Interdisziplinär und transdisziplinär forschen: Praktiken und Methoden 1.* Bielefeld, Germany: Transcript, 151–164.

Part IV

Failure in interdisciplinary and transdisciplinary educational programs

11 The challenges of studying place

Learning from the failures of an experimental, interdisciplinary and community-engaged environmental studies course

Valerie Imbruce and Miroslava Prazak

Introduction

The new millennium ushered in a growing recognition of the complexity of today's problems and the need to approach their solutions from multiple perspectives. The statement that complex problems require complex solutions is an unofficial mantra of our times. And how can the academy, with its traditional structure of independent and often isolated ivory towers reach out from its specialized knowledge centres and be a part of the creation of solutions?

The authors took part in an innovative initiative funded by the National Science Foundation (NSF) at a small, experimental, liberal arts institution, to bring together some of the crucial issues of our day and come up with solutions, drawing on multiple perspectives and areas of expertise to address a common problem in the Northeast of the United States. The initiative was called "The Future of the New England Mill Town." Having been at the heart of the Industrial Revolution in the nineteenth century, small towns straddling rivers and streams that supplied energy to all types of industries largely stagnated in the twentieth century and, so far, also in the twenty-first. In the era of interstate highways, the internet and international trade, what are the opportunities for these towns to flourish again, to be centres of population, employment and prosperity as they were for a couple of centuries in the past? What can a post-industrial Northeast look like? We believed that to address such questions we needed to construct a course of study that integrated understandings of the natural environment, human values and desires and historical and contemporary issues of importance to the locale. To achieve such an understanding, we brought together members of our academic institution and members of non-academic institutions in our community to discuss the town's culture, history and issues, and strategies to inform the course development and implementation phases of the project. In addition, we believed that our institutional fluidity, the lack of formal departments and of a fixed curriculum, and a mandatory winter field work term for students would enable community-engaged, interdisciplinary and experiential work to take place. We were not prepared for the disparities in our ways of thinking, or for the hidden rigidity of structures that undermined the group project.

182 *Valerie Imbruce and Miroslava Prazak*

We began to explore the past, present and future of our mill town with a small group of seven core members and occasional in-house visitors to the deliberations. We shared a common interest in environmental issues and studies, and the goal of creating a course sequence that would be interdisciplinary and community-engaged. First, we had to discover what questions to ask, and what issues the town was facing. Over a three-year timespan, our conversation involved a chemist, a social psychologist, a geologist, an architect, an ecologist, an anthropologist and an economic botanist. Our discussions were far-ranging and provocative, questioning how we know a place and what needs to be paid attention to, but also quibbling over basic definitional issues, falling back all too easily to our disciplinary strongholds. At the other end of the NSF grant period, we agreed that the most important gain from our endeavours was the enrichment we experienced and the appreciation we gained of the wealth of perspectives that we brought to bear on the core issues we started out with in our investigation of the role and life of small communities in a post-industrial America. As Pearce argues in Chapter 13 of this volume, we can see the complementarity of scientific and non-scientific approaches to understanding people in their environments, built and natural, and insist that both are needed to envision a sustainable future. The challenge is for team members within any interdisciplinary working group to think beyond their customary research methods and theories to those of others – to identify where commensurability or complementarity can be found. We did not find that place in our initial group of seven.

We found that through our process of interdisciplinary collaboration, fundamental tensions between the nature of science, technology, engineering and mathematics (STEM) disciplines and the ideal of a liberal arts education loomed large.[1] The empirical process of reducing complex systems to measurable and predictable patterns is very different to analyzing the ways that humans make meaning and create values through their lived experiences and observations. We failed: (1) to anticipate and overcome the disciplinary hierarchies within our group, particularly a bias towards scientific knowledge generation as the most valued approach, (2) to fundamentally mesh scientific with humanistic approaches and (3) to devise an evaluation strategy that included questions about our group members' views and values, and that did not rely on the quantification of qualitative data.

The lessons we want to offer through an examination of our course development and implementation process focus on how difficult it is to undo the tendencies towards disciplinarity and the "ivory tower" mindset of the academy that separates modes of knowing within its ranks as well as between academia and the rest of the world. If one discipline or sector (e.g., academia, industry, government) is given primary status by a group, or by individuals within a group, then the background knowledge, evidentiary standards, ways of understanding the world and research or other types of goals from that discipline or sector can gain primacy over others within a group, making co-production of knowledge very difficult or nearly impossible (Struck 2017). If these intergroup dynamics go unexamined, then the goal of solving complex problems in the world through interdisciplinary collaboration can be elusive. This was a particularly unexpected finding from our

The challenges of studying place   183

course development process because of the experimental structure of our institution – with no departments or majors, an unranked faculty and an emergent curriculum. The finding was also unexpected because of the college's experimental educational nature and history. It was designed to be more open to collaboration across disciplines, to supporting students' experiential learning through external internships in other sectors and to embracing exchange with communities outside of the conventional college structure. We found three main issues that stood in the way of bridging theory with practice of our interdisciplinary, community engagement goals: (1) there was a paucity of established mechanisms for collaboration between the college and the town; (2) town experts were not from town, so they also brought an outsider perspective; and (3) there was an unassailable hierarchy of types of knowledge and ways of knowing.

The course development process

The Mill Town Project: An interdisciplinary, community-engaged course sequence

The goal of our project was to develop a place-based course sequence, an introductory course and a projects course, that would teach students how to apply academic models and methodologies to deepen their knowledge of the places in which they live, study and work. The initiative was meant to leverage our college's unique educational structure of student-directed and experiential learning to develop students' capacities to understand pressing societal issues and become problem-solvers.[2] We believed personal engagement would build emotional as well as intellectual connections to a place – connections necessary to nurture students who don't just *know* about things but *care* about them. We used the concept of place to integrate our intellectual dispositions. The project was to be a centrepiece of the college's environmental studies programme.

Developing a new set of courses was an opportunity to further students' learning, strengthen faculty collaboration and build relationships with key people and organizations in town to advance the college's interdisciplinary programme in environmental studies. These goals were fulfilled in our project, but with unanticipated challenges and outcomes. At a broad level, we were trying to find a way to merge STEM approaches to education that teach empiricism with humanistic approaches that stress personal experience and contextual understanding. We also wanted to merge the expertise of practitioners from outside the academy with ours, and this was a tall order, one that remains at the heart of a debate on the purpose of higher education.

STEM disciplines are a common component of environmental studies programmes. They teach students how to make empirical inquiries and how to identify cause-and-effect relationships in the natural world. However, environmental problems play out in the human world where it is more difficult to isolate variables, make predictions and develop generalized theories about causation and correlation. Questions of human agency, cultural context, political process and

184　*Valerie Imbruce and Miroslava Prazak*

economic valuation muddle the (presumed) clarity of positivist science, but also bring the opportunity to develop critical thinking and interpretation skills that come with the exercise of assessing social patterns via theoretical social models. In reflecting on the dynamics of the year spent preparing the course, it is clear that there were several arenas in which negotiation was always necessary. The first is the chauvinism of the science faculty. Their understanding of the common goal was to make everyone think like a scientist and to call into question any proposal or understanding which according to them was not "scientific." As a result, we often heard the refrain, "that's well and good, but what does that have to do with science?," and in many cases there were complaints that the questions, readings, and activities proposed or undertaken were not "scientific." Anything not scientific was branded as inferior, even if our vision for an interdisciplinary course was given sanction by the NSF.

And perhaps most seriously, virtually everyone in the group spoke of the town as a problem, as a poor community populated by people who are uneducated, unemployed, and on a trajectory to nowhere. Only two faculty members of our group actually lived in town; the others lived in neighbouring towns over the New York border or further into Vermont's Green Mountains. This negative attitude is precisely what we wanted to problematize for the students, and it was hard to counter it in the faculty group. The desire on the part of some group members to consider townspeople's perspectives alongside academic perspectives was not a shared vision or value of the group.

As collaboration is a social process, the patterns we observed may be understood through the insights of organizational psychology. Deep-level characteristics of team members, such as personality, attitudes and values, affected team performance. One disagreeable team member can derail team performance, but deep characteristics that underlie agreeableness aren't always visible until there is a choice on the table (Bell 2007). When it came time to implement our project proposal, the degree to which we made our project community-engaged or more or less "scientific" uncovered the different sets of values in our group, causing a "fault line" to occur between those who believed in a multidisciplinary approach and those who did not (Lau and Murnighan 2005). This fault line caused subgroup formation and there was reduced trust and communication between the two subgroups, the quantitators and the qualitators. When we paired off as instructors to work on course syllabi and teach the courses, respect for different kinds of methodologies and for different ways of knowing was more easily established between those of us from the natural sciences and those from social sciences or arts or humanities than it was in the group setting.

Building relations between people from the college and the town

Despite our faculty group dynamics, we were able to engage productively with town members. We were fortunate to hire an excellent project manager whose role was to act as an intermediary between the course and the community. We realized the necessity for such a position after we failed at our first attempt to

The challenges of studying place 185

engage productively with townspeople. Part of the challenge of developing our course was the absence of literature other than works about the revolutionary war and the Battle of Bennington. How could we find out what issues are salient to our town? Most of the members of the Mill Town group didn't live in town, so couldn't claim a "native" or "indigenous" status. We decided to bring in "experts" on the topics we thought we needed to learn about. This led to a series of visitors focusing on their specific area of engagement, including forestry, geology, revolutionary history and governmental organization. Their presentations were lectures, open to students. None of these professionals were from the local area, and their presentations were narrow and esoteric. We judged that continuing this format didn't teach the faculty enough to warrant the time and effort involved, and was likely to turn off student interest. Furthermore, the formal presentation format reinforced their specialties instead of promoting a more general conversation about town dynamics. Indeed, the world, not just academia, is segmented by areas of expertise. We switched formats, inviting visitors to come and talk to the faculty group on areas of their individual expertise in a setting more informal than a lecture and more open to addressing questions the faculty actually had. We learned enough to begin identifying topics and people who would be interested in communicating information about them.

Given a series of topics that we wanted to cover in the course, the project manager helped the faculty identify the best places and people to connect with. Although some of this happened as a result of a serendipitous snowball effect, the persistence with which the connections were made led to an unprecedented involvement of members of the community in the building of knowledge within the college. The course itself received positive press coverage, both local and regional, and the townspeople's participation was made quite visible in this way (Carson 2015; McArdle 2015).

The structural features of the college

The idea for the course sequence addressed the needs at the college in relation to student learning, faculty collaboration and the structure of the environmental studies programme. We believed the educational philosophy of the college was conducive to our goals. It practices John Dewey's philosophy that students learn best through a hands-on approach, that reality must be experienced, and that students need to interact with their environments to learn and adapt. We were surprised by the limitations we found. Like other environmental studies programmes across the nation, ours operates in an interdisciplinary lacuna by sitting between the "discipline-groups" – our department-like structures that bind complementary fields together, set curricula, hire faculty and allocate resources. Faculty have primary responsibilities to their home discipline group and to contribute to an explicitly interdisciplinary programme largely voluntarily. With no set majors at the college, but instead an open plan process in which students articulate a set of questions to guide their individual courses of study, our challenge was to move beyond a potpourri of courses that students could assemble as they and

186 *Valerie Imbruce and Miroslava Prazak*

their plan committees saw fit, to the development of courses that in themselves were integrative and could provide students with a model for the design of their own educational plans. The NSF award provided a structured and remunerated opportunity for interested faculty from any discipline to engage in a course development process *together*. However, with a small faculty and single-person disciplines, faculty members were reluctant to abandon their disciplinary teaching for an experimental, integrative course. Much like the participants in the Living Lab that Fam et al. describe in Chapter 12 in this volume, after the grant period, faculty went back to their disciplinary homes.

Implementing the course

The course: Studying place by metes and bounds

After a year of group discussion, debating the concept of place from disciplinary perspectives, identifying the skills, questions and topics that should be addressed through the course, engaging with people from town, and suggesting readings and activities for the course, the authors made the final sprint towards completion of a syllabus for the first iteration of the course in January of 2015. We agreed that what differentiates "space" from "place" is people, so we put people's perspectives about the town at the centre of the course. This orientation meshed well with our desire to engage people from the town in the design and delivery of the course. We wanted students to hear directly from townies about their lived experiences and opinions about the town, to showcase various viewpoints, which would hopefully be different from their own. We saw this approach as a model of how social scientists learn from people. We taught students research methods that undergird this approach – observation, participant observation, interviewing, data collection design and analysis – to enable students' engagement with people and facilitate their experiential learning.

Half of our four hours per week were to be spent "in the field" practising a research method, such as participant observation or interviewing. The morning half of the class was used to discuss class readings, usually on epochs in the town history, concepts and methods of focus for the week. Homework assignments included writing up and analyzing results from those excursions, or further practising the method at hand, as well as reflections about student experiences in the form of blog posts for the course website and entries in a journal. To reinforce the community engagement aspect of the course, we assigned students to read the local daily newspaper, to form their own relationship with someone in town through volunteering at an organization, and finally, requesting and conducting an interview with that person. Our project manager played an essential role in bringing to bear the expertise of professionals and residents in the town, and a variety of individuals and enterprises were identified. The town participants shaped both what we studied and how we studied it, so that we could fulfil the core principle of the course: for the students to experience what was being studied.

The challenges of studying place 187

The course was titled "Studying Place by Metes and Bounds" to highlight a form of measurement that integrated natural and social features of the landscape, an approach we wanted to emulate in the course.[3] The course comprised three historically chronological sections: the early settlement period, the transition from an agrarian to an industrial economy, and the contemporary, mostly post-industrial, period. Each had vivid readings from many disciplines and publication types, town experts and field trips to illustrate the dynamics of the topics under study. The methods that we chose to teach were both qualitative and quantitative in nature. They included: making meaning from existing and collected quantitative data sets (e.g., cemetery data to describe demographics and water flow in Paran Creek to calculate potential water power); and generating descriptive and analytical writings from observation while walking through town, participant observation in a religious ceremony and an interview with a member of town that they had interacted with throughout the term in their community engagement assignment.

At our first class meeting, we discussed land acquisition and the primary natural features of our region, and looked at a variety of historical maps including the first land grants drawn up by New Hampshire Governor Benning Wentworth. In the afternoon, we took a van trip around the six-mile square perimeter of the town to see how the boundaries and features of these maps corresponded to the reality of the physical landscape. Our guide was a ninth-generation descendant from the first pastor of the original Congregational church, a landscape architect and amateur historian, who pointed out features of the landscape and built environment that would otherwise not be easily seen, or seen at all. During the tour we stopped at his home to view a painting of the agricultural landscape of the early settlement period. It contained pastures that have long since reverted to forest. We connected what we observed directly in the physical landscape with historic representations.

We also learned about town through direct observation and engagement with residents to bring to life our topics of study. We visited the well-preserved remains of the first blast furnaces that smelted iron ore from mineral deposits in the area to make pig iron, a basic material of the American industrial revolution that caused the landscape to be denuded of forests to make charcoal. We studied the settlement period through the work of historians and archaeologists, and also through the eyes of a man who lived in those times and kept copious journal records, known as the "Harwood Diaries," a treasure of the town's historical society. We visited the ancestral home of the Harwoods, one of the first colonial homes and farms built in the fledgling town, now owned by a descendant who described the preservation and stewardship of the house and property over two and a half centuries, what this entailed, and what it means to her and her family. Later in the course we visited a working, artisanal cheese farm and considered the female farmer's agricultural practices and views about the land alongside contemporary issues in agriculture. In this way, we connected the past and the present, the cultural and the environmental, introducing a variety of information sources and modes of constructing knowledge as the through points of the diverse set of course topics.

188 *Valerie Imbruce and Miroslava Prazak*

The course finished with a reception for all students and participating community members to foster further dialogue informally. At the reception, as at many other points during the term, it was clear that community members benefited from the ongoing opportunity to network among themselves in new ways, appreciating each other for community expertise they had previously been unaware or unappreciative of and finding new opportunities to advance their own professional and place-related agendas.

Evaluating the course

Evaluation is a significant aspect of NSF funding as well as of STEM education initiatives. In some ways, it became an all-too-important element of the course and played too significant a role in determining what data were collected. The evaluation and the capacity to evaluate various elements of the course steered us towards the elements more readily accessible via quantification, as opposed to fully assessing the more qualitative, experiential and subjective elements of the course and the learning processes.

An external evaluator worked with us to ensure that the learning objectives of the course – to develop an understanding of the town, to learn and practice various research methods and to develop an approach to studying any place – were met. The Student Assessment of Learning Gains survey[4] that we used provided quantitative measures of pre- and post-course learning gains and attitudes, a standard method in course assessment. These measures are limited in that students tend to be overconfident when self-reporting their abilities, and the magnitude of change in learning over the course is relative to the level at which students first report their knowledge at the course's start, making large gains more likely for students who report little knowledge at the outset. Finally, our data were not statistically significant due to the non-random nature of student selection for the course and the small sample size (Theobold and Freeman 2013). In fact, the measurement instruments were very sophisticated for a database of 13 cases. For all these reasons, additional qualitative data gathered through conversations, interviews and direct observations of student work were needed to provide a richer, more detailed account to explain and understand the course's outcomes.

One area of disjuncture between the quantitative and qualitative data about learning outcomes was in student interest in the course. According to the survey measures, which included such things as enthusiasm about course topics, interest in understanding the town and interest in discussing the course with others, students reported lower levels of interest at the end of the course than at the beginning. This sentiment, however, was not reflected in student summaries, focus groups or student course evaluations, where only one student expressed negative feelings about his learning experience. Comments like "Great course; unlike any I have taken … got students into the community in a way I have not experienced before – really loved it" and "I'd never studied a place before, so the entire class, pretty much, was new to me. … I found I love learning about places" provide a different picture than the survey data. Our evaluator interpreted this difference in findings as possibly being due to course fatigue that is known to lead to less interest at the end of a course, and suggested that such an effect be more adequately assessed in the future. But we are still left with the doubt this disjuncture cast on other quantitative findings.

We have observed that learning is connected to interest, experience and self-concept. The exercise in course evaluation that we were afforded through this project, above and beyond the norm for us as college professors, provided an enlightening foray into the complexities of defining and assessing learning, forcing us to examine what we mean when we talk about learning. We also see how the evaluation exercise in itself reflects some of the same tensions in the difference in approaches between STEM and liberal education that was at the heart of the entire project, embodied in questions like: Which data are valuable? Why? Are we asking the right questions? To whom? In her observations of the college's plan process, our evaluator noted that students' educational plans tended to evolve from their diverse interests, which may not necessarily have had any connections that could serve as the basis for meaningful interdisciplinary work. As well, she observed the tensions within three aspects of the college's plan process, a well-rounded liberal arts education organized around a central, integrative question, the requirement for students to designate interests that supported the pursuit of this question via disciplinary categories, and the concern held by faculty as to whether there was enough discipline-specific work in the plan to prepare students for graduate studies, should they chose that route. Such pushes and pulls – the desire for integrative, interdisciplinary thinking, the disciplinary structure of knowledge formation and stewardship in the academy, and the professionalization of specialties that occurs in graduate school – still operate within the college's educational processes, even though they are designed to reduce such tensions.

What happened with the project, and what we learned

Our project had successes and failures. We did develop and deliver an interdisciplinary, community-engaged environmental studies course, but not in the way we initially envisioned. Through this project, we can see how the microcosms of the course development process and the classroom are embedded in multiple spheres, the relationships, intellectual dispositions and structures of the institutions that are directly involved, but are also within those of higher education at large. This finding from the Mill Town Project experience show us that courses cannot operate in isolation of larger trends, and that institutions of higher education, no matter how small or distinct from others, are also subject to the influence of the norms of the sector. We had set out to create new linkages between the college and the town in order to reduce the proverbial town-gown divide and dispel the myth of the liberal arts bubble that suggests a college operates in isolation from broader societal struggles (Pierson and Riley 2017). Instead we exposed how a dominant structure of academia, the disciplinary unit, constrained our attempts to create an interdisciplinary and community-engaged course on our own terms.

190 *Valerie Imbruce and Miroslava Prazak*

Our experience challenged our assumption that institutional structures alone can reduce the hierarchies between disciplines and between the academy and the communities outside its gates. In our group, human-centred questions and approaches to knowledge generation were seen as less scientific, and the backing of the National Science Foundation to explore the idea of place in the interdisciplinary manner we proposed did little to alleviate this perspective of the natural scientists on our team. We also had frequent debates over how students should act in the community. Were they meant to solve problems, spread their course- and college-informed perspectives or simply observe as college students in our town? This debate represents a larger issue related to social science and activism, and town-gown relations more broadly. Are sources of knowledge that exist outside of the academy more or less valid, and how can academics begin and sustain constructive dialogues with community members? We were aware of differences in perspectives within our project but failed to predict the extent to which they would become latent barriers to our interdisciplinary, community-engaged work when this project got underway. We found the debate over the validity of knowledge – between disciplines and sectors – to be the primary point of negotiation, rather than the content and pedagogical approaches of the course sequence, the topics that the course development process was meant to discuss. Some of us worked successfully in paired units of faculty from different disciplines in the delivery of our course. But co-teaching was not sustainable. The model was abandoned because there were not enough faculty members to make the commitment to co-teach, care about place and care about environmental studies more than the other courses they routinely taught.

We did successfully engage community members in the construction of course content and in the students' learning experiences because we had the funds to hire a project manager who was well-connected and respected in the community, and well-versed in the approaches and goals of our course. In subsequent iterations of the initial course, this aspect of the course was abandoned due to the lack of funds; the projects course (the second in the sequence) is yet to be repeated. The course required consistent, skilled communication among instructors, the project manager and community participants. To commit to such communication required an underlying sense of importance of the pursuit. Our institution had few established mechanisms for collaboration between the college and the town. We were grateful that we had external support to hire a project manager to develop relationships with community partners and realized the implications of the lack of institutional support as funds ran out.

Despite the successful delivery of the course, community-engaged explorations and applications of place-based knowledges were not prioritized or supported by the administration and senior faculty as the centre of the environmental studies programme had initially envisioned. Imbruce left the college after her contract expired. Early career faculty take risks in interdisciplinary work because it is not as easily evaluated in promotion and tenure cases. Indeed, many early career faculty are advised against involvement in it by senior faculty until they become established or have tenure. How can higher education institutions change if the

The challenges of studying place 191

very energies that their members bring cannot be harnessed until well after their habits, networks and ways of work are entrenched? The importance of including interdisciplinary and collaborative work in tenure and promotion cases cannot be overstated (Klein and Falk-Krzesinski 2017).

We found that the integration of STEM approaches to learning with those that emphasize the insights of lived experience can be done in a complementary manner in the classroom. For example, measuring the speed of water flow can reveal how much power there potentially is to harness from a river. But equally important is learning a river's name, who named it and how that river was viewed and used through time (Busch, 2017). One exercise can lead to clear commercial outcomes, and the other can expose the continuity of human experience to build through affection and connection the case for stewardship of natural resources, an attachment and orientation needed if we are to continue scientific research and sustain our resource base for the future. Our experience affirms that interdisciplinary education can foster such thinking. By recognizing that the collaborative process to combine disciplinary approaches has common sticking points, those who begin such endeavours can be equipped to identify and solve problems that arise through the process and manage them towards effective outcomes.

The investment by the National Science Foundation in this project endures. Our college continues to engage with local and global environmental issues, as does the community it exists within. The NSF has extended several grants to the college for leadership in the fight against the PFOA contamination[5] that was discovered in several towns in the local area, and two of the three PIs were members of the Mill Town group. Prazak went on to teach "Studying Place by Metes and Bounds" again in 2018, editing a special edition of the local history journal the *Walloomsack Review* that featured her students' work. Imbruce has adapted the course as a two-course sequence that introduces students to environmental studies as part of a new first-year research programme. The main tenet of the project, that interdisciplinary knowledges and community engagement are fundamental to environmental studies, lives on.

Conclusion: The challenges and opportunities of moving away from a disciplinary approach in the classroom

The challenges students and faculty faced in developing and participating in this set of courses are found throughout higher education. The abstraction of classroom learning from the context in which human or natural problems play out is a familiar challenge of disciplinary teaching and learning. It is a central problem of environmental studies, and of STEM education in general (Clark et al. 2011a, 2011b; Project Kaleidoscope 2006). As STEM education becomes more focused on skills acquisition and job readiness to meet national economic needs, an interdisciplinary or transdisciplinary approach is increasingly being called for from the science policy world as the means to deliver professionals trained to meet society's grand challenges (President's Council 2012; Fry 2014; US Dept. of Education 2016). This effort needs to focus more on bringing in the perspectives

192 *Valerie Imbruce and Miroslava Prazak*

of humanists and social scientists who are skilled at understanding relevance, values, belief structures and skills needed to foster societal progress. The number of students graduating with humanities degrees has been on the decline since the 1970s, a decline that was recently renewed with the Recession of 2008. Students have been moving from the humanities to majors perceived as leading more directly to jobs, such as STEM majors, seen widely as education in work skills (National Academies 2018). This is education in service to the economy, rather than education for enlightenment, improved social welfare or greater levels of social justice. Together, current educational trends are putting liberal arts and professionally oriented educational programmes in tension once again (Lewin 2013; Shinn 2014; Flaherty 2015; Morris 2017). This is a false dichotomy: education needs to be holistic.

Interdisciplinary teaching and learning can expose the shades of grey, the ambiguities found in the world, and show how disciplines are, at the most basic level, a way to systematically organize empirical and theoretical knowledge (Goodman et al. 2014; Hursh et al. 1983; Newell 1992; Rives-East et al. 2013; Wilson et al. 2012). We need more synthesis. We also need more application of synthetic knowledge. The American Academy of Arts and Sciences (2013) and other national bodies call for moving beyond interdisciplinarity to a transdisciplinary, integrative approach, an approach whose ultimate goal is to promote collaborative work to address society's grand challenges, such as climate change, alternative energy and food security, to enable innovation beyond the bounds of academia by partnering with other sectors to accelerate the discovery and development process (National Research Council 2014; National Academies 2018). The core argument here is that complex problems require complex solutions – the mantra that we opened this chapter with. In our course, we strove to integrate disciplinary perspectives by teaching research methods based in empiricism and constructivism to model an approach to the study of any town in an effort to create more informed, respectful, tolerant and environmentally conscious residents.

Higher education is suffering from the fundamental contradiction between a well-defined normative understanding of the value of interdisciplinarity and the structural impediments to the implementation of interdisciplinary educational programmes. We expose the failures from our case study so that others can choose to embed interdisciplinary, liberal education within their colleges and universities with full knowledge of the tensions that exist. Foremost, we have learned that interdisciplinary programmes, like ours in environmental studies, often function outside of the main decision-making structures for resource allocation that prioritize disciplinary programmes (Shandas and Brown 2016; Vincent et al. 2015). Since our college has an open curriculum and broadly conceived discipline-groups instead of traditional departments, not a structure usual in liberal arts institutions, we assumed we would not succumb to territoriality. We failed to predict that disciplinary needs would be considered more important than interdisciplinary initiatives. The very small size of the faculty reinforced disciplinary teaching because individual faculty members felt compelled to teach in their discipline group first

The challenges of studying place   193

(since no one else could). They therefore teach interdisciplinary courses infrequently or only with the support of a visiting faculty member if resources are available so as not to disrupt their disciplinary sequence. This is especially true in math, science and languages, where courses are sequenced.

Structural barriers are not the only impediments to interdisciplinary, community-engaged education. In regard to the question of which form of knowledge is more valid, we found fundamental differences between faculty from the natural sciences and social sciences. This placed a strain on interpersonal relations within the group. The hierarchy of knowledges operating within our group, with science seen as more reliable and human-centred approaches more "squishy," led us to our second failure. We could not mesh scientific and humanistic approaches in our course as we had hoped.

Academic administrators often use structural changes and incentives to foster interdisciplinary collaboration, but it is not enough. While these tools can shape the social process of collaboration and lead to outcomes in the short term, like the delivery of the course in our case, they are not necessarily enough to create sustained institutional change. The intellectual divide that we experienced in the development of our environmental studies course, and the interpersonal conflicts that arose around that divide within the group, created obstacles to the team's collaborative process, and also affected the way that we brought in non-academic partners. Why this divide continued to exist despite the time, space and resources we had to devote to the problem cannot be definitively understood through this reflection; it could be due to the nature of the group dynamics throughout the process of collaboration, or it may indicate that we were not posing the right questions to help us find common understandings and uncover our common values about the ways that each of us approached knowledge building. That we (the authors) realized our fraught dynamics and could not overcome them in the group at large points to our third failure. We over relied on an evaluation strategy that employed a quantitative survey of students' learning gains. We could have used the expertise of our evaluator to pose questions that could deduce group dynamics and guide us towards common understandings, or at the very least, group-level acknowledgement of difference and how they would impact our course development.

This experience provides a case study that illuminates the intricacies and complexities of interdisciplinary, community-engaged education and demonstrates that while academic institutions and members of those institutions might support interdisciplinary education rhetorically, in practice it is very difficult to create and sustain curricula that truly integrate varying intellectual paradigms within topical domains that straddle academic units. We recognize that we are not alone in this work; there are many good case studies, reflections, guides and assessments on interdisciplinary teaching and learning (Carmichael and LaPierre 2014; Ryan et al. 2014; Newell 1994; Rives-East and Lima 2013; Drake et al. 2008). In our case, it took significant external resources to devote so many faculty members to the development and co-teaching of a course sequence. We experienced the

194 *Valerie Imbruce and Miroslava Prazak*

positive responses of our students to learning various methodologies, and their appreciation of gaining first-hand experience as researchers, and the enthusiasm of our community partners to engage with us. Like us, our students found the focus on the town in which they lived to be a compelling frame. They also found this aspect of the course to be unique in their college experiences thus far. For the instructors and course developers, this experience highlights the need to consider the ways that faculty members from various disciplines and fields develop knowledge. It also highlights the need to expose the methods that we use and explain the reasons for them to students, the need to show the boundaries of the methods, and the need to work with others collaboratively to expand them. By sharing our experiences, we hope to inform others grappling with the complexities of understanding the world through various disciplines, and combining approaches from different epistemologies. For environmental studies, this integration is crucial to finding truths about the world and ways to apprehend its complexities.

Take-home messages

- We need to acknowledge and tackle the structural impediments to interdisciplinary programmes to promote their creation.
- Hierarchies between disciplines are more powerful than institutional structures, and external contexts influence and colour the local arena.
- One way of knowing cannot be privileged over others in the course structuring and delivery, or the hierarchies of knowledge will be perpetuated.
- Differences in perspective become latent barriers to interdisciplinarity.
- To fully evaluate an interdisciplinary project, communicative, value-driven and process-oriented goals need to be articulated, and not just goals that can be assessed through quantification.
- A commitment to exploring the validity of different ways of knowing must be both ideological and practical.

Notes

1 We follow the Association of American Colleges and Universities' definition of liberal education as an approach to college learning that empowers students to deal with complexity, diversity and change, emphasizing a broad knowledge of the world. See http://aacu.org/leap/what-is-a-liberal-education.
2 We will refer to the college and town without naming it throughout the chapter.
3 The preamble of our syllabus reads: *Metes and Bounds is an English system of describing land that was used in colonial America. The [new town] was described this way in its charter: The* "Tract is to Contain Six Miles Square … Beginning at A Crotched Hemlock Tree Marked W: Six miles Due North of A White Oak Tree Standing in the Northern Boundary Line of the Province of Massachusetts Bay," quoted from the Vermont Historical Society website: http://vermonthistory.org/explorer/vermont-stories/becoming-a-state/starting-a-town.
4 See https://salgsite.net/.
5 PFOA stands for Perfluorooctanoic acid, a synthetic compound that has been used in the manufacture of prominent consumer goods in industrial quantities since the 1940s.

References

American Academy of Arts and Sciences. 2013. *ARISE 2: Unleashing America's research and innovation enterprise*. Cambridge, MA: Author. Available from: http://www.amac ad.org/content/Research/research.aspx?d=268.

Bell, S. 2007. Deep-level composition variables as predictors of team performance: A meta-analysis. *Journal of Applied Psychology*, 92(3), 595–615. doi:10.1037/0021-9010.92.3.595.

Busch, A. 2017, April 8. Learn a river's name before it's gone. *Sunday Review, The New York Times*. Available from: https://www.nytimes.com/2017/04/08/opinion/sunday/learn-a-rivers-name-before-its-gone.html?_r=0.

Carmichael, T., La Pierre, Y. 2014. Interdisciplinary learning works: The results of a comprehensive assessment of students and student learning outcomes in an integrative learning community. *Issues in Interdisciplinary Studies*, 23, 53–78.

Carson, D. 2015, May 27. Bennington College course finds "beating heart" of Bennington. *Bennington Banner*. Available from: http://www.benningtonbanner.com/stories/benni ngton-college-course-finds-beating-heart-of-bennington,287813.

Clark, S.G., Rutherford, M.B., Auer, M.R., Cherney, D.N., Wallace, R.L., Mattson, D.J., Clark, D.A., Foote, L., Krogman, N., Wilshusen, P., Steelman T. 2011a. College and university environmental programs as a policy problem (part 1): Integrating knowledge, education, and action for a better world? *Environmental Management*, 47(5), 701–715. doi:10.1007/s00267-011-9619-2.

Clark, S.G., Rutherford, M.B., Auer, M.R., Cherney, D.N., Wallace, R.L, Mattson, D.J., Clark, D.A., Foote, L., Krogman, N., Wilshusen P., Steelman T. 2011b. College and university environmental programs as a policy problem (part 2): Strategies for improvement. *Environmental Management*, 47(5), 716–726. doi:10.1007/s00267-011-9635-2.

Drake, T., O'Rourke, M., Panttaja, D., Peterson, I. 2008. It's alive! The life span of an interdisciplinary course in the humanities. *Journal of General Education*, 57(4), 223–243.

Flaherty, C. 2015. Major exodus: English departments at U. of Maryland and elsewhere respond to drop-offs—some of them major—in English majors. *Inside Higher Education*. Available from: https://www.insidehighered.com/news/2015/01/26/whe re-have-all-english-majors-gone.

Fry, C.L., ed., 2014. *Achieving systemic change: A sourcebook for advancing and funding undergraduate STEM education*. Washington, DC: The Association of American Colleges and Universities. Available from: https://www.aacu.org/pkal/sourcebook.

Goodman, B., Vaughn Huckfeldt, E. 2014. The rise and fall of a required interdisciplinary course: Lessons learned. *Innovative Higher Education*, 39(1), 75–88. doi:10.1007/s10755-013-9261-4.

Hursh, B., Haas P., Moore, M. 1983. An interdisciplinary model to implement general education. *The Journal of Higher Education*, 54(1), 42–59. doi:10.1080/00221546.19 83.11778151.

Klein, J.T., Falk-Krzesinki H. 2017. Interdisciplinary and collaborative work: Framing promotion and tenure policies. *Research Policy*, 46(6), 1055–1061.

Lau, D.C., Keith Murnighan, J. 2005. Interactions within groups and subgroups: The effects of demographic faultlines. *Academy of Management Journal*, 48(4), 645–659.

Lewin, T. 2013, October 30. As interest fades in the humanities, colleges worry. *The New York Times*. Available from: http://www.nytimes.com/2013/10/31/education/as-int erest-fades-in-the-humanities-colleges-worry.html.

196   *Valerie Imbruce and Miroslava Prazak*

McArdle, P. 2015, June 4. Bennington students focus study on town. *Rutland Daily Herald*, p. B3.

Morris, L. 2017. Letter to parents: The purpose of college. *Innovative Higher Education*, 42(3), 189–191. Available from: https://link.springer.com/article/10.1007/s10755-0 17-9398-7.

National Academies of Sciences, Engineering, and Medicine. 2018. *The integration of the humanities and arts with sciences, engineering, and medicine in higher education: Branches from the same tree.* Washington, DC: The National Academies Press. doi:10.17226/24988.

National Research Council. 2014. *Convergence: Facilitating transdisciplinary integration of life sciences, physical sciences, engineering, and beyond.* Washington, DC: The National Academies Press. Available from: https://www.nap.edu/catalog/18722/conver gence-facilitating-transdisciplinary-integration-of-life-sciences-physical-sciences-e ngineering.

Newell, W.H. 1992. Academic disciplines and undergraduate interdisciplinary education: Lessons from the School of Interdisciplinary Studies at Miami University, Ohio. *European Journal of Education*, 27(3), 211–221.

Newell, W. 1994. Designing interdisciplinary courses. *New Directions for Teaching and Learning*, 58, 35–51.

Pierson, J., Schaefer Riley, N. 2017, March 10. The liberal-arts "bubble" didn't always cause such trouble. *Wall Street Journal*. Available from: https://www.wsj.com/articles/ the-liberal-arts-bubble-didnt-always-cause-such-trouble-1489187214.

President's Council of Advisors on Science and Technology. 2012. Engage to excel: Producing one million additional college graduates with degrees in science, technology, engineering, and mathematics. Report to the President of the United States. Available from: https://obamawhitehouse.archives.gov/sites/default/files/microsites/ostp/pcast-e ngage-to-excel-final_2-25-12.pdf.

Project Kaleidoscope. 2006. Transforming America's scientific and technical infrastructure: Recommendations for urgent action. Report on Reports II. Washington, DC. Available from: http://www.pkal.org/documents/ReportOnReportsII.cfm.

Rives-East, D., Lima, Olivia K. 2013. Designing interdisciplinary science/humanities courses: Challenges and solutions. *College Teaching*, 61(3), 100–106. doi:10.1080/8 7567555.2012.752339.

Ryan, P., Sorenson Kurtz, J., Carter, D., Pester, D. 2014. Interdisciplinarity, qualitative research and the complex phenomenon: Toward an integrative approach to intercultural research. *Issues in Interdisciplinary Studies*, 32, 79–102.

Shandas, V., Brown, S.E. 2016. An empirical assessment of interdisciplinarity: Perspectives from graduate students and program administrators. *Innovative Higher Education*, 41(5), 411–423. doi:10.1007/s10755-016-9362-y.

Shinn, L. 2014. Liberal education vs. professional education: The false choice. Association of Governing Boards of Universities and Colleges. Available from: https://www.agb .org/trusteeship/2014/1/liberal-education-vs-professional-education-false-choice.

Struck, B. 2017. *Flagging problems of capture*. Available from: http://www.scienceme trics.org/flagging-problems-capture/#more-228.

U.S. Department of Education, Office of Innovation and Improvement 2016. *STEM 2026: A vision for innovation in STEM education*. Washington, DC. Retrieved from https://in novation.ed.gov/files/2016/09/AIR-STEM2026_Report_2016.pdf

Vincent, S., Dutton, K., Santos, R., Sloane, L. 2015. *Interdisciplinary environmental and sustainability education and research: Leadership and administrative structures.* Washington, DC: National Council for Science and the Environment.

Wilson, S., Zamberlan, L. 2012. Show me yours: Developing a faculty-wide interdisciplinary initiative in built environment higher education. *Contemporary Issues in Education Research*, 5(4), 331–342. Available from: https://search.proquest.com/docview/1418 450504?pq-origsite=gscholar.

12 Transdisciplinary learning within tertiary institutions – a space to skin your knees

Dena Fam, Abby Mellick Lopes and Cynthia Mitchell

Introduction

The rise of what Mulgan et al. (2016) term the "challenge-driven" university has emerged in Australia and internationally as a way of educating students to respond to complex real-world problems. These models of education invite students to respond to complex challenges for which there are no established or single solutions. Instead, students draw on a range of disciplines to solve or improve complex problems; they work in teams; and they collaborate with industry-relevant partners outside of higher education. Collaborative, industry-engaged and interdisciplinary and/or transdisciplinary models of education are well suited to preparing students for the needs of the world (Mulgan 2016), and as such constitute an important complement to traditional models of university education that involve mastering a single discipline. This collaborative, engaged approach to research, teaching, and learning has the potential to complement the controlled, experimental context of a positivist paradigm which tends to limit or reduce the scope of projects and disciplinary perspectives, or subsume disciplinary perspectives to a scientific worldview. In practice, mobilizing disciplinary knowledge in an *applied* setting necessitates disciplines to coalesce and learn from each other.

While there are many definitions related to the crossing of disciplinary boundaries, Petrie's (1992) review of interdisciplinary education identifies the extent to which integration of knowledge occurs across boundaries. Petrie considers multidisciplinary efforts to be akin to groupwork drawing on different disciplines for the purpose of solving a specific problem, whereas he argues that interdisciplinary approaches seek to integrate different views. Transdisciplinary approaches create a space for multiple, co-existing viewpoints and utilize the discontinuities between views as a source for further inquiry and emergent understanding. These latter approaches also support the systemic collaboration needed to address complex societal challenges (Senge 2006).

The case study presented in this chapter informed the development of a transdisciplinary living lab (Crosby, Fam et al. 2018; Fam, Lopes et al. 2019). This approach to education aims to transcend disciplinary boundaries by utilizing the university campus as a living laboratory in which students engage with a complex

Transdisciplinary learning 199

problem, in this case the introduction of an alternative sanitation system on campus – a urine diversion system. The living lab concept – collaborative learning in a living, social setting – has roots that go back to the experiential, problem-focused approach to learning championed by John Dewey in the early years of the twentieth century (Dewey 1938). His key claim of a continuity between learning and society has underpinned recent developments in living labs, engaged research, "work integrated learning," and the development of a research and teaching nexus. These developments attempt to roll back the abstraction of knowledge in academic institutions, and to enhance the contemporary relevance of knowledge in applied contexts. Living labs are now commonly understood as collaborative test beds for an innovative approach to problem solving occurring in a living, social environment where end-users are involved (Daniel 2017, p. 2). The living lab concept is increasingly being used to explore multi-dimensional and dynamic (or "wicked") sustainability-related problems in a university setting. A university community has the unique potential to nurture innovation by absorbing risk and valuing the endeavour as a learning experience. The socially and geographically bounded context can help to contain complexity and render it observable. This also introduces an approach to learning where students can "discover [...], examine and fail" in a "safe environment" and where the exchange of knowledge supported by living labs taps into the under-utilized "brain power" of the entire university, including its stakeholders (Graczyk 2015, p. 32).

"Skinning our knees" – trialling innovation in sanitation

In the context of this case study, "failure" refers to the inability of the sustainable sanitation project to move to the next phase of anticipated wider implementation and scale-up. As the original proposal stated:

> The project has an exploratory intent because we view it as the first tangible step in a long-term programme of research and practice. We will pilot urine diversion, recovery and reuse here at UTS with the aim of illuminating the range of interdependent factors that determine successful uptake and potential scale-up of radical sustainable urban sanitation. … Our intention in this project is to open up this very fertile space for further research and practice, and to enable implementation elsewhere, including UTS' new buildings.

The goal of the Sustainable Sanitation Project at the University of Technology Sydney (UTS) was to facilitate the development of urine diversion systems by trialling a system in an urban, multi-story building and investigating what it would take for the system to become viable in an urban environment. The two-year action research project involved the installation of a urine diversion system on campus to collect and treat urine at UTS before processing and reusing the nutrients in urine in agricultural trials at Western Sydney University (then the University of Western Sydney (UWS)). The project is premised on the potential value of urine as a substitute for phosphate rock, the primary component of chemical fertilizers used in agricultural food production. Mined phosphate rock is a rapidly depleting, finite mineral resource that underpins global food security (Cordell, Drangert et al. 2009). At the same time, phosphorus is widely understood as an environmental pollutant which is costly to manage and treat. Ultimately, the project had the aim of developing a proof-of-concept concerning the idea that urine could and should be seen as a resource that could be diverted, captured, transported, and reused in food production and subsequently contribute to closing the phosphorus loop locally (see Chapter 5 by Beal et al. in this book for another perspective on the emergence of UD in Australia). To capture, value and reuse urine in this way requires a significant transformation in how we think about and manage sewage: viewing it as a resource rather than a waste product. The project presented many technical, institutional and regulatory challenges in implementing sustainable innovation, as well as social and cultural challenges. These included embedded perceptions of sewage as a waste product, by everyone from toilet users to regulators to agriculturalists.

The project took an action research approach to supporting collaborative learning and to explicitly challenging the cultural fear of failure by acknowledging up-front that we could not know, and indeed did not need to know, everything before we began. The project prepared project partners in two ways: first, by making explicit our expectation that we likely would and in fact should plan to "skin our knees" along the way and, second, by making the argument that the university campus was the perfect place for such an experiment. The metaphor, "skinning our knees" inferred that we would encounter minor incidents from which we could readily recover and keep going, having learned something from the process of falling over. A significant parallel goal of the core research team was to demonstrate the value to industry and academic partners of an emergent approach to research: one where the overarching goal is clear – to trial an innovative, sociotechnical system – and where the details of not only the design and the methodology but also the project management milestones were less clear and needed to be flexible enough to respond to insights revealed along the way.

By taking a transdisciplinary approach, the project engaged with social, technical, cultural, representational, regulatory and economic issues, in both isolated and integrated ways. Project partners and collaborators included representatives from academia, industry and government (see Table 12.1 for details). The value

Table 12.1 Collaborators involved in the UTS trial across academia, industry and government

Academia
Law, agriculture, design, engineering, sustainability, systems thinking
Industry
Toilet manufacturer, nursery and garden association, water industry
Government
Department of health, facilities management, plumbing regulator

and significance of creating a new stakeholder conversation in this project was that it opened a domain of possibility for all stakeholders of "what could be," creating a surer footing for further experiments and validating learning from failures.

Living labs – or the experimental sites for learning-by-doing – are somewhat risky enterprises as they can be resource intensive and often fail to produce the "disruptive innovation" anticipated by industry stakeholders at the beginning of the process (EU 2015). In the current case study, embracing complexity, the utilization of early generation technology and the unpredictable nature of social participation meant that the project was inherently risky and likely to veer off track. The contained context of the university campus offset some of this risk, since the university could absorb it as research enterprise (Mellick Lopes et al. 2012; Allen et al. 2009). However, while the research presented an acceptable risk for stakeholders invested in innovation and "discovery learning" (Warburton 2003), the research was more of a challenge for university facilities management and practitioners bound by strict regulations and codes of practice, such as plumbers. Staff responsible for campus operations generally deal with the effective acquisition and use of resources in managing facilities, major projects and information systems on a daily basis. Our experience mirrored Hoffman and Axson's findings: The project management priorities of operational staff means their view of acceptable risk differs significantly from the views of faculty researchers (Hoffman and Axson 2017). An important dimension of this project therefore was the early involvement of facilities management staff *as* researchers. This required a collaborative process of framing shared goals, as well as an openness to negotiating tensions that might emerge in the conduct of the research. It was important that the facilities management staff were already committed to sustainability and were invested in improving the sustainability outcomes of campus operations.

In positioning the project as a transdisciplinary initiative, a diverse range of outcomes emerged throughout the project. We have mapped these outcomes against Mitchell et al.'s (2015) Outcome Spaces model which includes: (1) changes in the situation, (2) changes in stocks and flows of knowledge and (3) mutual and/or transformational learning which occurred for both researchers and research participants (see Figure 12.1).

Failure or adaptation to changing circumstances?

While the project was clearly designed to trial the social, technical and regulatory issues associated with installing innovation in sanitation, unexpected failures and successes emerged and are discussed below.

Project failure to enable scale-up

While the above discussion demonstrates the sustainable sanitation project did achieve a remarkable set of laudable outcomes in just two years (Figure 12.1), it failed at its central goal of enabling scale-up by "opening up the space to further research and practice." That is, in terms of managing transitions towards more

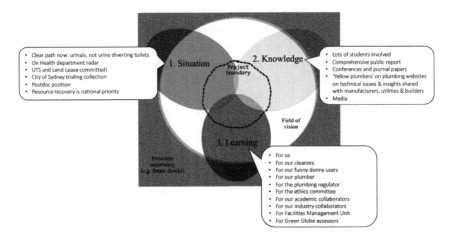

Figure 12.1 Outcomes achieved in the trial of urine diversion systems at UTS.

sustainable systems (Loorbach 2010), the project failed to expand the niche system of sanitation beyond a single experiment, or to influence the broader regime of wastewater management.

The community of practice generated through the project was insufficient to sustain the next phase of research and practice. Each of our project partners either was, or increasingly became, enthusiastic about the need for and potential of urine diversion as a mainstream alternative to conventional sewerage. However, all partners were practitioners – none were in leadership roles, very few were in influential positions within their organizations, and all had the project as an "extra responsibility" – that is, it was above and beyond their "real" jobs.

With the benefit of hindsight, it is evident that we failed to invest adequately in building a broader local platform for change that could translate what we did inside the university to an external process (Hansson and Polk 2018). We focused our efforts at two levels. For our niche experiment, we progressed the detail of the research pilot itself, learning what we did not know about UD systems in practice and shattering many myths in the process, creating transformational learning opportunities for ourselves, our project partners, and for our UD research participants. At the broader landscape level, we were involved in media and communications for wide-ranging outlets, as well as publishing journal articles and presenting research findings at industry events. However, we did not engage at the leadership level with key institutions locally. So, even though our project and its outputs embodied relevance, legitimacy and credibility for internal and external stakeholders, the combination of institutional barriers and lack of seniority contributed to a lack of uptake (Hansson and Polk 2018).

When the project ended, and new sources of funds were sought to continue the work, we had a group of collaborators who could now see and articulate for themselves the value of continuing to explore how to make urine diversion a practical reality, but none of them felt it was their responsibility institutionally to take it forwards. When faced with criticism of the idea of urine diversion by others in their fields, our supporters were not confident enough to argue the case. This also relates to the fact that our supporters were not influencers and key decision-makers in their fields. So, whilst they did not shy away from what they had learned, the lack of institutionalization of UD meant that neither did they step forward with their new knowledge to make a different case.

For example, one way to have scaled up to the next phase of research would have been to implement larger-scale trials of urine as a fertilizer on non-food crops to demonstrate efficacy and explore demand for a more sustainable product. Our nursery industry project participant was entirely supportive of this concept and provided industry contacts for various products so that we as researchers could seek support. However, the socio-cultural taboos associated with using bodily wastes proved too much for these uninitiated industry leads, and every approach by us as researchers was met with a refusal to participate from the horticultural industry. On reflection, this could have been due to the inability to overcome the "yuck factor" and taboos associated with the use of wastewater in horticulture/agriculture, or it could have been due to the failure of our media communication models to clearly provide justification for niche approaches in the face of embedded centralized norms of wastewater management.

The situation was similar across the project partners. For example, whilst the water utility saw value in the work, and arranged for the outputs to be presented at the general manager level in the organization, there was limited institutional support for further research funding to support the next phase, given a reduction in organizational research funds. The experience gained by the toilet manufacturer made it clear to them that their efforts to develop UD technology should remain focused on urinals, and not expand to toilets. That meant their interest going forward remained on avoiding blockages in pipework. For the local government representative, whilst they had a general commitment to sustainability, their specific issue with managing urine concerned public urination during summer festivals, which they solved in subsequent years by employing transportable urine storage tanks in temporary urinals across the centre of Sydney.

As a "failed innovation," the sustainable sanitation project proved to be a successful learning exercise on a number of levels. It drew attention to conflicting views about phosphorus that were embedded in the regime of water management – for example, urine was seen as a potential fertilizer but also as a pollutant causing blockages in sewerage pipes. This provided unexpected insights into likely failures occurring behind the scenes in the current system. Pipe blockages due to struvite precipitation are often quoted as a problem for urine diversion activities which is, at a minimum, significant and at times, insurmountable (Li et al. 2019). In this project, we revealed that potentially catastrophic struvite build-up was already occurring in conventional urinal piping systems within the university, but it was unknown, undocumented and therefore unmanaged. The spectacular and slightly gruesome images below speak for themselves (see Figure 12.2).

Figure 12.2 Images of documented pipe blockages from struvite build-up in piping for conventional urinals.

Within UTS, the combination of an aggressive building programme, an institutional commitment to sustainability, and our access to and support from facilities leadership meant that we were able to have an impact. We synthesized the learning from our project, our partners, and international experience into guidance materials for the design and installation of urine diversion pipework and plumbing in multi-story buildings. We created the opportunity to make this available to the project managers for a new, AUD$40 million university building being constructed on campus. As a result, the university requested the contractors install urine diversion plumbing and storage facilities, leading to two 10,000 L tanks connected to waterless urinals across ten floors of the new building for a cost of less than 0.1% of the building. However, the contractors had no experience with urine diversion plumbing. Whilst we had experience, we had limited opportunities to influence them: our relationships were with staff from the facilities management unit, rather than with the new building project managers directly, so we were given only a limited opportunity to provide advice. The result was that significant errors and omissions occurred during construction of the system, leading to significant operational difficulties and shortcomings. These problems undermined the confidence of facilities management leadership and staff in urine diversion. On reflection, this project required an intervention in the decision-making and procurement process, ideally by providing support for the university in developing specifications for project bidders. In recent years, the existence of the tanks and the ability to collect and store large volumes of urine on campus has enabled a new generation of wastewater treatment research on urine treatment and phosphorus precipitation by colleagues in the engineering faculty (see Volpin, Heo et al. 2019).

For most of our academic colleagues, this project was a side-interest. On its completion, most of them returned to their respective disciplinary homes and extant lines of inquiry. Colleagues at Western Sydney University were the exception – they went on to conduct further small-scale research on the application of urine as a fertilizer, and to further explore design's contribution to transdisciplinary research (see Mellick Lopes et al. 2012). This group, in collaboration with a subset of the original group, has moved further into the development of

Transdisciplinary learning 205

experimental learning models with an emphasis on transdisciplinarity, and has collaboratively developed a model of transdisciplinary education for teaching and learning (Crosby, Fam et al. 2018; Fam, Mellick Lopes et al. 2019).

All of this meant that transdisciplinary research on urine diversion systems was not adequately planned for, and thus fell between the cracks in terms of resourcing. The Australian Research Council remained focused on disciplinary research, industry research funds were focused on applications that were closer to implementation and no partner felt sufficient responsibility for the topic to step into a leadership role. In other words, our assumption that the experience of the project and the knowledge and practice discoveries revealed by the project would be sufficient as a platform to move forwards was not well founded.

There was a second confounding factor on top of this lack of an obvious source for the next phase of funding, and that was the business model of the institute that housed the lead investigators. It operates on a self-funding arrangement, which means the researchers must bring in funded research projects. Investment in new business development is possible, but only to a degree. By the time it became apparent that we had underestimated the need to invest during the project itself in building a coalition of partners who would back further investment, two competing pressures combined to stop further work. First, the level of effort required to seek alternative funds was becoming too high and, second, the PI's success in winning research projects in other areas meant there was no capacity to continue a significant involvement in UD research. In short, projects that undertake ambitious tasks of facilitating system change of embedded infrastructures require long-term support encompassing financial, human, and institutional resources.

Engaging a diversity of knowledge regimes

Limited research and knowledge on early generation urine diversion systems (Fam, Mitchell et al. 2009) at the time of the pilot project revealed the importance of considering not only the technological system but also the contextual nature of technological "solutions." The pilot revealed that it is not only a matter of installing the "right" technology but importantly the technology needs to be situated and socialized by those using, cleaning and maintaining the system if it is to be successful over the long term (Lopes, Fam et al. 2012).

Operational knowledge, including the practical insights provided by cleaners, plumbers and facilities staff, emerged as a critical form of knowledge in relation to identifying problems in practice that were important to resolve to ensure the ongoing viability of the new system being piloted. While, for example, the plumber was an enthusiastic participant in the research, it was not easy for him to go against years of compliance with the Plumbing Code in adapting plumbing pipework to accommodate the urine diversion toilets and system. While the code requires an odour trap to be installed with all sanitary fixtures, the researchers had hypothesized that in order for the urine to drain effectively, the S-bend odour trap needed to be removed. As Mitchell et al. (2013, p. 25) state "[the plumber's] first response was to enlarge the trap, and then to simplify the trap, and finally, to

206 *Fam, Lopes and Mitchell*

assuage our relentless requests, to remove the trap altogether." The impacts of the new system on plumbing practices required a critical analysis of current codes to determine points of flexibility and support for practitioners, including briefs for communications about installation practices and pipe gradations.

While no toilet design "survived" the trial as a radical innovation intact, these deliberations had a positive impact that made inroads into the plumbing community, and led to the framing of a new professional identity: the "yellow plumber" (Kyriakou 2010). Mitchell et al. (2013, p. 25) write: "this experience highlighted that even the best plumbers need training to appreciate and apply the distinctive principles for urine pipework when they depart from conventional plumbing codes." This example illustrates the necessity of involving a diversity of knowledge regimes in transdisciplinary experiments as it expands the project "field of vision," particularly as it pertains to innovation in the critical areas of adaptation and retrofitting. See Figure 12.3 for the layout of the urine diversion toilet and sampling system installed.

Clarifying roles and expectations of team members in transdisciplinary projects

The current model of tertiary education tends to focus on knowledge creation emerging from current disciplinary paradigms rather than transformational learning (Schön 1987). Academic partners in the project were influenced by the "politics of research" (Altman 1995) and the need to publish research through peer reviewed publications to fulfil expectations of their academic institutions. The expectation that academic members would produce research outputs had not been clearly articulated in the early stages of the project but was clarified as the project progressed. When it became apparent that academic members were, in many cases, disinclined to participate due to lack of institutional support, the facilitating team renegotiated incentives for academics to meet institutional requirements, for example by offering financial incentives, opportunities for research outputs and research assistance. Evidence from the project suggests that articulating both individuals and institutional expectations helps identify potential barriers to the sustained engagement of academic members (Fam 2017).

Working in transdisciplinary teams requires adopting a posture of collaboration which requires openness, a willingness to share knowledge and expertise outside disciplinary silos, and to accept that intellectual property and project results are being shared and collectively owned. It also means a willingness to encounter the limits of one's own knowledge and expertise which could be another example of "skinning the knees." Collaboration and an open approach to research discovery is novel for many academic researchers more familiar with working in disciplinary silos, building disciplinary expertise and seeking individual recognition and reward for their input.

While cross-disciplinary collaboration and decision-making was perceived by the facilitating team as necessary for trialling innovation, it was not universally accepted by all community members as a legitimate form of research

Transdisciplinary learning 207

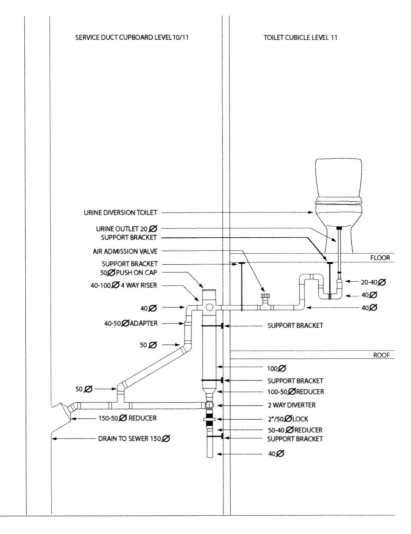

Figure 12.3 Illustration of UD toilet and sampling system (Mitchell et al. 2013).

collaboration. For example, one member viewed participatory input into decision-making as unnecessary and unprofessional, suggesting that *"being participatory to arrive at an outcome may sound democratic but ends in compromise ... that serves no-one. It's also an abdication of professionalism which is totally unnecessary"* (academic team member). While cross-disciplinary decision-making was widely accepted in theory, it was not until implementing participatory decision-making processes in practice during the design phase of the project that issues arose with certain team members perceiving disciplinary expertise to be compromised by participatory processes (Fam 2017).

208 *Fam, Lopes and Mitchell*

Learning through failure and unexpected successes along the way

An unexpected outcome was the role of visual communication design in transdisciplinary research and collaboration. Visual communication in research often plays a representational role, entering the field after "knowledge creation" to produce information graphics or diagrams to support the translation and dissemination of the research in the public domain. However, in this project, visual communication was brought in at an early stage to facilitate social engagement for the duration of the research. This was a direct result of an identified absence of the end-user voice in previous "top-down" UD experiments (Fam and Mitchell 2013), leading to critical questions about the engagement of everyday social actors in facilitating system change (Mellick Lopes et al. 2012). Part of the impetus of involving visual communication was the prevalence of poor visual assets in previous pilots. In the early stages of this project, it became clear that user manuals, signage and other artefacts would help facilitate new social practices of plumbers, cleaners and everyday toilet users, and would be a significant element of the investigation, demarcating and providing indices for a new territory of practice. It was also deemed important to involve visual communication in promoting system literacy to engage the university community and the broader public in the "story" of the project. At the start of the project, it was assumed that visual artefacts produced by two student groups involved in the project would be exhibited. However, what eventuated was a much more open-ended set of tools, including an in situ graffiti board that became a key instrument of social data collection over the eight months of the trial, capturing frank, practical, and creative inputs of everyday users (see Figure 12.4) and that visual communication design could provide insight into the range of collaborative input across strands of research (see Figure 12.5).

The importance of social learning

The transdisciplinary approach adopted in the project highlighted the importance of creating space for social interaction and social learning. Originating from concepts of organizational learning (Argyris and Schön 1978; Senge 1990; Wenger 1998), social learning has at its core a sense of the importance of the co-generation of knowledge. In the example of the graffiti board, participants noticed that the project team was taking action in response to comments. Said one participant, "*It seems comments are taken seriously and results in new little tweaks!*" "Tweaking" the system to align with user needs and expectations demonstrated the co-generation of knowledge and the truly socio-technical nature of the experiment (Fam and Lopes 2015). Rather than truth-seeking instruments, the social research tools used in this project were much more like "minor tools of situated demand management" to draw on an idea from Sofoulis (2005). This approach enabled the project to model an everyday politics of transitions (how to *do* transitions in practice) and highlighted the significance of situated, applied and operational knowledge in system change.

Social learning was highlighted by team members as an important characteristic of the project. Team meetings were deliberately structured to support

Transdisciplinary learning 209

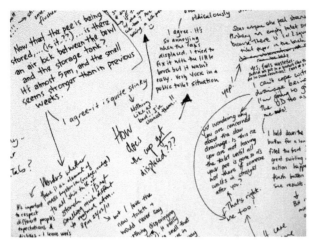

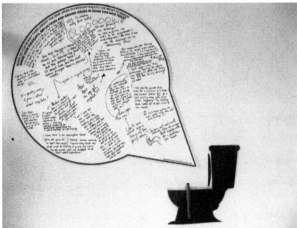

Figure 12.4 Graffiti board in situ and detail: used to collect end-users' feedback on the system, Designer: Yana Mokmargana (WSU).

conversation between cross-disciplinary members and the relationship between them and, in the process, to develop collective problem definitions and identification of potential solutions. Most team members interviewed as part of the project wrap-up (9 of the 11 members) noted that conversation between members was a significant learning experience, with one team member reflecting that "*The social dimension of the project has been a very important instigator of my learning. It's not me going off and reading something on my own necessarily. It's that plus the conversation ... plus, the interactive experience*" (academic team member). The academic investigators forming part of the wider research team were also conscious that didactic, autonomous, discipline-based courses rarely seek to foster

210 *Fam, Lopes and Mitchell*

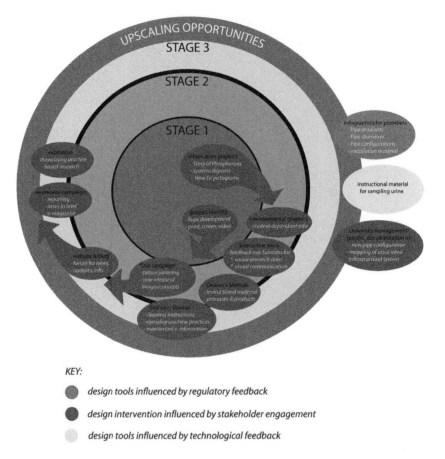

Figure 12.5 Development of a visual communication strategy building collaborative input across strands of research (Mellick Lopes et al. 2012).

an advanced social networking culture among students – a culture which is commonly credited with promoting deep learning (Gray, Williams et al. 2014).

As the experiment broached new territory, new productive relationships amongst stakeholders were also charted, with an unforeseen mode of interaction emerging in the form of collaborative writing as a process of learning. The importance of collaborative writing, not only as a research contribution and academic output, but also as a mode of learning, had not been recognized in the early stages of the project. Over the two years of the project, academic conference/journal publications were written across the fields of systems thinking, design education and transition management, design studies and transdisciplinary collaboration involving both industry and academic contributors. The social nature of academic writing with cross-disciplinary partners could be defined within the UTS project as a particular mode of social learning (Fam 2017). One industry partner highlighted that "*in working with purely agricultural scientists ... [writing together in the project] stretched my imagination a bit and made me think a little bit differently in how we approach the issue [of trialling a new system]*" (industry partner). The opportunity to utilize academic writing as an interdisciplinary mode of learning was enhanced by the fact that half of the members of the community were academics, each with a distinct and unique disciplinary background.

Learning to run a transdisciplinary project while incorporating a research-teaching nexus

The UTS project was an opportunity for the authors to design an educational programme for undergraduate students closely linked to an industry-funded project aimed at transitioning to an alternative sanitation system. One of the key outcomes for the project team was learning how to run a transdisciplinary project with a diverse range of partners while at the same time involving students as participant researchers. The challenges to disciplinary knowledge experienced by researchers were also experienced by students, as the project demanded an organic, adaptive approach to learning not often encountered in traditional disciplinary training. The project created novel spaces for creative student engagement, which promoted deep learning and sophisticated intellectual interactions in the sustainability sphere (Gray et al. 2014). What emerged as a result of this project was the development of a model for transdisciplinary education, in particular the evolution of the "Transdisciplinary Living Lab Model" (TDLL) (Fam, Lopes et al. 2019) with a research-teaching nexus at its core. Building on the collaborative and applied learning context of the sanitation project, which had a high degree of affinity with design as an interventionist and future-oriented discipline, the TDLL seeks collaboration with industry, government and university operational staff to provide transdisciplinary learning opportunities for students in relation to campus-focused sustainability research. The TDLL provides an opportunity for students to engage with the Sustainable Development Goals (SDGs) and the concept of planetary boundaries (or the safe operating space for humanity based on the biophysical processes regulating earth systems) while designing system interventions in fulfilment of their course requirements. The decision to incorporate the SDGs and the concept of planetary boundaries into the TDLL model was made to encourage students to critically reflect on the impact of their solutions to complex problems on global systems.

The TDLL is problem-focused and action-oriented, and deploys participatory approaches to support collaborative transdisciplinary input into improving complex problems such as waste and water management. The development of the TDLL was unapologetically "interventionist" in the way it framed, structured, and organized the discourse about the problem being addressed. That is, the research-teaching nexus took an interventionist approach to ask "what could be" (Brown 2010), with the view that system change is not simply technical but also social and cultural, with material infrastructural and immaterial symbolic dimensions. The

212 *Fam, Lopes and Mitchell*

student/researchers are therefore required to develop a rich understanding of the sustainability problem being investigated, starting with their own everyday practices, and they are required to identify a point of intervention from inside the system. Utilizing the campus as a living laboratory provides the context for students to engage with waste and sanitation systems daily, and to further investigate both the visible and commonly invisible components of the system including technologies, actors (cleaners, facilities personnel) and practices (Fam et al. 2019).

In the higher education context, on-campus living labs are one way to create an environment that supports transdisciplinary research, bringing members of the public, business, government, and researchers together to co-create services, systems, technologies and societal solutions. Linking curriculum, operations and research via the mechanism of a living lab offers a holistic and systemic way to support the university and its researchers, students, and graduates to practically meet sustainability goals.

Discussion*: How should tertiary institutions support learning through failure in transdisciplinary projects?*

Universities need to change from functioning primarily as service providers to the (current) labour market, which inherently diminishes a future-focused perspective, to taking more of a cultural leadership role and deliberately facilitating cultural change. This project was less about "work integrated learning" than about facilitating a grander social learning project that needs to be undertaken by the culture at large if we are to transition to more sustainable futures.

In this respect, the industry and government partners in the project were partners in discovery learning, rather than clients seeking the university's services to problem solve. As sustainable designer Ezio Manzini writes:

> The transition toward sustainability is a massive social learning process. The radical nature of the objective (learning to live better while leaving a light ecological footprint) requires vast experimentation, a vast capacity for listening and an immense degree of flexibility in order to change. … Sustainability and the conservation and regeneration of environmental and social capital means breaking with the currently dominant models of living, production, and consumption, and experimenting with new ones. A social learning process on this vast scale must involve everybody.
>
> (2008, p.16)

This is becoming all the more urgent, as indicated by the 2018 Intergovernmental Panel on Climate Change (IPCC) report which notes that, "Limiting global warming to 1.5 degrees C would require rapid, far reaching and unprecedented changes in all aspects of society" (IPCC 2018), including in how we manage our waste, water and energy services. All of these services have the potential to be explored on campus as part of a research-teaching nexus, which deliberately places students inside a complex living socio-technical system.

Transdisciplinary learning 213

Importantly, the project enabled the space, not only for social learning amongst project partners, but also for exploring future possibilities and the "unknowns" associated with UD systems. An important characteristic of transdisciplinary research is, of course, creating the space to explore the "unknowns" and emergent issues/matters of concern as they arise (Bammer 2013). A number of unexpected lessons were learned throughout the project. For example, the core project team would not have theorized the agency of visual communication in transdisciplinary projects so usefully if not for the opportunity for this practice-oriented discipline to participate in, rather than merely provide services to, the research. This enabled questions about the role of disciplinary knowledge and expertise in transdisciplinary project teams to emerge (Mellick Lopes et al. 2012).

Unexpected knowledge was also gained by working closely with key operational staff such as builders, plumbers and cleaning staff who managed the everyday maintenance of the UD toilets. What became increasingly apparent from feedback from cleaning staff in particular was the importance of catering to a culturally diverse community and the culturally specific toilet practices they observed. With a significant proportion of UTS students coming from Asian and South-East Asian backgrounds, a preference for using squatting rather than seated toilets was identified by cleaners. Cleaners had highlighted to the team that approximately 20 toilets were broken per week from students squatting on toilet seats. This involved a cost of approximately $150,000/year as well as significant risk of harm to the user if the porcelain toilet shattered in the process. This cost could be significantly reduced by installing culturally acceptable squatting toilets to cater for differing toilet practices amongst students. While this project was not focused on identifying diverse toilet practices, the need for culturally diverse input into future research is needed, reflecting the increasing cultural diversity of the Australian population. Approximately half of the current Australian population consists of either people born overseas or people with one or more parent born overseas (Australian Bureau of Statistics 2016). UTS reflects national statistics with approximately 50% of current students born overseas in (UTS 2018).

The project led to the installation of pipework in large new development in urban Sydney – an example of how this project did lead to a "scaling up" of sorts, if not of the kind envisioned at the beginning of this project – and to new lines of research in agriculture and law on the reuse of waste streams as fertilizer products. It also led to insights about new professional identities, such as the "yellow plumber." And, importantly, it exposed the provisional and contingent nature of promising technologies and the need for significant research investment to negotiate the tension between what has worked in the past and exploration of new fields of knowledge (Gherardi 2012).

Conclusion

One challenge encountered in conducting transdisciplinary courses and subjects within university programmes is that generalizability is actively sought, yet under current models, frameworks, and approaches it is not always possible to transfer

214 *Fam, Lopes and Mitchell*

"lessons learned" to other transdisciplinary projects which may cross sectors, disciplines and views of what constitutes valid knowledge and research. What this project provided was the space to "skin our knees" together, and productively learn from the experience. However, the capacity to sustain the learning engendered by the project was hampered by the failure to invest adequately in building a broader local platform for change from project inception, which could translate what we did inside the university to an ongoing, external process. In hindsight, this is particularly important for a project so far ahead of the current status of the complex system of sanitation, including its social, cultural, and material elements. In addition, if transdisciplinary research exploring the potential of innovative infrastructural solutions is to be valued, funding bodies need to recognize the need for longitudinal research and collaborative participatory approaches, and the difficulty in determining the finish line of experimental projects.

Take-home messages

- Provide a space where those involved in transdisciplinary projects can "skin their knees" so that both project partners and students are primed to value challenges and failures as key opportunities for learning. Create an understanding among collaborators that they are likely to "skin their knees."
- When considering project legacy, build a broader local platform for change from the very inception of the project to ensure that project findings have impacts beyond the boundaries and limited timeframe of the project.
- In experimenting with innovative infrastructural solutions radically different from the mainstream (particularly in sanitation systems), ensure that social, cultural and material elements are all considered in the process of transdisciplinary inquiry.

References

Allen, J. et al. 2009. Futures west: A design research initiative promoting sustainable futures for western Sydney. In: *Proceedings of the Cumulus Conference: 38°South: hemispheric shifts across learning, teaching and research*, Melbourne, Australia.

Altman, D.G. 1995. Sustaining interventions in community systems: On the relationship between researchers and communities. *Health Psychology*, 14, 526–536.

Argyris, C., Schon, D. 1978. *Organizational learning: A theory of action perspective*. Reading, MA: Addison-Wesley.

Australian Bureau of Statistics. 2016. Census of population and housing.

Bammer, G. 2013. *Disciplining interdisciplinarity: integration and implementation sciences for researching complex real-world problems*. Canberra: Australian National University E-Press.

Cordell, D. et al. 2009. The story of phosphorus: Global food security and food for thought. *Global Environmental Change Journal*, 19, 292–304.

Crosby, A. et al. 2018. Trandisciplinarity and the "living lab model": Food waste management as a site for collaborative learning. *In:* F. D. N. L and P. Gibbs, eds.

Transdisciplinary theory, practice and education: The art of collaborative research and collective learning. London: Springer.

Daniel, A. 2017, December. *Strategic opportunities for sustainability-focused living laboratories at Western Sydney University*. Western Sydney University, Penrith.

Dewey, J. 1938. *Experience and education*. New York: Collier.

EU. 2015. Practical guidelines for establishing and running a city logistics living lab. Available from: http://www.citylab-project.eu/deliverables/D3_1.pdf [Accessed 20 January 2020].

Fam, D. et al. 2009. From removal to recovery: Critical stakeholder involvement in implementing pilot projects of urine diversion systems in Sweden. In: *The first annual Asia-Pacific science technology and society conference – our land, our waters, our people*. Brisbane, Australia: Griffith University.

Fam, D., Mitchell, C. 2013. Sustainable innovation in wastewater management: Lessons for nutrient recovery and reuse. *Local Environment*, 18(7), 769–780.

Fam, D., Lopes, A.M. 2015. Designing for system change: Innovation, practice and everyday water. *Acme*, 14(3), 735–750.

Fam, D. 2017. Facilitating communities of practice as social learning systems: A case study of trialling sustainable sanitation at the University of Technology Sydney (UTS). *Knowledge Management, Research and Practice*, 15(3), 391–399.

Fam, D. et al. 2019. The transdisciplinary living lab model (TDLL). *In:* W.L. Filho et al. *Universities as living labs for sustainable development supporting the implementation of the Sustainable Development Goals*. London: Springer.

Gherardi, S. 2012. Why do practices change and why do they persist? Models of explanations. *In:* P. Hager, A. Lee and A. Reich, eds. *Practice, learning and change: Practice-theory perspectives on professional learning*. Dordrecht, Germany: Springer Verlag.

Graczyk, G. 2015. Master's thesis – Embedding a living lab approach at the University of Edinburgh, Scotland. Available from: https://www.ed.ac.uk/files/atoms/files/embedding_a_living_lab_approach_at_the_university_of_edinburgh.pdf [Accessed 20 January 2020].

Gray, J. et al. 2014. Lessons learnt from educating university students through a trans-disciplinary project for sustainable sanitation using a systems approach and problem-based learning. *Systems*, 2, 243 –272.

Hansson, S., Polk, M. 2018. Assessing the impact of transdisciplinary research: The usefulness of relevance, credibility, and legitimacy for understanding the link between process and impact. *Research Evaluation*, 27(2), 132–144. doi:10.1093/reseval/rvy004

Hoffman, A., Axson, J. 2017. *Examining interdisciplinary sustainability institutes at major research universities: Innovations in cross-campus and cross-disciplinary models*. Ann Arbor, MI: Cynthia and George Mitchell Foundation.

IPCC. 2018. Global warming of 1.5°C. An IPCC special report on the impacts of global warming of 1.5°C above pre-industrial levels and related global greenhouse gas emission pathways, in the context of strengthening the global response to the threat of climate change, sustainable development, and efforts to eradicate poverty V. Masson-Delmotte, P. Zhai, H. O. Pörtner, J. Skea, P. Zhai, D. Roberts, P.R. Shukla.

Kyriakou, D. 2010. The yellow plumber. *Plumbing Connection*. Available from: https://plumbingconnection.com.au/yellow-plumber/.

Li, B. et al. 2019. Phosphorous recovery through struvite crystallization: Challenges for future design. *Science of the Total Environment*, 648, 1244–1256.

216 *Fam, Lopes and Mitchell*

Lopes, A. et al. 2012. Designing sustainable sanitation: Involving design in innovative, transdisciplinary research. *Design Studies*, 33(3), 298–317.

Manzini, E. 2008. Design context: Enabling solutions for sustainable urban everyday life. *In:* E. Manzini, S. Walker and B. Wylant, eds. *Enabling solutions for sustainable living: a workshop.* Calgary, AB: University of Calgary Press.

Mitchell, C., Cordell, D., Fam, D. 2015. Beginning at the end: The outcome spaces framework to guide purposive transdisciplinary research. *Futures*, 65, 86–96.

Mitchell, C.A., Fam, D., Abeysuriya, K., Institute for Sustainable Futures, UTS. 2013. *Transitioning to sustainable sanitation: a transdisciplinary pilot project of urine diversion*, pp. 1–137. Sydney.

Mulgan, G. et al. 2016. The challenge-driven university: How real-life problems can fuel learning. NESTA. Available from: https://www.nesta.org.uk/blog/the-challenge-driven -university-how-real-life-problems-can-fuel-learning/.

Petrie, H.G. 1992. Interdisciplinarity Education: We are faced with insurmountable opportunities? *Review of Research in Education*, 18(1), 299–333.

Schön, D.A. 1987. *Educating the reflective practitioner: Toward a new design of teaching and learning in the professions.* San Francisco, CA: Jossey-Bass Publishers.

Senge, P.M. 1990. *The fifth discipline : the art and practice of the learning organization.* New York: Doubleday/Currency.

Senge, P.M. 2006. *The fifth discipline: The art and practice of the learning organization.* London: Currency Doubleday.

Sofoulis, Z. 2005. Big water, Everyday water: A sociotechnical perspective. *Journal of Media and Cultural Studies*, 19(4), 445–463.

UTS. 2018. *Facts, figures and rankings.* Available from: https://www.uts.edu.au/about/u niversity/facts-figures-and-rankings.

Volpin, F. et al. 2019. Techno-economic feasibility of recovering phosphorus, nitrogen and water from dilute human urine via forward osmosis. *Water Research*, 150, 47–55.

Warburton, K. 2003. Deep learning and education for sustainability. *International Journal of Sustainability in Higher Education*, 4(1), 44–56.

Wenger, E. 1998). *Communities of practice: Learning, meaning, and identity.* Cambridge University Press.

13 Learning to fail forward – operationalizing productive failure for tackling complex environmental problems

BinBin J. Pearce

Introduction

In this chapter, I demonstrate how engaging with "productive failure" can be used to develop students' capacity for complex problem-solving in the area of sustainable development. The context of the discussion is a compulsory, year-long course for first-year university students in the Department of Environmental Systems Science (D-USYS) at the Swiss Federal Institute of Technology in Zurich (ETH Zürich), "Tackling Environmental Problems" (TEP, or "Umweltproblemlösen" in German). Students' capacity for solving real-world problems is developed at the intersection of society, environment and the economy by an iterative process of insight finding, problem framing, brainstorming and prototyping, systems modelling, and engaging with stakeholders and experts in the real world that makes use of a newly developed methodology, known as Integrated Systems and Design Thinking. This approach integrates qualitative systems modelling with design thinking to enable students to analyze environmental systems and its results to identify and confront possible problems within the system. In this chapter, I demonstrate how this approach helps to encourage "productive failure" in students and thereby builds their capacity for complex problem-solving.

The motivation for exploring and developing a methodology for complex problem-solving aimed specifically at issues of sustainable development comes from the mission statement of D-USYS. Its aim is to educate researchers to "investigate the effects of global warming, examine possibilities for protecting ecosystems and search for ways to prevent the spread of harmful pollutants. Our aim is to preserve the world as a place where everyone can live by taking protective measures and using natural resources in a responsible way" (D-USYS 2019). This mission statement reveals the intention to foster analytical skills for investigating the natural world and educate students to "preserve the world" and take effective action in the real world.

This institutional-level aim is commensurate with global recognition for the need to focus on issues of sustainable development in education. Education for Sustainable Development (ESD) as defined by UNESCO as education that integrates sustainability issues into teaching and learning. The concept was first widely acknowledged in the Agenda 21 document (UN 1993) that identified education

218   *BinBin J. Pearce*

as an essential aspect of moving the world towards sustainable development. It is characterized by participatory teaching and learning methods that motivate and empower learners to act for sustainable development (UNESCO 2005, 2012).

The approach is not without critics. It has been seen by some as reinforcing the economic and social structures that have contributed to environmental problems (Huckle and Wals 2015; Jickling and Wals 2008) and as offering a narrow anthropocentric view of sustainable development (Kopnina 2012). Much of the tension lies in the broad scope of the concept and its lack of specificity. To address this tension, the specific variety of ESD that this chapter will adopt is what I will term transdisciplinary education for sustainable development (TD ESD). This is in line with what Jickling and Wals (2008) have described as a form of ESD that is socio-constructivist, action-oriented, socially critical and focused on the co-creation of knowledge. Building on the principles and competences of transdisciplinary learning (Pearce et al. 2018), rather than focusing on sustainable development (SD) as an aim in itself, it serves rather as the starting point for cultivating students' ability to engage with complex, societal problems. This view is exemplified by bringing perspective and feedback of real-world actors into key components of the course, through integrating knowledge from different disciplines and fostering students' ability to be aware of self and others. What distinguishes TD ESD is that it focuses on enabling students, not only to gather information and knowledge *about* the world but also to create effective change *in* the world.

But how can these aims be achieved in reality? What does it mean to take "effective action" in the realm of sustainable development? In the rest of this chapter, we demonstrate how the concept of productive failure, as a key element of the Integrated Systems and Design Thinking methodology, helps students take effective action in the world. We describe how our course operationalizes a concept of productive failure within the context of TD ESD, and finally, what was learned from this experience that advances our understanding how to create learning environments, and activities that meet the goals of an education that is geared towards training students who are poised to contribute to problems of sustainable development in the future.

What is productive failure?

Taking effective action for sustainable development requires an understanding of both natural and human systems and the interaction between the two. These coupled human and natural systems (CHAN) systems are complex, and they are characterized by nonlinearity, unknown transition points between alternate states, surprises, time-lagged effects, and variable degrees of resilience (Liu et al. 2007). Complex systems are characterized by incomplete information, cognitive bias, emergence and path dependency. These properties increase the uncertainty and unpredictability of these systems. In the context of decision-making for environmental systems and finding solutions to problems within such systems, failures are inevitable (Little 2011; Edmondson 2011). Although methodologies including systems modelling and systems dynamics can help to mitigate consequences

Learning to fail forward 219

of failure by drawing awareness to unintended consequences (Meadows 2008; Dörner 1996), these tools cannot eliminate the possibility of failure.

The people who will be designing the technologies, policies and environments for this complex future will require more than just a set of facts and information. They will need to learn to live with failure, because "growing apprehension of failure encourages methods of decision-making that make failure even more likely and then inevitable" (Dörner 1996). Failure, then, cannot be something that is avoided or swept under the rug. Rather, it should be a source of learning, and it should be dealt with in a meaningful and anticipatory way. Before we can learn from it, failure has to be embraced.

Standing in the way of embracing failure is its stigmatization in our daily lives. Failure is something we are conditioned to avoid from a young age. Failure triggers the fear of being ostracized and the shame of not being "good enough." Rather than perceiving failure as a probable and potentially helpful motivation for change under conditions of complexity, it is seen as a personal or organizational flaw that indicates a lack of competence and worthiness (Martin 2012). This perception has to be overcome if we are to benefit and grow from failure.

The key to this change is recognizing that not all failures are created equal. Failure occurs on a spectrum from "blameworthy" to "praiseworthy" (Edmondson 2011). Blameworthy failures are avoidable. They can result from violating a prescribed procedure, inattention to detail, a lack of ability or following a prescribed but faulty procedure. Praiseworthy failures are unavoidable. They result from carrying out a task that is inherently challenging, dealing with unexpected and emerging properties of complex systems, having to make decisions and carry out actions with limited information about future events and intentionally experimenting to test an idea or to expand knowledge and break new ground.

Productive failure as a learning design does not mean embracing avoidable failures and lowering standards for excellence. Instead, it involves increasing the acceptability of *unavoidable* failures so that students are able to learn from them. For this to be possible, course designers and instructors should be aware of: (1) the potential reasons for failure in each particular situation and what can be done to prevent avoidable failures and what is unavoidable and (2) what knowledge might be gained by engaging with a situation, regardless of the outcome.

Bringing this perspective to students in higher education means that we can start building the skills and competences for students who will have to take on a future that is growing in complexity – a future that demands that we be perceptive, flexible and conscientious human beings.

How is productive failure linked to TD ESD?

Productive failure is linked to TD ESD in that it provides a means of addressing and developing competences that are normally not targeted in higher education. These are affective competences, which have been correlated with student success and recognized to be important transferable skills for the workforce in the twenty-first century (Robbins et al. 2009; NRC 2012; Richardson et al. 2012). Attaining these competences is a part of "deeper learning" (NRC 2012), a process in which individuals adapt what is learned in one situation to another. This includes knowing how to connect different areas of content knowledge, and how, why and when to apply content knowledge to solve problems. Higher education curriculums supporting affective competences and assessment of students' attainment of these competences are not widespread (NRC 2012; Markle and O'Banion 2014; Myers and Goodboy 2015). The National Research Council (2012) in the United States identifies the affective learning domain with "intrapersonal" and "interpersonal" competences. Intrapersonal competences include intellectual openness, work ethic and conscientiousness and positive self-image. Interpersonal competences include communicating clearly, an ability to work with others, being responsible and knowing how to resolve conflicts. The importance of the affective domain is evident when considering competences relevant for ESD, which require not only knowledge about the systems under study, but also emotional capacity, values and an ability to perceive self and others. Currently, there is not a common set of definitions for affective competences or a clear means of assessing affective competences (NRC 2012; Markle and O'Banion 2014). This results in additional instructional time and resources needed to incorporate them into a curriculum when compared to cognitive competences.

The framework that identifies the cognitive, affective and psychomotor as the three main learning domains is known as Bloom's Taxonomy. It was first defined by Bloom et al. (1956), expanded upon by Krathwohl et al. (1964) and updated by Anderson et al. (2001 2009). The cognitive domain is defined by the acquisition of knowledge and analytical abilities. The affective domain is defined by the perception of, response to and prioritization of values, emotions and motivations. The psychomotor domain defines physical or embodied skills. While the cognitive learning domain emphasizes the development of intellectual skills (recall, recognition, application and the synthesis of facts, patterns and concepts), the affective domain defines the body of skills needed to deal effectively with the emotions, values and perceptions which accompany actions taken in other domains. Table 13.1 shows that many of the ESD competences either belong solely to the affective learning domain or belong to both the affective and cognitive domains, rather than belonging solely to the cognitive domain.

Productive failure is a learning process that can be harnessed within TD ESD to nurture underdeveloped affective competences. It is an approach that provides support for students as they experience unavoidable failures for the sake of long-term growth and learning (Kapur 2008; Clifford 1984). It is an empirically tested learning design that delays structure in the process of instruction so that students are allowed to develop their own problem representation and solution development in groups (Kapur 2008; Kapur and Bielaczyc 2012). No correct solutions are expected, but students are encouraged to explore and imagine possible alternatives. Later, after the students' own solutions are reported, concepts are introduced, which may verify or correct these original solutions. It has been shown that compared to students who receive direct instruction on how to solve problems, students who are pushed to first solve problems on their own show more creativity

Table 13.1 ESD competences in Bloom's Taxonomy

Learning Domains	De Haan (2006)	Wiek et al. (2011)	Rieckmann (2012)	Wals et al. (2017)	Pearce et al. (2018)
Cognitive	–	Systems thinking	Systems thinking	–	–
Cognitive + Affective	Anticipatory thinking	Anticipatory thinking	Anticipatory thinking	–	–
	Participate in decision-making Work in interdisciplinary settings Assess and utilize resources for action	Apply visioning and multi-criteria assessments Design and implement interventions (strategic competence)	Critical thinking	Crossing boundaries	Frame problems using diverse perspectives Apply concepts in the real world Imagine solutions and their consequences
Affective (intra/interpersonal competences)	Transcultural understanding and cooperation	Collaborate with stakeholders (interpersonal competence) Motivate and facilitate action	Handling of complexity	Handling diversity; Moving between perspectives	Communicate values
	Motivate self and others for behavioural change Reflect on one's own and others' actions Access empathy and compassion	– Understand ethics/justice/equity		–	– Reflect about self and others –

in problem representation, make more realistic assumptions, and demonstrate more careful consideration of contextual parameters in solving complex problems (Kapur and Bielaczyc 2012).

How can productive failure be operationalized in a curriculum?

The course, Tackling Environmental Problems (TEP), creates conditions under which students experience the complexity of real-world problem-solving. Crucial to this process is working each year with a specific case study within Switzerland related to the topic of sustainable development, and with the stakeholders who are affected by this topic. The goal of the course is to build students' capacity to negotiate complexity, not only through expanding their knowledge base of environmental systems but also through reflecting on the diverse perspectives that affect how a problem might be framed. In the following section, I describe how the learning goals, learning environment, and learning activities of the course are related to the concept of productive failure and how this learning ecosystem helps students develop capabilities for the real world (see Figure 13.1).

Learning goals

This course is meant to provide a comprehensive foundation for students in an environmental systems science department. We focus on providing students with a basic introduction to scientific thinking, including cognitive skills like writing scientific papers, conducting literature reviews and collecting and analyzing quantitative data. We also focus on developing competences with affective dimensions, such as working collaboratively with others, knowing how to apply and adapt academic concepts in specific contexts, communicating and integrating

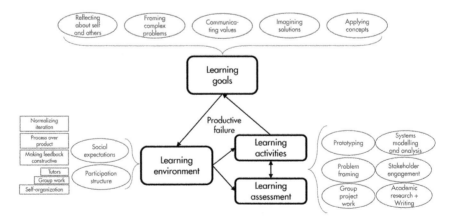

Figure 13.1 A learning ecosystem for productive failure.

diverse values, and imagining creative solutions to problems. The learning goals can be summarized as follows:

1. *Reflecting about self and others* – Students reflect critically on their own and others' perceptions and biases.
2. *Framing complex problems using diverse perspectives* – Students identify and frame clear, relevant problems using information that may be unstructured and which comes from diverse sources.
3. *Communicating values* – Students identify, ground and communicate assumptions and normative values related to sustainable development.
4. *Imagining solutions and their consequences* – Students develop solutions for real-world problems while being aware of any unintended consequences of these solutions and taking responsibility for these consequences.
5. *Applying concepts in the real world* – Students apply conceptual knowledge to specific contexts, and, in parallel, apply practical skills (such as project organization and time management) to deliver the required end products.

These learning goals are based on identifying important elements of transdisciplinary education that provide transferable skills in environmental science and sustainable development principles (more details are provided in Pearce et al. 2018). These abilities are matched to successfully completing the steps of problem-solving adapted from Newell and Simon's theory of problem-solving (1972). This is a process that includes (1) developing a mental representation of the problem situation, (2) defining and formulating the problem, (3) identifying goals and criteria for solutions, (4) searching for solutions and (5) choosing solutions (more detailed discussion is provided in Pearce and Ejderyan 2019).

The learning environment and productive failure

The learning environment and learning activities of TEP enable students to reach the goals which we have been set out for this course. The learning environment, activities and assessments can be understood in relation to productive failure, as illustrated in Figure 13.1.

The learning environment is created through the social expectation of learning and the participation structures set up for the course. First for social expectations, there are three practices that support students in learning from failure:

1. Normalizing iteration
2. Valuing process over product
3. Making feedback constructive

Normalizing iteration. The first practice of normalizing the iterative process is based on the observation that ideas do not come into the world fully and perfectly formed (Faste 1993; Brown 2019). Ideas are starting points only. It is through engagement with the idea – prototyping it, getting feedback for it – that it becomes

224 *BinBin J. Pearce*

concrete and realized in the world. The iterative mindset fully accepts that ideas have to be reworked and that they benefit from external scrutiny and diverse perspectives. In this process, the creator of the idea *expects* that there will be important aspects of the idea that have been overlooked or misunderstood. At this point, failure is productive because it becomes a learning tool rather than something to be afraid of. This iterative approach has been the de facto working process in the most innovative organizations in the world (Kolko 2015) and should therefore be made available to students in a formative period of their education.

Valuing process over product. The second practice of creating a productive failure learning environment is the focus on process as much as the end product. Students are prompted regularly to reflect on how they are working together and what can be improved in the collaboration process. The assignments are positioned not as hoops to jump through, but rather "scaffolding" to help with gradually reaching the end goal. We also provide opportunities to access tutors, conflict management strategies and frequent meetings with the instructors. As instructors, we emphasize that we *expect* difficulties to emerge. Students focus on the process by recording and reflecting on the work process each week as a part of a graded "learning journal."

Making feedback constructive. The third practice is creating opportunities for students to receive feedback from the real world. They are given input on how to receive and integrate both positive and negative feedback from stakeholders such that all feedback can be constructively incorporated into the works in progress. The course gets students in front of stakeholders who would be affected by the ideas they are developing. In doing so, students receive unexpected feedback and broaden their perspectives about how their ideas would function and be received in the real world. In this way, the students are able to develop a "thick skin" to criticism and become more resilient in taking negative criticism. They also develop their own sense of which feedback is helpful to listen to, and which is not. They are able to do so, however, in a protected and supportive environment with instructors and tutors who have gone through similar experiences and who are able to guide them in dealing with such situations. Instead of interpreting negative feedback as a personal attack and being defensive, we encourage students to let go of their egos and try to listen to what is behind the criticism and to keep in mind that all criticism comes from a specific point of view, that it is not always relevant, and that if it is relevant, it should be integrated into the work at hand.

We think that these three practices set social expectations that allow students to fail forward. In providing a safe space to make mistakes, we see students gaining courage and confidence in following their own ideas. This psychological safety has been shown to be the key for high performing groups within Google, for example (Delizonna 2017). It allows them to face what is true about themselves and others, to be open to and accept perspectives which are different from their own, to identify their own values and communicate them to others and to bring their ideas into reality.

The participation structure of the course also supports students in reaching learning objectives. Core to this structure is the use of student tutors as course assistants. Tutoring has been shown to effectively guide learning by tailoring feedback and information to individual or group needs (Merrill et al. 1995). All tutors are former students of the course and future tutors are selected by the previous cohort of tutors. The lecturers have no say in who is chosen. Each year 12 tutors commit to accompanying the course for two years, and they help make peer teaching and learning a core aspect of the course. Half of the tutors already have one year of experience being a tutor, and the other half are new to the job. The tutors take part in teaching workshops for the students on specific topics, such as project management and system modelling. They are also responsible for organizing two presentation events in which the public is invited to see the work of the students. They also organize social events which are a part of the course. The students are also able to go to tutors for advice on any challenges related to the working process within the group. The tutors are living examples of the outcomes of "productive failure." They show that it is possible to survive the course and are able to give current students an idea of what can be gained when one persists in overcoming the challenges of the course.

Learning activities and productive failure

In addition to the learning environment, the learning activities of the course also support students in reaching learning goals. The activities are connected to the concept of productive failure. There are four main learning activities in the course:

- Academic research and writing for systems knowledge
- Problem framing
- Systems modelling and analysis
- Stakeholder engagement and prototyping

None of these learning activities requires reaching the one "right answer." Students are encouraged to explore different solutions and take creative risks, as long as they can provide an adequate rationale for why they have approached the problem in a particular way. For all activities, students are expected to make transparent their thought processes and assumptions and show how they arrived at their ideas. Students are also given the opportunity to compare and contrast their own outcomes with those of their peers.

Failure potential of an activity

There are different ways students can "fail" each type of learning activity. This is what we define as the *failure potential* of an activity. It can be determined by the structure and goal of the specific learning activity (see Figure 13.2). For all learning activities, there are a variety of reasons for why failure might occur. As mentioned earlier, productive failure comes from "praiseworthy" failure (Edmondson 2011). Non-productive failure comes from "blameworthy" failure. Though failure potential spans both the negative and positive aspects of failure, the specific

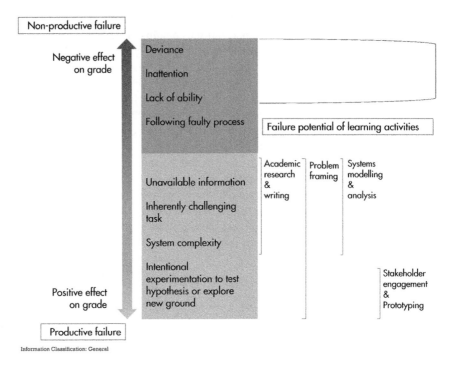

Figure 13.2 Failure potential of learning activities.

reasons for failure differ between learning activities. The differences are dependent on the content, process and format of the output from the learning activity.

In our course, "blameworthy" failures stem from deviance and inattention. These reasons define the negative failure potential for a learning activity. All learning activities share the same *negative* failure potential in this course, defined by deviance and inattention. Deviance is defined as the intentional neglect of the course or disruption of others' learning. Inattention is paying insufficient attention to what needs to be learned and not spending enough time studying the material that needs to be learned in order to make progress. Non-productive failures negatively impact students' grades in the course, while productive failures either have no impact or positively impact their grades. The causes of productive failure include: working without sufficient information, the inherently challenging nature of the task, the complexity of the system in which students are working, and intentionally testing a hypothesis or an idea for which the outcome is unknown.

While the negative failure potential of the course is identical for all the learning activities, the positive failure potential varies. This means that productive failure is productive for different reasons, depending on how the learning activity is designed. Reasons for productive failure can determine differences in individual engagement and performance within the course. For example, even though failure

Learning to fail forward 227

resulting from a lack of information and system complexity is understandable and shows that the students have wrestled with difficult topics, likely leading to learning regardless of the outcome, some students are able to deal with this uncertainty and complexity better than others. Those students who are able to produce an outcome that is convincing in spite of these challenges will receive a better grade than those who face those same challenges and arrive at a less convincing outcome. Productive failure is a concept that is multifaceted when it is operationalized. It is not associated with one particular type of learning; rather, it can lead to different learning outcomes.

In the following section, we demonstrate how positive failure potential is exhibited in each learning activity.

Academic research and writing for systems knowledge. Based on a different environmental systems case study in Switzerland each year, students are separated into different disciplinary or thematic areas in order to write a scientific report about the area. In the first semester, the students are asked to conduct a literature review and undertake a stakeholder analysis and find all available information on their areas of focus. The output is a collaboratively written scientific report. This information serves as the starting point and knowledge base for the second semester. Positive failure potential is exhibited when students have to engage with a lack of available and suitable information for writing the report. It is also exhibited when they have to characterize the complexity of a system within given time and knowledge constraints. They also struggle with mastering writing itself, an inherently difficult craft that cannot bypass investment of time and effort. When assessing students' work, we read through of the weekly learning journal that each group uses to record their challenges, accomplishments and new realizations. Evidence of explicit struggle with defining the boundary of the task and in-depth group discussion about different options for framing the assignment, for example, would have a positive effect on grading.

Problem framing. Building on the systems knowledge acquired in the first semester, students are asked to identify insights and build problem statements relevant to the environmental systems they have been studying. They do this via the integrated systems and design thinking methodology (details in Pearce and Ejderyan 2019) During one intensive week, students are introduced to design thinking and systems modelling and groups are reshuffled. Students who have specialized in different theme areas are mixed to share and integrate their specific areas of knowledge. The integration occurs through the identification of insights, which must be statements which reveal an AHA! moment for students about how or why the system functions the way it does. These insights are then the basis for both creating the problem statements that students will work on later in the second semester, and the systems model they have to build. The problem statements are developed from the perspective of multiple stakeholders in order to help students develop a systems view of the case study. Positive failure potential is exhibited when students struggle with the identification of the insight, and when they are evaluating what counts as an insight. They also struggle with the specificity of the problem statement and with seeing the problem from multiple perspectives. In

228 *BinBin J. Pearce*

most groups, the insights and problem statements have to be revised innumerable times throughout the second semester, usually in conjunction with the creation of solutions to these problems. Evidence that a group goes through multiple versions of the insight and problem statements, until hidden assumptions are clarified, would contribute to a positive effect on the overall grade. This progress is recorded during several meetings students organize with instructors throughout the semester.

Systems modelling and analysis. The students use aspects of soft-systems methodology and the software System Q to create a qualitative model of the system under study. These models originate from the insights and problem statements already identified, and changes are made to them throughout the semester. Positive failure potential is exhibited by the iterative approach they take to building the system model. When students first start to build a system, they do not have complete information. Yet they are expected to set the boundaries of the system and identify important variables. Only when they have developed solutions to the problems and integrated these solutions into the systems, do they know how effective their models are for capturing the relevant interactions under study. Another failure potential is that this is an inherently complex task that does not have a clear "right" answer, which means students are always grappling with a means of evaluating the quality of their work based on their growing understanding of why systems thinking is relevant to solving real-world problems. Engaging with system complexity is the final positive failure potential. Due to the density and number of linkages that are possible in the creation of a system model, it is not possible that each group will capture all of them. In spite of this inevitable "failure," students are asked to justify subjective choices made, including the variables and linkages in each system model. The quality of this rationale, as well as evidence of multiple iterations of the system model, would contribute to a positive effect on the grading.

Stakeholder engagement and prototyping. Students brainstorm and prototype solutions to address their insights and problem statements. They spend a significant portion of the second semester, creating and refining these prototypes. The prototypes are repeatedly tested with stakeholders to whom the solutions might be relevant (see Figure 13.3). The students integrate this feedback into the final version of the prototype that is presented at the end of the semester during a "Prototype Market." The positive failure potential of this activity is the act of intentional experimentation to test a hypothesis or to explore new ground. The iterative process of improving a concept by making it concrete opens the idea up to criticism and scrutiny at an early stage of development. The goal of prototyping and testing is to find what does not work yet, and the process uses the certainty of failure to proactively improve an idea. The intentional aspect of this iterative process is what makes "failure" productive. This means that rather than focusing on receiving positive stakeholder feedback, clear evidence of how the feedback (either positive or negative) led to improved prototypes would contribute positively to the grading.

Figure 13.3 Modelled prototype of a "floating mosaic" to enhance biodiversity in the Birs River software. (Source: Report from Clivaz, Eberli, Furrer, Holman, Hotz, Luz, Scherrer 2019)

Learning assessment tasks and productive failure

In TEP, we use nine assessment tasks to evaluate the learning processes and performances of students. There are two main types of assessment tasks – cumulative and one-off assessments. Cumulative assessments come from a series of interactions and work outputs that occur regularly and frequently throughout a semester. One-off assessments occur at the end of each of the two semesters. Striking a balance between cumulative and one-off assessments allows us to focus on how students are learning and the quality of their output. Most learning activities are assessed using both cumulative and one-off assessments to evaluate both the quality of the process and the output from an activity. This reinforces the notion that the ability to learn from mistakes is just as valuable as creating a deliverable that looks perfect.

There are assessment tasks for both group and individual performances. The final grade is weighted equally between the individual grades for individual performance, group process and group output (see Table 13.2).

On balance, more cumulative assessment tasks keep track of group processes than one-off assessment tasks. On the other hand, group output and individual performance are evaluated more often with one-off assessment tasks. About 40% of assessment tasks do not contribute to the final grade and are completed only to provide students with feedback. The ungraded assessments are events in which

Table 13.2 Corresponding learning activities and assessment tasks. Activities marked with a "*" are ungraded. Shaded assessment methods are graded cumulatively

Learning activities / Assessment Tasks	Academic Research and Writing for Systems Knowledge	Problem Framing	Systems Modelling and Analysis	Stakeholder Engagement and Prototyping	Group Project Work	Methods Integration and Application
Group process – Scientific report	X					
Indv. performance – Oral examination	X	X	X			X
Group process – Stakeholder feedback		X*		X*		
Group process – Instructor feedback		X*	X*	X*	X*	
Group process – Progress meetings with instructors		X*	X*	X*	X	
Indv. performance – Peer-to-peer feedback					X	
Group process – "Learning Journal"				X	X	
Group output – Final presentation (graded by instructors and experts in practice)		X	X	X	X	X
Group output – Project documentation		X	X	X	X	

the instructors or tutors interact with the students to get a sense of their progress and to give feedback on the work completed so far, but the students are not judged on the quality of the output presented. This opens up the possibility for students to pursue riskier ideas that may not end up as a part of the final project. From this assessment structure, we show students that assessments are not judgements about whether students are performing to an abstract standard, but rather vehicles for improving their own learning. In this way, we try to embed the message of failing forward in the assessment structure of the course.

What can we learn from operationalizing productive failure?

Operationalizing productive failure in the course brings up the following four questions:

*   What allows students to risk failure?
*   Does productive failure "work" for all students?
*   Is it possible to assess the "productivity" of failure?
*   What should be the appropriate institutional context to support productive failure?

The answers that we provide in this section are based on the experiences and observations of students over the course of four consecutive years of carrying out the TD ESD curriculum using the integrated systems and design thinking methodology.

What allows students to risk failure? When students know that judgements about the quality of their work are based not only on the outcome and others' judgements of that outcome but also the amount of effort that they have invested in creating the outcome, they come to realize that there is no "risk." They have complete control over their own efforts. What they learn during this process contributes to their personal growth, in spite of external judgement. A learning environment which focuses on processes over product, and where students are habituated to giving and getting feedback, contributes to minimizing this feeling of "risk." In addition, when students are motivated by ideas based on their own original insights, rather than acting on secondhand knowledge, they are more willing to risk failure in order to realize those ideas. The motivation to perform is internalized. The risk of failure becomes secondary to what they would like to accomplish in the world.

Does productive failure "work" for all students? One-on-one support and coaching are needed for students who find it especially difficult to change their perception of failure. While we strive to create an overall learning environment that provides psychological safety to students, it still may not be sufficient for all students and should be supplemented with individual support. Even with this, we do not claim that this is a way of teaching which works for 100% of students. However, after accompanying over 450 students through our curriculum, we do see during the individual oral examinations that the majority of students become aware of the benefits of working iteratively.

232   *BinBin J. Pearce*

Is it possible to assess the "productivity" of failure? The productivity of failure might be better assessed if learning activities were designed with this concept in mind. It may be worthwhile for educational designers to consider the meaning of failure in each activity that is introduced to the students, and what could be the causes of this failure that would contribute to a student's development if it was made the focus, rather than something to be ashamed of. The productivity of failure can be seen if the progress of students throughout the course can be tracked, rather than using single-point evaluations to judge only one outcome. By being transparent and diversifying the types of outputs being assessed, the aim is to ensure that students are able to learn and actually benefit from the assessment process.

What should be the appropriate institutional context to support productive failure?

It is possible to create a micro-learning environment for students in which failure is destigmatized, even when the students have to keep on navigating in an institutional context where failure is still largely unacceptable. At ETH Zürich, all students with an academic high school diploma (*"Matura"*) are accepted. However, after the first two years, if they wish to continue, students are required to pass a series of examinations and about 40% are not able to do so (*"Basisprüfungen"*). The subject for our course is included in this testing phase. As a result, our students are under enormous pressure to do well in the most conventional academic sense. Our course can only provide a very small reprieve from the ever-looming possibility of disappointment. However, we think that even small pockets of psychological safety might transform students' perspectives of what it means to "fail."

However, it remains true that the impact of a productive failure learning design is limited when it is not reinforced within the broader institutional context. If in one context they are encouraged to be creative, take risks and focus on processes, and, in another context, they are judged solely on the score they receive on one test, one cannot expect students to really believe that failure is *really* acceptable. We are transparent with students in explaining to them that what is expected from them in our course is not always aligned with what is expected of them in all their other courses and that this is, indeed, not an ideal situation. Ultimately, even if our course is the only one that supports the notion of productive failure within the institution, we believe that it creates an alternative way of thinking about failure and success in the world, and allows for students to be better prepared for the real world (Schmidt and Bjork 1992).

What are the implications of productive failure for ESD?

There are two main sets of implications for adopting productive failure in an ESD curriculum. First, implementing productive failure as a learning design highlights how we need to rethink the way students are assessed and for what kinds of competences they are being assessed. The difficulty of changing assessments should

Learning to fail forward 233

not be underestimated. At the very heart of this issue is how society at large perceives success. To change societal perceptions of success, institutions will need to take risks by supporting teaching formats and designs that explore new perceptions of success and failure. It is never easy to change embedded social norms. If, however, any institution has the obligation to lead the charge in bringing about this change, they are educational institutions, especially highly recognized institutions at the top of international rankings. These institutions are supposed to be at the cutting edge of human thought, science and progress and, therefore, they also have a responsibility to take part in solving the long-term problems of the future by educating the students for the tasks ahead. Rather than perpetuate existing standards for academic success, they should be exploring new concepts about what it means to reach one's full potential in life and to contribute to a better society.

Second, a mindset of productive failure is useful, not only for students as individuals but also for confronting complex problems of sustainable development in institutional and policy contexts. Sustainability problems exist within complex systems that are non-linear, have emerging properties and embody significant uncertainties. Students who are trained to be comfortable with mindful experimentation, to give responsible consideration to unintentional consequences, and to be adaptable, are the best people to work and lead in the field of sustainable development. Adaptive environmental policies, carrying out and scaling pilot projects, creating more accurate and holistic evaluation tools for environmental projects could all benefit from a mindset which accepts and incorporates productive failure as a part of their design from the onset.

Our course is an initial step connecting the idea of productive failure to education for sustainable development. We believe that this concept has the potential to be further developed and adapted to many other subject areas of higher education. Further work needs to be done to evaluate the longitudinal effects of a productive failure curriculum for students' future development. These results could then be used to refine our assumptions about the importance of experiencing failure within higher education, and this could lead to improved strategies for assessing the productivity of failure.

To address the critical issues of sustainable development in the future, failure is something we cannot turn away from. Without the courage to confront our own inevitable failures and helping our students to do the same, we will never find the way to face the complexities of the world.

Take-home messages

- Students can learn to engage with complex problem-solving in the real world when they learn how to fail forward.
- Students learn how to fail forward when productive failure is operationalized through learning goals, activities and environments (such as integrated systems and design thinking methodology) in which students are assessed on their *process* as well as output.

234   *BinBin J. Pearce*

- Focusing on work *process* contributes to delineating and building affective competences that prepare students to confront complex societal dilemmas in the future. This should be a core contribution of a transdisciplinary education for sustainable development.

References

Anderson, L.W., Krathwohl, D.R., ed., Airasian, P.W., Cruikshank, K.A., Mayer, R.E., Pintrich, P.R., Raths, J., Wittrock, M.C. 2001. *A taxonomy for learning, teaching, and assessing: A revision of Bloom's taxonomy of educational objectives* (complete edition). New York: Longman.

Bloom, B., Englehart, M. Furst, E., Hill, W., Krathwohl, D. 1956. *Taxonomy of educational objectives: The classification of educational goals. Handbook I: cognitive domain.* New York and Toronto: Longmans, Green.

Brown, T. 2019. *Change by design.* New York: HarperCollins.

Clifford, M.M. 1984. Thoughts on a theory of constructive failure. *Educational Psychologist,* 19(2), 108–120. doi:10.1080/00461528409529286de.

Clivas, K., Eberli, M., Furrer, S., Holman, R., Hotz, B., Luz, F., Scherrer, J. 2019. *Schwimmmosaik.* Zürich: Umweltproblemlösen Bachelors Studium, 1–56.

Delizonna, L. 2017. High-performing teams need psychological safety: Here's how to create it. *Harvard Business Review.* Available from: https://hbr.org/2017/08/high-performing-teams-need-psychological-safety-heres-how-to-create-it [Accessed 03 October 2019].

Department of Environment Systems Science (D-USYS). 2019. ETH Zürich. [Accessed 3 July 2019].

Dörner, D. 1996. *The logic of failure (English translation).* New York: Metropolitan Books.

Edmondson, A.C. 2011. Strategies of learning from failure. *Harvard Business Review,* 89(4), 48–55.

Faste, R., Roth, B., Wilde, D.J. 1993. Integrating creativity into the mechanical engineering curriculum. *In:* C.A. Fisher, ed. *ASME resource guide to innovation in engineering design.* New York: ASME.

Haan, G. 2006. The BLK "21" programme in Germany: A 'Gestaltungskompetenz'-based model for education for sustainable development. *Environmental Education Research,* 12(1), 19–32. doi:10.1080/13504620500526362.

Huckle, J., Wals, A.E.J. 2015. The UN decade of education for sustainable development: Business as usual in the end. *Environmental Education Research,* 21(3), 491–505. doi: 10.1080/13504622.2015.1011084.

Jickling, B., Wals, A.E.J. 2008. Globalization and environmental education: Looking beyond sustainable development. *Journal of Curriculum Studies,* 40(1), 1–21. doi:10.1080/00220270701684667.

Kapur, M. 2008. Productive failure. *Cognition and Instruction,* 26(3), 379–424. doi:10.1080/07370000802212669.

Kapur, M., Bielaczyc, K. 2012. Designing for productive failure. *Journal of the Learning Sciences,* 21(1), 45–83. doi:10.1080/10508406.2011.591717.

Kolko, J. 2015, September. Design thinking comes of age. *Harvard Business Review,* 66–71.

Kopnina, H. 2012. Education for sustainable development (ESD): The turn away from "environment" in environmental education? *Environmental Education Research,* 18(5), 699–717. doi:10.1080/13504622.2012.658028.

Learning to fail forward 235

Krathwohl, D.R., Bloom, B.S., Masia, B.B. 1964. *Taxonomy of educational Objectives: The classification of educational goals.* New York and London: Longman.

Krathwohl, D.R., Anderson, L.W. 2009. *A taxonomy for learning, teaching, and assessing: A revision of Bloom's taxonomy of educational objectives.* New York and London: Longman.

Little, A. 2011. Political action, error and failure: The epistemological limits of complexity. *Political Studies*, 60(1), 3–19. doi:10.1111/j.1467-9248.2011.00901.x.

Liu, J. et al. 2007. Complexity of coupled human and natural systems. *Science*, 317(5844), 1513–1516. doi:10.1126/science.1144004.

Markle, R., O'Banion, T. 2014. Assessing affective factors to improve retention and completion. *Learning Abstracts*, 17(11), 1–16.

Martin, A.J. 2012. Fear of failure in learning. *In:* N.M. Seel, ed. *Encyclopedia of the sciences of learning.* Boston, MA: Springer.

Meadows, D. 2008. *Thinking in systems.* White River Junction, VT: Chelsea Green Publishing.

Merrill, D.C., Reiser, B.J., Merrill, S.K., Landes, S. 1995. Tutoring: Guided learning by doing. *Cognition and Instruction*, 13(3), 315–372. doi:10.1207/s1532690xci1303_1.

Myers, S.A., Goodboy, A.K. 2015. Reconsidering the conceptualization and operationalization of affective learning. *Communication Education*, 64(4), 493–497. do i:10.1080/03634523.2015.1058489.

National Research Council. 2012. *Education for life and work: Developing transferable knowledge and skills in the 21st century.* Washington, DC: National Academies Press, 1–257.

Pearce, B.J., Adler, C., Senn, L., Krütli, P., Stauffacher, M., Pohl, C. 2018. Making the link between transdisciplinary learning and research. *In:* D. Fam, L. Neuhauser and P. Gibbs, eds. *Transdisciplinary theory, practice and education.* Dordrecht: Springer, 167–184.

Pearce, B.J., Ejderyan, O. 2019. Joint problem framing as reflexive practice: Honing a transdisciplinary skill. *Sustainability Science*, 15(5), 1–16. doi:10.1007/s11625-019-00744-2.

Richardson, M., Abraham, C., Bond, R. 2012. Psychological correlates of university students' academic performance: A systematic review and meta-analysis. *Psychological Bulletin*, 138(2), 353–387. doi:10.1037/a0026838.

Rieckmann, M. 2012. Future-oriented higher education: Which key competencies should be fostered through university teaching and learning? *Futures*, 44(2), 127–135. doi:10.1016/j.futures.2011.09.005.

Robbins, S.B., Oh, I.-S., Le, H., Button, C. 2009. Intervention effects on college performance and retention as mediated by motivational, emotional, and social control factors: Integrated meta-analytic path analyses. *Journal of Applied Psychology*, 94(5), 1163–1184. doi:10.1037/a0015738.

Schmidt, R.A., Bjork, R.A. 1992. New conceptualizations of practice: Common principles in three paradigms suggest new concepts for training. *Psychological Science*, 3(4), 207–217. doi:10.1111/j.1467-9280.1992.tb00029.x.

UN. 1993. *Agenda 21: Earth summit—the United Nations programme of action from Rio.* New York: United Nations, Department of Public Information, 1–351.

UNESCO. 2005. The DESD at a Glance. Paris: UNESCO. Available from: http://unesdoc. unesco.org/ images/0014/001416/141629e.pdf.

UNESCO. 2012. Shaping the education of tomorrow – abridged version. Paris: UNESCO. Available from: http://unesdoc.unesco.org/images/0021/002166/216606e.pdf.

236   *BinBin J. Pearce*

Wals, A.E.J., Mochizuki, Y., Leicht, A. 2017. Critical case-studies of non-formal and community learning for sustainable development. *International Review of Education*, 63(6), 783–792. doi:10.1007/s11159-017-9691-9.

Wiek, A., Withycombe, L., Redman, C.L. 2011. Key competencies in sustainability: A reference framework for academic program development. *Sustainability Science*, 6(2), 203–218. doi:10.1007/s11625-011-0132-6.

14 Failing and the perception of failure in student-driven transdisciplinary projects

Ulli Vilsmaier and Annika Thalheimer

Introduction

Phenomena associated with failure can best be described as liminal experiences. The German philosopher and psychiatrist Karl Jaspers introduced the term "limit situation" (German: "Grenzsituation") to describe existential experiences as opportunities for humans to transcend the immanent world – that is, the existing horizon of experiences (Jaspers 1919). Alvaro Vieira Pinto, a Brazilian intellectual, emphasized the nascent aspect of limit situations as "the frontier which separates being from more being" (Vieira Pinto 1960, cited in Freire 1996). By responding to limitations with "limit-acts," a given situation can be overcome. Paulo Freire picked up the concept of limit situations in his *Pedagogy of the Oppressed* (1996 [orig. published in 1970]) as a constitutive element of learning. For him, experiencing boundaries is key to being human, as it is in liminal experiences that we become conscious beings and, by acting upon these experiences, become more conscious beings. According to Freire (1996), limit situations imply tasks for those who form part of the situation and bear untested feasibilities.

Situations can be experienced as limit situations in multiple dimensions and scales. They are radically relational as they only exist as such for someone who experiences a situation against the background of limiting factors (which we refer to as boundary conditions) and specific objectives. Thus, a situation will only be experienced as a limit situation if there is consciousness about externally or internally set boundaries, and if the aim is to act upon them in order to change them. What we can learn from Vieira Pinto's conceptualization of limit situations is instructive when conceptualizing failure.

Failure is always related to a concrete case (Aydt 2015), and it can only occur based on action (Junge und Lechner 2004). It is the result of an action on something, and can thus be considered a re-action. As a result of this (re-)action, failure can be considered as the difference between will and possibilities (Aydt 2015). Where failure happens, something is closing down – a wish, a vision, a hope or an expectation. Thus, failure is a subjective perception of the result of an action, but it is not purely subjective. Whether something is perceived as a failure depends on subjective *and* social value conventions (Aydt 2015). Aydt distinguishes between gradual and absolute failure. According to the possibilities of (re)action, failure

238 *Ulli Vilsmaier and Annika Thalheimer*

can be absolute, indicating a total inability to act, or it can be gradual – that is, a temporal or partial inability (Aydt 2015). In learning situations, failure bears the potential to pave the way for further learning.

In this chapter, we present research on failure and students' perceptions of failure in a learning situation. We are dealing with conceptualizations of failure that are conceived within the boundary conditions of a scientific field, a study programme, a specific course, as well as a specific époque and world region that sharpen our image of ourselves, and of what we can and ought to archive. The situatedness within multiple frames (i.e., boundary conditions) informs our self-concept and (self) expectations, which, as a corollary, trigger our perceptions of failure. Boundary conditions can be distinguished as internal factors, depending on the individual personality, and external factors, like social value conventions or institutional guidelines (Aydt 2015; Junge and Lechner 2004).

Failure, as addressed in this chapter, is gradual, not absolute. All students passed the course and none of the students perceived the course to be an absolute failure – to anticipate one important outcome. The students study Sustainability Science, which is a highly normative field. Many students aim to contribute to societal transformation that enables sustainability. Beyond personal learning goals, this strongly informs their perception of failure. A key subject of this course is a research-based learning project at the science-society interface called the "Transdisciplinary Project." The students implement the transdisciplinary project during one year of their Master's programme, together with their lecturers and societal actors. The courses are peppered with excitement and frustration. Some succeed and produce valuable outputs and outcomes for all those involved, at the level of both content and learning. Others are perceived as a loss of valuable time and effort, do not come up with substantial outputs and carry the flavour of failure.

We, the authors, have contributed significantly to the boundary conditions for the learning situations. Ulli Vilsmaier has been responsible for the module and one of the lecturers. Annika Thalheimer has been student, teaching assistant and coordinator of the teaching assistants' team over several years. During the period of the study, we have been experimenting with different teaching elements and have further developed the structure of the module, and we have conducted evaluations and quality circles (an internal feedback instrument based on dialogue) with the students. To complement our insights, we analyzed research reports of the student research groups and individual essays of 115 students who participated in the module between 2015 and 2018, reflecting on them against the background of the course objectives (Vilsmaier and Meyer 2019; Vilsmaier and Lang 2015).

This chapter is organized as follows: in the next section, we provide an overview of the literature on transdisciplinary and student-driven projects in the field of sustainability science, exploring research on challenges and failure. We then provide information on the boundary conditions set by the format of the module before presenting the method applied in this study. In the results section, we present how failure is being addressed, to which frames of reference students refer and we elaborate on dimensions of the research process that the perceived failure is related to. In the discussion, we explore the students' perceptions of failure, how failure is constructed and what students perceive as failure, alongside what was learned from these results.

Challenges and failure in transdisciplinary and student-driven projects

Collaborative research projects, especially transdisciplinary research projects, are highly complex and multidimensional (Freeth et al. 2019; Freeth and Caniglia 2019). Multiple factors make it challenging to conduct such research projects successfully (Freeth and Caniglia 2019; Binder et al. 2015; Stokols 2014; Lang et al. 2012; Stauffacher et al. 2006). This is particularly true when transdisciplinary research is implemented in a study programme to prepare next-generation researchers, as the plurality of objectives increases. In addition to scientific research aims and practice-relevant objectives, various learning goals are pursued, such as the design of a transdisciplinary research project, the application of specific methods and collaboration skills (Vilsmaier et al. 2005).

In the literature about interdisciplinary and transdisciplinary project- and problem-based learning, a series of challenges and factors of success are discussed which are associated with experimental approaches and field work within sustainability studies, while a debate about failure is lacking (Engbers 2019; Jarchow et al. 2018; Di Giulio and Defila 2017; Wiek et al. 2014; Bacon et al. 2011; Fortuin and Bush 2010; Hansmann et al. 2009; Muhar et al. 2006; Scholz et al. 2006; Stauffacher et al. 2006; Steiner and Posch 2006; Brunetti et al. 2003). However, there is an awareness that it is important to evaluate the successes and failures of products and experiences to improve these formats (Wiek et al. 2014). Frequently mentioned challenges relate to the collaborative dimension of teamwork on the communication, social-organizational and epistemic levels (Vilsmaier and Lang 2015; Fortuin and Bush 2010), structural constraints (Bacon et al. 2011; Brunetti et al. 2003) and the expectations of different parties involved (Engbers 2019; Bacon et al. 2011; Fortuin and Bush 2010). In addition, the orientation of individuals in terms of the personal attitudes that are required for transdisciplinary research – such as values, beliefs and behaviours – has been discussed (Stokols 2014).

The module's background

Since 2002, transdisciplinary projects have been included in the Master's programme in Sustainability Science at Leuphana University Lüneburg, Germany. Students asked that these projects be included in our courses, and as a result they were incorporated into the formal curriculum (Burandt et al. 2003). Each year, research and learning spaces are established for approximately 40 students who are organized in two to three courses. Each course consists of about 15 students, two lecturers, one to two teaching assistants and several non-academic societal actors. Over two terms (equivalent to one-sixth of the entire study programme) students work on a transdisciplinary project and experience the entire research process.

240 *Ulli Vilsmaier and Annika Thalheimer*

The topics of the projects range from resource-oriented sustainability problems, such as sustainable phosphorous management, to issues such as the participation of marginalized groups in urban development. All projects deal with cases in the city or district of Lüneburg and Lower Saxony. The research and learning process is organized in three phases, described as "ideal-typical transdisciplinary research processes" by Lang et al. (2012): (a) problem framing and team-building; (b) co-creation of solution-oriented and transferable knowledge; and (c) (re-)integration of the co-created knowledge. The collaborative research process is realized in three different team constellations: the student team (composed of students with diverse disciplinary backgrounds), the academic team (including teaching assistants and lecturers from diverse knowledge fields) and the transdisciplinary team (including societal actors from outside academia) (Vilsmaier and Lang 2015).

Self-organization by the students plays an important role in the module. Students take responsibility for fundamental tasks. They conduct the framing process of the sustainability problem and determine the research area, develop the research design and carry out the production and integration of knowledge in co-operation with their lecturers, teaching assistants and societal actors. In addition to an introductory lecture, the lecturers provide input and guidance to the student teams throughout the course. In parallel, a programme of workshops on different issues (e.g., research management, methods of boundary work, gender and diversity) is offered to support capacity building and to strengthen the knowledge base of the students (Vilsmaier and Meyer 2019).

Methods and material

For this chapter, we analyzed eight courses of the module "Transdisciplinary Project." We scrutinized 15 research reports of the student groups and 230 individual reflections that were presented in the form of essays between 2015 and 2018. The research reports consist of a research plan presented at the end of six months and a combined document that comprises the manuscript of a scientific paper (envisioned to be submitted to the GAiA Master-Students-Paper-Award), a summary of results for praxis partners and a framing paper that integrates the two and provides additional insight into the research process, the group work and the learning process. These are submitted at the end of the course. In addition, each student hands in an essay that emphasizes a specific aspect of the transdisciplinary research process which the students self-select. All parts of the assignment critically reflect on the collaborative research process and its transdisciplinary character. However, the fact that the material we analyzed forms part of the final assignment has to be considered a limiting factor for this analysis as it is likely that students' openness in sharing perceptions of failure is limited for strategic reasons due to being graded based on these texts.

In analyzing the data, we undertook inductive qualitative content analysis according to Kuckartz (2016), screening the material with regard to the use of the words "failure" and "failing." As the terms were rarely used, we focused on reflexive parts of the texts and conclusions for in-depth analysis. We coded paragraphs containing expressions related to failing and failure, such as "didn't work

Failing and the perception of failure 241

well" or "something was missing or not sufficient," to systematize the perceptions and to keep the framing context of these estimations. We approached the students' perspectives with maximum openness, while being aware of our perspective, being lecturers in the courses and scholars in this analysis, pursuing certain objectives in both teaching and research – which has been a balancing act.

Results: The perception of failure from the students' point of view

How failure is addressed

The students very often stated that things had been challenging or problematic. When the term "failure" was used, they stated that the project "can be called a failure," or they emphasized their hope that the project would continue after the completion of their own involvement "so it can't be called failed." Some students reported aspects of the project they considered to have been failures, but no student or team claimed their project had been a total failure. Still, they often mentioned aspects that did not "work out," "missed the aims," "lacked something," "haven't been enough," "didn't happen," or "haven't been successful."

Frames of reference and dimensions of the research process

In their statements about failure, we found that the students used the following frames of reference:

a) student teams' objectives (i.e., collective research objects and the code of conduct)
b) individual objectives (i.e., personal goals)
c) objectives of societal actors or communities (i.e., expectations and demands of practice partners)
d) objectives of the scientific community (i.e., literature about ideal-typical transdisciplinary research and scientific standards)
e) general learning objectives (i.e., the module's learning objectives and structure)

In the analysis, different dimensions of failure were perceived and identified. Students perceived failure mainly with regard to (i) co-operation in different team constellations, (ii) in the application of methods and (iii) in the production of outcomes. In what follows, we exclude the extensive results regarding failures related to methods due to the limited scope of this chapter. These will be published elsewhere.

Failure in co-operation in different team constellations

Students perceived failures of co-operation to have occurred in various team constellations. We systematized their perceptions of failure according to the three

242 *Ulli Vilsmaier and Annika Thalheimer*

team constellations that constitute the course: the student team, the academic team and the transdisciplinary team.

Student team

When students talked about failure within the student team, they referred to different frames of reference such as collective research objects, the code of conduct, scientific standards, team objectives and demands and individual objectives and demands.

In the documents, it is mainly the students' team objectives which were used as a reference, rather than students' individual objectives. Still, some students reported that they did not meet their personal goals. Some students indicated that they had problems developing their roles within their teams. Some students reported that they were good at playing familiar roles but not at developing new ones which involved new tasks and responsibilities. Others were dissatisfied with their performances within their teams. One student concluded that "the different personalities [of team members] haven't been analyzed enough to include them efficiently into the research process."

Lots of students and student teams perceived that there had been failures in the *coordination* of their teams. This was particularly the case where sub-teams were created to meet the multiple tasks of the research process. Creating sub-teams working in parallel (i.e., parallel working structures) caused various problems such as a loss of working capacity, a lack of project management and discontinuity in process planning. Communication platforms (e.g., Slack™, Teamspace4students™), for example, were in some cases not used appropriately. After a main workshop in one of the projects, the lack of planning structures led to disorientation and "after-workshop-blues," which lasted a few weeks. Others reported that miscommunication led to inconsistent results.

There were diverging results with regard to the *team-building* process. One group stressed that the team-building process took too much of their time. Some students claimed that there was too much focus on group formation, whereas others perceived too much focus on content-related tasks without paying enough attention to group formation, reflection and evaluation. One student stated that reflection and evaluation were considered to be disruptive factors, which led to conflicts.

Concerning *feedback culture*, some students felt that there should have been an opportunity for feedback in student teams. They felt an extended exchange of ideas and feedback amongst students would have helped them to complete tasks in a more efficient way. Others stated that performance and motivation were diminished by the lack of feedback between students.

The *unequal contribution* of workload was seen to be another source of failure within student teams, with different priorities and time constraints leading to conflicts and loss of individual satisfaction. Others stated that the code of conduct that stipulated a fair contribution by all students was not met. According to one project team, the inequality of students' contributions was the reason for fading

Failing and the perception of failure   243

motivation and declining performance by the end of the project. This was also mentioned with regard to the proportion of time allowed for each student to speak. Some groups observed that the communication rules written in the code of conduct failed to be applied by all students.

Failure was also perceived to have occurred when *shared understanding* was lacking. In some teams, a shared vision for the project was missing, which led to disorientation. Another group failed to develop a shared understanding of the research design in the first part of the project, with the consequence being inconsistency throughout the whole project. One student stated that the team members had different ideas of transdisciplinarity, which made the integration of societal actors according to mode 2 research (Nowotny et al. 2001) impossible.

Where *heterogeneity* concerning study backgrounds was not provided in the distribution of team members in the student group, students also perceived this as a source of failure. Lacking diversity biased the research process. Where group heterogeneity was provided, many students reported a lack of boundary work within the student team that would have helped to bring into fruition that heterogeneity. One student regarded the heterogeneity of the team as a disruptive factor.

With regard to their *expertise*, students claimed that an ideal-typical transdisciplinary project was impossible because of the preparation time needed at the beginning of the module to become familiar with the transdisciplinary research methodology and the subject of their specific project. This, for instance, slowed the development of the research question and led to weak research designs. Lack of knowledge and incompetency among students was considered a severe problem. Some stressed this as the reason for difficulties in the co-operation with societal actors, as they did not feel prepared for or comfortable in their roles as scientific experts. Students on one project even felt they were seen as foreigners in their study area due to their lack of local knowledge. In the view of one student, this contributed to mistakes throughout the whole study design.

Academic team

Very few statements addressed collaboration in the academic teams. Points raised diverged significantly between the student teams. Some claimed that the teachers could have helped to satisfy demands for knowledge with more guidance, which would have prevented their team from experiencing time-consuming difficulties. A similar request was raised by a student when she asked for more assistance during the boundary work process. On the other hand, one student claimed that teachers were too engaged and provided too much help, which weakened the students' roles as the experts, leading to mistrust of the students' group by the societal actors.

Transdisciplinary team

When students talked about failure within the transdisciplinary team, they referred to objectives of the scientific community, in particular the literature about

244 *Ulli Vilsmaier and Annika Thalheimer*

ideal-typical transdisciplinary research processes and objectives, and the expectations of social actors or communities, as well as the module's structure.

Students of all projects perceived transdisciplinary teamwork to have (partially) failed. Very often, they claimed that they did not pass through the ideal-typical transdisciplinary process. They referred to the pertinent literature and sometimes to the module's framework. They especially focused on the intensity and style of co-operation with societal actors and the (re-)integration of results.

In most of the courses, the *composition* of the transdisciplinary team was decided by the students and often did not fit the thematic scope of the study or the ideal heterogeneity of a transdisciplinary team. Various teams had a gender bias in favour of male participants, and a lack of diversity in age, level of education and disciplinary and institutional background. Some teams did not include politicians, representatives of civil society, ordinary citizens or critical voices concerning the issue of concern. Methods or procedures to identify relevant societal partners were claimed to be insufficient. In one case, the disproportional representation of actors from different societal fields alarmed some participants who were concerned that the academic team could be exploited by the overrepresented group of actors. In addition, the withdrawal of societal actors or conflicts between them led to imbalanced team compositions. According to one student team, governmental reliance on long-term and regulated processes clashed with the innovative and creative approach used in transdisciplinary processes.

The restricted *timeframe* of one year limited transdisciplinary working dynamics. For several groups, final workshops, evaluation sessions and the implementation of results were impossible. The circumstances required parallel working structures even if the processes and methods demanded that the work be conducted successively, and often societal actors were excluded in some phases of the projects, especially in the early or late phases. Often, only selected team members made decisions about the research objects, research design and research methods, and only some team members were involved in organizing workshops. In some cases, projects were evaluated without the involvement of societal actors.

Where failure in collaboration was experienced, it was mainly related to *insufficient and discontinued collaboration* with societal actors. Reasons for this included a lack of experience on the part of the students, time constraints of the team members and spontaneous cancellations and discontinuity in participation in events. One group experienced severe difficulties when a vital member of the transdisciplinary team spontaneously cancelled their participation in the key workshop when he became aware of a conflict of interest with his political activity. In two cases, the physical distance between the academic workplace and the study area hindered continuing collaboration with societal actors from the study area.

Several project groups missed out on working with societal actors at the beginning of the project due to their participation in team-building exercises. This was considered to have inhibited co-leadership with societal actors and led to a *lack of trust* and an *asymmetric distribution of power*. The students often named one or two interactive workshops and sometimes preparatory interviews to be the core transdisciplinary formats of their research. The preparation, analysis and assessment of these formats were mainly the responsibility of the students. Some students perceived this process to be pseudo-participation. Some stated that the societal actors were relegated to a passive-affirmative role, and that a substantial, enduring contribution from societal actors was mostly impossible. The consequences were incomplete results with deficient validity and social robustness. Especially when vital actors were missing, students claimed low legitimacy of the results. One student team assumed that societal actors might have lost interest and motivation as they had not enough opportunities to engage actively and creatively in the process.

Failure was also perceived where co-operation was not *on equal footing*. According to one project group, the superficial exchange between societal actors and students ended in a shallow bond of trust between the research partners. Students perceived that the dichotomy between an *active researcher* and a *passive research object* was not abolished. One student reported that equivalence between scientific and non-scientific knowledge, and the questioning of the scientific expert status (according to Hanschitz et al. 2009), did not happen completely. According to this student, it was more like the students interviewed the societal actors instead of collaborating with them. In two cases, students had the impression that the societal actors did not take the student team seriously, or attached little importance to the project. Some considered the projects to be contract research instead of collaborative research. Students in every project stated that they felt uncomfortable about not having worked with societal actors as closely as they planned and wished, and according to the literature, should have. A joint steering group was an explicit aim of several groups but was conducted in none.

Failure in the production of outcomes

Many students struggled with the outcomes of their projects. Some considered the results to be incomplete, unrealistic, unsound, unscientific, non-essential, impractical and insufficient for both students and societal actors. They referenced their collective research objects, the objectives of the scientific community regarding transdisciplinarity and other scientific standards, the objectives of the community, individual demands and the module's structure.

Many students stated that the *(re-)integration of knowledge* failed completely or happened in a shallow way. At the end of the projects, knowledge (re-)integration often remained obscure in their recommendations and action plans. In some groups, societal actors were not well included in the assessment of the results and joint discussions of the recommendations for action were missing. This led to incomplete and unsatisfying results and no (re-)integration of knowledge in the respective fields of practice. The perception that the project was not finished was shared by various students. One student claimed she had expected to implement the measures developed during the project and had hoped to make a difference with the project. A similar view was expressed by one student, who stated that he had hoped to continue the project, to implement the gathered knowledge and for the project not to fail.

246   *Ulli Vilsmaier and Annika Thalheimer*

One group stated that the *quality of results* was not as meaningful as they desired, and that the results were instead incomplete and unrealistic. This was also noted by the societal actors involved, students reported. One student even perceived societal actors to be disappointed by the quality of the outcomes. The students mentioned time constraints and missed opportunities for exchanges with societal actors, the limited number of societal actors, the homogeneous nature of the cohort of societal actors and the irregular and shallow collaboration within the transdisciplinary team as reasons for the unsatisfying quality of results. In addition to the standards of transdisciplinary research, students also referred to common scientific standards in describing their results as weak. Furthermore, students of one project were afraid that their own assumptions and estimates biased their research. Another group struggled with inconsistency of results because of difficulties in team communication. In two cases, students observed that the results did not correspond with the ideals of the team due to lack of expertise and the inappropriate framing of questions and choices of methods. This led to results that did not correspond with their ideas of sustainability. One student team stated that the multiple demands of the module – the simultaneous efforts in team-building, theoretical and methodological orientation, and implementation of the different tasks of the transdisciplinary research process – forced the students to contemplate sustainability issues in a shallow way and that the outcomes did not meet the team's sustainability goals.

Many students were also very critical about the *suitability of generated knowledge*. Some even doubted that their project generated any suitable, scientific knowledge, while others claimed that they met few if any targets and/or did not produce any transformative knowledge. One student team stated that they did not fully exploit the possibilities to generate specific local knowledge due to unsuitable methods. One student team did a sustainable life-cycle assessment and planned a final ranking of the products at hand but claimed that the assessed system was too complex to make a final evaluation and ranking possible. Students perceived a lack of strategies for transformation on a societal level and wondered if the outcomes generated socially viable solutions. According to one student, their project would not cause any significant changes and thus did not have any societal impact.

Discussion

How students construct failure

In our introduction we highlighted that failing is relational and only exists against the background of frames of reference. Thus, subjective and social value conventions that trigger the perception of failure (Aydt 2015) are entwined and mutually constitutive. The frames of reference students constructed have different degrees of institutionalization. The collective research objects and the codes of conduct of student teams are internally constructed conventions and are an expression of the team's self-expectations. The module's learning objectives that were set by the

Failing and the perception of failure 247

faculty and lecturers, the state-of-the-art literature and scientific standards and the objectives of societal actors or communities, are external conventions and boundary conditions that are tangible to different degrees. These frames of reference are similar to the sources of pressure that impact student-driven transdisciplinary research according to Stauffacher et al. (2006), such as peers, societal partners, professors and multiple learning goals.

Students' perceptions of failure in transdisciplinary research projects

The results show a high degree of critical reflexivity, a strong commitment to the principles and practices of transdisciplinary research and very high self-expectations. Students mainly perceived themselves as being responsible for the failures they saw in their transdisciplinary research projects. The multiple frames of reference students constructed display the multiplicity of objectives and the degree of complexity of such research and learning endeavours. Students perceived failure in multiple dimensions of transdisciplinary research, many of them having been discussed extensively as challenges in the literature (Binder et al. 2015; Lawrence 2015; Vilsmaier et al. 2015; Lang et al. 2012; Stauffacher et al. 2006). The following reasons for failure were stressed: time constraints and different institutional tempos, inadequate organizational expenditure, the lack of experience of all persons involved in conducting such kind of research and the absence of shared objectives and responsibilities. While the perception of failure is diverse with regard to the learning processes of individuals or student teams, there are strong parallels with regard to the establishment, consolidation and continuation of the transdisciplinary teams in all courses. The results show that, to a certain extent, all teams experienced failure in the operationalization of transdisciplinary research processes.

What is instructive for the particular case of transdisciplinary learning projects is that many students considered failure against the background of an ideal-typical transdisciplinary process. An ideal transdisciplinary process serves as a benchmark and can only be approximated due to the singularity of any transdisciplinary research constellation (Krohn 2010). However, the students' perceptions of failure reflect what is discussed in the literature as being the core challenges of transdisciplinary research. When the research process was not jointly driven by societal actors and the student team – that is, when the framing of the research field or the assessment of results was performed by students only – students perceived failure. The results show the serious attempts by the majority of groups to work on equal footing, to acknowledge different forms of knowledge equally, and to distribute power among all those involved in the transdisciplinary team. Failure on the level of outcomes was mainly perceived when these objectives were not met.

The various types of tensions that emerge in student-driven transdisciplinary projects became apparent. First, there is a tension between students' freedom and the guidance provided by lecturers in the courses. The results confirm that students have highly differing needs, and meeting for these varying needs is a core

248 *Ulli Vilsmaier and Annika Thalheimer*

balancing act for lecturers, as already highlighted in previous studies (Vilsmaier and Lang 2015; Stauffacher et al. 2006; Muhar et al. 2006; Hmelo-Silver 2004). Fortuin and Bush (2010) emphasize the balancing act between providing a "challenging environment for students" and the danger of "democratic fatigue." While some students claimed the teaching was too liberal or not rigorous enough, others complained of there being too much structure and a lack of autonomy in the research process, which is also reported by Fortuin and Bush (2010) and Pfirmann and Martin (2010). Second, the results highlight the tension between students' learning goals and the orientation towards societal needs, which has also been observed in similar projects at other universities (Stauffacher et al. 2006). From this perspective, student reflection on the project roles in the student teams is particularly interesting. While students tried to do their best in taking responsibilities for the process and performing tasks with which they were familiar, some failed to use the course as a learning opportunity to experiment with new roles. Third, a tension is created between solid scientific research and the suitability and applicability of outcomes. Where objectives and expectations of societal actors (and students' transformative goals) dominated the research process, students struggled to produce scientifically robust outcomes.

Consequences for student-driven transdisciplinary projects

What can we – the authors and lecturers – learn from these results? Have we failed to provide sound boundary conditions? Do we overburden students by creating space for student-driven transdisciplinary research projects? Or is the state-of-the-art in transdisciplinary research not yet sufficiently consolidated to realize such projects in a student-driven way? Obviously, there are no easy answers. But in addition to the perception of failure, the material indicates excitement, huge learning experiences and – in part – substantive and valuable outcomes. Therefore, it seems worth continuing to work on improving boundary conditions and on further developing such learning spaces.

The module "Transdisciplinary Project" is still an exception in the landscape of study programmes. An entire year of the Master's programme is devoted to student-driven transdisciplinary research. But still, students considered time constraints to be a major reason for failure. A way to meet this constraint is to reorganize the study programme to make other courses fit with the transdisciplinary projects. Contents such as research management, methods courses, and theoretical lectures on sustainability science should be more strongly linked to the module to better prepare students. Furthermore, more structure for the working process should be provided by the lecturers, for example by not only introducing but also setting up a specific research management methodology in collaboration with the students (Defila et al. 2006) to enable successful and efficient communication and co-operation in the different team constellations. In relation to parallel working structures, the model introduced by Scholz and Tietje (2002), which includes a synthesis group that integrates the working process and results from sub-groups,

Failing and the perception of failure 249

might be a promising means to address difficulties with integration. With regard to collaboration in transdisciplinary teams, it has become apparent that stronger support from the lecturers in setting up stable conditions for collaboration is needed. This is intertwined with the identification and framing of the sustainability problem and accordingly the research questions. Strong guidance and support from lecturers are particularly needed in the first phase of the transdisciplinary projects. This should also be the case in the formation of the interdisciplinary student teams to make the different knowledges and abilities within the team visible, to bring heterogeneity into fruition and to frame transdisciplinary research fields that correspond with students' expertise.

Last but not least, the fact that the students rarely mentioned challenges concerning collaboration within the academic team indicates that the way student performance is assessed in these student-driven transdisciplinary projects has to be questioned. Grading creates distance within the academic team, which is likely to be counterproductive for a joint research process. More heterarchical, group-based forms of assessments might be a way to move forward to meet this challenge.

Conclusion

Learning situations are limit situations that trigger students to perform limit-acts (Freire 1996). In so doing, students can fall short on social value conventions (i.e., externally set boundary conditions), and fail to meet their own expectations (i.e., their personally set boundary conditions). However, transdisciplinary research projects can also fail to contribute to societal transformation and accordingly, to meet the expectations of societal actors and communities involved in the research process. This makes a significant difference. Compared to courses that provide learning in a protected university-learning sphere, students are exposed to real situations and their performances have consequences that go beyond the learning situation. This is particularly serious in the study field of sustainability science where many students feel a moral responsibility to contribute to a more sustainable world.

What has become apparent in this study of failure and the perception of failure in student-driven transdisciplinary projects is the responsibility of lecturers to set suitable boundary conditions and to provide sufficient space for dialogue on (self-)expectations and students' needs in the academic team. To accompany and support them more strongly may lead to more acknowledgement of their own performance and lessen the perception of failure. This seems to be necessary in developing research objectives and designs, and in stabilizing the transdisciplinary team, but also to support students in critically reflecting on the novelty of the transdisciplinary approach and the related upheaval in scientific value conventions, because in fact, none of the courses was graded with a lower mark than "good" (2) which is an acknowledgement of the students' performances in these highly complex learning endeavours by the professors.

250 *Ulli Vilsmaier and Annika Thalheimer*

Take-home messages

- Actively deal with paradoxes and contradictions, such as meeting both scientific and societal robustness or collaboration between students and teachers grading them.
- Be aware of and discuss the novel and radical character of transdisciplinary research at the science-society interface and be patient about failure. It is more than an inter-generational endeavour!
- Take time to clarify aims and criteria of success, explore individual expectations and define shared expectations, and set up a steering board in every transdisciplinary research process where continuous dialogue and decision-making takes place.
- Have in mind that research *in vivo* entails a lot of unexpected dynamics and incidents that are not described in ideal transdisciplinary research processes in the literature, particularly when introducing them in lectures.

Acknowledgements

We would like to thank all the students that participated in the module "Transdisciplinary Project" between 2015 and 2018 for their engagement, huge efforts and critical reflexivity. Thanks also to our colleagues for their willingness to accompany the teams, and for providing the assignments. We are thankful to our colleagues at the Methodology Center, Esther Meyer and Moira Skupin, for their critical comments and proofreading of the text, and to Michael Dellwing, who discussed the methodological design used to study failure several times with us.

References

Aydt, S. 2015. *An den Grenzen der interkulturelen Bildung: Eine Auseinandersetzung mit Scheitern im Kontext von Fremdheit*. Bielefeld, Germany: Transcript.

Bacon, C.M., Mulvaney, D., Ball, T.B., DuPuis, E.M., Gliessman, S.R., Lipschutz, R.D., Shakouri, A. 2011. The creation of an integrated sustainability curriculum and student praxis projects. *International Journal of Sustainability in Higher Education*, 12(2), 193–208.

Binder, C.R., Absenger-Helmli, I., Schilling, T. 2015. The reality of transdisciplinarity: A framework-based self-reflection from science and practice leaders. *Sustainability Science*, 10(4), 545–562.

Brunetti, A.J., Petrell, R.J., Sawada, B. 2003. SEEDing sustainability: Team project-based learning enhances awareness of sustainability at the University of British Columbia, Canada. *International Journal of Sustainability in Higher Education*, 4(3), 210–217.

Burandt, S., Döscher, K., Fuisz, S.-K., Helgenberger, S., Maly, L. 2003. Transdisziplinäre Fallstudien in Lüneburg: Beschreibung eines Entwicklungskonzepts hin zur angewandten Erweiterung des Curriculums an der Universität Lüneburg. Center for Sustainability Management, Universität Lüneburg, Lüneburg, Germany.

Failing and the perception of failure 251

Defila, R., Di Giulio, A., Scheuermann, M. 2006. *Forschungsverbundmanagement. Handbuch für die Gestaltung inter- und transdisziplinärer Projekte*. Zürich: vdf Hochschulverlag.

Di Giulio, A., Defila, R. 2017. Enabling university educators to equip students with inter- and transdisciplinary competencies. *International Journal of Sustainability in Higher Education*, 18(5), 630–647.

Engbers, M. 2019. *Kultur und Differenz: Transdisziplinäre Nachhaltigkeitsforschung gestalten*. Wahrnehmungsgeographische Studien 29. Oldenburg: BIS Verlag.

Fortuin, I.K.P.J., Bush, S.R. 2010. Educating students to cross boundaries between disciplines and cultures and between theory and practice. *International Journal of Sustainability in Higher Education*, 11(1), 19–35.

Freeth, R., Caniglia, G. 2019. Learning to collaborate while collaborating: advancing collaborative interdisciplinary research. *Sustainability Science*, 14(48), 1–15.

Freeth, R., Clarke, E.A., Fam, D. 2019. Engaging creatively with tension in collaborative research: Harnessing the "I" and "we" through dialogue. In: V.A. Brown, J.A Harris and D. Waltner-Toews, eds. *Independent thinking in an uncertain world: a mind of one's own*. London: Routledge.

Freire, P. 1996. *Pedagogy of the oppressed*. London: Penguin.

Hansmann, R., Crott, H.W., Mieg, H.A., Scholz, R.W. 2009. Improving group processes in transdisciplinary case studies for sustainability learning. *International Journal of Sustainability in Higher Education*, 10(1), 33–42.

Hmelo-Silver, C.E. 2004. Problem-based learning: What and how do students learn? *Educational Psychology Review*, 16(3), 235–266.

Jarchow, M.E., Formisano, P., Nordyke, S., Sayre, M. 2018. Measuring longitudinal student performance on student learning outcomes in sustainability education. *International Journal of Sustainability in Higher Education*, 19(3), 547–565.

Jasper, K. 1919. *Psychologie der Weltanschauungen*. Berlin: Springer.

Junge, M., Lechner, G. 2004. Scheitern als Erfahrung und Konzept: Zur Einführung. In: M. Junge and G. Lechner, eds. *Scheitern - Aspekte eines sozialen Phänomens*. Wiesbaden, Germany: VS Verlag für Sozialwissenschaften, 7–14.

Krohn, W. 2010. Interdisciplinary cases and disciplinary knowledge. In: R. Frodeman, J.T. Klein and C. Mitcham, eds. *The Oxford handbook of interdisciplinarity*. Oxford: Oxford University Press, 7–14.

Kuckartz, U. 2016 *Qualitative Inhaltsanalyse: Methoden, Praxis, Computerunterstützung*. 3rd ed. Weinheim and Basel, Gerrmany: Beltz Juventa.

Lang, D.J., Wiek, A., Bergmann, M., Stauffacher, M., Martens, P., Moll, P., Swilling, M., Thomas, C.J. 2012. Transdisciplinary research in sustainability science: Practice, principles, and challenges. *Sustainability Science*, 7(1) 25–43.

Lawrence, R.J. 2015. Advances in transdisciplinarity: Epistemologies, methodologies and processes. *Futures*, 65, 1–19.

Muhar, A., Vilsmaier, U., Glanzer, M., Freyer, B. 2006. Initiating transdisciplinarity in academic case study teaching: Experiences from a regional development project in Salzburg, Austria. *International Journal of Sustainability in Higher Education*, 7(3), 293–308.

Nowotny, H., Scott, P., Gibbons, M. 2001. *Re-thinking science: Knowledge and the public in an age of uncertainty*. Cambridge: Polity Press.

Pfirman, S., Martin, P.J.S. 2010. Facilitating interdisciplinary scholars. In: R. Frodeman, J.T. Klein and C. Mitcham, eds. *The Oxford handbook of interdisciplinarity*. New York: Oxford University Press, 387–403.

252 *Ulli Vilsmaier and Annika Thalheimer*

Scholz, R.W., Tietje, O. 2002. *Embedded case study methods: Integrating quantitative and qualitative knowledge*. Thousand Oaks, CA, London, and New Delhi: Sage Publications.

Scholz, R.W., Lang, D.J., Wiek, A., Walter, A.I., Stauffacher, M. 2006. Transdisciplinary case studies as a means of sustainability learning: Historical framework and theory. *International Journal of Sustainability in Higher Education*, 7(3), 226–251.

Stauffacher, M., Walter, A.I., Lang, D.J., Wiek, A., Scholz, R.W. 2006. Learning to research environmental problems from a functional socio-cultural constructivism perspective: The transdisciplinary case study approach. *International Journal of Sustainability in Higher Education*, 7(3), 252–275.

Steiner, G., Posch, A. 2006. Higher education for sustainability by means of transdisciplinary case studies: An innovative approach for solving complex, real-world problems. *Journal of Cleaner Production*, 14(9–11), 877–890.

Stokols, D. 2014. Training the next generation of transdisciplinarians. In: M. O'Rourke, S. Crowley, S. Eigenbrode and J. Wulfhorst, eds. *Enhancing communication and collaboration in interdisciplinary research*. New York: Oxford University Press, 56–74.

Vilsmaier, U., Freyer, B., Muhar, A. 2005. Transdisciplinary goal finding in regional planning processes. Transdisciplinary case study research for sustainable development, Proceedings of the 11th annual international sustainable development research conference 2005, Helsinki, 215–226.

Vilsmaier, U., Lang, D.J. 2014. Transdisziplinäre Forschung. In: H. Heinrichs and G. Michelsen, eds. *Nachhaltigkeitswissenschaften*. Berlin/Heidelberg: Springer-Verlag, 87–113.

Vilsmaier, U., Lang, D.J. 2015. Making a difference by marking the difference: Constituting in-between spaces for sustainability learning. *Current Opinion in Environmental Sustainability*, 16, 51–55.

Vilsmaier, U., Meyer, E. 2019. Inquiry-based learning in sustainability science. In: H.A. Mieg, ed. *Inquiry-based learning - undergraduate research: the German multidisciplinary experiences*. Cham, Switzerland: Springer, 331–229.

Wiek, A., Xiong, A., Brundiers, K., van der Leeuw, S. 2014. Integrating problem and project-based learning into sustainability programs: A case study on the school of sustainability at Arizona State University. *International Journal of Sustainability in Higher Education*, 15(4), 431–449.

Coda

15 Failure *is* an option

Lessons for success

Julie Thompson Klein

At first blush, this book seems unnecessary. Decades of recommendations from science-policy bodies, educational commissions, professional organizations and a growing number of case studies have identified reasons for failure in projects and programmes that cross both disciplinary and sector boundaries. At second blush, their redundancy justifies the volume. The same factors keep appearing ... and reappearing. Thus, despite widespread agreement on how to counter causes of failure, projects and programmes continue to falter. This chapter begins by condensing barriers and impediments into a digest of common reasons for failure of cross-disciplinary work encompassing interdisciplinarity and transdisciplinarity and cross-sector work that bridges the academy, government, industry and communities in the North/West and Global South. It then combines lessons from four case studies beyond this book with insights from earlier chapters, with the aim of understanding the political economy of knowledge, the centrality of learning and stakeholder engagement in cross-disciplinary and cross-sector work. The chapter concludes by presenting six overarching principles for success that emerge from a deeper understanding of failure and a closing reflection on lessons from the composite of case studies.

The reportage of failure

Failure is not a straightforward concept. In their introduction to this book, Michael O'Rourke and Dena Fam identify a number of meanings, including not meeting expectations, setting unrealistic goals, being derailed by unexpected developments, not meeting funders' requirements and lacking adequate human and material resources. Perceptions of what constitutes failure also vary by individuals, and authors of chapters in the volume contributed their perceptions as well. O'Rourke, Crowley, Eigenbrode and Vasko deemed it a heterogeneous concept that is open to interpretation. Martina Ukowitz observed the enigmatic nature of failure means it may be a total breakdown, falling short of an ideal or simply a mistake; it might also result from an accident or other misfortune, or just be a sense of disquiet. And Ulli Vilsmaier and Annika Thalheimer observed failure might mean something was missing or insufficient or simply "didn't work well."

Carelessness, lack of requisite skills and even outright incompetence are added reasons for failure, as well as other factors identified in the editors' preliminary survey and affirmed in case studies reviewed in this conclusion. They include lack of momentum, inadequate communication, conflict among team members,

256   *Julie Thompson Klein*

uneven participation, discipline-based commitments and reward systems, lack of leadership, loss of personnel, inadequate timeframes and limited or no co-production of knowledge with stakeholders.

Given the variety of forms failure takes, consequences range from complete collapse of a project to minor glitches requiring adjustments. Beyond this book, others have also commented on the meaning of the concept. In an online exchange, Roderick Lawrence questioned criteria for determining failure, given the co-existence of multiple kinds of interdisciplinarity (pers. comm., 5 December 201). In response, Cynthia Mitchell added that diminished outcomes may not spell outright failure and in fact may yield tools and strategies for success (pers. comm., 7 December 2018). Even with multiple connotations, however, authors in this collection join O'Rourke, Crowley, Eigenbrode and Vasko in conceptualizing failure as an "engine for change" while making good on Neuhaser, Brettler and Boyle's exhortation in their chapter to move past binary thinking in terms of strictly negative versus positive outcomes.

We can start our consideration of failure by asking whether there are factors in common across instances of failure. Benchmark reports on cross-disciplinary and cross-sector work have identified in passim and in their formal recommendations strategies for overcoming specific obstacles, including the US-based National Research Council's *Facilitating Interdisciplinary Research* (2005) and *Convergence* (2014), Hilton and Cooke's *Enhancing the Effectiveness of Team Science* (2015), the INTREPID series on bridging humanities and social sciences (2017a, 2017b), the British Academy's *Crossing Paths* (2016) and the Global Research Council's *Interdisciplinarity* (2016). This roster is not an exhaustive one. However, it provides a foundation for Table 15.1, which presents a composite of reasons for failure in cross-disciplinary and cross-sector work.

Although the reports emanated from different contexts, they were all prompted by a gap between widespread rhetoric of endorsement and realities of practice. The continuing dominance of disciplinary organization in academic policies and procedures is a major reason for the gap. Ad hoc efforts outnumber comprehensive change in institutional cultures, and shallow capacity building leaves members of these institutions ill-equipped for dealing with the complexities of cross-disciplinary and cross-boundary work. Figure 15.1 casts light on top impediments to interdisciplinary research in academic environments, based on responses to a preliminary survey for the 2005 report on *Facilitating Interdisciplinary Research*. Provosts and individual faculty and staff differed in their assessment of which impediments were more important, although promotion criteria ranked top for both groups. Prominent though it is, however, one factor alone does not impede success. Co-chairs of the report cautioned that multiple institutional customs create "a small but persistent 'drag' on individuals wanting to engage in crossdisciplinary work" (p. 4).

The focus of the 2005 NRC report is not solely academic. It also recognized cross-sector work in industry and national laboratories. Over the past two decades, greater attention is being paid to research and problem-solving initiatives that cross the boundaries separating the academy and public and private spheres. Table 15.1 reflects that development, extending from my earlier composite of barriers and disincentives to interdisciplinarity in academic environments to include cross-sector work (Klein 2010). The factors are divided between primarily academic ones and factors appearing both within and across sectors.

Table 15.1 Barriers and disincentives related to failure in cross-disciplinary and cross-sector work (Klein 2020)

Barriers and Disincentives

Organizational Structure and Administration

Primarily academic	Discipline- and department-based silos
	Territoriality and turf battles
	Ambiguous status of projects, programmes and units within an institution
	Insufficient control over budget, research and curriculum
Within and across sectors	No clear and authoritative report lines for dedicated programmes and units
	Rigid one-size-fits-all model of organizational and/or professional structure
	Ad hoc and dispersed infrastructure
	Lack of experienced leaders
	Resistance to innovation and risk
	Shortage of incubator space for working across boundaries

Procedures and Policies

Primarily academic	Inflexible rules for approval of new programmes and courses
	Unfavourable policies for allocating workload credit in teaching
	Rigid and exclusionary degree requirements
	Targeted programmes and electives for particular cohorts rather than mainstream practice
	Lack of inclusive guidelines for hiring, tenure and promotion and salary
	Unfavourable policies for intellectual property indirect cost recovery from grants
Within and across sectors	Prioritizing of some approaches over others
	Narrow strictures of resource allocation
	Dominance of and defaulting to particular disciplinary, professional and sector perspectives
	Competing rules across domains and sectors

Funding

Primarily academic	Budget allocations favouring discipline-based units
	Inadequate funding for seeding new projects and programmes
	Dependence on soft money without hard budget allocation
	Lack of access to overhead from grants

(Continued)

Table 15.1 Continued

Barriers and Disincentives

Within and across sectors	Narrow criteria for funding and siloed categories Shortage of sources for financing Reliance on volunteerism and overload Joint funding by multiple agencies/research councils with differing demands

Resources and Infrastructure

Primarily academic	Inadequate resources for activities including space and equipment Inadequate personnel for education and research including faculty lines Restricted access to internal incentives and seed funds for ID research and curriculum Insufficient time to learn language and culture of another discipline and to form collaborative relationships in team Insufficient support for student assistantships and fellowships
Within and across sectors	Weak or no professional development system Ignorance of pertinent literature and networks Insufficient time for planning and implementation cross-boundary projects Demands for evidence of impact on short timescales

Recognition and Reward

Primarily academic	Lack of support at department, college and/or university levels Invisibility and marginality of individuals and teams Lack of appropriate criteria in tenure and promotion system Ineligibility for awards, honours, incentives and development programmes
Within and across sectors	Lack of long-term sustainability, rendering projects and programmes ephemeral Negative bias against cross-disciplinary, interprofessional and/or cross-sector work Weak networking channels and communication forums Inadequate incentives for participation

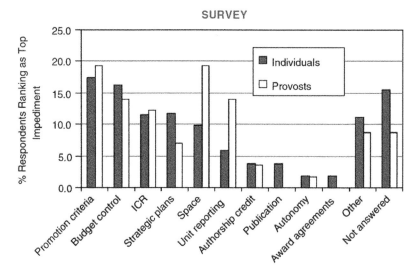

Figure 15.1 "Top Impediments to IDR," *Facilitating Interdisciplinary Research*, 2005, p. 76.

To reiterate, one factor or category alone does not impede success. Organizational Structure and Administration influence budget allotments, decision-making, attitudes towards change and prospects for innovative projects, programmes and units. Procedures and Policies often limit flexibility, impede autonomy and enforce values and criteria that do not fit the complex needs of working across boundaries. Funding typically favours dominant forms of expertise in prescribed organizational slots, follows standard procedures and perpetuates inadequate support that undercuts the potential of even the most highly touted initiatives. Resources and Infrastructure also frequently favour dominant disciplines and professions. They are often insufficient for both cross-disciplinary and cross-sector work, and do not support long-term sustainability, professional development and making good on widespread claims of transforming the academic system while educating the "next generation" of researchers and educators. And, finally, Recognition and Reward re-inscribe dominant values, lack sufficient criteria for evaluating pertinent work and marginalize or outright ignore related accomplishments. As a result, change in one area alone is insufficient to create a culture shift. This outcome is the case whether we are talking about an entire institution or units within it such as centres and programmes. A deeper look at lessons from case studies sheds further light on the lived experience of failure.

260 *Julie Thompson Klein*

Case studies

In addition to previous chapters, case studies beyond this book yield relevant insights. Some are restricted to academic contexts, others to particular professions or communities and still others bridge sectors. Their locations also differ within and across countries and continents. Three case studies from the literature resonate with three overarching themes, thereby broadening and deepening understanding of failure. Why introduce new examples at this point? No single case, however powerful, captures the magnitude of cross-cutting themes that emerge from located practices. Moreover, merging insights underscores their importance, highlighting in this instance the political economy of knowledge, the centrality of learning and stakeholder engagement.

The political economy of knowledge

The first example beyond this book is Dena Fam and Zoe Sofoulis's (2017) case study of a waste management project, supported by an Alaskan Water and Sewer Challenge from the state's Department of Environment and Conservation. It introduces the impact of status hierarchy, not only in the academy but also across sectors of society. Both the external example and Fletcher and Lyall's chapters in this book, in a different context of producing red blood cells for transfusion, illustrate priorities of positivist science and engineering over social sciences and humanities. Comparable to Fam and Soufoulis's chapter, Imbruce and Prazak's chapter on introducing an environmental studies course illustrates minimizing of community-based knowledge, even when yielding valuable insights into the fit between a proposed solution and local feasibility. Perceptions of failure and success hinge, then, on both shortfalls in integration and the differing stakes particular groups have in a project.

The project team in the Alaska case study brought pertinent experience. Two members were knowledgeable about decentralized and arctic engineering of water and sanitation systems. One was a microbiologist with Indigenous and public health expertise. Other contributors included design consultants who had experience in STEM, participatory design and transdisciplinary projects. However, despite the inclusion of language of design thinking and community engagement in the call for proposals, positivist science was prioritized. Moreover, no team member had formal qualifications in social sciences and humanities, and the budget reflected engineering priorities. Social research is often deemed crucial to solving complex problems. Yet, Fam and Sofoulis cautioned, plugging social data into a predictive model along with technical, environmental and economic information is a narrow form of integration that prioritizes quantitative methodologies. In contrast, interpretive researchers attempt to get "inside the situation" by contextualizing a problem from the actors' points of view, using "bottom-up" qualitative research methods such as fieldwork and observational studies, surveys, conversations, interviews, diaries and photo journals.

The political economy of scientific priorities also diminished local knowledge. In an effort to learn more about local conditions, the team spent two weeks in conversations with participants from two remote Alaskan villages, regional health consortiums

Failure is *an option*   261

and statewide organizations. However, the call for proposals did not allow in-depth community engagement, even though villagers possessed expertise about their water and sanitation, the economic viability of alternatives and the long-term acceptability of any changes. A portion of funding was allotted for social research, but limited funds were exhausted before the final stage and the team opted for a workshop on the proposed design and a questionnaire faxed to community leaders for feedback on technical solutions. Engineers and scientists appreciated exposure to other kinds of knowledge. Yet, design thinking that could have tailored contextualized solutions for a sanitation system was countermanded by a one-size-fits-all, top-down Big Water logic. Differences between positivist and interpretivist paradigms, Fam and Sofoulis added, were further evident when the technical design group tried to separate from the social design group, which favoured a broader transdisciplinary approach that strengthened links between social and technical factors. The Alaska project is not an isolated example of competing values.

Isabel Fletcher and Catherine Lyall focus in their chapter on a different context: producing industrially generated red blood cells for transfusion. The Novosang project was not a complete failure, but it was an "unsatisfactory" and "disappointing" experience for social researchers. Natural scientists acknowledged learning about social sciences, but interview data revealed that social scientists were not involved in the initial problem framing. Thus, their work package was distanced from core activities. Bill Bellotti and Fred D'Agostino's chapter in this book also identified reasons for falling short of full integration. Their transdisciplinary research programme in food systems at the Global Change Institute had only a small pool of cross-disciplinary researchers, ad hoc status, inadequate capacity to engage stakeholders and insufficient time. Despite some positive outcomes, the cumulative result was an undertow of uncertainty and stagnation amplified by departure of staff, budget reductions, low morale among those remaining, lack of a strong common vision and narrow metrics of success.

Valerie Imbruce and Miroslava Prazak's chapter focuses on a different goal than the prior three examples: creating community-engaged environmental studies courses on post-industrial life in the northeastern United States. Yet, it too encountered differing priorities. The Mill Town Project took place at a small liberal arts university that had no departments or majors and an emergent curriculum. So, it seemed ideally suited for innovation. Yet, discipline-based priorities still lessened commitment to an experimental interdisciplinary course, driven in no small part by the challenge small campuses face in sparing faculty from teaching mandatory courses in essential subjects. Three years of grant-funded conversations yielded a rich understanding of people in their environments, involving a social psychologist and an anthropologist as well as a chemist, a geologist, an architect and a botanist. Yet, once again positivist sciences enjoyed higher status, diminishing prospects for incorporating more qualitative data. Moreover, despite a positive relationship with a project manager charged with interfacing between the course and the local community, cancellation of a seven-week term in January and February resulted in loss of a time and a format that could have accommodated internships related to the project. Interest in environmental concerns continues, including some coursework, but in an ad hoc manner.

262   *Julie Thompson Klein*

Learning

Learning is also a key theme in both the broader literature and pertinent chapters. A case study from the literature draws lessons from a failed innovation in Swedish schools that faced the greater priority of traditional discipline-based curricula. Dena Fam, Abby Mellick Lopes and Cynthia Mitchell's account of limits to curricular innovation in Australia amplifies insights from the external example in a niche experiment that fell short of scaling up an innovative socio-technical system for urine diversion, recovery and reuse. Like BinBin Pearce's chapter on a curricular experiment in environmental studies at the ETH-Zurich, it also illustrates the importance of creating a space where productive failure results in learning without punitive risk. Neuhaser, Brettler and Boyle's chapter, in turn, illustrates the importance of providing time for adjustments when problems arise, and it frames institutionalizing learning from failure as a positive value. The final three examples illustrate learning from problems with methodologies. They are: O'Rourke, Crowley, Eigenbrode and Vasko's analysis of failures in four US-based Toolbox workshops; Irena Leisbet Ceridwen Connon's account of resistance to a charrette-based method of engaging participants in a UK-based project focused on extreme weather events; and Ulli Vilsmaier and Annika Thalheimer's examination of feedback on student-based research projects in Germany.

Magnus Hultén's (2013) case study of "Spheres of Work" analyzed a thematic child-centred concept introduced in 1969 as part of a new national curriculum. It consisted of syllabus content for one or more school subjects aimed at a more integrated approach to grades 7–9. Typical of projects in the literature and this book, Spheres of Work was interpreted differently by individuals and groups with their own agendas and materials. Yet, it was an active concept at the organizational level and a boundary object for steering past disagreements on a subject-based versus an integrated approach. The group working on Technological Orientation was the first to recognize the Spheres of Work concept, while groups working on social studies and science developed a more elaborate structure moving from a single-subject approach to Spheres of Work units integrating either science or social studies with an overall level that includes content from both. Survey data, though, revealed differences by grade level, teachers' experience and location. Moreover, syllabi and schedules were still typically structured around subjects, so teachers had to construct integrated teaching units themselves. In the end, outcomes did not match hopes, and in 1980 a new national curriculum replaced Spheres of Work with another thematic idea.

Even so, Hultén concluded, Spheres of Work had a "massive impact" on the structure of knowledge in the 1969 reform, textbooks written in the 1970s, and classroom practice. The project failed to achieve widespread implementation, but it pushed educational discourse in Sweden further in the direction of integration. It also united stakeholders with differing allegiances while bringing scattered pedagogical discourse into a common focus, even though textbooks and literature still favoured progression in a single subject, especially in sciences. And, it introduced aspects of progressive education into subject-based teaching. This

Failure is an option 263

case is not isolated either, Hultén added. Many pedagogical ideas have enjoyed support, including project method, groupwork, collaborative learning and networked learning. At present the STEM movement is also promoting integrated approaches to science, technology, engineering and mathematics. Yet, some contend STEM will increase student learning and employability while others critique its underlying social and economic rationales. Others yet caution against marginalizing the humanities, arts and social sciences.

In their chapter for this book, Fam, Lopes and Mitchell reported limits to curricular innovation at a "challenge-driven" university in Australia. As a category a "challenge" institution focuses on real-world problems. This example, though, illustrates difficulties, even in a problem-oriented institution, caused by discipline-based priorities. The project, which aimed at introducing an alternative sanitation system in a multi-story building, was both cross-disciplinary and cross-sector, involving academic and industrial partners. The Living Laboratory experiment was also in effect a "collaborative test bed" that provided a place, as the authors put it, to "skin your knees." Academic resistance to participatory decision-making, though, impeded progress. The project was a side interest for researchers who returned to their regular homes afterwards. Furthermore, facilities management practitioners such as the plumber had regulations and codes to follow. And, no provision was made for long-term funding that could have created a broad platform for larger-scale trials. Nonetheless, the experiment was not a complete failure. It launched a community of practice at the university and new research.

The experiment in "learning to fail forward" that Pearce describes took place in a first-year required course in the Department of Environmental Systems Science at the Zurich-based Swiss Federal Institute of Technology. Entitled "Tackling Environmental Problems," the course cultivates values of curiosity and inquiry over certainty and correctness, while integrating qualitative systems modelling with design thinking. The concept of productive failure entailed in this and other chapters distinguishes praiseworthy failure as steps in a process from blameworthy failure due to factors such as deviance and inattention. Classrooms are not the only site of productive failure, either. Neuhaser, Brettler and Boyle's account of the Changzhou Worker Wellness Project illustrates the value of allowing for adjustments rather than continuing to impose an a priori plan, and the IDEO company's formal embrace of failure as a form of "constructive learning," illustrated in improved design of breast pumps.

Productive use of negative feedback on methodology also appears across three chapters. O'Rourke, Crowley, Eigenbrode and Vasko report how the purpose of four Toolbox workshop was thwarted by criticism of the method. Feedback led to a new version improving prompts for dialogue, but it still exposed widespread reluctance to dealing with differences in underlying philosophical assumptions. In her UK-based chapter on power outages, Connon drew lessons from resistance to a charrette-based method of engaging participants, leading to an alternative qualitative approach using ethnographic research and semi-structured interviews. Conceptualizations of identity, the project team learned, are tied to local knowledge and political parameters along the rural/urban divide as well as communities

264 *Julie Thompson Klein*

versus government institutions. In their chapter on sustainability science at Leuphana University, Ulli Vilsmaier and Annika Thalheimer drew lessons from analysis of research reports and essays, yielding feedback for making teamwork in student-driven projects more equal and for building shared understanding. It is important, Vilsmaier and Thalheimer concluded, to set boundary conditions for collaboration and students' expectations and needs.

Stakeholder engagement

The topic of stakeholder engagement has gained prominence in literature on transdisciplinary research. The opening example for this final theme continues to illustrate why projects do not fully engage stakeholders, framed by Gabriele Wuesler and Christian Pohl's analysis of projects aimed at sustainable development. Added insights from literature on public engagement underscore further challenges, along with Beal, Fam and Clegg's chapter affirming the importance of acknowledging differences in stakeholders' positions informed by the Ecovillage trial of a urine diversion system. Martina Ukowitz's account of the Carinthia International project also affirmed the need for trust between researchers and partners in practice. The international scope of this volume expands with examples of Indigenous and local knowledge in Africa and Australia. Together, they reinforce the question of which forms of knowledge and expression count, shaping practices including Jason De Santolo's experience driven by the double obstacle of academic priorities and colonial logic.

Gabriela Wuesler and Christian Pohl's (2016) study of ten land-use projects introduces this topic. The projects they examine span ecosystem pollination, expansion of oil palm, biofuel crop production, mountain regions and forest development, water-related services and management, carbon sequestration and crop-livestock systems. They were also geographically dispersed across India, Indonesia, Madagascar, Ethiopia, Switzerland, Kenya/Tanzania, Panama and Nicaragua. The ideal model of transdisciplinarity holds that research should start from societal actors' problem perceptions and needs. However, needs and perspectives of societal actors came later in the process, so they only had an indirect influence. Some researchers possessed direct and indirect contextual knowledge, and in some cases enjoyed trust of farmers. Yet, the potential societal relevance of scientific contributions was short-changed. Gains in fundamental understanding should not be dismissed. However, the academic reward system precluded certain research questions while prioritizing existing infrastructure, previous research and funding opportunities.

The parallel topic of public engagement is also fraught with challenges. Tebes and Thai (2018) report that public engagement goes by many names, including participatory action research, citizen science, patient and public involvement, stakeholder engagement, community-engaged or community-based participatory research and participatory team science. Involving stakeholders at all stages, they add, is typically unrealistic, cost prohibitive, and unsustainable. Russell, Wickson and Carew (2008) further warn against idealizing the *agora*, given its

Failure is an option 265

heterogeneity, complexity and own imbalances of power. In their chapter on the Ecovillage trial of a urine diversion system, Beal, Fam and Clegg also stress the need for collaborative organization and/or management. End-users, plumbers, regulators and water utilities all possessed relevant knowledge that needed to be coordinated with action research. Ukowitz's illustration of the Carinthia International project, in turn, affirms the need for trust between researchers and partners in practice, requiring close attention to social dynamics. Even though the project on relationships and mobility within a globalized environment of work succeeded in producing insights, here too academic science prioritized generating new knowledge over the interests of practitioners. Culture is an added factor.

Knapp, Reid, Fernández-Gimenéz, Klein and Galvin (2019) include both Indigenous and local knowledge in a roster of collaborative approaches associated with transdisciplinarity. These approaches are multi-dimensional: encompassing traditional knowledge passed across generations, empirical expertise, revealed wisdom and contemporary perspectives based on experience, education and problem-solving. In making a case for decolonizing transdisciplinary research in Africa, Bagele Chilisa (2017) explains how local methodologies draw on philosophies, worldviews and histories that offer alternative ways of conducting research. Ethno-philosophy, for example, can explain how mythical concepts, ritual practices, language, proverbs, metaphors, folklores, stories, songs, artefacts and art inform epistemological assumptions. Yet, Michael Davis (2006) questions whether efforts are bridging a gap or crossing a bridge, in his case between Indigenous knowledge and the language of law and policy in Australia. Jason De Santolo's chapter in this book depicts the value of Indigenous rights and connective capacity of storywork through the personal lens of obstacles to earning a PhD in law, pitting land-based paradigms and community teachings against Western policies of ownership, authority and power.

Conclusion

In the online exchange mentioned at the beginning of this chapter, Frédéric Darbellay suggested much of what may be considered failure targets difficulties or obstacles that can be translated into conditions for success (pers. comm., 5 December 2018). No one-size-model fits all. However, studies of failure in this book and the larger literature furnish six overarching principles for success:

1. transparency in all aspects of boundary work
2. informed use of best practices, models, guidelines and authoritative reports
3. consistency and alignment of separate activities in a systematic approach
4. effective balancing of disciplinary, cross-disciplinary and cross-sector work
5. credit for rather than marginalization or dismissal of boundary crossing work
6. appropriate criteria and a multi-methodological approach to evaluation

The first principle underscores the centrality of communication. In introducing this volume, O'Rourke and Fam emphasize the importance of recognizing

266   *Julie Thompson Klein*

differences from the outset. Many projects falter when participants realize they may have common interests but differing conceptions and stakes. Based on trans-disciplinary initiatives in New Zealand centred on managing impacts of land-use, Robson-Williams, Small and Robson-Williams join others in affirming the need to be explicit from the outset. In the Selwyn Waihora Project, agreement was needed on standards for water quality and requirements for farmers, and in The Matrix of Good Management project definitions of good management in agri-cultural practice and a method for estimating nutrient losses at farms. Balancing research and community interests, the authors concluded, also requires transpar-ency about predetermined, non-negotiable aspects of a project and understanding sources of problems that arise.

The second principle reinforces the importance of learning from experience. In their chapters, Bellotti and D'Agostino, as well as Fam, Lopes and Mitchell, emphasize that leaders need to be familiar with interdisciplinary and transdis-ciplinary process, methodology and theory. Researchers also need to be famil-iar with processes of integration and collaboration. O'Rourke and Fam's caveat comes to mind, however: projects do not always follow step-by-step protocols and theories. Moreover, success in one context does not necessarily translate to success in others. The third principle minimizes fragmentation, defaulting to par-ticular domains and falling short in a multidisciplinary mélange of approaches. The fourth underscores the need for appropriate mixes of expertise driven by the nature of a particular problem or question. The fifth recognizes recognition and reward and, finally, the sixth principle moves beyond reliance on disciplinary criteria and proxy measures inadequate for assessing cross-disciplinary and cross-sector work.

A final question also looms across the principles. Who is responsible for mini-mizing the negative force of failure and maximizing learning from it? Benchmark reports target actions for individuals and teams, universities, professional associa-tions, funding agencies, government, industry and communities. Yet, all parties are responsible. Recalling Table 15.1, administrators are not the only ones respon-sible for addressing obstacles in organizational structure. They replicate the struc-tural logic of disciplines that sets expectations for faculty, staff and students. Cross-disciplinary and cross-sector work are rendered peripheral, limiting their power, status, and access to both human and material resources. Procedures and policies follow suit, limiting horizons for activities that do not fit inflexible pro-tocols. Even the most lauded initiatives are left in a weak position. Unfavourable funding priorities, both within and beyond the academy, also narrow prospects, while ignorance of pertinent literature deters the work of leaders and all partici-pants. Finally, lack of recognition and reward exacerbate visibility and legitimacy.

Case studies have also called attention to other factors. The political economy of knowledge in the waste management project in Alaska exposes reductionism that occurs when scientific and quantitative approaches dominate, minimizing qualitative insights from social sciences and humanities and the knowledge lay people have of their communities. The Mill Town Project, which aimed at cre-ating community-engaged environmental studies courses, reveals that even an

Failure is an option 267

institution committed to flexible structure must meet discipline-based priorities. Dominance of existing paradigms and epistemic cultures also curbs hopes for radical transformation while dividing parts of a whole into multidisciplinary segments. The UK-based case study of producing red blood cells for transfusion, and Wuesler and Pohl's study of ten land-use projects by Swiss researchers reminds us, as well, that participation in the problem framing phase is crucial for symmetry of power. And the research programme in food systems at the Global Change Institute demonstrates the proposition in Table 15.1 that multiple challenges overlap.

Repeated support for learning from failure also reinforces O'Rourke and Fam's admonition that intelligent failure can lead to change, not only in an immediate project but also in the underlying logic of an organization or institution. Although the Spheres of Work approach to curriculum, for example, was replaced by a new curriculum, it furthered the discourse of integrative learning in Swedish schools. Providing a place to "skin your knees" at an Australian university, "learning to fail forward" in a Swiss-based curriculum, and the formal valuing of "learning from failure" in the IDEO enterprise further combine to provide a safe environment for gaining from experiences, rather than being stigmatized. Engaging stakeholders also illustrates learning from failure is reciprocal for academics and community members alike, breaking the linear flow of application that privileges academic expertise. The history of failure recounted in this book, to recall a compelling reply in the preliminary survey reported in O'Rourke and Fam, is replete with "compromises, anxieties, disjunctures and misses" that mark the continuing gap separating "lofty idealism" and "nearly utopic ambitions" from the "actual messy reality" of cross-disciplinary and cross-sector work. However, the lessons it furnishes are vital to improved practices.

Acknowledgements

Parts of this chapter draw on draft material for a forthcoming book, "Beyond Interdisciplinarity: Boundary Work, Communication, and Collaboration." I thank Bethany Laursen, Integration & Implementation Specialist, Laursen Evaluation & Design, LLC. I also thank co-editors Dena Fam and Michael O'Rourke for their helpful feedback on an early draft.

References

British Academy. 2016. *Crossing paths: Interdisciplinary institutes, careers, education, and applications.* Available from: https://www.thebritishacademy.ac.uk/interdisciplin arity.

Chilisa, B. 2017. Decolonizing transdisciplinary research approaches: An African perspective for enhancing knowledge integration in sustainability science. *Sustainability Science*, 12, 813–827.

Davis, M. 2006. Bridging the gap or crossing a bridge? Indigenous knowledge and the language of law and policy. *In:* W. Reid, F. Berkes, T. Wilbanks and D. Capistrano,

268   *Julie Thompson Klein*

eds. *Bridging scales and knowledge systems: Concepts and applications in ecosystem assessments*. Washington, DC: Island Press, 145–182.

Fam, D., Sofoulis, Z. 2017. A "knowledge ecologies" analysis of co-designing water and sanitation services in Alaska. *Science and Engineering Ethics*, 23, 1059–1083.

Global Research Council. Statement of principles of interdisciplinarity (from 2016 annual meeting). Global Research Council. Available from: https://www.globalresearchcoun cil.org/fileadmin/documents/GRC_Publications/Statement_of_Principles_on_Interdis ciplinarity.pdf.

Hilton, M., Cooke, N. 2015. *Enhancing the effectiveness of team science*. Washington, DC: National Academies of Science.

Hultén, M. 2013. Boundary objects and curriculum change: The case of integrated versus subject-based teaching. *Journal of Curriculum Studies*, 45(6), 790–813.

Intrepid. 2017a. 1st Intrepid policy brief: Recommendations on integrating interdisciplinarity, the social sciences and the humanities and responsible research and innovation in EU research. Available from: http://intrepid-cost.ics.ulisboa.pt/wp-c ontent/uploads/2017/05/EU-research-ID-SSH-RRI-Policy-BRIEF.pdf.

Intrepid. 2017b. 2nd Intrepid report: Interdisciplinarity, the social sciences and the humanities and responsible research and innovation in EU research. Available from: https://www.academia.edu/34770813/2_nd_INTREPID_Report_Interdisciplinarity_ the_Social_Sciences_and_the_Humanities_and_Responsible_Research_and_Innovat ion_in_EU_Research.

Klein, J.T. 2010. *Creating interdisciplinary campus cultures*. San Francisco, CA: Jossey Bass and Association of American Colleges and Universities.

Knapp, C.N., Reid, R.S., Fernández-Gimenéz, M.E., Klein, J.A., Galvin, K.A. 2019. Placing transdisciplinarity in context: A review of approaches to connect scholars, society, and action. *Sustainability*, 11, 4899+ (25 pp. online).

National Research Council. 2005. *Facilitating interdisciplinary research*. Washington, DC: National Academies of Science.

National Research Council. 2014. *Convergence: Transdisciplinary integration of life sciences, physical sciences, engineering, and beyond*. Washington, DC: National Academies Press.

Russell, A., Wickson, F., Carew, A. 2008. Transdisciplinarity context, contradictions and capacity. *Futures*, 40, 460–472.

Tebes, J.K., Thai, N.D. 2018. Interdisciplinary team science and the public: Steps toward a participatory team science. *American Psychologist*, 4, 549–562.

Wuesler, G., Pohl, C. 2016. How researchers frame scientific contributions to sustainability development: A typology based on grounded theory. *Sustainability Science*, 11, 789–800.

Index

***Page numbers in *italics* reference figures.
***Page numbers in **bold** reference tables.

absolute failure 237–238
academic teams, perceptions of failure from students' point of view 243
ad hoc groups, Toolbox workshops 103–104
agriculture, UQ (University of Queensland) 72
AHSS (arts, humanities, and social science) 48
Alaskan Water and Sewer Challenge 260–261
Anderson, L.W. 220
ARC (Australian Research Council) 71, 205
Archibald, J. 149, 151, 158–160
arts, humanities, and social science (AHSS) 48
assertive self-determination 151
Australia: treaties 156; UD (urine diversion) systems *see* UD (urine diversion) systems
Australian Research Council (ARC) 71, 205
auto-ethnography 46
avoiding failure 22
Aydt, S. 237–238

barriers and disincentives in cross-disciplinary and cross-sector work **257–258**
Behrendt, L. 150–151
Bischoff, M. 167
blameworthy failures 219, 225–226
Bligh Tanner Pty Ltd 81
blood products, Novosang project 48–49
BloodPharma 50

Bloom, B. 220
Bloom's Taxonomy 220
boundaries, MGM (Matrix of Good Management) Project 140–142
breast pumps 34–35, 38
Brown, T. 32
Buchanan, R. 31
buy-in, Ecovillage at Currumbin 86–87

Callard, F. 54
Canterbury Water Management Strategy (CWMS) 131
capacity-building interventions, recommendations for 112
Carinthia International: lessons learned 175–177; research and development 167–175
"challenge-driven" university 198
challenges to implementing food systems research program 67–73
challenges to transdisciplinary and student-driven projects 239
CHAN (coupled human and natural systems) 218
Changzhou Worker Wellness Project 28–31, 37
charrette method 118–119
collaboration 184; interdisciplinary collaboration 193; perceptions of failure from students' point of view 244
collaborative learning 199
colonization 153, 157–160
commitment, Ecovillage at Currumbin 86–87
communication 265; visual communication 208, *210*

Index

community coping 118
community engagement, Mill Town Project 186–190
compassionate action, Indigenous research paradigm 158–160
complex problems of traditional research 23–24
consequences for student-driven projects 248–249
constructive feedback, learning environments 224
cooperation: interdisciplinary cooperation 166; perceptions of failure from students' point of view 245
coupled human and natural systems (CHAN) 218
course development process, Mill Town Project 183–191
cross-disciplinary and cross-sector work, reasons for failure 256–259
cultural differences, Toolbox workshops 104–105
CWMS (Canterbury Water Management Strategy) 131

D'Agostino, F. 71
decolonization 157
deeper learning 220
Department of Environmental Systems Science (D-USYS) 217
Department of Natural Resources and Water (DNRW), Queensland 81
design process 26
design sciences 25–26
design-thinking 31–35, 37
design-thinking and innovation Venn diagram 32
deviance 226
Dewey, J. 199
dialogue, TDI (Toolbox Dialogue Initiative) see TDI (Toolbox Dialogue Initiative)
Dickersin, K. 22
disciplinary approach, challenges and opportunities 191–194
disciplinary excellence 55
disciplinary knowledge, UD (urine diversion) systems 88–89
disciplinary perspectives on failure 4–5
disciplinary-based schools, resistance to implementing food systems 71–72
discipline groups 185
Dixon, N. 157
Dixon, R. G. 157

DNRW (Department of Natural Resources and Water), Queensland 81
Douglas, M. 167
Dunlap, R. E. 86
D-USYS (Department of Environmental Systems Science) 217
dynamics within social system of research, Carinthia International 171–172

Eat-Lancet Commission report (2019) 63
ecology 160
Ecovillage at Currumbin: formal institutional environment 82–84; informal institutions 85–89; methods of inquiry 81–82; UD (urine diversion) systems 79–80
Edison, T. 21, 31
Edmonson, A. C. 22
education 6
Education for Sustainable Development (ESD) 217–218; competences in Blooms' Taxonomy **221**; productive failure 232–233
educational philosophy 185
ELSI (ethical, legal and social implications) 54
emotional resonance of failure 152–158
empirical science 5–6
endogenous failures 101
engineering 5
Environment Canterbury 131, 133, 138
Environment Canterbury (Temporary Commissioners and Improved Water Management) Act 131
ESD (Education for Sustainable Development) 217–18; competences in Blooms' Taxonomy **221**; productive failure 232–233
ETH Zürich 232
ethical, legal and social implications (ELSI) 54
evaluating courses, Mill Town Project 188–189
Evans, T. L. 9
evolution of scientific inquiry 24–28
expectation management, TDI (Toolbox Dialogue Initiative) 106–107
expectations of team members, clarifying 206–207
experience 266
experiential knowledge, UD (urine diversion) systems 88
expertise, perceptions of failure from students' point of view 243

external stakeholders, challenges to implementing food systems research program 70
extreme weather (UK), research project 116–120

Facilitating Interdisciplinary Research 256
failure: absolute failure 237–238; avoiding 22; defined 2–7, 101–102, 237; endogenous failures 101; fear of 22; gradual failure 237–238; intelligent failure 7, 22; manifestations of 7–9; micro-failures 7; praxis failure 9; process failure 45; productive failure *see* productive failure; reflections on 160–161; reportage of 255–256; role of 24–28
failure analysis 5
failure management 6, 12
failure potential 225–229
falsifiable 5
Fam, D. 260
fast failure 6
fault lines 184
fear of failure 22
feedback 263; learning environments 224
feedback culture 242
Fire Sticks Alliance 161
Firestein, S. 101
Fitzgerald, D. 51, 54
food security 65, 72
food systems 63–64; challenges to implementing food systems research program 67–73
Food Systems Program 62–66, 70, 72; challenges to implementing food systems research program 67–73; responding to challenges 73–74
forensic engineering 5
frames of reference: how students construct failure 246–247; perceptions of failure from students' point of view 241
Frege, G. 5
Freire, P. 237
FSP (Food Systems Program) 64–66
funding 53, 90; challenges to implementing food systems research program 70–71; from host institutions, food systems 69; Novosang project 49–50
The Future of the New England Mill Town 181–183

GCI (Global Change Institute) 64; external review 66–67; Food Systems Program 62–66, 70, 72–74

GCRF (Global Challenges Research Fund) 71
GECAFS (Global Environmental Change and Food Systems) 64
Geher, G. 36
Global Challenges Research Fund (GCRF) 71
Global Change Institute (GCI) 64; external review 66–67; Food Systems Program 62–66, 70, 72–74
Global Environmental Change and Food Systems (GECAFS) 64
Global Nutrition Report (2017) 63
good management practice (GMP) 133
Götz, K. 167
gradual failure 237–238
green motivations, Ecovillage at Currumbin 86–87
guidelines, UD (urine diversion) systems 82–84

Haraway, D. 55
health, Changzhou Worker Wellness Project 28–31, 37
Health Research for Action Center (HRA) 28
Heintel, P. 167
heterogeneity 243
higher education 191–194
Hillersdal, L. 50
Hoosan, G. 149, 152, 157
Horizon 2020 program 47
host institutions, funding and resourcing food systems 69
HRA (Health Research for Action Center) 28
Hultén, M. 262
"human sciences" paradigm 25

i2S (integration and implementation sciences) framework, water management (NZ) 135–144
IDEO 38; design-thinking 34–35
IDR (interdisciplinary research) 2, 46–48, 55; impediments to *259*
IGERT (Integrative Graduate Education and Research Traineeship) 98
impediments to IDR *259*
implementation: of courses, Mill Town Project 186–91; handling of 173
inattention 226
incorporating research-teaching nexus, while running transdisciplinary projects 211–212

272 *Index*

incremental processes, Carinthia International 172–174
Independence Referendum (UK) 122–123
Indigenous doctoral journey: compassionate action 158–160; emotional resonance of failure 152–158
Indigenous research paradigm 149–151; compassionate action 158–160
individual failure 9
innovation 47
Institute for Sustainable Futures 161
institutional failures 8–9
institutional framing, UD (urine diversion) systems 80–81
institutionalization 167
Integrated Systems and Design Thinking 217
integration and implementation sciences (i2S) framework 135
integration of knowledge, perceptions of failure 245
Integrative Graduate Education and Research Traineeship (IGERT) project 98
integrative research 99
integrative-synthesis mode 48, 53
intelligent failure 7, 22
interactive and cyclical design-thinking process *33*
interdisciplinarity 53–54, 64, 71, 192, 255–256
interdisciplinary collaboration 193
interdisciplinary cooperation 166
interdisciplinary research (IDR) 2, 46–48; impediments to *259*
interdisciplinary teaching 192
Intergovernmental Panel on Climate Change (IPCC) 212
international survey, results 7–9
internationality, Carinthia International 167
internationalization, Carinthia International 168–171
interpersonal competences 220
intervention 25
intrapersonal competences 220
intuition 140
IPCC (Intergovernmental Panel on Climate Change) 212

Jackson, M. 155–156
Jaspers, K. 237

Klein, J. T. 8, 68
knowledge 24; operational knowledge 205; perceptions of failure from students' point of view 246
knowledge regimes, diversity of, urine diversion systems 205–206
Knowledge Transfer Partnership (KTP) project 117–121; failure to mobilize original plan 121–127
Kuckartz, U. 240

Landmatters Currumbin Valley Pty Ltd 81
Lang, D.J. 240
Läpple, D. 167
leadership, challenges to implementing food systems research program 67–69
learning 6, 262–264; deeper learning 220; from failure 6–7, 267; supporting through failure 212–213
learning activities, productive failure and 225–229
learning assessment tasks, productive failure 229–231
learning environments, productive failure 223–224
learning goals 222–223
Lee-Morgan, J. 161–162
lessons learned: Carinthia International 175–177; Mill Town Project 189; Sustainable Sanitation Project 208–212; transdisciplinary researchers *144*
Leuphana University (Germany), student-driven projects 239
liminal experiences 237
limit situations 237, 249
Lindvig, K. 50
Little Thunder, R. 161
Living Laboratory 263
living labs 198–199; Sustainable Sanitation Project 201
logic 5
Loscalzo, J. 21
Lowe, P. 72

malnutrition 63
Manzini, E. 212
Māori 155
Matrix of Good Management (MGM) Project 133–135, 138–139, 266; boundaries 140–142; timelines *134*
McDinny, N. 149
Medela Symphony breast pump *34*

Index 273

mediating between individual interest and cooperative project development, Carinthia International 169–171
meta-discussion 108
meta-skills 55
methods of inquiry, Ecovillage at Currumbin 81–82
MGM (Matrix of Good Management) Project 133–135, 138–139, 266; boundaries 140–142; timelines *134*
micro-failures 7
Mill Town Project 266; course development process 183–186; implementing courses 186–191
Millennium Drought, Ecovillage at Currumbin 83–84
Mitchell, C. 206
mobility programme, Carinthia International 171, 173
Moedas, C. 47
motivational values, differences between locals and large corporate industries 125–127
Mulgan, G. 198
multidisciplinary efforts 198
Mutu, M. 155–156

National Research Council (United States) 220
National Science Foundation (NSF), United States 98–99, 191
National Socio-Environmental Synthesis Center (SESYNC) 65
natural science inquiry 25
negative failure potential 226
negative feedback 263
negative results 5–6
New Environmental Paradigm tool 86
New Zealand, water management (NZ) *see* water management (NZ)
niche environments 81
non-productive failures 226
normalizing iteration, learning environments 223–224
Novosang project 48–49; failure 51–52; reflections on 53–56; serendipity 49–51
NSF (National Science Foundation), United States 98–99, 191

On the Move 168
operational knowledge 205
operationalizing productive failure 231–232

organizational behavior 6
O-Tu-Kapua 154
outcomes, perceptions of failure from students' point of view 245–246

paradigms of scientific inquiry 24–25
participants, KTP (Knowledge Transfer Partnership) project 119–121; influence of political processes 121–124
Pathfinder International 28
people, studying, Mill Town Project 186–187
perceptions of failure from students' point of view 241–246
Petrie, H.G. 198
Petroski, Henry 5
phases of design-thinking process *33*
Phillipson, J. 72
philosophy of science 5
phosphorus rock 80, 200
Pinto, A. V. 237
places, studying, Mill Town Project 186–187
plans 10
plumbing, UD (urine diversion) systems 205–206
Pohl, C. 115
policies, UD (urine diversion) systems 82–84
policy discourse 46–48
political climates, Ecovillage at Currumbin 83–84
political economy of knowledge 260–261, 266
political processes, influence on local views, KTP Project 121–124
politics 114–115; challenges to implementing food systems research program 72–73; pre-existing tensions between locals and national governments 124–125
Popper, Karl 5
positionality 108
power in research groups 110, 114–115
power outages (UK) 116–120
praiseworthy failures 219, 225–226
praxis failure 9
pre-existing tensions, between local communities and national-level governments, KTP 124–125
principles for success 265–266
problem framing 227–228
problem structuring methods 23

274 *Index*

problems, of traditional research 23–24
process failure 45
productive failure 218–219; ESD
  (Education for Sustainable
  Development) 232–233; learning
  activities and 225–229; learning
  assessment tasks 229–231; learning
  environments 223–224; operationalizing
  231–232; TD ESD (transdisciplinary
  education for sustainable development)
  219–222
professional mobility, Carinthia
  International 174–175
progress in transdisciplinary research 115
projects as sites of failure 10–12
prototypes 32
prototyping 228
psychomotor domain 220
purakau methodology 162
pursuits model 65

quality of results, perceptions of
  failure 246

Randerson, J. 154
random forests 25
RBCs (red blood cells) 45
reality, changes views of 24
red blood cells (RBCs) 45
reductio ad absurdum 5
REF (Research Evaluation Framework) 50
referred pain 141
reflections on failure 160–161
regulatory frameworks, UD (urine
  diversion) systems 82–84
relationships, building 184–185
reorientation 153, 161
reportage of failure 255–256
research, problems and weaknesses of
  23–24
research and development, Carinthia
  International 167–175
Research Evaluation Framework (REF) 50
research trials 80
resistance, challenges to implementing
  food systems research program 71–72
resource mobilization, Ecovillage at
  Currumbin 83–84
resourcing, from host institutions, food
  systems 69
RIRDCs (Rural Industry Research and
  Development Corporations) 71
risk 231

risk-averse attitudes 36
Rittel, H. W. 10
role of failure, scientific inquiry 24–28
roles, clarifying for team members
  206–207
Roslin Cells and NHS Blood and
  Transplant 49
Royal Society's 350th anniversary Festival
  of Science and Arts (2010) 52
Rural Industry Research and Development
  Corporations (RIRDCs) 71
Russell, Bertrand 5

scale-up, Sustainable Sanitation Project
  201–205
Scholz, R.W. 248
Schultz, K. 21
science of failure 21
scientific inquiry 36; evolution of 24–28
scientific research 175
Scientific Research Toolbox instrument
  104–105, 109
scientific revolution 24, 36
Scottish and Southern Energy Networks
  (SSEN) 117–118; differences in
  motivational values between locals and
  corporations 125–127
Scottish Funding Council (SFC) 49–50;
  differences in motivational values
  between locals and corporations
  125–127
Scottish National Blood Transfusion
  Service 45
self-determination 151–152, 155
self-organization, student-driven
  projects 240
Selwyn Waihora Project 132–133,
  135–138, 266; errors 139–140; timelines
  134; transparency 142–143
sense-making 151
serendipity, Novosang project *see*
  Novosang project
SESYNC (National Socio-Environmental
  System Center) 65
SFC (Scottish Funding Council) 49–50;
  differences in motivational values
  between locals and corporations
  125–127
shared knowledge principles 154
shared understanding 243
Simon, H. 25
skinning our knees 200
Smith, L. T. 153

Index 275

social dynamics, influence on projects 176–177
social learning 208–209
social networks, Ecovillage at Currumbin 85–86
social research involvement 90
social-communicative process 169
societal actors, perceptions of failure from students' point of view 244–245
socio-technical systems 79
Sofoulis, Z. 208, 260
soft skills 55
Spheres of Work 262
SSEN (Scottish and Southern Energy Networks) 117–118; differences in motivational values between locals and corporations 125–127
stability, within social system of research, Carinthia International 171–172
stakeholder engagement 228, 264–265
Stauffacher, M. 247
staying power, Carinthia International 174–175
Steffensen, V. 154, 157, 162
STEM approaches 183, 191–192
stem cells, Novosang project 48–49
story ready 149–150, 159
storytelling 150
storywork 151, 156, 160–162
strategic essentialism 55
Student Assessment of Learning Gains survey, Mill Town Project 188
student teams, perceptions of failure 242–243
student-driven projects 239–240; challenges to 239; consequences for 248–249; perceptions of failure 241–248
Studying Place by Metes and Bounds 191; Mill Town Project 186–188
subordination-service mode 48
success, principles for 265–266
success conditions across Toolbox contexts **98**
success/failure 21–22
supporting productive failure 232
supporting learning through failure 212–213
surveys, international survey results 7–9
sustainability 78
sustainable living 81
Sustainable Sanitation Project 199–201; lessons learned 208–212; project failure to enable scale-up 201–205

Swiss Federal Institute of Technology in Zurich (ETH Zürich) 217
systems modelling 228
Szostack, R. 54

Tackling Environmental Problems (TEP) 222
TD (transdisciplinarity) 27–28, 36–37; Changzhou Worker Wellness Project 28–31
TD (Transdisciplinary) Project 238, 248–249
TD ESD (transdisciplinary education for sustainable development) 218; productive failure 219–222
TDI (Toolbox Dialogue Initiative) 97; ad hoc groups 103–4; building workshops for participants 105–106; cultural differences 104–105; importance of dialogue and expectation management 106–107; lessons learned 107–111; Toolbox dialogue method 98–101
TDLL (Transdisciplinary Living Model) 211
team members, clarifying roles and expectations 206–207
temporary communities 103–104, 109
tensions in student-driven transdisciplinary projects 246–247
TEP (Tackling Environmental Problems) 222; learning activities 225–229; learning assessment tasks 229–231; learning environments 223–225; learning goals 222–223
Thalheimer, A. 238
Tietje, O. 248
time poverty 53
timeframes, perceptions of failure from students' point of view 244
toilets, UD (urine diversion) systems *207*, 213
Toolbox 1.0 101, 109
Toolbox 2.0 101, 106–7, 110
Toolbox Dialogue Initiative (TDI) 97; Toolbox dialogue method 98–101
Toolbox dialogue method 97, 98–101; ad hoc groups 103–104; building workshops for participants 105–106; cultural differences 104–105; failure 101–102; importance of dialogue and expectation management 106–107; lessons learned 108–111
Toolbox Project 99

276 Index

traditional research, problems and weaknesses of 23–24
transdisciplinarity (TD) 27–28, 36–37; Changzhou Worker Wellness Project 28–31
Transdisciplinary (TD) Project 238, 248–249
transdisciplinary approaches 198
transdisciplinary education for sustainable development (TD ESD) 218
Transdisciplinary Living Lab Model (TDLL) 211
transdisciplinary research 2, 68–69, 114; lessons learned *144*; progress 115; recommendations for 127–129
transdisciplinary teams, perceptions of failure from students' point of view 243–244
transformation 155
transparency, Selwyn Waihora Project 142–143
treaties, Australia 156
trust within social system of research, Carinthia International 172
tutoring 225

UD (urine diversion) systems 78, 90–91; Ecovillage at Currumbin *see* Ecovillage at Currumbin 79–80; engaging diversity of knowledge regimes 205–206; formal institutional environment 82–84; institutional framing 80–81; outcomes 202; Sustainable Sanitation Project 199–201
UI (University of Idaho) 98–99
unavoidable failures 219
uncertainty, water management (NZ) 143–144
UNDRIP (United Nations Declaration on the Rights of Indigenous Peoples) 156
United Kingdom: extreme weather 116–120; Independence Referendum 122–123; KTP (Knowledge Transfer Partnership) project 121–124; power outages 116–120; pre-existing tensions between locals and national governments 124–125
United Nations Declaration on the Rights of Indigenous Peoples (UNDRIP) 156
University of Dundee (UoD) 117
University of Edinburgh, Roslin Cells and NHS Blood and Transplant 49
University of Idaho (UI) 98–99

University of Maryland, National Socio-Environmental Synthesis Center (SESYNC) 65
University of Queensland (UQ): agriculture 72; challenges to implementing food systems research program 67–73; GCI (Global Change Institute) 62, 66–67
University of Technology Sydney (UTS) 199; incorporating research-teaching nexus 211–212; Sustainable Sanitation Project 199–201; urine diversion (UD) systems 204
unknowns 24
UoD (University of Dundee) 117
UQ (University of Queensland): agriculture 72; challenges to implementing food systems research program 67–73; GCI (Global Change Institute) 62, 66–67
urine diversion (UD) systems 78, 90–91; Ecovillage at Currumbin 79–80; engaging diversity of knowledge regimes 205–206; formal institutional environment 82–84; institutional framing 80–81; outcomes *202*; Sustainable Sanitation Project 199–201
urine-diverting toilet *79*
UTS (University of Technology Sydney) 199; incorporating research-teaching nexus 211–212; Sustainable Sanitation Project 199–201; urine diversion (UD) systems 204

Values module (Eigenbrode et al.) **100**
valuing process over product, learning environments 224
Vilsmaier, U. 238
visual communication 208, *210*

wastewater management, Alaskan Water and Sewer Challenge 260–261
water management (NZ) 131–2; i2S (integration and implementation sciences) framework 135–144; MGM (Matrix of Good Management) Project 133–135, 138–142; Selwyn Waihora Project 132–133, 139–140, 142–143; uncertainty 143–144
Webber, M. M. 10
Wehrden, H. von 174
Weigel, M. 56
Weingart, P. 64

Index 277

Wellcome Trust's Translational Award
 program 49
Wellness Guide, Worker Wellness Project
 (Changzhou, China) 29–30
Western Sydney University 204
wicked 10

Willow 34–35, 38
Worker Wellness Project (Changzhou,
 China) 28–31, 37
work-package, Novosang project 51
writing for systems knowledge 227

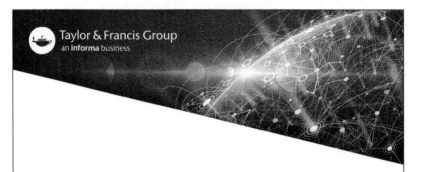

Taylor & Francis eBooks

www.taylorfrancis.com

A single destination for eBooks from Taylor & Francis with increased functionality and an improved user experience to meet the needs of our customers.

90,000+ eBooks of award-winning academic content in Humanities, Social Science, Science, Technology, Engineering, and Medical written by a global network of editors and authors.

TAYLOR & FRANCIS EBOOKS OFFERS:

- A streamlined experience for our library customers
- A single point of discovery for all of our eBook content
- Improved search and discovery of content at both book and chapter level

REQUEST A FREE TRIAL
support@taylorfrancis.com